Balkan as Metaphor

Balkan as Metaphor
Between Globalization and Fragmentation

Edited by
Dušan I. Bjelić and Obrad Savić

The MIT Press
Cambridge, Massachusetts
London, England

This book was set in Sabon by SNP Best-set Typesetter Ltd., Hong Kong.

Printed and bound in the United States of America.

Library of Congress Cataloging-in-Publication Data

Balkan as metaphor / Dušan I. Bjelić . . . [et al].
    p. cm.
    Includes bibliographical references and index.
    ISBN 0-262-02524-8 (hc : alk. paper)
    1. Balkan Peninsula—Politics and government—1989– 2. Balkan Peninsula—Ethnic relations. I. Bjelić, Dušan I.

DR48.6 .B3453 2002
305.8′00946—dc21
                                                                2002024697

For Miladin Zivotić and Radomir Konstatinović, founders of *Belgrade Circle*

Contents

Foreword

A persistent paradox infuses most of the negative stereotypes entertained in the self-styled West: the Other is hopelessly diverse, fragmented, and internally divided—so much so that in the end all such peoples seem radically alike. Who can make sense of so much difference? It is easier to dismiss it as all the same.

This is recognizably the other side of a familiar coin: the Western self-characterization in terms of individualistic genius. Whether celebrating the emergence of possessive individualism modeled on the ownership of material property or of transcendent intelligence metonymically reproduced in moral and intellectual properties, the politically and economically dominant nations of Europe (and, later, of North America) have had their cake and eaten it too. Nowhere is this clearer in the countries now subsumed under the redolent title of "the Balkans." It is here that the picturesque individualism of the European Other becomes the atomistic fractiousness and insubordination of the Oriental within.

Such characterizations have taken a deep hold on a disturbingly wide range of constituencies. Not only have they been paraded through a long series of justifications for intervention in the name of peace, rights, civil society, and economic development, but their success as both the expression and the instrument of hegemonic processes appears most clearly in the remarkable degree to which they have been locally accepted. That acceptance may be more rhetorical than psychological, although it is hard to be sure and harder still to generalize. No matter: the importance of these stereotypes and their astonishingly wide local currency lies in the ease with which they serve a massive international structure of self-absolution. Just as a bureaucrat and a client may collude in using a common set of excuses—appealing to "the system" lets both off the hook of failure—so, too, charges of innate Balkan evils not only appear to justify foreign intervention but also serve locally, in a sometimes cynical assumption of political agency, to bolster actions and attitudes that have low status in the now-dominant global cultural hierarchy of value. What can we poor Balkan types do? So runs the complicit logic of self-abjection.

The authors whose work is collected in this volume, however, avoid such easy options. An observer might interpret their variety and sheer number, as well as the range of styles and disciplinary orientations they represent, as evidence of the besetting inconsistency and complexity of the Balkan world. But what is to block an equally plausible (and equally essentialist) counter-claim to the genius of individualistic originality? Important as the differences are, however, we may also be struck by the similarities among these papers. Are we then to have recourse to the opposite stereotype, viewing Balkan scholarship as deadeningly lacking in internal differentiation—as failing to meet the European criterion of personal and cultural genius?

I raise these questions, not because I want to perpetuate such stereotypes, but—to the contrary—because the questions, conscientiously examined, expose the absurdity that for too long has characterized debates about the Balkans. It is extraordinary that, in an age in which stereotypes and prejudice have long been viewed with a jaundiced eye by those professing to be tolerant and open-minded, these particular attitudes should have persisted so successfully—often among the people, or in the academic circles, in which the condemnation of prejudice has been loudest. We are tragically familiar with the affectation of those who declare that in their country "people are not racists" but that "those people" (often Balkan people) deserve to be punished, not because of who they are ethnically or culturally, but as criminals or degenerates. Such mealy-mouthed pieties are not confined to the rhetoric of personal self-exoneration, but pervade the spaces of international politics, scholarship, and journalism.

The authors of the essays presented in this book have taken a notable risk in thus appearing to confirm—through the variety of their messages and their occasional reproduction of such familiar themes as the responsibilities of "the West"—key aspects of the prevailing stereotype of "the Balkans." Yet their message is clear and critical: the tropological representation of a geographically and historically defined cultural zone carries liabilities that must be addressed in a forthright and analytical manner.

This is the difficult task undertaken in the essays before you. It will be easy for the disingenuous reader to pounce on certain commonalities and say, "I told you so! These people really are all alike, especially in their desire to blame someone else!" But why not take those similarities as evidence of a problem the sources of which lie, in large measure, *outside* this evocative imagined space? Why not take the differences, not as evidence of inconsistency or incompetence, but as indications of a rich intellectual ferment—of what the self-styled "West" would praise in itself as evidence of its innate genius?

Once admitted, the pernicious character of such "otherings" also takes on heuristic and explanatory potential. I have suggested that these rhetorical devices of policy and scholarship are not only symbolic but also instrumental. In the jargon of modern linguistic philosophy and anthropology, I would call them "performative." The world leaders who use such rhetorical devices to justify "containing" and "pacifying" actions to tax-weary electorates know full well that the force of such devices is entirely material. And the discovery of how deeply these stereotypes have soaked into the aesthetic and moral landscapes of Balkan peoples, as well as those of the major international powers, highlights their entailment in a thoroughgoing hegemony. Forced to collude in the reproduction of their own "othering," Balkan leaders—intellectual as well as political—find themselves trapped in what often seems to be an inexorable logic: the more they protest, the more they confirm. But that, too, is evidence, not of the "truth" of the stereotypes, but of their material effectiveness as instruments of domination.

Read this book, not only as a critical analysis of the Balkan trope, but also as a commentary on its silent (what linguists call "unmarked") partner: "the West." Notice how much of what is attributed to the Balkans emerges in the populations that consider themselves to be Western. Notice, too, how those on the outside ignore the specificities of local history and culture, or reduce these to epiphenomena of what is considered to be the situation of the Balkans today. A church is of Byzantine origin? That "explains" its "medieval" responses. The language of blood and rape seems familiar? That is because it belongs to "our" past but to "their" present, according "us" the right to judge "them." Of such circularities and presuppositions are the rhetoric and practice of foreign policy frequently made. The claims of international power managers to be realistic in the face of an imputed Balkan inability to face reality is but another instantiation of their fundamental entailment in symbolic practices of political control. But such claims are powerful, and they are powerfully backed: they appeal to a world dominated by Cartesian logic and by the economic and military might of a few countries. Despite a groundswell of critique—of which this book is an exemplary illustration—the hermetic logic of representation means that the authors whose work you will read here have thus engaged in an uphill struggle.

That they will persevere seems clear: many of them already have clocked up long and distinguished trajectories of critical labor. The present set of essays is richly stimulating, raucously varied, and wonderfully blunt. Read the essays, digest what the authors have to say, above all *listen* to the authors' insights and *see* "the West" mirrored in their anguish and their exasperation, their bitter fury and their amused compassion, their analytical probing and their passionate engagement.

What's in it for "the West"? Must it submit to yet more ungrateful tirades? Probably those who have already decided that this is the issue will not be able to extract much knowledge from the essays before them here; and they will be the losers, for they will have failed to recognize, not "the Balkans," but themselves. But others, more honest or self-aware, will make the effort. Their willingness will be an important part of the process that this book carries forward: the audience, the reader, is a key player in the work of interpretation and the production of knowledge.

Without such a serious commitment to understanding what these writers have to say in all their suggestive diversity, the claims of the international powers to represent justice and civil society will ring increasingly hollow. Perhaps that is no bad thing, because then perhaps the disingenuous character of much interventionist rhetoric will stand exposed for what it is. On the other hand, are we willing to turn a blind eye? Will we refuse all responsibility for the situation? And, if we do so, what price, then, the stereotype of the Balkan "mentality" that "always" blames "us"?

This is a book that, to an unusual degree, makes reading not only a rich experience but also an ethically and politically responsible act. Take it in your hands, engage its complex and varied messages, and reflect on its relationship to the stereotypes that you have encountered. Above all, try to put it into the hands of those who have some responsibility for both creating the tragedies that have beset the Balkans and then exclusively blaming Balkan people for what has happened. Perhaps, in that way, this ostensibly cerebral discussion of metaphor will acquire a potent materiality in what those who make policy are pleased to regard as the "real world."

Michael Herzfeld
Harvard University

Acknowledgments

We would like to thank Anthony Giddens and Chris Norris for their enthusiastic support for this collection. Gratitude is also extended to Pamela Bellinger, Eric D. Gordy, Martha Lampland, and Laura Secor for reviewing the proposal, and to Ion Berindei, Vesna Bogojević, Corrie Calderwood, Lucinda Cole, Eda Čufer, Dušan Djordjevic Mileusnić, Susan Murch, Keneth Rosen, Maple Razsa, and David Wills for ongoing aid. A special thanks goes to Roger Conover, executive editor at the MIT Press, who presented us with his vision of the book and who worked with us to see it through to completion.

Introduction: Blowing Up the "Bridge"

Dušan I. Bjelić

During the summer of 2000 we (students from Serbian universities, representatives of various Serbian NGOs, and two professors from a U.S. university) sat in a small restaurant in Vladičin Han, on the border of Serbia and Macedonia. We were having lunch on our way to Macedonia for a meeting with students from Priština University, an event organized by the Helsinki Committee for Human Rights in Serbia. As we were being served beverages, a bearded multilingual Orthodox monk, his black robes marked by the Greek Orthodox insignia, approached our table apparently intrigued to hear Professor Lucinda Cole speaking English. In Oxford English he introduced himself as Petar; we offered him a seat. After a series of tense exchanges on Madeline Albright's "Jewish conspiracy" against the Serbs (at this point he identified himself as a Serb), on why the Roma should not be allowed to form their own church, on the general idea of multiculturalism, the conversation (for reasons now impossible to reconstruct) turned to Margaret Mitchell's *Gone with the Wind*. It turned out that the monk, who by that time had succeeded—in spite of his pious voice—to insult the political sensibilities of just about everybody on the terrace, had read the novel at least seven times. He proceeded to quote entire passages in a passionately romantic tone, and to express very strong opinions on why Scarlett O'Hara married her first husband, whose name he nevertheless misremembered. "Charles!" a young, pierced and tattooed representative of the Helsinki Human Rights Committee corrected, loudly and somewhat testily, from another table. The entire terrace—which unbeknownst to us, had been listening to this conversation in English—laughed, and soon enough a chorus of voices offered opinions about Scarlett's behavior and about whether or not she "truly" loved Rhett Butler. The editor of *The Belgrade Circle Journal* suggested, jokingly, that instead of focusing on Serb-Albanian relations, we should organize a conference on the socio-political impact of *Gone with the Wind*.

We laughed, too, but in retrospect this moment seems emblematic, and not only because prior to that point we had no idea how many in our radically diverse group spoke English. Clearly, what prompted the conversation across religious, political, gender, and ethnic lines was an *investment* in the relationship between Rhett Butler and Scarlett O'Hara—an identification, that is, with some aspect of this especially powerful American narrative of heterosexual romance. It was no accident, in other words, that a "trans-ethnic" Orthodox monk, an American post-structuralist feminist, two anti-nationalist Serbs, a Rom activist, a Communist feminist, and dozens of other participants were able to argue about Scarlett O'Hara's love life. Through the bourgeois romance-narrative, race, ethnicity, class, sexuality, and other markers of difference were temporarily occluded. *Gone with the Wind* appeared to offer a momentary release, on this terrace in Vladičin Han, from the imperatives of differences, and a momentary escape into the pleasures of a heterosexual love story. The obvious *jouissance* of self-commodification in the Eastern Orthodox monk's sentiments shocked yet challenged our stereotypes. The monk, who had trained in the ascetic disciplines of the desert fathers, appeared to contradict Fredric Jameson's orientalizing claim that East wishes to talk only in terms of "power and oppression" while "the West in terms of culture and commodification."[1] In retrospect, however, the monk had taught us an important lesson, of how those discourses which insist exclusively on "society as a whole," are bogus in the face of the concreteness of a life in crisis. Appreciating Terry Eagleton's observation about the diminished theoretical relevance of such discourses to "an irritating habit of existing,"[2] today we wonder whether or not Jameson's "hearing aid got switched off"[3] when he made his claim, glossing over the important fact, for example, that in both the United States and the Balkans the tradition of heterosexuality and of ethnic differentiation are historically linked, fusing procreation with nation, kin with territory, sexual pleasure with ethnic exclusion, with fratricide, and with rape.

The episode at Vladičin Han, we think, succinctly introduces the topic of this volume: Balkan identity and representation, its pleasures and its violence. Though the Balkans and the American South have very different histories, neither history can be understood without recognizing the impact of a colonialism that helped shape both regions' cultures, identities, and corresponding regimes of signification. In *Gone with the Wind*, a binary logic constructs the category of "Whiteness" as being parasitic on "Blackness."[4] Similarly, among nationalistic Serbs, the category "the Serbs" is parasitically dependent on the category "Albanians." The Balkans and the American South are constructed through a discourse that associates modernity and progress, however arbitrarily, with "the West" in the one instance, and "the North" in the other. Consequently, their identities are structured in relation to a spatio-political order that arrives from the "outside." The Balkans serve much the same function for global politics that the American South serves for the American national one. Whereas "the South" has traditionally been viewed as a backward, seething pit of racial and sexual violence against which the liberal and enlightened North defines itself, "the Balkans" have functioned as the fulcrum for Enlightenment Europe's self-image, or the means by which "progressive" Europe projects its anxieties and forbidden desires onto the other, as if onto "Cat People," that is, or onto those who constitute its antithetical periphery. In this sense, we can speak of an organized system of knowledge akin to what Edward Said has called *Orientalism*.

Like *Orientalism*, *Balkanism* has been organized around a sense of binaries (rational/irrational, center/periphery, civilization/barbarism) arranged hierarchically so that the first sign ("Whiteness" or "Europe"), is always primary and definitional of the second ("Blackness" or "Balkans"), and so that the second is always a grammatical, internal effect of the first. For example, "Byzantium" (referring to the Byzantine church) is not represented today in the same way as Protestantism and Catholicism—that is, in terms of what it meant to the members of that religion, the Byzantines—but rather in terms of what it meant to Protestants and Catholics. In "What is so Byzantine about the Balkans?" Milica Bakić-Hayden summarizes the binary logic of Western discourse on Byzantium, whereby Byzantium becomes marked as "authoritarian" or "crypto-nationalist," "corrupted" by a "convoluted politics" that is "cesaropapistic."[5] The question that remains, however, is whether or not *every* system of colonial representation based on binaries is by definition *Orientalism* or, more importantly, are the binaries of Said's *Orientalism* good for the marginals and outsiders?

Is *Balkanism* a Subsidiary of *Orientalism*?

Although influenced by Said's work, the Balkan scholars represented in this volume cherish Said's political humanism and would agree with Gayatri Spivak that Said's *Orientalism* "blossomed into a garden where the marginal can speak and be spoken, even spoken for."[6] Yet Balkan scholars would insist, however, that *Balkanism* is not a subspecies of *Orientalism*, but has its own unique properties, responding to rules that marginalized minority speech. Balkan scholars were not the first to develop a critique of *Orientalism*, but they contributed a unique host of arguments specific to their discursive locality.

In the middle of the nineties, Balkan scholars began to produce groundbreaking work in the English speaking world. Maria Todorova's seminal book *Imagining the Balkans*,[7] Vesna Goldsworthy's *Inventing Ruritania: The Imperialism of the Imagination*,[8] Stathis Gourgouris *Dream Nation: Enlightenment, Colonization, and the Institution of Modern Greece*,[9] and Milica Bakić-Hayden's "Nesting Orientalism,"[10] to mention just a few, have established Balkanism as a critical study of colonial representation distinctly different from *Orientalism*. Rather than representing the Balkans substantively, either as a geopolitical place or as a people with a "collective paranoia," these authors began to represent the Balkans as a "place" in a *discourse-geography*. That is, as the object of a coherent body of knowledge—*Balkanism*. Thus instead of telling us what the Balkans *are*, they diverted the question of the Balkans into the problem of imperial language. They asked, "how do we know what we know about the Balkans?" Without denying overlaps with *Orientalism*, the Balkan scholar insists that *Balkanism* has different representational mechanisms. While Said argues that the East/West Orientalist binary refers to a "project rather than a 'place,'" Bakić-Hayden claims that, in the former Yugoslavia, *Orientalism* is a *subjectivational practice* by which all ethnic groups define the "other" as the "East" of them;[11] in so doing, they not only orientalize the "other," but also occidentalize themselves as the West of the "other."

Indeed, postcolonial analysts noticed before Bakić-Hayden that pejorative stereotypes were strategically available not only to the empire, but also distributed among colonial subjects. Richard G. Fox demonstrates how Mahatma Gandhi utilized, for the purpose of anticolonial struggle, "Orientalist images of India as inherently spiritual, consensual, and corporate."[12] But while Gandhi and the Hindi internalized Orientalized stereotypes to resist their colonial identifications, something else happened in the Balkans, where people subverted their own identities by orientalizing one another.

These "nesting Orientalisms" seem to be as old as the split of the Christian Church. The Orthodox Church always presented itself as the West; that is, as part of Christendom in relation to the Islamic East. But in relation to Roman Catholicism, the Orthodoxy presented itself as rooted in the monastic East. Thus, *Balkanism*, Todorova maintains, must be evaluated in the light of *Occidentalism* as well—a discourse on the West's self-essentialization.[13] There are two reasons for this: first because the West's essentializing scheme of being the "opposite" to the "Orient" operates as a benchmark for "nesting-Orientalisms"; second because in inventing *Balkanism* as a discourse on the "opposite," the West essentializes Balkan identity. *Balkanism*, then, meanders between *Orientalism* and *Occidentalism*, once as a representational mechanism, again as a *subjectivational* process.

It should be clarified that the word *Balkanism* has changeable meanings. Sometimes it refers to the body of knowledge about the Balkans, and sometimes to the critical study of this very discourse. *Balkanism* in the first sense delivers substantive knowledge about the Balkans without examining the presuppositions upon which this knowledge has been generated—Robert D. Kaplan's book *Balkan Ghosts: A Journey Through History* is a prime example. *Balkanism* in the second sense examines the Balkans in relation to suppositions constitutive of *Balkanism* in the first sense—that is, as an epistemology. Maria Todorova's book, *Imagining the Balkans*, illustrates this approach.

K. E. Fleming's excellent paper "*Orientalism*, the Balkans, and Balkan Historiography" elucidates the above differences. Fleming maintains that to the extent that *Balkanism* creates a single popular image of the Balkans, which then becomes a matrix for all other representations of the Balkans, it resembles *Orientalism*. However, Said's *Orientalism*, and Balkan scholars' critique of *Balkanism*, significantly differ in theory and method. For Said, *Orientalism* "was meant to be a study in critique, not an affirmation of warring and hopelessly antithetical identities"[14]—a way of setting the stage for peaceful coexistence by dismantling differences in part by accepting the universal critique of the Western essence. *Balkanism*, in contrast, affirms constitutive differences and paradoxes for the sake of the Balkan's representational concreteness. This affirmation is the key to both the method and the cultural mission of *Balkanism*. Having said that, however, we do not mean to suggest that the *political goals* of *Balkanism* differ from Said's aspirations for multicultural coexistence. Rather, we are suggesting that especially for *Balkanism*, the political may also be in the method of representation, rather than in its content. Said hoped that if a discourse could eliminate differences, political reality would follow that discourse. But Balkan scholars have long recognized that though differentiation is a universal principle of domination, it does not make all differentiation the same. In other words, political differentiation and methodological differentiation for the Balkans are different operations. This is an important point of distinction, especially since the Balkans have all too often been confused with other parts of Eastern Europe: for example, before the introduction of automatic dialing, U.S. phone operators would often connect to Czechoslovakia when asked for Yugoslavia. Similarly, it is not unusual even for American academics to confuse the Balkans with the Baltics, or Slovenia with Slovakia. The editors of the book in which Slovenian philosopher

Slavoj Žižek's article "Enjoy Your Nation as Yourself!" was recently published, described him as a "Slovakian social theorist and psychoanalyst."[15]

Before addressing internal differences, then, Balkan scholars often stress a politics of signification, one of whose effects has been to erase a specific place, body, or history. The lack of differentiation in Said's *Orientalism* prompted Arif Dirlik to insist, like Todorova, on a full restoration of "historicity informed by the complexity of everyday life, one which accounts not only for what unites, but more importantly, for those diversities in space and time which are as undesirable to national power as to Eurocentrism."[16] It is precisely this lack of differentiation that jeopardizes the most vital aspect of Said's work, giving the voice to minorities, because as Bart Moore-Gilbert observes, Said's rush to unify the world under the common culture "may equally well confirm, or even engender, a whole series of margins and outsiders."[17]

What then is Balkan specificity? What were the historic contingencies engendering the Balkan specificities? Is this specificity in the nature of empirical evidence or of logical paradox? The Balkan scholars in this volume agree that the latter is the case. Historically, the paradox may be explained, by acknowledging that the Balkan region was never colonized in the modern sense, as the Orient was, despite being subjected to Ottoman rule. Rather than exploiting natural resources and human labor, the Ottoman Empire, Fleming reminds us, introduced policies of re-population, coupled with policies of religious conversion and polarization, underwritten by perennial military campaigns. Thus Balkan people perceived each other as both colonial rulers *and* as colonial subjects. Serbian nationalism, for example, both celebrates its medieval empire and remembers Ottoman slavery, a dual sensitivity which then gets translated into calling Bosnian Muslims "Turks"— that is, the colonizers—even while claiming Kosovo as an important part of the Serbian Empire. Whether Balkan nationalism is post-imperial or post-colonial, it is fair to say that it remains distinctly liminal.

The Balkans as a *Discursive Geography* and a Method for Liminal Space

In the critique of *Balkanism*, the Balkans gain specificity by virtue of this liminal status, of being neither here nor there, but in two places at the same time. Many scholars share a tacit understanding that, for outsiders, the Balkans "cannot be told apart or put together," which ultimately causes Balkan differences to melt into sameness. However, this Balkanist presupposition may also be turned into a heuristic device for concretizing the Balkans. As Fleming observes, discourse on the Balkans is one both of "sameness and of difference."[18] This liminal status must contribute not only to Balkan identity, but also to how we resist the representational stability that *Balkanism* implies. To this end, Fleming observes, "The Balkans' liminal status—at the interstices between worlds, histories, and continents—is tantamount not so much to marginality as to a sort of centrality."[19] This centrality has two consequences: First, the Balkans may reclaim their representational concreteness; second, the Balkans may be known through what Michel Foucault calls "subjugated knowledges." According to Foucault's notion of power and domination, knowledge of certain specific places, bodies, and histories is concealed and subjugated because such entities resist the discourse of universal rationality—indeed, their incorporation into that discourse would rupture it. Here another paradox of the Balkans looms. The intense internal polarities created by *Balkanism's* binary logic (Christianity/Islam, civilization/barbarism, etc.) infuses any reality imposed upon the Balkans by *Balkanism* with pernicious instability.

Another, no less important difference between *Orientalism* and *Balkanism*, Fleming insists, is the different institutional organization of these two knowledges. While *Orientalism* involves a long tradition of academic and "expert" knowledge, the same cannot be said for *Balkanism*. There is nothing comparable in *Balkanism* to the Napoleonic survey of Egypt; *Balkanism* traditionally consisted of travelogues, journalistic accounts, and occasional history books. Only very recently, with the disintegration of the former Yugoslavia, was "expert" knowledge introduced in *Balkanism*. Even this expertise is less related to academia than it is to journalism, diplomacy, and international law. Only a very small group of Western scholars are dedicated to Balkan studies. In contrast to *Orientalism* and its critical study, which originated in Western centers of knowledge, *Balkanism* and its study are primarily concentrated in the Balkans.[20] In this respect, *Balkanisms* are an intellectual export industry of the Balkans.

Although they agree on the general contours of *Balkanism*, Balkan scholars disagree on the proper methodology for its critical analysis. Unlike Said's *Orientalism*, which brackets the question of the Orient's historical concreteness in order to describe *orientalist* constructions, *Balkanism* as a critical study is a system of representation based on the historical perception of the Balkans by colonial rulers. These perceptions took root as schemes of self-recognition for Balkan peoples, so their study must be based on historical as well as discursive analysis. The very terms "Balkan" and "Balkanism," as Todorova convincingly argues, cannot be divorced from the history of the place.

Few scholars of the Balkans can ignore Todorova's work. But how can Balkan people account for their history if their history is also their personal tragedy, and the Balkans the site of their trauma? Petar Ramadanović takes up this issue in "Simonides of the Balkans," demonstrating the gulf between participants' and onlookers' accounts of war, and the contingent nature of memory. Ramadanović compares a recent attempt by an ex-Yugoslavian poet and writer, Dubravka Ugrešić, to compare the legend of Simonides, in the context of the Yugoslavian wars, with a Western journalist's accounts of the siege of Sarajevo, underscoring that both attempts fail to tell what actually happened, and may even create the narrative conditions for a new catastrophe.

Considering the claim that language is not a medium for transmitting information, but a mechanism for producing order, Ramadanović's essay brings to our attention the traumatic status of Balkan languages and their failures to recreate the past in a rational and stable fashion. An epistemological obstacle for a rational discourse, trauma is utilized most effectively by the ideological discourses for the production of reality. Always traumatic and unstable, Balkan reality invites discourses of domination. Bearing this in mind, Rastko Močnik, in his essay " 'The Balkans' as an Element in an Ideological Mechanism," accuses Todorova of falling into an empiricist bias by analyzing the Balkans only in terms of an "Ottoman legacy," and failing to fully account for the status and function of *Balkanism* within the context of an ideology of globalization. Močnik meanwhile insists that an a priori analysis of power relations may be necessary not only to explain the formation of Balkan representations but also to provide a nonbiased direction for empirical studies. He extrapolates from the public discourse on the Balkans two major a priori structures of domination and subordination that govern conceptual formations: first, a *horizontal* antagonism between the Balkan states and ethnic groups, in which each of them is a potential aggressor; secondly, a *vertical* system of co-operation between each of these parties and the European Union. Within this asymmetrical system of *antagonisms* and *co-operation*, stereotypes of Balkan character emerge as "knowledge" and as identities. Unlike Todorova, who insists on teasing out historic specificities of the Balkan societies and who employs her methods for the decomposition of presupposed social totalities, Močnik trusts existing, already unified discourses on ideology, textual rather than archival analysis, to speak on behalf of Balkan identity. Such a position Močnik inherited from the not so distant past. As a prominent member of a loosely structured circle of radical theorists and artists from Slovenia who during the eighties quite successfully challenged socialist ideology by taking it at its word, forcing its collapse and achieving national liberation, Močnik prefers specific experience over historic specificity because, in his view, it represents Balkan identity not as an artifact of the past, but rather as dynamic identity shaping itself by responding to the present ideology rather than to the past.

Balkanism as Cultural Exorcism

The Austrian philosopher Rudolf Steiner, born in Kraljevac, now part of Croatia, once prophetically said that the difference between natural and social parasitism is that in nature, simpler organisms live off more complex organisms, but in society, more complex societies live off simpler ones. Such a relationship, arguably, holds today between the more complex liberal democracies, or globalizing societies, and the Balkans.

Similarly, on the relation between liberal democracies and their peripheries, Slavoj Žižek has argued that the explosion of violent nationalisms in the Balkans, and particularly in the former Yugoslavia, should be attributed to the inner logic of Western capitalism. Although distant in space, the nationalistic reconstruction of Eastern Europe in general and the Balkans in particular is not external to the mechanisms through which liberal democracies invented and preserve themselves in history. "It is as if democracy," he writes, "which in the West shows more and more signs of decay and crisis and is lost in bureaucratic routine and publicity-style election campaigns, is being rediscovered in Eastern Europe in all its freshness and novelty."[21] The *"inner antagonism inherent in these communities"*[22] and the *"inherent structural imbalance,"*[23] Žižek casts into relief, may potentially open an internal collapse of a social consensus. But this collapse has been played out in the Southeastern peripheries of Europe as the conflicts of and on behalf of the center. Liberal democracies not only channel internal vindictiveness onto the periphery to preserve themselves from the inner conflicts endemic to the structure of capitalism, but more importantly, to fall in love with themselves, with a face-lifted capitalism without conflicts—a superficially purified, morally rejuvenated object of self-desire.

This process of self-beautification at the price of the other's ugliness goes back to the beginnings of democracy. Did not Athena in Aeschylus's *Oresteia* mastermind the first democracy by persuading the citizens of Athens to redirect their vengeance from each other to "the stranger" in order to establish the rule of law rather than of a tribal vengeance? Did she not in return guarantee to eliminate "grief and pain," grant them "some definite powers," and offer them a way of life worshiped by others? And did not a chorus in *Oresteia* chant: "But man with man and state with state shall vow the pledge of common hate and common friendship, that for man hath oft made blessing, out of ban, be ours unto all time"?[24] The heart of tragedy still beats in the chests of civilized Europe, while *Balkanism's* poisonous milk drips from her breast. And just as the collective vengeance of the liberal democracies holds European nation-states together in a mode of self-beautification and pleasure, it became the conceptual force behind both Slobodan Milošević's beautification of the nation-state by cleansing "Serb land" of "the Orient" and NATO's bombing of Yugoslavia to stop "ugly" Serbian nationalism. By the end of the nineties, *Balkanism* had permeated the media, military, and academic apparatuses of Western democracies, creating a consensus for what Noam Chomsky calls "the new military humanism"[25] of the world's former colonial masters, now united in NATO. As the war in Kosovo, Bosnia, and Croatia attests, *Balkanism* not only represents the Balkans as a place of violence, but also in part *introduces violence into the Balkans on behalf of its concepts.*

The authors in this volume do not overlook the fact that Balkan identity has been a potent channeling tool in the cultural exorcism of civilized Europe. They do not languish in passive blame. They seize the occasion to mount an important critique of liberal democracy and its violent self-beautification. Not a coincidence, then that these scholars find an ally in Carl Schmitt rather than Jürgen Habermas. Speaking from within the world's center of "formal rationality" Habermas's apology for liberal democracy and his justification of NATO's war against Serbia and Montenegro advanced the process of self-beautification, but had little to contribute to a critical understanding of the aesthetics of the Enlightenment and of European modernity, and their invention of Balkan as metaphor. In "Carl Schmitt on Kosovo or Taking War Seriously," Grigoris Ananiadis uses Schmitt's critique of liberal democracies to unpack the political history of liberal democracy and its contemporary moral rebirth. Challenged by Balkan irrational nationalism, European liberal democracies, in order to reaffirm their Enlightenment foundations and defend modernity, revamped the medieval concept of "just war." Ananiadis scrutinizes the consensus reached between such potential enemies.

Habermas and Myriam Revault d' Alonnes, on the one end and Wesley Clark, the NATO head general, on the other, converge at the notion of a "just war" based on principles of rationality and universal justice. Schmitt argued that this Medieval concept of war has been secularized by the Enlightenment and transformed into a "legal war," a legal instrument of a sovereign state. And yet, as Ananiadis points out, these Enlightenment premises about war and justice clash with the theological origin of the term "just war," which was employed by the Catholic Church to mount "total war" against infidels. In spite of NATO's "limited objectives in Serbia, the war's "collateral damage" was foreseeable and intentional. Contrary to the views of the above-mentioned philosophers, NATO reintroduced a "quasi-total war" under the cover of a "just war."

Some might challenge Ananiadis's argument as farfetched and inconsistent with the facts on the ground, or even question what Schmitt has to do with the theme of this book, with Balkan as metaphor. Did we not witness, such critics would press, one of the most polarized debates between interventionists and isolationists proving the lack of common consensus precisely in regard to this war? Indeed, one may point to, but also dismiss, the interventionists-isolationist "What should we do with the Balkans?" debate by observing that there was no genuine rupture of western social consensus. While interventionists clamored for military punishment to halt Serbian barbarism, isolationists reckoned that "the Balkans were not worth the bones of one healthy Pomeranian grenadier." Though superficially opposite, both viewed the Balkan people as less than civilized, an over-familiar, long-established, disingenuous, domestically self-congratulating and placating position which is a prelude to instructive vengeance and domination. We can thus conclude that a "just war" is a war with a face-lift, one whose ugly parts have been artfully adjusted and concealed; terms like "legal war," "limited objective," and "collateral damage" belong to the moral cosmetics of liberal democracies, equally beautifying the faces of NATO generals and German Greens.

Vampires Fight Back

In the introduction to her book *The Unmaking of Fascist Aesthetics*,[26] Kriss Ravetto unmasks precisely this mechanism of cultural exorcism found in the writing of such prominent liberal writers as Susan Sontag, who can simultaneously call upon NATO's plan to destroy the ugly face of Serbian fascism while aestheticizing "civilized fascism."[27] This "insidious disassociation" and reconstruction of Serbian fascism purifies not only the bombs that fell over Dresden, Hiroshima, or Hanoi, but helps pasteurize Eurofascism, ever incorporating it in the Western project of self-beautification. Where did the ugly blood of Europe go? Where are the Holocaust demons? The knowledge of Balkan violence, *Balkanism*, then, is also a knowledge of Western peace, both of which have historically figured in representations of the vampire, which British journalist Misha Glenny once called "the single most important metaphor in representations of the Balkans." Could it be then that Bram Stoker's *Dracula* can provide a clue to Europe's genealogy of violence? Unlike the trash on a barge in New York City harbor, which nobody wants to claim, the blood drained from Eurofascism is at home in the bodies in Balkan vampires.

Implicitly or explicitly, Balkan authors have begun to incorporate this imposed perception into their analyses. This is not because they wish to occlude responsibility for the atrocities committed by and upon the Balkans, but rather would complicate the question of responsibility. Two of the contributors to this volume, Vesna

Goldsworthy and Tomislav Longinović, focus specifically on the metaphor of the vampire in relation to mainstream media representation of the Balkan conflict. Goldsworthy argues in "Invention and In(ter)vention: The Rhetoric of Balkanization" that the "(young) lifeblood of the Balkans" has been sucked by an "old world sapped of all energy." This inverted relation between Western peace and Balkan blood reverses the stereotype of the Balkan vampire, with blood now streaming in the opposite direction. This image dominates Tomislav Longinović's essay "Vampires Like Us: Gothic Imaginary and 'the serbs.'" Mainstream Western media's perverse fascination with Serbian atrocities, Longinović argues, positions Serbian atrocities in relation to a Western audience's forbidden phantasms. To the extent that the killings committed by the Serbs activated the U.S. war machine only during the night, the stalker technology employed by U.S. planes dropping bombs on Serbia resembled immense bats, and the dead bodies visible on American electronic screens each morning invoked a vampire's now bloodless chamber. In Longinović's view, the Gothic semiotics of the U.S. military complex revealed the concealed pleasures of a reversed vampirism.

Goldsworthy's and Longinović's essay exemplify what could conditionally be called an *external* critique of Serb identity, that is, a critique of stereotyping external to Serbian identity formation. The other mode of critique, what could conditionally be called an *internal* method, does not take Serbian subjectivity for granted as a completed selfhood, but treats Serbian subjectivity and the symbolic order which forms it as its central problem. In the same way Edmund Husserl established a radical position by questioning philosophy's assumptions about the world it sought to understand and explain, the second method achieves the same radical move by establishing an object of cultural criticism within the nationalist narrative responsible for the interpellation of Serbian subjectivity. The study of Serbian subjectivity need not be understood as the reintroduction of the humanistic discourse on selfhood, nor even less as an apology for the nationalistic narrative, but rather as a strategic decoy to tease from it the enigmatic "psychic life of power."

This is exactly what the Serbian philosopher Radomir Konstantinović managed to do in his book *Filozofija Palanke* [*Philosophy of Provincialism*]. When the text of this book first aired on Belgrade radio in 1969, and appeared in print later that year, it immediately attracted a cult following among Serbian intellectuals and student activists fighting for reforms. Konstantinović was a prophetic reader of the signs around him in Belgrade in the 1960s; he understood that what looked from a superficial standpoint like the democratization and internationalization of Serbian society was not the real thing. As Slovene art theorist Eda Čufer has perceptively written in a personal correspondence, "Konstantinović speaks in this book about the secret fears of the provincial mind, the unspoken frustrations which lead to iron laws and hidden logics—the punishment of difference which makes individualism impossible within the parochial system. He saw the self-destructive and paranoid tendencies of Serbia in the 1960s, and was among the first to see what they would lead to in the 1990s—the completion of Belgrade's transformation of itself from metropolis to village."[28] Forty years after its first publication, this book enjoys the unusual status of being a virtually unique example of indigenous Balkan discourse independent of European philosophy, and as such it should be an essential component for the new cultural studies of the region which we hope this book initiates. Developed as a study of the spirit of the *palanka* or market-town mentality, Konstantinović's book discerns at the margin of Enlightened Europe an oppositional rationality, the provincial mind versus Hegelian cosmopolitan reason. While the latter is open to the world with relational subjectivity, the reasoning of the provincial mind closes itself into a subjectivity that excludes the world. To totalize itself as a closed world, the reasoning of the parochial mind must build a wall around itself. Never stated explicitly, Konstantinović's book is about Serbian *Geist*.

How does the rationality of the provincial mind constitute, for example, Serb nationalism? Branka Arsić takes up this question in her essay "Queer Serbs," arguing that the rationality of the provincial mind is deeply entrenched within the homosexual economy of Serbian nationalist power. An ancient Serbian poem describes three brothers building the walls of a city, who to secure the life of the wall must satisfy a female, perhaps lesbian fairy's request to brick one of their wives into the walls, leaving the brothers alone behind their walls, their remaining wives presumably demoralized and bonded by trauma, the fairy with the entombed woman in the symbolic world of the wall representing the requisite homosexual economy of pleasure constitutive of Serbian nationalism. When Serbian men shouted in response to Slobodan Milošević's famous call to Serb unity, "Slobodan we love you!" he replied "I love you too," which resonates with a line by a Serbian romantic poet Sima Pandurović, "It seems that we, the tired children of this century, are no longer interested in the other, beautiful sex. . . ."[29] In these expressions of sentiment by Serbian men, Arsić sees the building of a nation by the sacrificial exclusion of women. "But to build the woman into the city walls," Arsic writes, "does not mean to get rid of her. For her body will go through a miraculous process of 'transsubstantiation'; her body will become the body of the city or of the territory. The dead women lives as the very body of the bodiless nation and the so-called 'national spirit' is nothing other than the life of a dead woman." Thus the national territory marked by the city walls has been claimed, conquered or defended in the name of "dead women."

Although written in the sixties, *Filozofija Palanke* anticipated to a large extent Foucault's discourse on sexuality and knowledge. Longinovic and Arsić complicate, each in different ways, Konstantinović's propositions regarding the ratios of power and pleasure in the representation of a Serb national identity. Foucault argued that not only rationality but also pleasure organizes concepts into systems of knowledge and power. Insofar as the Balkans represent the inverse and forbidden desire of the West, the region is, in the Foucauldian sense, the object of a perverse pleasure. In his chapter "Serbian Discourse on Method," Konstantinović develops the thesis that a philosophical method in the closed world of a provincial rationality must confront procreative sexuality as a norm of tribal rationality and collective identity. In "Sexualizing the Serb," Dusan I. Bjelić, and Lucinda Cole demonstrate how *knowing* Serb sexuality as a new *scientia sexualis* generates what Foucault calls the "pleasure of analysis." The sexuality of South Slavs and especially Serbs has thus served, at particular historical moments, to stabilize Western schemes of sexual self-representation as well as the Serb sexual self-orientalization. Consistent with Konstantinović's position of elucidating a rationality of Serb parochialism from within its own totalizing logic rather than from outside as an occidental tourist, Arsić, Bjelić, and Cole emphasize, following Konstantinović's "Serbian Discourse on Method," that sexual identity must be placed at the core of any serious cultural criticism of the region.

Yet the role of pleasure in *Balkanism* also allows Balkan scholars to mount resistance to the imperial culture of globalization. Balkan food, films, music, and literature have all shaped the representation of the Balkans. It is not uncommon to hear in conversation among those who have toured the Balkans that Balkan food is too fatty, that Balkan movies glorify irrationality and violence, that Balkan music is trashy, or that Balkan literature is tribal. Indeed, Balkan film and film music is studiously resistant to both Western cinematic and musical aesthetics. Thus Stathis Gourgouris, in "Hypnosis and Critique (Film Music for the Balkans)," analyzes the ecstatic as a narrative strategy of suspension in Theo Angelopoulos's *Ulysses' Gaze* and Emir Kusturica's *Underground*, as well as in music composed by Eleni Karaindrou and Goran Bregović. Unlike most Western movies, music here is not a decorative complement to the film narrative, but an autonomous element of cinematic structure. This status permits composers not only to resist the global codes of film music established by Hollywood's imperial culture, but also to mount an aesthetic critique sensitive to the Balkan cultural locale. Karaindrou's music induces moments of suspension in Angelopoulos's meditation on Balkan history; Bregović's music induces ecstasies in Kosturica's narrative on the war in the former Yugoslavia. Yet both lead to hypnosis. For Gourgouris, such hypnosis is a moment of self-formulation, a nation's imaginary performative, or evolution as a dreaming nation.

It is unusual, however, for Balkan scholars to praise Kusturica's movies, a peculiar cultural phenomena which needs a brief unpacking. Rejecting the worldwide success of Kusturica's films and Bregović's music is *de rigeur* for many Balkan intellectuals. They fear that, in glorifying Balkan stereotypes of violent gloom and reckless extravagance entertaining the West with their "reverse racism,"[30] Kusturica and Bregović interfere with their process of disidentification with nationalism and with their efforts to decontaminate their cultures from nationalistic signifiers. Western scholars who recognized in Kusturica's movies an alternative to Hollywood and a refreshing attempt to reshape the codes of global culture remain puzzled by this attitude. Perhaps the modernity of Western scholars was secured and not threatened by Kusturica's films, or perhaps they located the cultural battlelines for defining global community elsewhere, and were able to focus on a different set of issues. In any case, many Balkan intellectuals reflexively distanced themselves from Kusturica's portrayal of the Balkans as part of their resistance to nationalism. Whether this was an oblique manifestation of "nesting orientalism" remains to be investigated. However, when Kusturica's movies, Bregović's music, or other signifiers of former cultural wars are pitted against the emerging codes of global cultural shallowness, as Gourgouris does, they may be resignified as cultural sites of genuine resistance and triumphant critique, rather than as an apology for nationalism.

Indeed, the rapid acceptance of the cultural codes of a global society is enormously tempting for Balkan intellectuals eager to be recognized as members of the world discursive community. But this universalized globalism, as has been long established, is ethnic too: it emanates from "whiteness" as concealed ethnicity.[31] The challenge for Balkan scholars, despite their desire for a modern non-ethnic identity, remains one of recognizing how resistance to consumerist globalism is corollary to their resistance to nationalist myopia.

Unstable Identity

As a regime of knowledge production, *Balkanism* relies on figurative language and metaphor. For the Ottomans, as well as for Western colonial cultures, the Balkans formed the "bridge" between the East and the West, a metaphor naturalized by Ivo Andrić in his Nobel Prize–winning novel, *The Bridge over the Drina*. That metaphor of the "bridge" induces endless hermeneutical circles which transform a "bridge" into a "wall," dividing rather than connecting. It is imperative that we critically examine the history of figurative language and its relation to the Balkans.[32]

Just as they have with the vampire, Balkan writers have appropriated other Western metaphors to define themselves. For Todorova, for example, the bridge metaphor is central. A bridge between East and West reveals the Balkan experience of in-betweenness. Other writers emphasize the instability of the Balkans themselves as a sign. What "Balkan" names, according to Todorova, is neither here nor there but always in-between.[33] Yet during the Kosovo war and the introduction of the Stability Pact for the region, the name "Balkans" suddenly disappeared from the media and was replaced with "Southeast Europe."

Such nominative instability is likewise evident in the construction of particular ethnic identities. Yet perhaps the contradictions of Balkan identity can be traced most clearly through Serbian history: Serbs have comprised an empire and a colony, holocaust victims and holocaust victimizers. The representational schemas deployed by themselves and others reflect these contradictions. Sometimes they are represented as either threats or guardians at the gates of Western civilization-others, as the only remaining European barbarians, equally susceptible to bribery and betrayal. And perhaps no other ethnic group has received so much external scrutiny (and orientalistic treatment) as the Serbs in the last decade of the twentieth century, when they mounted ethnic wars against almost everybody. But similar contradictions exist in other Balkan ethnic identities. Adrian Cioroianu examines the history of the paradoxical Romanian identity in "The Impossible Escape: Romanians and the Balkans." Cioroianu argues that Romanian identity has been historically torn between a desire to escape and a desire to stay in the Balkan region. He concludes that to "run away from the Balkans would be but a stage in the Romanians' much wanted escape from the East; the more persistently they are pushed back to the Balkans and the East, the more difficult their endeavor." Vesna Kesić, in "Muslim Women, Croatian Women, Serbian Women, Albanian Women . . . ," makes similar claims concerning Balkan gender identity. Caught between their men's wars and their ties to other women, women from the former Yugoslavia are themselves split between their gender and their ethnic identities, between their emancipation and their demographic service to the nation.

Subjectivity is framed in relation to both symbolic and institutional identity, but it is never fixed. The Balkan subject constantly oscillates between internalizing and distancing him or herself from group symbols. In "The Dark Intimacy: Maps of

Identities, Acts of Identification," Alexander Kiossev does not settle for the veneer of semiotic stability, introducing instead a "politics of questioning" by asking how Balkan identity is possible in the first place. War shapes Balkan ethnic identity, replies Ugo Vlaisavljević. Following Jean-Luc Nancy's claim that war is a total *event* (cultural as well as military), Vlaisavljević writes in "The South Slav Identity and the Ultimate War-Reality" that the periodic reconstitution of *ethnie* in the Balkans can be achieved properly only through war. In wars, the ethnic Self operates as an imaginary symbolic body that invents its entire (subjective) reality. By establishing a peculiar relation between the imaginary and the real, war becomes an event promoting the self-metamorphosis of identity, one in which identity is trapped between the desire to fit into larger geopolitical schemes of power, or to preserve a nationally distinct version of modernity. The Balkans, Ivaylo Ditchev argues in "The Eros of Identity," have joined the global market of identity with their enormous "natural" resources of victimization and horror, the other side of their *jouissance*—leisure, cuisine, and exoticism. But what appears to be a choice merely plays into the dialectics of the system. "Victimary capitals (post-communist countries, then Bosnia, Kosovo)," he writes, "are moneyed on the media market; thus it was the bloody succession of wars in former Yugoslavia that changed the attitude towards the region, obliging the EU to adopt a quicker procedure of integrating it, developing the Stability pact for financial aid, etc." Henceforth, Ditchev concludes on a critical note that Balkan modernists like dramatist Eugene Ionesco, literary theorist Julia Kristeva, or director Angelopoulos, these figures of universalism are being replaced by "exclusive resellers of local color like writer Ismail Kadare, musician Goran Bregović, or director Emir Kusturica."

In assembling this book, we have primarily enlisted authors born and educated in the Balkans. We do not mean to suggest that Balkan authors have exclusive rights, or even a contextual (regional) mandate, to competently present and represent the Balkans. We do hope to offer, however, a corrective counterpoint to currently circulating representations of the Balkans. At best, these authors attempt to show how an ancient place—the Balkans—became the center of a deep contemporary cultural, political, and identity rupture between the "global" and the "local," a rupture which, having grown increasingly confrontational, now involves the "global" and the "local" turning horrifying caricatures upon each other. No one feels the discursive impact of this rupture as dramatically as these authors.

For most of these authors, the Balkans are not merely a discursive construct but part of their intellectual, cultural, and personal identity. Through their work and public presentations, others recognize these scholars, sometimes as objects of *Balkanism*, to be floating clouds of the Balkan metaphor which occasionally create melodramatic storms. In their daily lives, however, these authors invariably resist this self-generated or imposed metaphoric identity. Without that identity has one barely a proper name, whether in the Balkans or in the West. And so the authors in this volume maintain a radical mode of being in the world. They do not succumb to the disjunctive stereotypes of either the global or local position, those perennial reductive prejudices so often operative in representing the Balkans. None of the authors speak on behalf of the abstract homogeneity of the Balkans in order to confront a homogeneous West; nor does anyone attempt to promote or impose an exclusive or exceptional geo-political identity. When pressed, these writers would probably disagree, for example, about the NATO bombing of Serbia, and they would do so for unpredictable reasons. They examine two differentiated and pluralistic conceptions of the Balkans: a "colonial" and "postcolonial" perspective. The latter comprises a new, self-critical mode of reflection about the Balkans by those from the Balkans, one which many of their essays explore. Our overarching goal is to strike a delicate balance between competing visions and representations of the Balkans and the West, or more generally speaking, of the Orient and the Occident. And yet despite this effort, we must acknowledge that the authors' differentiated positions are not immune to the contradictions of a Balkan identity. While disagreeing on many issues, such as whether the Balkans are a metaphor, or whether Westerners or Serbs are vampires, the authors suggest there is a need to homogenize the West in order to de-homogenize the Balkans. Whether this is a postcolonial irony, a moment of fortuitous occidentalization, or just another paradoxical avatar of the Balkan identity-enigma remains to be seen.

Although discursive and theoretical resistance to *Balkanism* is a largely domestic (Balkan) phenomenon, the discursive strategies of that resistance primarily belong to Western academicians. Post-structuralism, post-modernism, deconstruction, psycho-analysis, post-colonialism, and critical multi-culturalism, in different ways and through parallel efforts, have opened new frontiers of resistance to the traditions concomitant to the Western Enlightenment, namely patriarchy, racism, colonialism, and sexism. In *Balkanism*, theorists have produced a useful account of the proliferation of power relations, which emanates from the center and radiates throughout the periphery. This volume assists in achieving a necessary view on the mechanisms of domination from the view of minority, peripheral, and marginal groups multiplying every globalizing day in uncountable numbers, far from our homes, yet also in and around them. For this changing reality Eagleton has an important warning to announce to those in the center who still may have their "hearing aid switched off":

> While this crisis has broken out with a vengeance on the troubled margins of Europe, the Western heartland can still for the moment indulge the luxury of not seeing themselves from the outside, as a particular, minority form of life, as a specific culture rather than as civilization itself.... The United States in particular has always had extreme difficulty in seeing itself from the outside, and something of this self-opacity is revealed in Richard Rorty's richly provocative essay, which finds no difficulty in enlisting in the "human rights culture" a nation (his own) which has constantly flouted the rights of its own minorities, not to speak of those of cultures far from its shores.[34]

Consistent with Eagleton's warning, the authors and editors of this volume not only wish to enhance the center through improved understanding of the dynamics of their region of origin, but when considering the internal optics of globalization and fragmentation, to *gaze* back at those who *gaze* at them in order to reverse the panoptical process of the center. In this respect, *Balkanism* has bestowed on Balkan scholars an opportunity to mount representational resistance against the imperial depredations and shallowness of global culture. These authors resist any representational strategy that leads to the decomposition of the Balkans into functional fragments—as NATO army bases, as digital maps, or as the "Mall of the Balkans"— to wire them into the global market as an e-Balkans. Since the Balkan countries lack both wealth and might, the region's best resistance to globalization and fragmentation may not be to obstruct the inevitable process of the world community, but to foster an alliance of cultural critics across ethnic and professional lines. The authors in this volume aim to institute new discursive conditions for the formation of Balkan identity around which cultural fragments of Balkanhood abandoned as road kill on the highway of globalization may be reassembled into a vital parliament of our hybrid Balkan cultures.

Notes

1. Fredric Jameson, "Conversation on the New World Order," in Robin Blackburn, ed., *After the Fall: The Failure of Communism and Future of Socialism* (New York: Verso, 1991), 260. Had Jameson genuinely focused on the East rather than on his own discourse— or if he did not see the other as the "East"—Jameson would have realized, as we did that afternoon, that if one is willing to listen to the "other" then there is no real struggle for "discursive rules" between the West and the East because people of the Balkans and of

the United States, as Ludwig Wittgenstein would say, already agree in "forms of life." About the extended critique of Jameson's troublesome notion of the "other" see Aijaz Ahmad's "Jameson's Rhetoric of Otherness and the 'National Allegory,'" *Social Text* 17 (fall 1987).

2. Terry Eagleton, Preface to *The Politics of Human Rights*, ed. Obrad Savić (New York: Verso, 1999), vi.

3. Complaining about the Eastern European intellectuals' ability to understand the Western's intellectual concerns, Jameson claims: "The more their truths are couched in Orwellian language, the more tedious they become for us; the more our truths demand expression in even the weakest forms of Marxian language—that or simple social democracy say, or even the welfare state or social justice, or equality—the more immediately do the Eastern hearing aids get switched off." (Blackburn, *After*, 260.) Also see Susan Buck-Morss's *Dreamworld and Catastrophe: The Passing of Mass Utopia in East and West* (Cambridge, Mass.: The MIT Press, 2000), and how Jameson's orientalization of Eastern European intellectuals in its ability to sweep over the heterogeneous intellectual territory of the "East" may still gain a theoretical authority even when the author claims an open minded ethnography in surveying the "Eastern" intellectual landscape.

4. Cornel West, "The New Cultural Politics of Difference," *The Cultural Studies Reader*, 2d ed., ed. Simon During (London: Routledge, 2000), 264.

5. A recent book by Branimir Anzulovic, *Heavenly Serbia: From Myth to Genocide*, in which he explains Serbian acts of genocide by invoking Byzantine ties between the Orthodox religion and the Serbian state, is a fresh example of the application of Byzantism (New York: New York University Press, 1999).

6. Gayatri Spivak, *Outside in the Teaching Machine* (New York: Routledge, 1993), 56.

7. Maria Todorova, *Imagining the Balkans* (Oxford: Oxford University Press, 1997).

8. Vesna Goldsworthy, *Inventing Ruritania: The Imperialism of the Imagination* (New Haven: Yale University Press, 1998).

9. Stathis Gourgouris, *Dream Nation: Enlightenment, Colonization and the Institution of Modern Greece* (Stanford, Calif.: Stanford University Press, 1996).

10. Milica Bakic-Hayden, "Nesting *Orientalism*: The Case of Former Yugoslavia," *Slavic Review* 54, no. 4 (winter 1995), 917–931.

11. Ibid.

12. Richard G. Fox, "East of Said," in *Edward Said: A Critical Reader*, ed. Michael Sprinker (Oxford: Blackwell, 1992), 151.

13. See James G. Carrier, ed., *Occidentalism* (Oxford: Clarendon Press, 1995).

14. Edward Said, *Orientalism* (New York: Vintage Books, 1997), 334, 338.

15. Les Back and John Solomons, eds., *Theories of Race and Racism: A Reader* (London: Routledge, 2000), 475.

16. Arif Dirlik, *The Postcolonial Aura: The World Criticism in the Age of Global Capitalism* (Boulder, Colo.: Westview Press, 1997), 123.

17. Bart Moore-Gilbert, *Postcolonial Theory: Contexts, Practices, Politics* (London: Verso, 1997), 72.

18. K. E. Fleming, "*Orientalism*, the Balkans, and Balkan Historiography," *American Historical Review*, October 2000, 1215.

19. Fleming, ibid., 1232.

20. A partial list of periodicals on the Balkans published in English follows. Bulgaria: *Balkan Neighbours* (monthly). Greece: *Thesis* (monthly); *Balkanism* (quarterly). Macedonia: *Balkan Forum* (quarterly); *The Macedonian Times* (monthly). Turkey: *Turkish Review of Balkanism* (annual); *Balkanism* (annual). Serbia-Montenegro: *Review of International Affairs* (quarterly); *Newsletter* (bimonthly), CSS Survey (monthly).

21. Slavoj Žižek, *Tarrying with the Negative: Kant, Hegel, and the Critique of Ideology* (Durham, N.C.: Duke University Press, 1993), 200.

22. Žižek, *Terryng*, 206.

23. Ibid., 209.

24. Aeschylus, *Oresteia*, translated by E. D. A. Morsehead (http://classics.mit.edu/Aeschylus/eumendides.html).

25. Noam Chomsky, *The New Military Humanism: Lessons from Kosovo* (Monroe, Me.: Common Courage Press, 1999).

26. Kriss Ravetto, *The Unmaking of Fascist Aesthetics* (Minneapolis: University of Minnesota Press, 2001).

27. Susan Sontag, "'There' and 'Here': A Lament for Bosnia," *Nation* 261, no. 22 (December 25, 1995), on the web: http://www.bosnet.org/archive/bosnet.w3archive/9601/msg00037.html; "Why are we in Kosovo?," *New York Times,* May 2, 1999, on the web: http://www.nbi.dk/~predrag/projects/SontagKosovo.html.

28. Eda Čufer, personal correspondence.

29. Sima Pandurović, "Mrtva Draga" ("A Dead Darling"), quoted in Radomir Konstanti-nović, *Filozofija Palanke* (Philosophy of Provincialism) (Belgrade: NOLIT, 1969), 216.

30. Slavoj Žižek writes: "Finally, there is the reverse racism which celebrates the exotic authenticity of the Balkan Other, as in the notion of Serbs who, in contrast to inhibited, anaemic Western Europeans, still exhibit a prodigious lust for life—this last form of racism plays a crucial role in the success of Emir Kusturica's films in the West." (*The Fragile Absolute, or why is the Christian legacy worth fighting for?* [New York: Verso 2000], 5).

31. Richard Dyer, "The Matter of Whiteness," *Theories of Race and Racism*, ed. Les Back and John Solomons (New York: Routledge, 2000), 539–548; Peter McLaren, "White Terror and Oppositional Agency: Towards a Critical Multiculturalism," *Multiculturalism: A Critical Reader*, ed. David T. Goldberg (Oxford: Blackwell, 1997), 45–74.

32. Eric Cheyfitz has given an instructive historical account of this relation. The beginning of British colonial history, he argues, fundamentally transformed the English language; its structures split into two hierarchically ordered languages, one figurative and the other literal. The British empire emphasized the eloquence of English, rather than its dialogic and figurative tradition. As a result, democratic dialogue, with its figurative, equivocal, and conflictive play, rigidified into the literal, proper, or univocal language of eloquence. (*The Poetics of Imperialism: Translation and Colonization from Tempest to Tarzan* [Philadelphia:

University of Pennsylvania Press, 1997], 38). "When this equivocality is repressed," Cheyfitz continues, "the literal and the figurative aspects of language became hierarchized into absolute and oppositional entities, with the masters occupying the territory of the literal or proper and consigning the slaves to that of the figurative" (38–39). For Roland Barthes, this division of language falls under the division of "national/foreign," and "familiar/strange," making a national language strange to itself. Within this imperial hierarchy of language closed into a nation state, imperial language metaphorically represented the rest of the world, including the Balkans, as a colonial subject, even though not one with a modern colonial history.

33. Todorova, *Imagining the Balkans*, 18.

34. Eagelton, Preface, vi.

What forces were really at work here? I didn't mean by that the obvious ones. . . . I meant—or thought I meant—what basal forces, what innate characteristics, what elements of competing Balkan histories and cultures and ethnicities could ever have led to such a situation as this?

For there was nothing new here. . . . What was actually happening here at Blace's swamp-camp, and all the tales we were hearing from the refugees of what had been happening up in Kosovo, was merely—as if the word *merely* could really be used in so awful a context—a manifestation of what had been going on in the Balkans for a thousand years or more.[8]

As he tries to unlock "the savage mysteries of this wretched peninsula,"[9] Winchester opens his book with a lengthy epigraph on Balkan geology and continues to resort to geological parallels between the land and the people who inhabit it: "The two chains [i.e., the Balkan Mountains and the Dinaric Alps] smashed into one another to create a geological fracture zone that became a template for the fractured behavior of those who would later live upon it."[10] Just as the peninsula—"these strange and feral Balkans"[11]—is outlandish and unlike the rest of Europe, its inhabitants, "the wild and refractory peoples of the Balkans,"[12] are seen almost as a different species: "One might say that anyone who inhabited such a place for a long period would probably evolve into something that varied substantially, for good or for ill, from whatever is the human norm."[13]

American journalist Robert Kaplan proposes similarly exotic explanations of Balkan hostilities in an account of Balkan "ancient hatreds" that is said to have had a particular influence on President Clinton.[14] The Balkan peoples are so deeply immersed in their bloody history, Kaplan argues in *Balkan Ghosts*, that their world is barely comprehensible to an outsider: "This was a time-capsule world: a dim stage upon which people raged, spilled blood, experienced visions and ecstasies. Yet their expressions remained fixed and distant, like dusty statuary."[15] The British army colonel Bob Stewart puts it more simply in his account of his time in Bosnia-Herzegovina in the 1990s, *Broken Lives. A Personal View of the Bosnian Conflict*: "Historically, relations between Serbs, Croats and Muslims had been appalling for centuries. . . . The place has always been considered a powder keg."[16]

While the vision of the Balkans as a permanent, or "natural," source of instability in Europe—the continent's powder-keg—predates the First World War,[17] it gained new currency in the wars of the Yugoslav succession in the 1990s. Particularly when invoked alongside the "ancient hatreds," the metaphoric notion of the peninsula as a powder-keg proved useful in exonerating outsiders of culpability for the crises in the Balkans. It represented the peninsula as a source of instability, a threat to the outside world rather than a victim. The paradox of how the Balkan peoples could be so obvious in their cat-and-dog-like passions, while at the same time igniting the more sober parts of the world (i.e., acting as a powder-keg) is rarely examined.

Whatever merits such metaphors might have as a shorthand for particular aspects of Balkan history, their uncritical repetition has ensured that conflicts of very different origins and outcomes could blur into a generic "Balkan" war, the intermittent letting of blood which releases the pressure of "ancient hatreds." Some of the more recent studies of the Balkans—including Misha Glenny's *The Balkans 1804–1999: Nationalism, War and Great Powers*[18]—have attempted to redress the balance against such repeated simplifications by focusing on the frequently divisive role of the Great Powers or the "international community" in the peninsula. Nonetheless, relatively simple images such as fault lines, ancient hatreds, and powder kegs continue to offer the advantage of beguiling simplicity to those confronted with Balkan history, which is, as Richard Holbrooke pointed out, "too complicated (or trivial) for outsiders to master."[19]

Romancing the "Balkan" Wars

"To the outside observer, the Balkans appear to be a puzzle of confusing complexity. A geographic region inhabited by seven major nationalities [sic!], speaking different languages, it has usually impinged on the Western consciousness only when it has become the scene of war or acts of violence," the American historian Barbara Jelavich wrote in 1983.[20] As if to confirm her words, the Balkan wars of the 1990s produced a tide of books: new histories of Serbia, Croatia, Bosnia-Herzegovina, and Kosovo;[21] countless memoirs by politicians, diplomats, and soldiers engaged in the region; accounts by foreign correspondents and relief workers; the testimonies of victims, survivors and camp inmates; diaries kept during the siege of Sarajevo; anthologies of poetry and prose; reissues of long out of print titles;[22] and a variety of academic explorations of the Balkan peninsula, including the present volume.[23]

An interest in the Balkans that lasts only as long as war—or the rumor of war—persists might well help create the impression that the Balkan peoples, like metaphorical Rip Van Winkle of Europe,[24] sleepwalk their way through brief interludes of peace only to come to life in a series of bloody ethnic struggles. An intermittent focus on the peninsula has meant that perceptions that originated in the decades of turbulence during the gradual withdrawal of the Ottoman empire from most of the peninsula in the nineteenth and early twentieth century could persist both in the periods of Balkan peace and the times when the Balkans were swept by conflicts of (West) European provenance such as the Second World War. The defamiliarizing of accounts of Balkan conflicts in the Western media—describing ethnic wars as unthinkable elsewhere in Europe while supplying gory details of singularly "Balkan" butchery to an eager audience—contribute to the perception of the peninsula's ambiguous, "not-yet" or "never-quite," Europeanness. They also, however, reveal an ambiguous attitude toward war itself. Editorials profess horror at blood-spilling and yet an enormous, and frequently voyeuristic, media output (newspapers, TV, publishing, and film industries have all developed their own "Balkan" production-lines during the 1990s) offers daily testimony to a fascination with war and killing about which we have as many taboos as the Victorians did pornography. We claim to abhor war, and yet we romanticize the professionals—foreign correspondents, cameramen—who enable us to partake in the experience. Pictures for which photo-journalists risk their lives, and video footage taken by "smart" bombs as they hit their target have a large, enthusiastic audience in the West. Some of the dullest backwaters in the former Yugoslavia have acquired a dubious romantic resonance over the past ten years while reporters searched for the Balkan heart of darkness, in order to return with tales of "unspeakable" horror. The relative anonymity of those parts of the Balkans outside the (currently) war-torn areas—in comparison with the overwhelming exposure of the former Yugoslavia—is another indication of this particular fascination.

Recent books, such as Joanna Bourke's *An Intimate History of Killing* and Niall Ferguson's *The Pity of War*,[25] which attempted to break some of the taboos related to the First World War by suggesting that many of the participants actually enjoyed the experience of fighting, have been the subject of a great deal of controversy. The ambiguous Western attitude toward Balkan wars is an even more difficult subject to tackle as it reflects the values and preoccupations of our generation. Western "horror" at what is going on in the Balkans contains, like Gothic horror, a frisson of pleasure that is difficult to own up to—an opportunity to re-enact the imperialist fantasy of drawing frontiers and "sorting the troublesome natives out" without being accused of racism (because all the people involved are white), a supply of raw material for the expanding industries of conscience (manifest in a plethora of multinational NGOs and pressure groups), a chance to pass the "tests of history" on what the British Prime Minister Tony Blair described as the "doorstep of Europe," or—for a few—simply a possibility to experience war at close quarters. In a situation in which our Balkan war heroes are blue-helmeted peacemakers, tough-talking negotiators, or indignant correspondents, it might seem awkward to suggest that individual Westerners are drawn to Balkan wars by anything beyond the call of duty or humanitarian instinct. Yet as the British journalist Paul Harris admitted in *Somebody*

Else's War: Reports from the Balkan Frontline, "there is the awe-ful[sic] realisation that you can actually enjoy, physically and mentally, the heat of battle, the taste of fear and the actuality of survival. And, as a writer you realise that the extremes of emotion, to which you are so brutally and suddenly exposed, release the ability to string together the words in a way you hitherto hardly dreamt possible."[26]

A century ago, British writers were prepared to be more forthcoming about this particular attraction of the Balkans. In "The Cupboard of the Yesterdays," a short story written during the Balkan wars of 1912–1913, H. H. Munro (Saki)—who was the correspondent of the *Morning Post* from Macedonia in the early years of the twentieth century—remarked:

The Balkans have long been the last surviving shred of happy hunting-ground for the adventurous, a playground for passions that are fast becoming atrophied for want of exercise. In old bygone days we had the wars in Low Countries always at our doors, as it were. There was no need to go far afield into malaria stricken wilds if one wanted a life of boot and saddle and licence to kill and be killed. Those who wished to see life had a decent opportunity for seeing death at the same time.[27]

Saki's fictional characters frequently complain about "an intrusion of civilised monotony" into the Balkans: "after every important war in South-Eastern Europe in recent times there has been a shrinking of the area of chronically disturbed territory, a stiffening of frontier lines."[28] Byronic spleen before the dullness of the "non-Balkan" Europe crops up again and again in his writing. As he enlisted to join the army in 1914, Saki actually admitted to a friend that he had "always looked forward to a romance of the European war."[29] The novelist Joyce Cary was similarly open about wanting "the experience of war" when he volunteered to join the Montenegrins in the war against Turkey in October 1912: "I thought there would be no more wars. And I had a certain romantic enthusiasm for the cause of the Montenegrins; in short I was young and eager for any sort of adventure."[30]

The idea that war lends not only a sense of adventure, but a greater sense of reality to lives in the Balkans, can be encountered in writings from the peninsula itself. In this context, the experience of war is described as providing a privileged viewpoint, a position of deeper insight. In his account of a tour on the "European Literary Express 2000," when he traveled from Lisbon to St. Petersburg with 99 other European writers, the Sarajevan author Nenad Veličković describes the vacuousness of much of West European prosperity. At a chateau near Bordeaux, to which the hundred writers are taken for a wine-tasting session, Veličković comments: "You need to survive a war, or come here from a *small European colony*, to have the thought that there is more spirit at one single table on the pavement in front of the Rafaelo Inn in Sarajevo than in all this wine which will turn into poetry on poets' lips."[31] Later on, he observes English football supporters in Brussels on their way to the European championship. He comments that they try to compensate for the lack of war experience through hooliganism and street violence:

Weekend, Saturday afternoon, a cloudless sky, the time and the terrain ideal for war. Thousands of Englishmen born a hundred years too late, without a real chance of losing an eye, an arm or a life for the homeland, like proud lions fed on Soya steaks, stretch their nostrils at the smell of blood. Tonight, someone will pay the price of all their humiliations and injustice, of a boring life through which they pass without a medal on their chest or a wooden leg below the knee. Tomorrow, tame—like after an epileptic fit—they will sit on the floor of the railway station. . . .[32]

The notion that experiencing a war offers a deeper, more meaningful perspective on life might be an understandable response from a writer who has experienced the siege of Sarajevo. A suggestion, however, that war might be a covetable experience (that, in Saki's words, "nearly every red-blooded human boy has had war, in some shape or form, for his first love,"[33] or—in Nora Ephron's—"for correspondents, war is not hell. It is fun")[34] reveals the kind of romanticization of the battleground which seems to make the Balkans interesting for as long as the fighting lasts.

Like Jonathan Harker, the English solicitor hero of Bram Stoker's novel *Dracula* (1897), who goes to the Balkans to conclude a property deal but ends up locked in a life-and-after-death struggle with the vampire count, many Westerners of our generation—whatever their notional reasons for getting involved with the problems of the peninsula in the first place—have set out to "solve the problems of the Balkans" and ended up espousing particular causes with a passion and partisanship which are normally ascribed to Balkan peoples. Indeed, the issues related to the conflicts of the 1990s have produced a degree of viciousness, name-calling, and mutual character assassinations among the champions of different sides in the West that demonstrates that there is nothing peculiarly "Balkan" about the Balkan wars. Moreover, while the description of the wars of Yugoslav succession as "Balkan" has highlighted the continuum of ethnic strife in the peninsula, it has obscured the particularly Yugoslav context of these wars. Many of the Western historians and political commentators who have accused Balkan peoples of being in thrall to ancient history have shown the same preference for the exciting narrative of "ancient hatreds" rather than analyzing the more mundane but just as devastating failure of Yugoslavia's economic and constitutional experiments after 1945.

Globalizing Balkanization

The fact that the wa[r] [...] as "Balkan" rather than "Yugosla[via]" [...] he peninsula, is to a significant deg[ree] [...] name. Now the attention of the [...] n states and territories—all those [...] nt Clinton's speech—the notion o[f] [...] nd mutually hostile fragments, ha[s] [...] quency. One Internet search engin[e] [...] ht examples of the term's usage: f[...] the Chinese legal system, the terri[...] city grid, the transit system in San [...] politicians, even the United Sta[tes] [...] tion for the Balkanization of Am[erica] [...] ericans" by Brent A. Nelson is titl[ed] [...] g and every-where seems to be in [...] proportion of these cases taking place in the Balkans themselves.

[handwritten marginal note: "globalization may in fact enable and promote balkanization"]

If Balkanization means a particular kind of fragmentation where the fragments are mutually hostile and in competition with each other, then it is by no means clear that fragmentation and globalization are really opposites as the subtitle of this volume implies. Globalization may in fact enable and promote Balkanization. Although Fredric Jameson has argued that contemporary societies face a choice between nationalism and global American postmodern culture,[36] it is also possible to see nationalism as having evolved in response to increasing globalization. While embracing some aspects of global culture, it has offered a sense of safety by promoting a particular identity against the new anxieties of creeping homogeneity. On the simplest level, where particular Balkan identities might once have been defined against each other, they now incorporate a sense of difference from Americans, Western Europeans or Asians. (A nationalist from a Balkan country can thus continue to say that "we" are more civilized than the Serbs or braver than the Croats, while adding that "we" are leaner and fitter than the Americans, are more individualistic than the Japanese, or have stronger family structures than the British.) Globalization has also, for the first time, divorced the nationalist from the particular territory by offering preconditions for "virtual" nationalism. The network of global communications has enabled expatriate communities throughout the developed world to maintain closer links with their countries of origin and to influence the political scene at "home" in a variety of new ways. Some of the most radical Balkan nationalists are thus to be found among American tax-payers and American voters. The world-wide web, while being the ultimate expression of globalization, has also enabled the dissemination of nationalist material to an unprecedented degree and encouraged a variety of Balkanizing processes. Globalization might have undermined particular types of national identity—in federalist, unionist, or "melting pot" societies such as the former Yugoslavia, Canada, urban Britain, and, paradoxically, the United States (the world might be becoming more American, but a right-wing politician such as Pat Buchanan clearly worries that the United States is becoming less so)—but it might well, at least in the short term, have encouraged ethnic nationalism and Balkanization.

The B-Word: Escape from the Balkans

In Western popular fiction and film, the Balkans have often provided a threatening space—the mysterious and unhomelike (*unheimlich*) Eastern location for the unfolding of Western adventure.[37] That space frequently remained blank: there was no need to evoke much local color if the sheer resonance of Balkan toponyms could suffice. Agatha Christie's *Murder on the Orient Express* (1934) is a typical example. In lieu of any precise description of time and location, the white windows of a snowbound luxury train, onto which the reader is expected to project his or her own images of horror, can evoke the "wild Balkans" outside. The train is delayed by snow near the small Croatian town of Vinkovci, a railway junction in the middle of the Slavonian plain—hardly the Gothic stuff of which the "Wild East" is made. Ironically, while the plot of Christie's novel hinges on the idea of being stuck in a threatening Balkan space, "the murderer" is a group of Westerners (conveniently sharing the guilt). Sharing their Balkan deed in a similar way, a "troika" of Western men (an Englishman, an American and a Dutchman) destroys the Transylvanian count in Bram Stoker's *Dracula* in order to save England (Europe) from the Balkan undead. In a rare reversal of this kind of imagery, the idea of Europe as a vampire, the old world sapped of all energy which sucks the (young) lifeblood of the Balkans, appears as a mirror image in Balkan writing. Writes Veličković: "France represents the smile of Europe—a smile affected and dangerous, as kind as strictly useful, as wide as strictly necessary. When she laughs, her jaws and her vampire teeth click. A wrinkled face of a frightened miserly old lady hides behind the expensive make-up."[38]

The kind of symbolic geography which opposes Europe and the Balkans seems to have become more pervasive in the 1990s. "After 1989, which was assumed by some to mark 'the end of history', came a kind of 'rebirth of geography,'" Wendy Bracewell and Alex Drace-Francis remarked in their "Southeastern Europe: History, Concepts, Boundaries," as they attempted to find "a way out of the spiralling vacuum of metaphors" that affected much of the thinking about Southeastern Europe over the past decade.[39] That this "born-again" geography is primarily symbolic is all too evident in President Clinton's speech on the eve of the Kosovo campaign. While he stood in front of an actual map, he described the Balkans in the language of images and metaphors—fault lines and collisions of civilization—rather than "real," physical geography.[40] If the Balkan peoples are frequently accused of being trapped in their own history, many of the outsiders dealing with the region have also shown an unwillingness to think beyond a symbolic, formulaic representation, to the point where—to paraphrase this book's title—the Balkans have become nothing but a metaphor for conflict, incivility, and violence.

Unsurprisingly, few wish to remain in the peninsula whose very name—"the B-word"[41]—became unmentionable for fear of bad luck, "toil and trouble," like "the Scottish play."[42] While Yugoslavia fell apart, the peninsula around it gradually emptied as (formerly) Balkan countries sought to demonstrate that their true allegiance lay elsewhere (in Central or even Western Europe), in what the Romanian politician Elena Zamfirescu described as "Flight from the Balkans."[43] Zamfirescu argues that Romania belongs to Central Europe. Croatian president Franjo Tudjman made his 1997 campaign slogan "Tudjman, not the Balkans."[44] Similarly, in a speech at a Balkan conference, the Bulgarian president Petar Stoyanov reminded his audience that the Yugoslav president Slobodan Milošević is "not dividing Europe from the Balkans but Europe from Europe."[45]

In academic debates, the "politically correct" term Southeastern Europe has more or less replaced the Balkans, because it has become impossible to define a country as "Balkan" without having to explain oneself. Indeed, Serbia under Slobodan Milošević seems to be the last country in the peninsula that is regularly described as Balkan, with obvious symbolic connotations. It is telling that, at the reopening of one of the bridges on the Danube destroyed in NATO's bombing raids, Milošević himself proclaimed Serbia the most European of European countries. Attending the reopening alongside hundreds of Serbs bussed in for the ceremony, Predrag Matvejević mused over the paradox of Europe being both the enemy and the measure of Serbia's "success."[46]

What Milošević's speech demonstrates is that any set of values can be inscribed in the metaphorical taxonomy, but that the superiority of Europe in opposition to the Balkans tends to remain a constant. This is equally true whether the heart of

Europe is placed in Brussels or in Belgrade, whether the Balkans shrink to a single country (as in current perceptions of Serbia) or expand northward to the edge of the English Channel (as is the case in the pronouncements of some British "Eurosceptics" who see the whole of Europe as the Balkanized other). This kind of symbolic hierarchy and its practical political consequences have been the subject of increasing scrutiny since 1989.

Out of the Balkans: New Directions

A number of new strategies developed over the past decade and inspired by movements in postcolonial and subaltern studies, most notably Edward Said's *Orientalism*, have been used to explore perceptions of the Balkans. John Allcock's 1991 examination of Balkan "multiple marginality" in "Constructing the Balkans" was followed by numerous studies of "the way West looks East"[48] throughout the 1990s. Milica Bakić-Hayden's "nesting orientalisms" and Maria Todorova's notion of *Balkanism* were particularly influential. I attempted to encapsulate the ever changing oppositions between the Balkans and (the rest of) Europe using the metaphor of Ruritania, an imaginary country which is always either "not yet European" or "what Europe has already been."[49] While I was primarily interested in the imperialism through which imagination comes to occupy the map, I was aware that the map itself would require a different type of examination if Balkan studies were to avoid the pitfalls of Orientalist enquiry.

In his influential book *In Theory: Classes, Nations, Literatures*,[50] the Indian Marxist Aijaz Ahmad, one of Edward Said's most vocal critics, has accused *Orientalism* of an obsession with Western knowledge. Ahmad pointed out that *Orientalism* was primarily developed by West-oriented Third World scholars working within Western universities and Western scholars who emulated them. Might the examination of the Balkans similarly have become too wrapped up in the way "the West looks East" if its most influential directions are being defined in Western universities by scholars of Balkan origin—such as many of us contributing to this book? Here, globalization has proved to be the hero rather than the villain of the piece. Because of the Internet and a host of other channels of academic exchange that have developed since 1989, scholars resident in the Balkans are taking part in the debate, in spite of often difficult circumstances, much more meaningfully than in the late seventies and the early eighties when Orientalist studies were being defined. With a new generation of Western historians of the Balkans debunking the "myths" that Balkan peoples may have about themselves, and Balkan scholars pulling the rug from beneath some complacent Western certainties about the Balkans, there is now, for the first time since the Second World War, an ongoing dialogue and an unprecedented exchange of ideas. Should a new set of definitions of the Balkans emerge out of this debate, they might, perhaps for the first time, be a shared creation of East and West—provided, that is, that once the wars of former Yugoslavia have run their bloody course, the peninsula is not forgotten, as it so often has been in the past.

Notes

1. David Owen, *Balkan Odyssey* (London: Victor Gollancz, 1995).

2. President Clinton's televised address to the nation from the Oval Office. March 24, 1999. 8:01 PM EST.

3. Samuel P. Huntington, "The Clash of Civilizations?" *Foreign Affairs* 72, no. 3 (Summer 1993): 23–49.

4. Edith Durham, *The Burden of the Balkans* (London: Thomas Nelson, 1905), 20.

5. Jason Fields, "Historical Perspective: Yugoslavia, a Legacy of Ethnic Hatred," Associated Press web-site, wire.ap.org/Apnews/center_package.html?Packageid=flashpointyugo (19 February 1999).

6. Michael Nicholson, *Natasha's Story* (London: Pan, 1994), 16. (First published 1993. Nicholson's book inspired a popular film version titled *Welcome to Sarajevo* directed by Michael Winterbottom in 1997.) I am grateful to Simon Goldsworthy for bringing this to my attention.

7. Simon Winchester, *The Fracture Zone: A Return to the Balkans* (London: Viking, 1999), 26.

8. Ibid., 29.

9. Ibid., 31.

10. Ibid., 60.

11. Ibid., 21.

12. Ibid., 3.

13. Ibid., 61.

14. Richard Holbrooke, *To End a War* (New York: Random House, 1998), 22.

15. Robert D. Kaplan, *Balkan Ghosts. A Journey through History* (New York: St. Martin's Press, 1993), xxi.

16. Colonel Bob Stewart, *Broken Lives. A Personal View of the Bosnian Conflict* (London: Harper Collins, 1994), 6.

17. See Maria Todorova, *Imagining the Balkans* (Oxford: Oxford University Press, 1997), pp. 119–20 for the background to this type of imagery.

18. Misha Glenny's recent book has challenged this by drawing attention to the Great Power's involvement in the area. See Misha Glenny, *The Balkans 1804–1999. Nationalism, War and the Great Powers* (London: Granta Books, 1999).

19. Holbrooke, *To End a War*, 22.

20. Barbara Jelavich, *History of the Balkans. Eighteenth and Nineteenth Centuries* (Cambridge: Cambridge University Press, 1983), ix.

21. Examples include: Tim Judah, *The Serbs. History, Myths and the Destruction of Yugoslavia* (New Haven: Yale University Press, 1997); Tim Judah, *Kosovo. War and Revenge* (New Haven: Yale University Press, 2000); Noel Malcolm, *Bosnia: A Short History* (London: Macmillan, 1994); Noel Malcolm, *Kosovo: A Short History* (London: Macmillan, 1997); Marcus Tanner, *Croatia: A Nation Forged in War* (New Haven: Yale University Press, 1997).

22. Among these are some of the following: memoirs by politicians, such as David Owen, *Balkan Odyssey* (London: Victor Gollanz, 1995); Holbrooke, *To End a War*; Carl Bildt, *Peace Journey. The Struggle for Peace in Bosnia* (London: Weidenfeld and Nicholson, 1998); soldiers: General Sir Michael Rose, *Fighting for Peace. Bosnia 1994* (London: Harvill, 1998); Colonel Bob Stewart, *Broken Lives* (London: Harper Collins, 1994); relief workers: Larry Hollingworth, *Merry Christmas, Mr Larry* (London: Heinemann, 1996); journalists: Anthony Loyd, *My War Gone By, I Miss It So* (London: Doubleday, 1999); Eve Ann Prentice, *One Woman's War: Life and Death on Deadline* (London: Duckworth, 2000); Michael Nicholson, *Natasha's Story* (London: Pan, 1993), Fergal Keane, *Letters Home* (London: Penguin, 1999); Janine di Giovanni, *The Quick and the Dead: Under Siege in Sarajevo* (London: Phoenix House, 1994); John Simpson, *Strange Places, Questionable People* (London: Pan, 1999); Ed Vuillamy, *Seasons in Hell: Understanding Bosnia's War* (London: Simon & Schuster, 1994); survivors: Zlata Filipović, *Zlata's Diary: A Child's Life in Sarajevo* (London: Penguin, 1995); Rezak Kuhanović, *The Tenth Circle of Hell*, London: Abacus, 1993); Elma Softić, *Sarajevo Days, Sarajevo Nights* (Toronto: Key Porter Books, 1992).

23. Including Maria Todorova, *Imagining the Balkans* (Oxford: Oxford University Press, 1997); Stevan K. Pavlowitch, *A History of the Balkans 1804–1945* (London: Longman, 1999); and my own *Inventing Ruritania: The Imperialism of the Imagination* (New Haven: Yale University Press, 1998).

24. I borrow this image from Edith Durham, *The Burden of the Balkans* (London: Thomas Nelson, 1905), 14.

25. Joanna Bourke, *An Intimate History of Killing* (London: Granta Books, 1999). Niall Ferguson, *The Pity of War* (London: Allen Lane, 1998).

26. Paul Harris, *Somebody Else's War. Frontline Reports from the Balkan Wars* (Stevenage: Spa Books, 1992), 44.

27. H. H. Munro, "The Cupboard of the Yesterdays," in *The Penguin Complete Saki* (London: Penguin Books, 1982), 528–529.

28. Ibid., 529.

29. Quoted in A. J. Langguth, *Saki: A Life of Hector Hugh Munro. With Six Short Stories Never Before Collected* (London: Hamish Hamilton, 1981), 251.

30. Joyce Cary, *Memoir of the Bobotes* (Austin: University of Texas Press, 1960), ix.

31. Nenad Veličković, "Više duha ima za jednim stolom sarajevske birtije Rafaelo . . . ," Dnevnik sa putovanja (3), *Slobodna Bosna*, 22 June 2000, 54. (My translation and my italics).

32. Ibid., 55.

33. Langguth, *Saki*, 258.

34. Harris, *Somebody Else's War*, 45.

35. Brent A. Nelson, *America Balkanized: Immigration's Challenge to Government* (American Immigration Control Foundation: Monterey, Va., 1994).

36. See Fredric Jameson, *Postmodernism, or, The Cultural Logic of Late Capitalism* (London: Verso, 1991).

37. In *Inventing Ruritania* I examine literary images of the Balkans over the past two hundred years.

38. Veličković, "Više duha ima za jednim stolom sarajevske birtije Rafaelo . . . ," 54.

39. Wendy Bracewell and Alex Drace-Francis, "South-Eastern Europe: History, Concepts, Boundaries," in *Balkanologie* 3, no. 2 (December 1999): 48.

40. At around the time President Clinton was making this speech, in a joke that was making the rounds in Belgrade, the Serbs complained that they were about to be bombed by a country that has no history. To that the American president replied: "Soon, you'll have no geography."

41. Bracewell and Drace-Francis, "South-Eastern Europe," 58.

42. Shakespeare's *Macbeth*.

43. Elena Zamfirescu, "The Flight from the Balkans," in *Südosteuropa* 44, no. 1 (1995): 51–62.

44. See Maple Razsa, "Balkan Is Beautiful," in *Arkzin*, no. 87. Available on <http://www.arkzin.com/actual/balkan.html> 20 July 2000.

45. Petar Stoyanov, keynote address, Crisis or Stability in the Balkans Conference, Washington, United States Institute of Peace, 23 April 1999. <http://www.usip.org/oc/BIB99/stoyanov_keynote.html> 20 July 2000.

46. Predrag Matvejević, "S puta po Srbiji (I): S druge strane evropske civilizacije," *Dani*, no. 160, 23 June 2000, 23–27.

47. John B. Allcock and Antonia Young, eds., *Black Lambs and Grey Falcons. Women Travellers in the Balkans* (Bradford: Bradford University Press, 1991), 170–191.

48. See Bracewell and Drace-Francis, "South-Eastern Europe," for a useful overview of these studies.

49. Vesna Goldsworthy, *Inventing Ruritania: The Imperialism of the Imagination* (New Haven: Yale University Press, 1998), 202–212.

50. Aijaz Ahmad, *In Theory: Classes, Nations, Literatures* (London: Verso: 1992).

Yugoslav writer Danilo Kiš reminds us that the realm of horror is close to all Europeans, since they inhabit the space where ethnic others were sacrificed to the idea of ideological and racial purity. In the chapter of his *Tomb for Boris Davidovich* entitled "The Magic Card Dealing," criminals in Stalin's Gulag play a card game similar to the Marseilles Tarot. The stakes in the game called Devil or Mother are the lives of Stalin's political opponents.[9] In the former Yugoslavia, both the quest for racial purity (embodied in the Ustaše, a separatist Nazi regime that sacrificed Serbs, Jews, and Roma) and the Titoist form of communism led to massive violence during the Second World War.

Milosz remarks, with bitter irony, that the West is paying the price for technological sophistication by regressing into historical and cultural amnesia. This tendency to forget what is not in one's "vital self-interest" is the dominant ideological discourse in the United States, and it is evident in the popular "vagueness of any notions related to history."[10] Milosz juxtaposes the sense of "proper place and time" that shapes the small nation's historical imagination to this politics of oblivion. Today, it seems that the last remaining superpower needs no memory, since it resides in a perpetual present driven by economic expansion at home and peace-keeping operations abroad.

For most European-based collective narratives, the need for blood circulates through stories about the past, etched into memory like a holy sign of martyrdom. That sign bears the weight of sacrifice and returns in the form of a vampire who lurks in obscurity beyond expression. The horror effect of the gothic imaginary reminds the Western viewer of the past Europeans are struggling to overcome and forget. The ethics of "human rights," which the U.S.-led West uses to enforce the peace and to erase and reshape the past and present, is called into question when confronted with the abject power of small nations. These nations are forced to relive their postcolonial victimization through the vengeance of "the serbs."

According to Milosz's poetics of memory, the historical imagination of small nations is constantly being written and erased by the imperial logic of large nations who lack this specific, victim's sense of history. In other words, small nations suffer and imagine, while large ones rule by pushing the question of historical imagination into a purely academic background. In the nineteenth century, the historical imagination of "Other" Europe was formed by the longing of the emergent middle classes for the days of their nation's imperial glory, a past imagined as a full presence of one's own national being and belonging.

Over the course of that very long century, the fall of smaller nations under the imperial rule of great powers was reinterpreted in the agonistic key of liberation at any cost. Before that moment of national emergence, the Balkan peoples were largely invisible to the West, like a vampire's reflection in a mirror. However different the specific conditions of imperial enslavement have been for each particular nation of "Other" Europe, the reinvention of the nation and its culture in the nineteenth century took place in the context of a post-colonial legacy that strove against this global invisibility.

Skeleton in the Closet

The process of national reinvention glorifies the past, creating an uncanny relationship with the present, which is always seen as uncertain and ready to collapse under the heroic burden of *Dracula's* "old centuries." This emptiness of the present is characteristic of emerging national cultures and perhaps a reason why Harker can see "no sign of a man" in the mirror as he watches the eternal count. "The whole room behind me was displayed; but there was no sign of a man in it, except myself."[11] The void that those "Other" Europeans saw reflected in the magic mirror of history during the ages of Turkish, Austro-German, and Russian colonialism was quickly filled with narratives of blood and belonging.

The return of the vampire and the rule of "old centuries" is achieved through the imaginary reconstruction of past glory, as well as through the codification of the "national" tongue and canonical literature that sings the people's praises. The desire to record the folkloric vision of the people and their "glorious" past naturalizes the agonistic vision of one's particular cultural identity. While still invisible to the present inhabitants of Western Europe, these "Other" Europeans strive to close the temporal gap and assume an identity apart from the agonistic vision to which their leaders and the outside world subject them.

When he observes that the old centuries cannot be killed by "mere modernity," the notorious Transylvanian resurrects a temporality symptomatic of Balkan phantasms. The words are recorded in diary written by Jonathan Harker, the protagonist-narrator of Bram Stoker's *Dracula*. The vampire figures in Stoker's gothic imagination as a channel for the blood and evil that stain European stories about the past, and which determine the temporal context for understanding the otherness of "Other" Europe. The European East is reflected in the mirror of the gothic imagination with a temporal delay of several centuries; they appear alien yet familiar to Harker's Western imagination.

The Balkans are represented as the transitional region between Europe and Asia, at once alien and backward by virtue of the unclear and hybrid identities that inhabit the peninsula. Not unlike the vampire, the West cannot see its own reflection in the mirror of Balkan temporality, and it buries its fears of intrusion from the East in the dark chambers of Dracula's castle. Intellectuals in "Other" Europe, meanwhile, were always torn between the mirror of the West and their own "nativist" tendencies. Also like the reflection of the Transylvanian count, the "nativist" drives of the nationalist elites were better obscured and buried deep in the cellars of medieval castles.

The native imagination of late colonial Eastern Europeans was formed by the feeble bourgeois longing for the days of freedom before the fall into the hands of the Ottomans, the Habsburgs, or the Romanoffs. This dynastic triangle colonized the "native" cultures in ways the Enlightenment could never fully erase, and it contributed to the longevity of the vampiric legacy. As a creature of history, the unfortunate count is formed by the colonial gaze of the West, which senses the presence of its own bloodthirsty past reflected in non-parodic aspects of the vampiric imagination. One should not forget this specular displacement of identity when analyzing the media's display of perverse fascination with the atrocities in the former Yugoslavia during the first half of the 1990s.

The fact that Vlad Dracul learned the art of torture while a hostage of the Turks reinforces another important phantasm among the Balkan populations. For the nationalists, the continuous presence of Islamic populations among the Balkan Christians is a sign of the latter's shameful backwardness. After the collapse of the Ottoman empire, the emergence of Slavic Christians from virtual slavery to the Turks was followed by strong identification with the colonial masters and their scorn for "Christian dogs and infidels."

Eastern and Western Europe share a fascination with the old, with the ancient time that continues to haunt literary imagination and refuses to die a natural human death. "Mere modernity," which is clearly the property of those technologically superior Western nations, is entrusted with the task of killing that memory and erasing the narratives of a people's collective identity. Bram Stoker's gothic response to the Balkan vampiric plagues of the eighteenth century invokes the killing of one temporality by another. Western Europe is the agent of a superior force that nevertheless encounters the resistance of those who are already dead.

The deliberate fracturing of Yugoslavia's post-communist civilian body, following the programmatic failure of worker self-management and non-aligned foreign policy, marked the rise of neo-medieval political practices. The broken bonds of my homeland are the result of the simultaneous desire of Slavic others and their ethnic others to separate and to stay together. Different ethno-religious figurations that rose after the demise of the old Titoist order based on "brotherhood and unity" threatened "the serbs," who would lose a common ethnic state after the end of Yugoslavia.

The resurrection of the colonial dimension, which comes after "other" starts killing "other," was expressed in the narratives of intellectuals. Not only did these intellectuals suddenly discover their Medieval roots, but they supplemented that discovery with the consumerist desire for more that currently constitutes the hegemonic discourse of the U.S.-led West. The modernizing social influences Tito and his comrades had achieved were to be removed simultaneously with communism, while religion and its proponents gained unprecedented influence in all post-Yugoslav states. The particular nationalist visions caused the Yugoslav skeleton to fracture along the lines of former empires. The sole exception was "the serbs." The secret to their obstinate resistance to bombs and starvation is a vampiric one, since it is the secret of those who stand outside of reason and the light of day.

Domestic ethnic terror was legitimated by foreign diplomatic and military interventions, as "brotherhood and unity" turned into a territorial war. The conflict erupted along the same civilizational fault lines that divided the former Ottoman and Habsburg empires. The terms set by the emergent nationalist elites differed: "The serbs" defended Yugoslavia as a creation that enabled them to live in one state, while the rest of the Yugo-others preferred separation and independence. The U.S.-led West favored the enemies of "the serbs," since the country's dissolution meant the defeat of a lesser Cold War enemy, in which communism was not imposed from the outside by the Soviet Union. Yugoslavia was the homegrown variety of the worker's state, having patched up its skeleton after the horrors of world wars and mutual genocides. The secret of horror and its success in both East and West lies in the complex relationship between the global and local forms of vampirism.

In fact, the violence implicit in the universal rejection of any form of a common state after communism, and in the "othering" of "Oriental" Europe, is most evident in the media portrayal of the recent wars of Yugoslav succession (1991–1995). Brothers no more, all experts agreed, after such genocidal rage. The U.S.-led West refused to see the role its own distorted vision of the Balkans played in the "errors" it committed during the unhinging of the Yugoslav skeleton; that refusal was itself part of the strategic takeover of the region. Real atrocities were committed in the Balkans, and they were supplemented by "peace-keeping" operations and media coverage that singled out the most vampiric of vampires, "the serbs." The very concrete military, political, and diplomatic measures of NATO governments served to excise the part of Europe inhabited by "the serbs" from the symbolic domain of the West, although a cynical observer could certainly claim that the seventy-seven days of "humanitarian bombing" brought the U.S.-led West very close to "the serbs" and their vampiric obsessions. A new form of techno-supremacist discourse arose in the U.S.-led West during the Clinton years to justify the punishment of these less civilized peoples who inhabit the central Balkan peninsula.

The genocidal practices that were resurrected during the wars of Yugoslav succession turned the names of Yugoslavia, Bosnia, Kosovo, and "the serbs" into markers of abominable practices, including murder, rape, and ethnic cleansing. But these practices are all part of the common Euro-Western heritage: Western colonial powers tested them on overseas subjects and "racial" enemies inside Europe itself. The very identity of most NATO nations is in fact constituted through the suppression and rejection of these "others," whose existence is seen as alien to the common ancestry of the West. "The serbs" are a perfect phantom. They are violent yet minuscule, and they perform the cultural role of a scarecrow for the U.S.-led West. In the post–Cold War rhetoric, this spectral collective has replaced both Marx and his big Soviet brother as the threatening apparition of human nature gone astray.

Modern European national identity emerged based on the overtly simplistic definition of the state as a territory belonging to a single ethnic group. The same process of territorialization of ethnic identity was activated in the Balkans during the last decade of the twentieth century. What Derrida calls "the secret of European responsibility" stands at the center of various forms of Balkan justice executed during the past decade.[12] The time delay of more than a century has allowed enlightened Westerners to conveniently repress the fact that struggles among nations shaped the European continent through numerous wars and much bloodshed. That vampiric specter has indeed reinforced Stoker's vision of the Balkans as a site where "the old centuries/had, and have powers of their own which/mere 'modernity' cannot kill." Yugoslavia is the skeleton in the closet of Europe, a place where the otherness-that-creates-me is repressed, sanctioned, and bombed.

The Imaginary Lens

The gothic imaginary has outgrown the writers who produced it in the English language at the end of the nineteenth century, transforming into a lens for contemporary geostrategic perceptions of the Balkans. Vesna Goldsworthy speculates that "probably the most common words of Balkan origin in the English language— 'bugger,' 'Balkanization,' and 'vampire'—all reflect, in a sense, the fear of the Other, the threat of possible invasion and corruption."[13] The last decade of the twentieth century has added one more collective figure visualized through the lens of the gothic imaginary: The bloodthirsty Serbs.

Media networks in the U.S.-led West have established "the serbs" as the postmodern incarnation of the vampire. Represented as the major predatory race in Europe, "the serbs" have resurrected the vampire's eternal hunger in its Balkan home, or so the producers of our daily world of information would have us believe. Most of the present knowledge of the Balkans is tied to this excessive violence, which marks the return of "old centuries." The sacrificial mechanism of collective becoming has been made visible on the bloody altar of Kosovo, a locality "the serbs" guard as a precious wound that is also a reminder of slavery to Islam.

Because "the serbs" desire freedom at any cost, the U.S.-led West discounts their notion of a common state as a dangerous fantasy. The real war crimes committed during the wars of Yugoslav succession (1991–1995) and the NATO bombing of FR Yugoslavia (1999) are viewed through the lens crafted by the gothic imaginary, so that the collective phantasm of "the serbs" emerges as a justification for the existence of NATO. Written between quotes and with a lowercase initial letter, the noun defining the largest Balkan nation demotes "the serbs" from a proper name to the media incarnation of evil. This vampire-inspired collective entered the new millennium led by international war crimes suspects, its castle ruined by NATO bombs and missiles. Since "the serbs" are represented by the global media as a monolith of ethnic hatred, the so-called "international community" has withdrawn the notion of the nation from this imagined community.

The breakup of Yugoslavia contributed to the gradual erasure of the capital letter in the name of "the serbs." Their "others" escaped Yugoslavia, leaving them with quotation marks around their name as a sign of the quarantine imposed on them for their vampiric behavior. The identity of "the serbs" has shifted from the nominal (Serb as a proper noun) to the verbal (to serb [srbovati], which denotes actions ranging from celebrating the glory of one's ethnic pain to brutally annihilating one's ethnic others) in the post-communist era. Both the local and the global media have participated in enforcing a vision of this nation as an essential, monumental, and historically stable entity. The global media grammar has classified "the serbs" as a symptom of the return of that ancient being that thrives on the suffering of others.

Samuel Huntington's notion of the clash among different civilizations is a predatory projection of the U.S.-led West, which is itself a vampire of vampires, structuring every desire of the average global consumer. Huntington redefines race as a non-biological construct: Belonging has become a matter of religious and cultural heritage instead. While it is literally true that this scenario materialized in the former Yugoslavia, such developments were more the result of the gothic political imagination of outside decision makers than of local power struggles. Despite the fact that "the serbs" have been defeated and cleansed in Croatia, quarantined in Bosnia-Herzegovina, and punitively bombed by NATO in Serbia, they continue to be targeted by the U.S.-led West because they have been doubly Orientalized. As members of the shrinking world of Orthodox Christianity who also bear the post-colonial legacy of Ottoman servitude, they have been transformed into the Other of Europe within Europe.

The global media has made an example of "the serbs" for their ethnic crimes, creating a climate in which the notion of collective responsibility could be resurrected by figures such as Daniel Jonah Goldhagen. Native intolerance was imputed to "the serbs," while their neighbors were portrayed as objects of forced ethnic displacement, mass rapes, massacres, and torture in detention camps. The endless stream of refugees displayed on global television was used to justify any form of struggle against this nation of vampires. With "the serbs" hung out front as a scarecrow, client states of the United States (Israel, Turkey) could, with near invisibility, brutalize their own minorities on a scale comparable to the suffering of Kosovar Albanians.

Thus, given the media coverage of the horrors of war in Croatia and Bosnia, the U.S.-led West felt justified in committing crimes against the vampiric "Serbs," whose smallness and weakness was more than made up for by the rabid fierceness with which they attacked their ethnic others. Milošević's transformation of ethnic pride into a tool of neo-nationalism during the 1980s, coupled with the country's undecided strategic status, has resulted in political, economic, and cultural exclusion from the global community. The implosion of Yugoslavia has turned "the serbs" into a population in a shrinking common state, where they used to play the role of the "ethnic glue." The United States subjected "the serbs" to corrosive solutions: purposeful destruction, the poisoning of an entire population with depleted uranium, and bombed-out petrochemical plants.

The grotesque disproportion between the military puniness and the swollen national identity of "the serbs" made them a perfect sacrifice on the altar of NATO unity, which was celebrated during the bombing of Yugoslavia in 1999. It should not be forgotten that "the serbs" as a collective phantasm were strategically positioned as a substitute for an older enemy, against which the monumental transatlantic alliance was built to preserve the foundations of the U.S.-led West.

This older enemy does not dwell only in the ruined Transylvanian castle of Count Dracula. Rather, it occupies other imaginary territories and invokes other spectral phenomena as well, most recently that of "world communism," a specter of total-itarianism that forced the noble knights of the U.S.-led West to arm themselves to the teeth and lead the charge against whatever communist strongholds survived the fall of the Berlin Wall in 1989. "The serbs" were an excellent surrogate other for the larger Orthodox nation of Russia: They were small enough never to fight back, and dark enough to be effectively excluded from humanity based on the crimes for which they'd been tried in the media.

"The serbs" continue to haunt the global media imagination as a new outlaw nation, a collective whose vampiric return from the "old centuries" is deemed to deserve only one, decisively powerful response from what Madeline Allbright has called "this splendid military," which suffered from serious lack of action after the dissolution of the Soviet Union. The arsenals of Western democracies provided the stake of justice and the wings of airpower that managed to detach Kosovo from "the serbs" in 1999, despite Kosovo's alleged status as the object of supreme value to a population the media described as stuck in Stoker's "old centuries" that have a "power of their own."

What motivates "the serbs" to cling to their "historic territories"? The gothic imaginary in Dracula originates in an anti-Islamic worldview that is deeply rooted in the heritage of Europe. Europe's young moderns spent the nineteenth century lamenting the destiny of Balkan Christians under the "Ottoman yoke." While not properly Orientalist in Edward Said's sense of the term, this perspective projects a hegemonic claim on Europe as the realm antagonistic to "the Crescent" and "the Turk" in the same way that the nationalist ideology of "the serbs" labels their Bosniak and Albanian others. Nineteenth century Europe lived to see the Islamic withdrawal from the Balkans, which was to be followed by the "mere modernity" of the Great War to end all wars. It was then again that the specter of "the serbs" was invoked by Austria-Hungary, the last imperial power to die in Mitteleuropa. On the eve of the First World War, Clara Zetkin wrote:

The horrible specter before which the people of Europe tremble has become reality. The war is ready to crush human bodies, dwelling places and fields. Austria has used the senseless outrage of a twenty-year-old Serbian lad against the Successor to the Throne, as a pretext for a criminal outrage against the sovereignty and independence of the Serbian people and in the final analysis, against the peace of Europe.[14]

The lowly peasant race that dared to spread its vampiric nationalism into the imperial province of Bosnia-Herzegovina and to challenge the last Central European empire was again targeted by the U.S.-led West for its barbaric propensities. Is it a mere coincidence that Vlad Dracul Tzepesh got his name through the Vlax bastardization of the order of Drakon, which his father received from the Habsburg Holy Roman Emperor for stopping the Ottoman armies at the edge of Europe? Once again, Central Europe and the Balkans are joined in the figure of the historical count and through the cross they defended from Islamic incursions. Dracula's aristocratic heritage is supplemented by the nationalist verbosity of Stoker's day. When Jonathan Harker asks the mysterious count about his origins, Dracula, who is otherwise terrified of the Cross, identifies himself as a crusader who has avenged "the shame of Kosovo."

When that great shame of Cassova [i.e., Kosovo] was redeemed, when the Wallachian and Magyar flags went down beneath the Crescent, who was it but one of my own race who, as Vojvode, crossed the Danube and defeated the Turks on his own ground? This was a Dracula indeed.[15]

Dracula's age transcends the bounds of a single human life, projecting back into a past that provides him with sustenance to avenge "the shame of Kosovo." At the time, that myth was still quite active, not just among "the serbs" but also throughout the West. Stoker's gothic imagination treated Kosovo as the symbol of a pan-European struggle against "Turkey in Europe" in the name of Balkan Christians who lived in subjection to their Muslim masters. The "humanitarian intervention" of the U.S.-led West to save the Kosovar Albanians from "the serbs" in 1999 reverses that civilizational pattern, because the West intervened in the name of a predominantly Muslim minority. The phantom of "the serbs" as the vampires of the new world order is ostensibly sustained by this reversal, which allowed the West to portray itself as a model of ethnic tolerance while at the same time destroying the last remnants of "communism."

The gothic imaginary functions as a time-delayed reflection of past traumas of European collectivities, and this image is then projected onto "the serbs" through the narratives of global news networks as they recount their Balkan histories in real time. Dracula's speech about the need to avenge "the shame of Kosovo" derives from the same repertoire of discourses as the speeches of Western leaders during the NATO bombing of Yugoslavia. At that time, Bill Clinton even invoked Joseph Conrad in the *New York Times* to remind us that in his vision of the world, "the Balkans are not fated to be the heart of darkness."[16] The Balkans are here invoked as a place that has the potential to be worse than Conrad's imaginary Africa. In the lexicon of the global media, the innocence of human life was constantly being violated by "the serbs," a phantasm represented by the decisions of their suicidal leader, Slobodan Milošević.

The vampiric myth of exemplary cruelty was revived in the figure of the Serbian president, who gave Europe and America a perfect alibi to embark upon yet another civilizing mission to pacify the reawakened postcolonial rage of "the serbs." The name of the last communist president in Europe has often been invoked to justify interventions against "the serbs," especially because of his willingness to sacrifice innocent civilians for the sake of his own bloodthirsty race. In the book *Balkan Ghosts*, Robert Kaplan makes the direct connection between Dracula's heritage and the present-day behavior of the corrupt postcommunist elites in the Balkans.[17]

The distance between Kaplan's and Stoker's "reality" grows narrower every day, as "the serbs" begin the new millennium under the yoke of Milošević's version of communist power in its last throes. After the Kosovo defeat in 1999, all media viewers begin to ask themselves when the stake of justice would put to its final rest the vampire Milošević resurrected in Kosovo in 1989. As Larry Wolff and Todorova have already established in their excellent books on the topic of "othering" Eastern Europe and the Balkans, the West tends to construct these imaginary localities as collectivities that display a "less civilized" version of proper European identity. Starting in the eighteenth century, these perceptions were enforced by enlightened travelers who ventured into the proverbial "lands-in-between" of "Other" Europe to discover the superiority of their own, Western civilization. It is not surprising that the narrative of Dracula begins with Jonathan Harker's journey to the Balkans, where he encounters this eternal being who embodies the contradictions of European identity and its metaphysical foundations.

In his *Vampiric Lectures* (1999), Laurence Rickels uses the psychoanalytic mechanism of projection to account for the schizoid split at the very roots of the West. The hunger of being leads to a process of perpetual mutual devouring, and this lies at the bottom of European identity:

Even as I attack Eastern Europe, it is the East that threatens to attack the West; it is not we who are actively colonizing (and in effect cannibalizing) the East: it is the East that is packed with animals and subhumans whose drive Westward we must stop in our tracks back East. The threat, embodied, for example, as vampirism, always comes from the East (from Eastern Europe, for example), even when at all times it is the West that is doubling over with hunger.[18]

Hunger for the other's blood is not limited to the subhuman race of "the serbs." Rather, though it is repressed, it fuels the imagining of *all* communities, since others serve as a screen for the projection of the eternal hunger of the vampire. According to Rickels, Western others are often imagined as agents of that eternal being who is so intent on robbing us of our precious life force, of our individual and group identities. If we don't act preemptively against the vampire, he threatens to lodge himself deeply inside us, to taint our blood and race with his illicit desires.

The global identity of the U.S.-led West is currently constituted through the imaginary gaze at the Balkans, a region that begins to function as the representation of the European unconscious, as a locus where the secrets of violence and sexuality are openly displayed, and as the reminder of the "old centuries" before civilization. The vampiric phantasm transforms "the serbs" into a prototypical Balkan nation, featured by the global media as the community, stuck in ancient history, whose survival can be assured only by the perpetual sacrifice of its ethnic others.

This vision of lesser and barbaric identity is disseminated across the Balkan ethnoscape, which is then contaminated by the violent proximity of "the serbs." The peninsula's inhabitants possess a heart of darkness that marks their cultures as temporally lagging and civilizationally inferior. Harker perceives the peasants he encounters along the way to Dracula's castle in the same manner: as autistic creatures who "have neither eyes nor ears for the outer world."[19] This coding of the Balkans is symptomatic of the gothic imaginary, which Jonathan Harker reads into this part of Europe unaffected by "mere modernity." The narrator of *Dracula* suggests that the power of technology is not able to kill the archaic blindness to progress and resistance to enlightenment within the bounds of proper European identity.

The political and military conflicts which erupted within the former Yugoslav federation were interpreted by global media in the same vein, as events motivated by "ancient and irrational ethnic hatreds." This implied a need for military intervention that would provide those peoples unable to rule themselves with the guidance and protection of "Western democracies." Needless to say, the colonially motivated genocides those same democracies have been engaged in for centuries hardly provided them with adequate moral tools to mediate in the Balkan conflicts.

Televised narratives about the Yugoslav war contributed to the awakening of fear and hatred, because they displayed the effects of "ethnic passions" rooted in stories about a bloody, yet glorious past, which is not compatible with the "new world order."

Racism without Race

Few analysts have considered the racist implications of the current political discourse about "the serbs," perhaps for fear of being equated with them in their bloodthirsty quest for ethnic purity. I write with that risk in mind, but also with the hope that I will be able to deconstruct the effects of the intentional misreading of "the serbs" by the media and the public relations industry. The most successful coup carried out by the information industry in the West has been the conflation of the war crimes committed by "the serbs" during the 1990s with those of the German Nazis during the 1930s and 1940s.

When the media invokes the historical holocaust of the European Jews as a metaphor for reading the Balkans, it transforms "the serbs" into a collectively genocidal nation intent on the wanton destruction of its neighbors. However, this not only misrepresents the actual events in the Balkans but also demeans the unique nature of the historical holocaust. The populations of the Balkan countries, whose "white" inhabitants were nevertheless regarded by the West as "lesser" Europeans, hardly present a blueprint for a master race.

In fact, these "other" Europeans have been tainted with shades of cultural "blackness" which are most often tied to their Slavic origins or their belonging to the religious cultures of Orthodox Christianity and Islam. Cultural difference begins to function as a marker of lower civilizational standards, practically equating all the people to the east and south of a particular nation as subject to a set of practices that is tacitly deplorable to the particular nation in question. This subtle form of racism is operative throughout Europe, as already noted by Freud in his characterization of nationalist chauvinism as a narcissism of minor differences.

Without the gaze of the Western media and the good intentions of NATO leaders, the gothic imaginary could have stayed limited to horror films and pulp fiction. Imperial rule and colonization have transformed the "native" cultures in ways that the feeble importation of Enlightenment could never fully erase, contributing to the longevity of the vampiric temporality and imagination. The descendants of the bloodthirsty count are structured by the persistent colonial gaze of Europe, which senses the presence of its own less-than-enlightened past reflected back in the figure of the vampire. One should not forget this specular displacement of identity when analyzing the Western public's perverse fascination with the media display of atrocities in the former Yugoslavia throughout the 1990s.

At the end of the twentieth century, the legacy of the Transylvanian count has been revived with the all too real tragedy of Yugoslavia. The uneasy blending of laughter and horror that greets the dissemination of the vampiric imagination testifies to the possibility of a simultaneous cultural representation of the Dracula figure's parodic and non-parodic elements. The horror of the vampiric era is supplemented by the laughter of the Western viewer. Completely non-parodic representations of Dracula are no longer possible, since Jonathan Harker's gaze at Eastern

Europe is symptomatic of the centuries-old bias nurtured by the gothic imaginary. The increasing popularity of the vampire in Hollywood movies throughout this century speaks of the fascination with blood and violence that has marked the millennial present.

Funny violence has become a Hollywood genre following the success of Quentin Tarrantino's *Pulp Fiction* (1994). This genre provides an adequate marketing response to the "compassion fatigue" Western viewers suffered after the media display of real Balkan populations gripped by poverty and ethnic strife during the 1990s. The laughter produced by a number of vampire remakes, including Francis Ford Coppola's *Bram Stoker's Dracula*, always bears the mark of real violence that is being parodied. While innocent civilians die at the hands of their post-communist masters, the global spread of the vampiric imagination exemplifies the new/old cultural formations that regulate the relationships among the various pieces of the European imaginary.

The return of racism under a different sign is consistent with the role of the enemy, which "other" Europe played for the better part of the twentieth century under the sign of communism. The military-party complexes that ruled those countries in the name of the "working class" were portrayed by the Western public discourse as the "evil empire's" cabals of totalitarian masters, who were ultimately intent on brutalizing the comfortable lives of Western citizens. After Gorbachev's reforms removed the ideological barriers between the two parts of Europe in the 1980s, the West quickly reverted to the modes of control it had already tested in the "third world," subjugating the Balkan peoples through colonial and neocolonial practices of military, economic, political, and cultural control.

British Prime Minister Tony Blair explained the seventy-seven days of NATO bombing, and the subsequent takeover of Kosovo in the spring of 1999, as necessary steps toward defeating a barbarism that will no longer be tolerated on the European continent. The remote control bombing that enabled this NATO victory was portrayed in the media as a humanitarian intervention, necessary to save an endangered minority (Kosovar Albanians) from the irrational and rabid behavior of "the serbs." While destroying Yugoslavia's industrial infrastructure and contaminating its environment with chemical and radioactive pollutants, the Western military alliance touted the superiority of its technology, claiming the moral high ground through various forms of psychological operations and electronic warfare that news consumers in the West accepted as "reality."

This emerging form of racism is often couched in the progressive language of human rights, but the supposedly unbiased and universal system of international justice, exemplified by the work of the International War Crimes Tribunal in the Hague, displays a clear moral double standard. Robert Hayden has coined the term "humanrightsism" to account for this phenomenon, especially regarding the treatment of war crimes in the former Yugoslavia as compared with the same type of war crimes committed by the NATO pilots during its 1999 bombing campaign against "the serbs."

Hallucinatory Bhabism

The "idea of pure national identity" is not what guided "the serbs" into the excesses of murder and torture that insulted the innocence of the Western gaze. The war crimes were committed by the nomadic clones of post-communist territoriality, regardless of ethnic and religious origin; "the serbs" were both the fiercest perpetrators and the most numerous victims of these anti-Yugoslav forces. The fact that "the serbs" were the ethnic glue that kept the skeleton of socialist Yugoslavia together drove them to wage war and commit crimes in order to preserve a common territory after the demise of that country. In fact, "the serbs" were the most common ethnic denominator in the former state, since they made up only two thirds of Serbia itself and lived mixed with the other ethnic groups in all other former Yugoslav republics, with the notable exception of westernmost Slovenia.

The reawakening of the gothic view of the Balkans in the first half of the 1990s was tied to conceptions of time and identity that are seemingly "out of joint" with the Western hegemonic vision of human rights. The most hallucinatory forms of collective memory, which are currently articulated in the Western discourse on the Balkans, cannot omit "the serbs" as the arch villains of the new world order. It is understandable that the former Yugoslav populations' political discourses of belonging to the faiths and cultures of the former imperial masters have been intentionally overlooked by the intervening Western governments. But it is odd that this postcolonial (and at the same time deeply anti-modern) turn has escaped the attention of theoreticians like Homi Bhabha, who nevertheless felt obliged to devote a single sentence of his 1994 book *The Location of Culture*, to the specter of "the serbs" as the agents of "psychotic fervor":

The hideous extremity of Serbian nationalism proves that the very idea of a pure, "ethnically cleansed" national identity can only be achieved through the death, literal and figurative, of the complex interweavings of history, and the culturally contingent borderlines of modern nationhood. This side of the psychosis of patriotic fervor, I like to think, there is overwhelming evidence of a more transnational and translational sense of the hybridity of imagined communities.[20]

The logic and hegemony of the gothic imaginary forces the *New York Times*-informed Bhabha to buy into the narrative of "the serbs" as the agents of ethnic purity. Despite Bhabha's assurance that "the serbs" are the exception and that subjects "this side of the psychosis of patriotic fervor" may articulate a different vision of the nation, one is forced to ask a very difficult question concerning the validity of such conclusions. Could there really be a "this side" that evades the grasp of desire for the imagined community after it has been plunged into the rage of war for "one's own" territory and national survival? Doesn't the truth strike much closer to home? In Derrida's words: "what is happening there translates what happens here, always here, wherever one is and wherever one looks." If the ethics of "infinite responsibility" could be enacted globally, the specter of the "vampires like us," "the serbs," needs to be supplemented by the "vampires like U.S.," the specter of the well-intentioned viewers and interveners in the Balkans.

It is obvious that what Bhabha calls "the hideous extremity of Serbian nationalism" is not the only path of communal struggle for emancipation. Yet, the failure to recognize that hideousness is not an innate and essential quality underlying Serbian "national character" so much as a projection of the West and its own phantasms about national purity is a fallacy, and it emerges from Bhabha's submission to the hegemonic media gaze of the West. However "humanitarian" the motivations for the Western military interventions in the Balkans may have been, the outcome has been the destruction, impoverishment and dependence of both "the serbs" and their ethnic enemies.

Therefore, the processes that result in the "death, literal and figurative of the complex interweavings of history, and the culturally contingent borderlines of modern nationhood" have been inherent in the logic of separation that was applied by the U.S.-led West in the former Yugoslavia since 1991, not in the ideology of conquest for the sake of Kosovo and Greater Serbia. It is startling that this misreading by the foremost postcolonial critic exhibits the same traits as the global imagination responsible for framing "the serbs."

Used as an example of civilization's other by CNN and the other global media networks, "the serbs" continue to languish in the shadow of their wanted leader at the very end of the second millennium. The cradle of vampirism in Europe is once again displayed to the eye of the camera through massacres, death camps, and mass graves. The evil attributed to the vampire returns with the media representation of "the serbs," while the NATO violence used to stop them is projected as a sterile, surgical display of superior technology and military power.

While transforming real human suffering into a unit of information, the expected televisual erasure of "old centuries" turned into their instant replay. The world watched a war unfold in Europe for the first time since the end of the Second World War. The wild ones sacrificed the innocent ones on the altar of blood and soil, in the name of a past that refused to die. The non-parodic nature of the historical event crushed and displaced thousands of humans, fueled by stories of civilizational differences among the Yugoslavs. Once again, memories of past historical traumas were invoked and old wounds reopened to feed the old creature of history.

The vampiric phantasm of "the serbs" functions like a time-delayed mirror image of the West itself, processed by the televisual technology of real-time history and disseminated by the news networks. The evil of real war crimes against those who are perceived as a threat to the territory of "the new world order" causes displacement, "both literal and figurative" of both the nomadic clones signified by "the serbs" and their numerous others. The bite of the vampire infects the national imaginary with pain and the desire for an impossible return to the glory before the fall at Kosovo. The life that has not been subjected to decay and forgetting sustains itself as the violence built into the very notion of the subject and its eternity. The ruins of Dracula's castle hide this dirty secret; they hide the hunger for life displayed by "the serbs" as the beings who ostensibly represent the bad other of the West. The infinite technological superiority of the West, demonstrated by the remote control bombing of Yugoslavia and its militarized media coverage, is then another symptom of the vampiric infection. Evidently, "the serbs" have spread their vampirism beyond the Balkans, into the very centers of the U.S.-led West, which appeared to be acting against "the serbs'" bloody practices but at same time preserved its own secret thirst for power.

Notes

1. Matthew Brunson, *The Vampire Encyclopedia* (New York: Crown Publishers, 1993), 64.
2. Bram Stoker, *Dracula* (New York: Modern Library, 1897), 40.
3. Jacques Derrida, *Specters of Marx* (New York: Routledge, 1994), xv.
4. H. C. Artman et al., "The Budapest Roundtable," *CrossCurrents* 10: 18.
5. Ibid., 21.
6. Maria Todorova, *Imagining the Balkans* (Oxford: Oxford University Press, 1997), 82.
7. Artman, "The Budapest Roundtable," 20.
8. Ibid., 18.
9. Danilo Kiš, *Tomb for Boris Davidovich* (New York: Penguin, 1980).

10. Artman, "The Budapest Roundtable," 21.

11. Stoker, *Dracula*, 25.

12. Jacques Derrida, *The Gift of Death*, trans. David Wills (Chicago: The University of Chicago Press).

13. Vesna Goldsworthy, *Inventing Ruritania* (New Haven: Yale University Press, 1998), 74.

14. Clara Tzetkin, "Proletarian Women Be Prepared" in *Women Writers of World War I*, (London: Penguin, 1999), ed. Margaret Higgonet, 6.

15. Stoker, *Dracula*, 29.

16. William Jefferson Clinton, "A Just and Necessary War," *New York Times* (May 23, 1999), A17.

17. See Robert D. Kaplan, *Balkan Ghosts: A Journey through History* (New York: Vintage Books, 1996).

18. Laurence Rickels, *The Vampiric Lectures* (Minneapolis: University of Minnesota Press, 1999), 12.

19. Stoker, *Dracula*, 20.

20. Homi Bhabha, *The Location of Culture* (London: Routledge, 1994), 5.

3

What's So Byzantine About the Balkans?

Milica Bakić-Hayden

From the West of the Former Byzantium: A General View

In the battle between truth and prejudice, waged on the field of history books, it must be confessed that the latter usually wins. . . .

   At the hands of such prejudice many historical epochs have suffered, and most of all the epoch known as the after Roman or Byzantine Empire. Ever since our rough crusading forefathers first saw Constantinople and met, to their contemptuous disgust, a society where everyone read and wrote, ate food with forks and preferred diplomacy to war, it has been fashionable to pass the Byzantines by with scorn and to use their name as synonymous with decadence. In the eighteenth century, refinement was no longer considered decadent; but decadence remained the Byzantine characteristic. Montesquieu and his more brilliant contemporary Gibbon, searched for new justification. Taking the superstition and bloodthirsty intrigues that were typical of all medieval Europe, and harnessing them to Byzantium, they gave new life to the synonym. . . . All the historians in chorus treated a thousand years of empire as a short sinister unbroken decline.[1]

Thus Sir Steven Runciman begins his study of tenth-century Byzantium, originally published in 1929. What makes his introductory words worthy of our attention is not necessarily their unbiased truthfulness, for in its thousand and so years of existence, Byzantium had its share of deposed Emperors and Patriarchs,[2] as well as all kinds of courtly intrigues, murders, and interfamilial strife. But the empire also had a distinctive worldview—one manifest in its dyarchical structure of government (worldly and spiritual), its encouragement of many forms of religious experience, and its remarkable achievements in art, architecture, music, and literature. Hence, it would be misleading to underscore only the negative aspects of Byzantine reality as though these were its only distinguishing attributes.[3]

   Runciman, by contrast, willingly breaks with the mainstream, simplistic representations of Byzantium summed up in the idea of *decline*, or, as Hegel more graphically put it, "the rotten edifice of the Eastern Empire"—"a disgusting picture of imbecility" where "insane passions" stifled "the growth of all that is noble in thought, deeds and person."[4] Such discourses on Byzantium are hardly value-neutral; on the contrary, they have dramatically falsified historical realities and rendered "Byzantinism" comparable to *Balkanism* and *Orientalism*.[5] These are not just surviving prejudices from the past; they also structure the present scholarly consciousness, which is often poorly informed about Byzantine ways and unaware of its own ideological heritage and motivation when discussing them. Modern scholars seem to take the rationality of their own culture for granted. And yet, it takes little more than a glance at reports on high school shootings, breast implants, and the daily horoscope in the local newspaper to see why we cannot, without self-critical hesitation, consider ourselves to inhabit a world of reason more than other peoples before us and elsewhere, whether in Byzantium or in any other moment of antiquity.

The unfortunate tendency of early Byzantinists to subsume Byzantine history and culture under the history of the Roman Empire or of the Hellenic world has until recently prevented Byzantium from being socially localized as an authentic civilization, which deserves to be understood through its own categories. Similarly, Byzantine art is consistently classified in a manner that dissociates it from the art of western Europe, "to which it is connected in many ways from the early Middle Ages into the Renaissance."[6] One wonders exactly how two coeval periods in the history of Christian art can be deemed unrelated. The classification of Byzantine art as ancient, rather than medieval (and thus coeval with Western art), has been implanted at the very basic level of art historical education for the past 150 years. And while we continue to add to the canon, "less often do we re-think how and why it is constructed as it is."[7] For the same reason, various aspects of Byzantine experience are entitled to be considered in terms other than those of political history. This is particularly relevant for Orthodox Christianity, which is today probably the most visible legacy of what used to be known as the Byzantine *oikoumene*, a single Cosmopolis of the inhabited world.

In a recent study of the collapse of communism in Eastern Europe, Ilya Prizel, an East Europeanist writing for a learned but non-academic audience, makes several references to the "situation in Byzantine Europe," to "Byzantine societies" and "Byzantine countries of Eastern Europe," as if Byzantium exists today as some kind of viable or unified political entity.[8] What could be the common denominator among such current references to non-existent Byzantium? Obviously, "the Byzantine church." But today few Orthodox Christians would consider their church Byzantine, even though they would all acknowledge that various aspects of their worship are grounded in the Byzantine past. John Meyendorff, an authority on Orthodox and Byzantine matters, notes: "It is not Byzantium which 'made'

Orthodoxy, but rather the opposite . . . , so that today, faithfulness to Orthodoxy cannot be identified with or reduced to a servile and mechanical preservation of Byzantine relics of the past."[9] Hence it is misleading to refer to modern (formerly communist) societies of Europe, which used to be part of the Byzantine commonwealth over half a millennium ago, as "Byzantine," especially given the raft of connotations that the term has acquired over the course of time.

Ironically, Prizel does not include Greece, the former champion of the Byzantine cultural space, in his references to "Byzantine societies." What's more, those societies he does classify as Byzantine are far more immediately Ottoman (in the Balkans) or Austro-Hungarian (in parts of central and eastern Europe). And even though the Orthodox church, primarily through its liturgical vision of the kingdom of God, ensured the continuity of the Byzantine idea of Christianity, the Ottoman period created a number of discontinuities in other areas of social and cultural life. Thus, there is no direct connection between them and the alleged failure of the post-communist "Byzantine societies" to create civil societies.

Further implications of this misconstrued "Byzantine connection" can be seen if, with Prizel, we follow the putative frontiers on Samuel Huntington's map, and conclude that "the social difference along the Byzantine-Catholic axis is far more profound than is often recognized."[10] Of course, no one can seriously deny the differences between various cultures and societies of Europe, because those very differences are constitutive of the specific European identities. However, one should explore those differences beyond the level of partial knowledge and hasty generalizations.

We can look, for example, into one difference that turned a process of gradual cultural, political, and economic estrangement between Greece and Rome into the dramatic eleventh-century schism: the issue of Papal claims. Two theological matters stand out among the factors that led to the schism between the eastern, Greek-dominated church and the Roman Latin one of the west:[11] the attempt of the Roman patriarch to bring the east under his jurisdiction as well as the west, and the *Filioque* (the issue of the procession of the Holy Spirit from the Father, as in the original Creed, as opposed to the addition "and the Son" [*filioque*] accepted later in the Latin church).

It is ironic from today's perspective to realize that the anti-authoritarian voice was raised by eastern Christians, whose Orthodox church has been commonly identified as authoritarian and caesaropapist. Many Orthodox today would find their opinion of the Papacy in full accordance with the one expressed by the twelfth century writer and Archbishop of Nicomedia, Nicetas:

My dearest brother, we do not deny to the Roman Church the primacy amongst the five sister Patriarchates; and we recognize her right to the most honorable seat at an Ecumenical Council. But she has separated herself from us by her own deeds, when through pride she assumed a monarchy which does not belong to her office. . . . How shall we accept decrees from her that have been issued without consulting us and even without our knowledge? If the Roman Pontiff, seated on the lofty throne of his glory, wishes to thunder at us and, so to speak, hurl his mandates at us from on high, and if he wishes to judge us and even to rule us and our Churches, not by taking counsel with us but at his own arbitrary pleasure, what kind of brotherhood, or what kind of parenthood can this be? We should be the slaves, not the sons, of such a Church, and the Roman See would not be the pious mother of sons but a hard and imperious mistress of slaves.[12]

We see here a fundamental difference in the conception of the outer organization of the Christian churches: The four ancient Patriarchates of the east (Antioch, Alexandria, Jerusalem and Constantinople) understood the Church as hierarchical in its structure (through the Apostolic Succession of bishops), but more counciliar and more collegial, with a sense of equality among bishops and the Patriarch as *primus inter pares*, first among the equal. But in Rome, the only Apostolic see in the west, historical circumstances shaped the idea of the Church as a monarchy and thus strengthened her centralized character. From Prizel's argument about the relation between religious and political culture, wouldn't one expect that the more decentralized and collegial eastern Church, in which "neither Patriarchs nor Councils could ever introduce new teaching, for the guardian of religion is the very body of the Church, that is the people (*laos*) itself,"[13] would be more compatible with civil and democratic ideas then the highly centralized western Catholic church? In other words, wouldn't the Church that claims that all bishops are fundamentally equal—where patriarchs, metropolitans, and archbishops enjoy primacy of honor *among* their brother bishops, but not *above* them, where decisions are made by consensus, not by issuing peremptory decrees—be more likely to generate democratic political culture than an authoritarian church would be?

Thus, the real question here is not about difference as such, but about the *legitimacy of the valorization of differences*, about the ability to acknowledge and respect those differences rather than structuring them in hierarchies that favor less different over more different. After all, it is the more different that challenges us to understand [i.e., to stand-under] a universe of meaning differently constructed than our own. Finally, we must ask by which criterion we select one difference as more "profound" or decisive for the relationship than another, and why.

In our example, Prizel singles out religious differences between the Byzantine and Catholic churches as fundamental, and he uses them to explain differences in the general political culture of post communist East and Central Europe. He evaluates both religions' traditions primarily according to their supposed political efficacy and their ability to affect or to adjust to new social circumstances. It is no wonder, then, that the Orthodox church of the Balkans and Russia "failed to foster civil society"; for in the past fifteen centuries, according to Prizel, the Byzantine church "functioned as a state institution," "preaching passivity and submission to the worldly government as a manifestation of divine will," showing *"little if any evolution in intellectual terms,* resulting in an absence of dialogue between the intellectuals and the church hierarchy. . . ."[14] (emphasis mine).

One could view these kinds of assumptions of Byzantine legacy in the Orthodox church—which practically deny any Orthodox contribution to Europe's intellectual and spiritual heritage—as another example of "Byzantinism," placing them in the larger context of *Balkanism* and *Orientalism.*[15] In this essay, I propose to shift attention from the rhetorical level, which emphasizes the (mis)representation of Byzantine civilization, to the conceptual level, through which we can explain those concepts that have defined the distinct world of *homo byzantinus* for centuries. This route not only leads us to acknowledge common misunderstandings and preconceptions regarding religious developments in Byzantium and by extension in the Orthodox church; it also challenges us to make a renewed effort at understanding religious phenomena in general, and at more competently including them in historical and social scientific research. Thus, not only do we broaden one specific kind of comprehension, but we also come to understand the implications of our own position as modern scholars with respect to traditional forms of religious experience and expression that no longer speak to us with real immediacy.

Outside the discipline of religious studies, scholars seldom regard religious attitudes as diverse modalities adopted by humans who contemplate the divine, so much as they analyze them as social and political manifestations:[16] *Zoon politicon* writes the history of *homo religiosus.* This is not to say that one cannot write meaningfully about religious phenomena from a secular perspective, but rather that in order to achieve understanding today, we must mediate the symbolic religious consciousness through the critical one, in a relation Paul Ricoeur refers to as a "second naiveté."

Since we can no longer, in a post-religious world, have immediate openness to the sacred and participate in its meaning in the pre-modern manner, nor can we ignore symbolic understanding altogether, we have to engage in an interpretive relation that would be "the postcritical equivalent of the precritical hierophany."[17] Otherwise we might fail to make three crucial distinctions. The first is between the *totalizing* worldview of a religion-dominated society, such as Byzantium, which attempted to translate Christian transcendent vision into a political structure, and the political reality of a modern *totalitarian* state, which asserts total control and power. Second, the balance and conflict between the two "powers" within the Christian Commonwealth must be distinguished from the tensions or conflicts between church and state in modern society. Third, the challenges of the post-Christian Balkans of the mid-nineteenth century must not be confused with those facing post-communist Eastern Europe at the end of the twentieth.[18] Seeming parallels between these situations should not be taken as more than parallels: In their ultimate meaning, they never intersect.

Double-headed Eagle: Ambivalence as Reality

Perhaps no other single word encompasses the perception of Byzantine reality as fully as the word *ambivalence*. In Byzantium, write Kazhdan and Constable, ambivalence was not just a matter of poetic expression, but a "normal trait of reality" encountered at every step and realized "with unparalleled consistency in the various spheres of Byzantine social, political, and cultural life."[19] Whether it be the economy, in which barter and monetary systems existed side by side (the monetary system was itself ambivalent, serving as both a means of accumulation and a medium of exchange), or the geographical environment ("mountains were both dreadful and holy; the sea was both threatening and attractive"),[20] or the ambivalence of the oral and written culture, which reflected the "inner" and the "outer" wisdom of saints and scholars,[21] having either or both of two contrary values or qualities[22] was a part of the Byzantine worldview.

This manifestation of ambivalence is consistent with the Orthodox rendering of Christian cosmology, at the center of which is the antinomical person of Incarnate Christ, a being both fully human and fully divine who serves as a bridge between God and humanity. It is also consistent with Christian anthropology, in which human beings act as a bridge between the intangible things of spirit, or *noetos*, and the material objects of the sensory world, or *aisthetos*. In some traditions, like the Hindu, a similar relation between "atemporal order and temporal shift" recently has been discussed in terms of "the inner conflict."[23] But in the Byzantine tradition, the dyarchy of imperium and sacerdotium, embodied by the patriarch and the emperor respectively, was referred to as *symphony*.

In theory, and as symbolicly depicted by the double-headed eagle of the Byzantine code of arms, the domains on which the Church and the State imposed their authority were clearly distinguished (two heads) while still bound in a single organic unity (one body): "The Church and the Kingdom were in effect but One

Society, indivisible and undivided, One *Civitas—Republica Christiana*."[24] Hence both the emperor and the patriarch derived their respective *meanings* from, and were encompassed by, the same Christian narrative. Neither stood outside of it to question it; rather, each was expected to apply the narrative's meaning to the concrete realm of which he was in charge. Perhaps no document illustrates this better than the preamble of the emperor Justinian's edict issued in 535: "The greatest blessings of mankind are the gifts of God which have been granted to us by the mercy on high: the priesthood and the imperial authority. The priesthood ministers to things divine; the imperial authority is set over, and shows diligence in, things human; but both proceed from one and the same source, and both adorn the life of man."[25]

The nature of the established Christian narrative was clearly totalizing (for religion's concern is the world *in toto*), as was its rhetoric. Thus, again consistent with general ambivalence, the emperor, though a repository of secular power, was at the same time associated with the providence of God.[26] This would make imperial power seem almost unlimited, encompassing the realm of the patriarch and the church. But the ambivalence of the church itself safeguarded against total imperial control. For in Orthodoxy, the church is conceived as both visible and invisible, divine and human: "It is visible, for it is composed of specific congregations, worshipping here on earth; it is invisible, for it also includes the saints and the angels. It is human, for its earthly members are sinners; it is divine, for it is the Body of Christ."[27] These distinctions within the church, however, do not imply separation between the visible and the invisible church, which together constitute a single and continuous reality.[28]

It must be remembered that even when the Byzantine church, as visible and human, did surrender the supervision of its external affairs and administration to the emperor (i.e., to the state), that state was Christian and the emperor, himself subject to divine law, was in a sense limited by the Christian faith and the teachings of the Apostles and Holy Fathers.[29] Even though the emperor had the right to appoint and dismiss the patriarch, to call the church councils, and to enjoy special ecclesiastical privileges (such as communion in the sanctuary) ordinarily reserved for the bishop and priests, he nonetheless could have no impact on doctrinal issues or the teachings of the church.[30] The patriarch himself, it should not be forgotten, had his own resources, such as suspension and excommunication, to curtail or resist the emperor's power.[31] In other words, the emperor had no power over the church's "inner wisdom." As Papadakis writes, "the emperor may have been an absolute Caesar but he was never pope—ultimate custodian of the Christian faith."[32]

True, in concrete historical circumstances, this "symphonic" model of conceptual interdependence between spiritual authority and temporal power often resounded in disharmony and the effect on the church was usually negative. Nonetheless, in its own mind, the church never lost its salvific mission and inner freedom.

In the context of an overriding Christian narrative, submission, that term of opprobrium in modern times, was seen as a matter of discipline, a measure of spiritual endurance, and the dictate of (outer) circumstances wrought by providential will. The temporal realm was seen as distinct but not ultimately separated from the spiritual realm, and so it was never given autonomy apart from spiritual which is atemporal.[33] Instead, a common link was acknowledged to exist between God and the emperor, who was responsible for the well-being of the state, as well as between the God and the citizens.[34] Consequently, derogatory charges of *caesaropapism*, that is, the allegation of the Orthodox church's submission to the state, which still undergirds many historical and political writings on Byzantium or the Balkans as well as analyses of church-state relations in communism, cannot but be seen as biased anachronism.

The situation of the Orthodox church in the communist totalitarian state—or, for that matter, in the Balkan national states of the past century—was quite different. Nationalism, a new, western, secular ideology, was a greater threat to the inner meaning of the church than the theocracy of either Byzantine or Ottoman times. Even the non-Christian Ottoman Empire embraced the idea of one God, a world that derived meaning from Him, never questioning the religious universe as such. What it did change, however, was the dyarchical Byzantine system and the ambivalence that went with it. The unfortunate result of the Ottoman legacy for the Orthodox church was that during this period "the things of Caesar" became almost indistinct from "the things of God": as the institution of the Christian emperor disappeared with the fall of Constantinople to the Turks in 1453, the patriarch was appointed not only as a spiritual but also as a civil authority in charge of all Orthodox Christian population or *Rum Millet*, the Roman nation.[35] On the one hand, the indifference of the Ottomans to the ethnic, cultural, and linguistic distinctions between the various peoples of the empire helped affirm the catholicity, or universality, of the Orthodox church; but on the other hand, since the Church became the chief organizer of political and civil life at every level, it became crucial to the national survival of various peoples in the empire, thus merging and confusing in their minds the sense of religious and national belonging.

In the newly independent Orthodox nation-states of the nineteenth century Balkans, national churches welcomed their independence from the ecumenical patriarchate in Constantinople, which remained under Turkish rule.[36] In this sense, the individual churches were supportive of national independence movements as anti-Ottoman sentiment grew in the eighteenth century; but since the protagonists of those movements, inspired by the ideals of the Enlightenment, were generally anti-clerical, the place of religion in the newly emerging nations was defined, as in the West, in subordination to the secular power of the state.[37] Nationalization of the churches in the nineteenth century (Greece, 1833; Romania, 1865; Bulgaria, 1870; Serbia, 1879; and much later Albania, 1922–1937) exposed the conceptual incompatibility between Orthodoxy and nationalism. In August 1872, a major synod consisting of the Ecumenical Patriarchate in Constantinople, the patriarchs of Alexandria, Antioch, and Jerusalem, plus the archbishop of Cyprus, condemned racist (meaning nationalistic) discrimination within the Church as *phyletism*: "We renounce, censure, and condemn racism, that is racial discrimination, ethnic feuds, hatreds, and dissensions within the Church of Christ, which is contrary to the teaching of the Gospel and the holy canons of our blessed fathers which support the holy Church and the entire Christian world, embellish it and lead it to divine godliness."[38]

Of course, each of the Orthodox churches in the Balkans has a story of its own, and the Russian Orthodox church is a separate story altogether. The point here is to note that the Church as such was really threatened when its inner (salvific) mission and its *meaning* were threatened; and in the increasingly secular, post-Christian, modernizing Balkan nation states of the second half of the nineteenth century (and with the advance of communism in the twentieth), this was exactly what had begun to happen. It was the expression in the Orthodox East of these new ideologies—which considered the " 'will of the people" and "national interests" supreme and unquestionable values—that was "utterly incompatible with the mental and social structures of the Byzantine Middle Ages."[39]

Paradoxically, then, it was modernization, not imperium, that brought the Orthodox church to the position of so-called submission to the worldly government. That government was no longer ruled by the (medieval) ideology of a universal Christian empire, but it was endorsed to a lesser extent by the independent Orthodox churches, a fact reflected in their respective modes of survival under such governments. Modern patriarchal pluralism, and the independence of the Orthodox churches as national churches, may resemble the ecclesiastical regionalism of the past, which the ancient canons sanctioned in the context of a universal unity of faith, but the fact is that modern nation-states radically changed the character and meaning of this regionalism with their parochial approaches to ethnicity, language, and territoriality.[40] The change in the overall context—that is, in the social structures within which the reality of the Christian world was taken for granted and individuals were socialized such that this world was real to them—had direct bearing on the meaning of Orthodoxy, if not on its survival, in the post-Ottoman Balkans.[41]

Amplifying Ambivalence: *via contemplativa* and *via activa*, and unlike the monastic orders of Catholic Europe, which undertook a vast array of social activities that became the foundation of a civil society, Byzantine monasticism tended to emphasize asceticism, self-denial, and outright withdrawal from society. As such, Byzantine monasticism has had a far more limited role in the formation of civil society than has Roman Catholicism elsewhere.[42]

One could broadly say that eastern monasticism was exclusively contemplative, if the distinction between the two ways, active and contemplative, had in the East the same meaning as in the West. In fact, for an eastern monk the two ways are inseparable. The one cannot be exercised without the other, for the ascetic rule and the school of interior prayer receive the name of spiritual *activity*.[43]

The views presented above may be seen as making much the same point: that Eastern Orthodox monasticism puts great(er) emphasis on contemplative life. But the former view places that fact in the context of its relevance for the development of contemporary political and social institutions, whereas the latter interprets it in terms of Orthodox religious practice and modes of expression. Even though, in the first case, religion is allotted an important place in the process of historical change, its meaning is interpreted exclusively in the context of (overtly materialistic) political history, thus privileging its economic and political dimension while treating those aspects of monastic experience that are religious *par excellence* as irrelevant if not as drawbacks. Hence we need to look into the religious dimension of meaning in order to open it up to other discourses and establish dialogical understanding.[44]

The second view actually takes us in that direction as it presents us with the ambivalent idea—that *via contemplativa* and *via activa* are not separated in a simplistic way along the lines that Western monks are "active" and Eastern ones are "contemplative." Rather, in good Byzantine style it makes the ambivalent claim that in the Orthodox tradition contemplation *is* an activity, not at all inferior to the activities of the world. From today's perspective these may appear as seemingly incompatible views of faith and knowledge, of the metaphysical question of "the truth of religion" and "the empirical question of its effects on the life of humanity and its meaning for society."[45] From the Byzantine perspective, however, human activity was seen as a continuum, on the one hand relating humans to divine, and on the other, to other humans in society. The "truth of religion" is eschatological: It reveals the difference between the kingdom of God and the concrete reality of the world, but also the way the two relate to each other. "The kingdom, therefore, is to be experienced sacramentally, ritually, mystically, and not by exercising political power, or engaging in social activism, to make the world better than it is."[46]

"White" clergy (married priests and deacons) and confraternities of layman may engage in social work and related outward activities, but the monk's primary activity is prayer. Whether he lives the solitary life of a hermit, or in a loosely organized, small, semi-eremitic community of monks under the spiritual supervision of an experienced elder, or in a larger cenobitic monastic community, it is not what the monk *does* that matters, but what he *is*.[47] Monks can occupy themselves with a variety of activities—historically, these have ranged from physical labor to manuscript copying, icon painting, wood carving, singing, composing, and spiritual counseling.

These days, the results of such activities tend to be incorporated into what we call culture (from which religion is distinguishable but not separable). Much more than the imperial church, it was monasticism, with its ascetic endeavor, that preserved and advanced a spiritual creativity that found its expression in various forms of learning and art. And yet, such achievements do not themselves give worth to the monks' calling so much as does the quality of spiritual life they reach through them. Just as inward prayer and contemplation are activities, so are all outward activities contemplative. Monks and nuns of the Eastern church, in which no multiplicity of orders exists, are traditionally viewed as people who are part at once of the "present age" and of the anticipation of the "age to come." As such, they embody the transition to another social plane and dimension of living—one expressed in the Christian paradox that humans are to *become* what they *are*: the image and likeness of God.

From the very beginning, and that means from the time of the establishment of the Christian empire, there were Christians who were suspicious of the Christian conquest of "this World" and so attempted to set a model of the new society, the true Christian community, outside the city gates, in the desert. Early Christian monasticism, which originated in the East, was a spontaneous movement whose purpose was not to escape into wilderness and solitude to avoid social burdens (as if life in the desert were somehow "easier"), but to pursue union with God by removing oneself from the existing social structures (family, people, Empire) and starting fresh in another community, namely, the Church.

The outward pattern of the monastic life in Byzantium indeed included a period of withdrawal and solitude during which a monk learned the truth about himself and developed the gift of discernment of things human and divine. Only then could he open the door of his cell to the world, or return to it himself. Thus the solitary life may be a phase, or the chosen path of the few; the prevailing form of monastic life, however, has never been anti-social so much as "coenobitical," or communal. St. Basil the Great, considered to be the first legislator of Eastern monasticism, saw the formation of monastic communities as "an attempt to rekindle the spirit of mutuality in the world which seemed to have lost any force of cohesion and any sense of social responsibility."[48]

The tension between the Empire and the Desert, or the City and the Desert, was another ambivalence that marked much of Byzantine religious history, generally leaving the impression that monasticism preserved the early Christian principles frequently compromised in the Empire. Georges Florovsky makes that point clear: "As in the pagan Empire the Church herself was a kind of 'Resistance Movement,' *Monasticism was a permanent 'Resistance Movement' in the Christian Society.*"[49] Because of that, in every Orthodox tradition, monastics, and especially the "elders" (Greek *geron*, Russian *starets*), with their spiritual discernment and wisdom, have enjoyed great veneration and attracted attention from the lay public in both rural and urban settings.[50] However, the scope of their subtle social influence on culture and history has generally remained unrecognized, since it pertains to inward self, to self-creativity, and to the transfiguration of human nature rather than to the more tangible social and economic circumstances of life.

If such circumstances become the only criteria for evaluating the monastic calling in the Byzantine tradition, then its depreciation in comparison to the monastic orders of the Roman church is not surprising. But if one uses "the truth of religion" as a criterion, the same set of facts gain a different meaning: It is precisely because of western monks' involvement in the world, and the adjustments they made to its social, political, and economic environment, that they put themselves in danger of compromising "the call of the Desert," forgetting that their true "citizenship," *politeuma*, is not here but in heaven (Phil. 3:20).

The parable of Martha and Mary (Luke 10:38–42) provides a scriptural paradigm for the two modes of activity: When Jesus visited the house of the two sisters, Martha welcomed Him and was busy serving Him while Mary sat at His feet and heard His word. Realizing that she was doing all the work, Martha demanded her sister's help from the Lord. And He said: "Martha, Martha, you are worried and troubled about many things. But one thing is needed, and Mary has chosen that good part, which will not be taken away from her" (Luke 10:41–42). Thus, "that good part" for monks, and indeed all Christians, must indeed be His word—a priority which by no means excludes serving Him. We see from this viewpoint an asymmetrical synergy between the concreteness of life and its ultimate concerns. This asymmetry is in favor of the ultimate concern: The economy of life is encompassed by the biblical *oikonomia* (from which the term *economy* originates), or God's *plan* for the salvation of humankind (Eph. 1:9–10, 3:2–3). This is a Byzantine model of ambivalence, but within the shared "universe of discourse."

Today, ambivalence is replaced with certainty and there is no shared "universe of discourse." The resulting misunderstandings and recriminations call for greater caution and responsibility. Habitual use of religion and religious qualifiers to explain, for example, economic development or the lack thereof usually raises more questions than it answers. This is particularly evident in regard to Eastern Orthodoxy, about which many Western journalists and analysts exhibit remarkable incompetence.

What is one to conclude from the following statement of "fact"? "Since 1989, the economies of the Catholic and Protestant countries of Poland, Hungary, Slovenia and the Czech Republic have all grown faster, or at least have been less stagnant, than those of Orthodox Romania, Bulgaria and Macedonia, and largely Muslim Albania."[51] What is being qualified here? Economy as Catholic, Protestant, or Orthodox? Or, Catholicism and Protestantism as faster growing or less stagnant than Orthodoxy? In what way, one wonders, can these religious designations be helpful in understanding the logic of investments in post-communist Eastern Europe? Why, indeed, has Hungary had more investment than Romania? Can politics perhaps explain more than religion in this case?

Consider the observation that "we should not delude ourselves that the spread of open societies in the Balkans and elsewhere is necessarily a natural development: It is a direct result of the expansion of American imperial authority—albeit soft and undeclared—with which local populations now see it in their self-interest to get along."[52] There is no ambivalence here; no Byzantine recognition of *oikonomia*, the divine *plan* for the salvation of humanity. Only the certainty of an *economic plan* of "American imperial authority" to save those societies in the Balkans to whom this kind of "openness" does not come "naturally," but must be induced in order for the "local people" to see their own self-interests. However, what happens when the "local people" do not share the vision of the imperial authority?

Ambivalence as Byzantine Legacy

And in our own days, when we are wrestling with the same problem, we may get some more light on ourselves through an impartial study of the Eastern experiment, both in its hope and in its failure.[53]

We have seen that ambivalence was a characteristic trait of Byzantine reality, defining it at every level of its outer and inner life. Byzantium was an attempt to accept and apply to history the antinomical idea of Christ's Incarnation, which is itself "beyond history." In the end (after a millennium of dedicated commitment), the idea of a "churchified" Empire failed. The Desert remained, witnessing in the last two centuries of the Empire the sudden flowering of mystical contemplation on Mount Athos[54] and "the last Byzantine Renaissance" in art, philosophy, and learning, whose echoes were to resonate through the Western Renaissance as well.[55] The epilogue of Byzantium may thus be as ambivalent as the reality on which it was premised: "The fall of the Empire and the Fulfillment of the Desert. . . ."[56]

The Byzantine legacy of ambivalence, that is, its recognition of reality as inherently ambivalent, may be precisely what contemporary Europe needs to recognize and reconsider in order to come to terms with its various selves, including its "Balkan self." Since the time of Byzantium, "the in-betweenness" and "neither-here-nor-there" position of the Balkans has disquieted the West. Negative attitudes do not, however, obliterate what is negated. In dialectical logic, negation is a form of relationship: "To negate is to indicate an alternative, a neglected complement."[57] Perhaps some ideas for an alternative relationship between Europe and the Balkans may be found in the experience of that neglected complement to other European civilizations—the one called Byzantium.

Let us suggest the complex phenomenon of *inverse perspective*, characteristic of Byzantine art, as a metaphor for the relation in question. Unlike the familiar linear perspective common in European painting since the Renaissance, which implies a single, external, static point from which the object is viewed, Byzantine (and other medieval and ancient) art used viewing positions from within the representation. While linear perspective excludes the viewer from the space represented, inverse perspective includes the viewer within the space of its representation.[58]

To the eye accustomed to linear perspective, this inverse perspective appears as "distortion," as two-dimensional and thus "primitive." However, where linear perspective creates the illusion of a window into a three-dimensional space external to the viewer, inverse perspective unites the represented space with the real space of the viewer. There is no break between represented space and real space.[59]

Acceptance of the viewer's internality to the representation reveals a third dimension of that which, by linear convention, is flat. It also demonstrates the insufficiency of the external perspective, which is not to say that the external perspective is false, but only that it is incomplete. Similarly, European depictions of the Balkans as an external space are insufficient. Europe and the Balkans are united in the same space; the question is which perspective reveals that unity to both.

Notes

1. Steven Runciman, *The Emperor Romanus Lecapenus and His Reign* (Cambridge: Cambridge University Press, 1995 [1929]), 9.

2. It is interesting to compare the thousand-year period in the history of the German empire with the thousand-year Byzantine history, in terms of stability of imperial power. In the German case the throne was occupied by about fifty rulers from five noble families, whereas in the Byzantine case—where half of the emperors were removed from power by force—we find about ninety emperors from thirty different families. How do we evaluate this? We see the instability of Byzantine imperial power, on the one hand, but we also see that the lack of strict hereditary rules of succession kept the throne open to anyone but a eunuch or a monk. See A. P. Kazhdan and G. Constable, *People and Power in Byzantium: An Introduction to Modern Byzantine Studies* (Washington, D.C.: Dumbartan Oaks Center for Byzantine Studies, 1982), 146.

3. After all, Machiavelli's portrayal of the prototype of the unscrupulous, treacherous, and cunning political ruler was not inspired by the Byzantine emperor, but by Caesar Borgia, illegitimate son of Rodrigo Borgia, who later became Pope Alexander VI.

4. G. W. F. Hegel, *Philosophy of History* (New York: Dover Publications, 1956), 340. In the age of Freud, as Robert Nelson notes, one may be tempted to interpret Hegel's ideas on assassination plots and poisoning of the Emperors, or his depictions of Byzantine women as lustful and easily surrendering themselves to all kinds of abominations, as "the rantings of an elderly man, projecting onto a safely distant Other his deepest fears." But, in fact, one need not go into such biographical psychoanalysis to ground attitudes like these since they were quite widespread from at least the eighteenth century ("Living on the Byzantine Borders of the Western Art," *GESTA* 35, no. 1 (1996), 8.

5. On various aspects of *Balkanism* and *Orientalism*, see Maria Todorova, *Imagining the Balkans* (New York: Oxford University Press, 1977); Vesna Golsworthy, *Inventing Ruritania: The Imperialism of the Imagination* (New Haven: Yale University Press, 1998); Milica Bakić-Hayden and Robert M. Hayden, "Orientalist Variations on the Theme 'Balkans': Symbolic Geography in Recent Yugoslav Cultural Politics," *Slavic Review* 51, no. 1 (Spring 1992), 1–15; Milica Bakić-Hayden, "Nesting Orientalisms: The Case of Former Yugoslavia," *Slavic Review* 54, no. 4 (Winter 1995), 917–931; Alexandru Dutu, *Political Models and National Identities in "Orthodox Europe"* (Bucharest: Babel Publishing House, 1998); and Alexandru Dutu, "Small Countries and Persistent Stereotypes," *Révue des études sud-est européennes* (Academie Roumaine) 31, nos. 1–2 (1993).

6. Nelson, "Living on the Byzantine Borders of Western Art," 3–4.

7. Ibid.

8. Ilya Prizel, "The First Decade after the Collapse of Communism," *SAIS Review* 19 (summer–fall 1999): 7.

9. John Meyendorff, *The Byzantine Legacy in the Orthodox Church* (Crestwood, N.Y.: St. Vladimir's Seminary Press, 1982), 9.

10. Prizel, "The First Decade," 4.

11. At the risk of some oversimplification, Kallistos Ware notes that in the early Church, which from the start implied unity of faith amidst diversity of theological schools, the Greek approach to the Christian mystery was more speculative, and the Latin more practical. For the Eastern church theology was never separated from mysticism and liturgical worship. In the Western church the concepts of Roman law and juridical ideas had a profound effect on its administrative style as well as on the development of Scholasticism and subsequent attempts to rationalize faith. In terms of doctrine, where the Greeks tended to emphasize Christ's divinity (Christ the Victor), the Latins stressed his humanity (i.e., Christ the Victim); the Greeks put emphasis on deification and the Latins on redemption, and so on (see Timothy Ware, *The Orthodox Church* (London: Penguin Books, 1993), 48–49.

12. Quoted in Ware, *The Orthodox Church*, 50.

13. From the letter of Orthodox Patriarchs sent to Pope Pius IX in 1848, quoted in Ware, 251.

14. Ibid.

15. Statements like these remind one of the observation of an English historian and politician, who asserted that all of the Indian literature (Sanskrit and Persian) was less valuable than a bunch of "paltry abridgements" used in English prep schools. See Wilhelm Halbfass, *India and Europe* (Albany: SUNY Press, 1988), 68.

16. Alexandru Dutu, "Orthodoxie et totalitarisme," in *Europa Orthodoxa* (Academia Romana: Insititutul de Studii Sud-Est Europene, 1997), 55.

17. Paul Ricoeur, *The Symbolism of Evil* (Boston: Beacon Press, 1967), 352.

18. Thus, Byzantine society may appear as a " 'totalitarian collectivity' in which 'individual rights' do not exist"; (cf. Vladimir Lossky, *The Mystical Theology of the Eastern Church* [Crestwood, N.Y.: St. Vladimir's Seminary Press, 1976], 175–176) but that means we are reducing the Church purely to its "earthly aspect," neglecting that what in its mind distinguishes it from every other human society, and we thus confuse her ultimate concern for the human *person*, made in the image and likeness of God, with that for *individuals* as elements of collectivities.

19. Kazhdan and Constable, *People and Power*, 142.

20. Ibid.

21. Ibid., chapter 5; see also Donald M. Nicol, "Saints and Scholars: The 'Inner' and 'Outer' Wisdom," in *Church and Society in the Last Centuries of Byzantium* (Cambridge: Cambridge University Press, 1979).

22. See the entry in *The Oxford English Dictionary*.

23. J. C. Heesterman, *The Inner Conflict of Tradition* (Chicago and London: The University of Chicago Press, 1985), 2.

24. See Georges Florovsky, *Christianity and Culture*, vol. 2 (Belmont, Mass.: Nordland Publishing Co., 1974), 75.

25. Quoted in Aristeides Papadakis, "Church-State Relations under Orthodoxy," in *Eastern Christianity and Politics in the Twentieth Century*, ed. Pedro Ramet (Durham, N.C.: Duke University Press, 1988), 39–40.

26. Averil Cameron, *Christianity and the Rhetoric of Empire* (Berkeley: University of California Press, 1991), 200.

27. Ware, *The Orthodox Church*, 243.

28. Ibid.

29. Aristeides Papadakis, "Church-State Relations under Orthodoxy," in *Eastern Christianity and Politics in the Twentieth Century*. Ed. Pedro Ramet. (Durham and London: Duke University Press, 1988), 43; Florovsky, *Christianity and Culture*, vol. 2, 77–79.

30. The attempts of some emperors to impose on the Church a compromise on theological issues such as Arianism, Iconoclasm or, later, a dubious 'reunion' with the Roman church, failed rather miserably (*Ibid.*, 80–81).

31. Ibid., 82.

32. Papadakis,"The Church-State Relations, 43. It is rather ironic that *caesaropapism*, the common allegation of the Orthodox Church's submission to the state, came from the West, whose institution of papacy represents a far more ambitious attempt to join imperial and ecclesiastical powers in a single office, of which the Byzantine emperor could not even dream.

It was only during the Ottoman period, when the institution of the emperor ceased to exist, that the office of the patriarch was vested with both ecclesiastical and administrative power, and the patriarch practically became an Ottoman official.

33. See Alexandru Dutu, *Political Models and National Identities in "Orthodox Europe"* (Bucharest: Babel Publishing House, 1998), 165.

34. Cf. Alexandru Dutu, "Small Countries and Persistent Stereotypes," *Revue des etudes sud-est europeene* (Academie Roumaine) xxxi, nos 1–2 (1993), 8.

35. Ware, *The Orthodox Church*, 88–89; Papadakis, "Church-State Relations," 46–49.

36. The autocephaly of the churches of Bulgaria and Serbia, for instance, was completely suppressed during the Ottoman period.

37. The Greek case was particularly paradoxical in that the newly appointed king of independent Greece (who was neither Greek nor Orthodox, and was brought there by the European powers after the assassination of the first Greek president, Capodistrias, in 1831) had power over the church, making it effectively an agency of the state (Pappadakis, "Church-State Relations," 49–51; Theofan G. Stavrou, "The Orthodox Church of Greece," in *Eastern Christianity and Politics in the Twentieth Century*. Ed. Pedro Ramet [Durham and London: Duke University Press, 1988]), 187–189.

38. Quoted in Paschalis M. Kitromilidis, " 'Imagined Communities' and the Origin of the National Question in the Balkans," *European History Quaterly* 19 ([April 1989], 181–182.)

39. Meyendorff, *The Byzantine Legacy*, 251.

40. *Ibid.*, 225; "All the Christian churches founded in the early years of the faith were local and contained the Christians of a specific town or a specific locality, without racial distinction." Quoted in Kitromilidis, " 'Imagined Communities,' " 181.

41. Cf. Peter Berger, *The Sacred Conopy* (New York: Anchor Books, 1967), 46.

42. Prizel, "The First Decade," 4.

43. Lossky, *The Mystical Theology*, 18.

44. Cf. *Ibid.*, 13. "For the 'historian of the Church' the religious factor disappears and finds itself displaced by others; such, for instance, as the play of political or social interests, the part played by racial or cultural conditions, considered as determining factors in the life of the Church."

45. Ricoeur, *The Symbolism of Evil*, 359.

46. John Meyendorff, "Was there ever a 'Third Rome'? Remarks on the Byzantine Legacy in Russia," in *The Byzantine Tradition after the Fall of Constantinople*, ed. John Yiannias (Charlottesville and London: University Press of Virginia, 1991), 57.

47. Ware, *The Orthodox Church*, 37–38.

48. Florovsky, *Christianity and Culture*, vol. 2, 85.

49. Ibid., 88.

50. Peter Brown, "The Rise and Function of the Holy Man in Late Antiquity," *Journal of Roman Studies* 61 (1971): 81–101.

51. Robert Kaplan, "Yugoslavia's Fate, and Europe's," *New York Times*, op-ed (October 6, 2000), A31.

52. Ibid.

53. Florovsky, *Christianity and Culture*, vol. 2, 100.

54. In the center of this spiritual revival was Gregory Palamas, a fourteenth-century monk, scholar and, at one point, the Archbishop of Thessaloniki, whose (1) defense of the *hesychast* method of the "prayer of the heart" or the *Jesus Prayer*, involving breath-awareness and a particular bodily posture, and (2) teaching on the "energies" and the "essence" of God brought him recognition from one of the most revered Church Fathers in Orthodox Christianity.

55. "The Last Byzantine Renaissance" is the title of Steven Runciman's book (Cambridge: Cambridge University Press, 1970).

56. Florovsky, *Christianity and Culture*, 2: 130.

57. See Errol E. Harris, *Formal, Transcendental and Dialectical Thinking: Logic and Reality* (Albany: State University of New York Press, 1987), 157.

58. Boris Uspensky, *A Poetics of Composition* (Berkeley: University of California Press, 1973), 134–136.

59. Leonid Ouspensky, *Theology of the Icon*, vol. 2 (Crestwood, N.Y.: St. Vladimir's Seminary Press, 1992), 495.

4

The Balkans as an Element in Ideological Mechanisms

Rastko Močnik

Across the Alps, towards the Atlantic
Title of an editorial, *Delo* (Ljubljana), July 19, 1997

Simply speaking, these features are slyness, speculation, unreliability, relativity of the given word. These are concepts which . . . are beyond the civilizational caesura of Westernness, since between the two principles, the European and the Byzantine, the compromise has never been reached.

Delo, May 30, 1998 (description of the *Italian* foreign policy)

Behind the Turkish hill
there are many guys
fighting for us.
One is without an arm,
the other without a leg,
the third one is sitting on the soil
without the ass.

Slovene folk song

In this chapter, I will discuss the Balkanist stereotype and some of the ideological mechanisms that rely upon it. I will examine a selection of utterances that appeared in the Slovenian and Croatian mass media. I have selected this material for analysis due to its paradigmatic, that is, structural, value. Given the recent proliferation of Balkanist discourse, this approach does not originate exclusively in my personal preferences and limitations. Rather, some kind of typological, that is, deterministic or semiotic work seems necessary as a preliminary step toward more ambitious empirical studies propelled by statistical or stochastic methods in the future. The chapter proceeds in two phases. In the first phase, I analyze *Balkanism* as an ideology of domination, demonstrating that within *Balkanism, two types of relations of domination* are articulated: the relations of geo-political and economic hegemony, and the relations of internal domination within the societies geo-politically stigmatized as "Balkan." *Balkanism* supports, that is, ideologically mediates and reproduces the economic, social, and political dependence of a certain semi-peripheral European region upon the Western European center, as well as the socio-economic domination of the ruling elites within the countries of the region. Immanuel Wallerstein[1] speaks of "ethnicization of the exploited classes": Here, we are concerned with the Balkanization of entire countries, submitted to a regime of unequal exchange or straightforward exploitation.[2] In the second phase, the paper examines the ideological mechanisms at play in the present Balkanist ideology, focusing on the functions performed by the Balkanist stereotype and arguing that these functions are predominantly pragmatic (and not semantic, as a common doxa would tend to indicate).

I.   Where Are the Balkans?

Many of the countries of Southeastern Europe, and especially those affected by the Dayton agreement, are currently engaged in an arms race. This is certainly not the best option for countries devastated by war, "transition," greedy states, and self-serving local elites. Neither is this the best possible arrangement of their mutual relations. Yet it seems to have been imposed upon them.

Each country can decide whether to arm itself or not. If a country decides against profligate military spending, it can free up important portions of its budget for more citizen-friendly uses. But that country also takes a considerable risk, because, *should other countries of the region not do the same*, it will be pushed into an inferior position, which opens it to blackmail and eventually aggression from its neighbors. The tragic experience of the Republic of Bosnia and Herzegovina is there to shake any pacifist considerations out of regional leaders' minds.

It is theoretically relevant that the situation would not change even in the improbable case that *all* the countries of the region, and all the local leaders, were to genuinely favor pacifist policies. The reasoning would remain the same. At a first stage, each of the parties implicated would be wary of the intentions of the others; at a second stage, everybody might well acknowledge the good intentions of the others, but would also realize that these intentions will never be acted upon. Every party involved would then follow the same discouraging reasoning: "Of course they do not want to start an arms race, just as we don't; but can they afford to abstain? No, they can't. It suffices that one party breaks the tacit agreement—and it will fall apart. So better to hurry and arm ourselves, since it is too dangerous to wait and lose time!"

The relations between the countries involved form a system: It is a system of confrontation, but nevertheless a system. It is the system of balkanization in its double colloquial sense: both of isolating an area against external influence and of dividing an area into small antagonistic states. Such a system can arise from a situation where each party involved plays the role of potential warmonger for all the others. Empirically, this is the most common situation. Theoretically, though, one can construe a *limit-situation* in which, regardless of the actual mutual perceptions of the parties, the situation would be defined by a *phantom* militarist. The *limit situation* would be structured as follows: From the point of view of each party involved, it is impossible to exclude the likelihood that some other party will identify one of the parties (including the one that is the subject of this reasoning) as the phantom militarist; therefore, it is necessary for every party actually to become a militarist. In other words: a possibility, first incorporated by an ideological phantom, intersubjectively translates itself into a necessity. Because each party cannot exclude the possibility that, in someone else's view, it is (ideologically) identified with the militarist phantom, it actually has to become militarist.

This is the classic prisoner's dilemma: Although an optimal outcome of the game exists, the players cannot reach it and have to opt instead for an outcome that is equally disadvantageous to all the players but that is nevertheless (precisely because it is *equally* disadvantageous) the second best option. In a simplified form, we can represent the situation as a matrix game for two players, each of whom has two options: to disarm (D) or to arm himself (A). The options of the second player are represented on the upper line, the options of the first player in the column. The gains (positive numbers) and the losses (negative numbers) for each player in each of the possible outcomes form the matrix (first figure for the first player, second figure for the second player) (see table 4.1).

Although the best outcome for both players would be reached if both play D (disarmament), the rational choice for both is to play A (armament), which yields the outcome −1 for both players.

So the best strategy for the Dayton signatories is to settle for antagonistic, non-co-operative behavior, and to engage in an arms race. Here comes the curious detail in the picture, though: In terms of the number of guns, tanks, aircraft, and so on each party can possess, the race is contained by an international agreement. Each country involved can consequently hope to acquire an advantage over the others

Table 4.1

1/2	D	A
D	1, 1	−2, 2
A	2, −2	−1, −1

not in quantity of military equipment but only in the quality of human potential and social organization. At the limit, the advantage a country can eventually gain depends upon its capacity to turn itself into a mammoth military barracks.

If the international agreement, by limiting the material military potential of the Dayton countries, indirectly encourages their societal militarization, why has the international community not set the limit of the arms race at zero? Since there is an international agreement, why is it not a construction of *demilitarization*? There may be thousands of answers to this question, but the bottom line is this: The alternative construction would not be one centered upon the contradiction between antagonism on the lower regional level and cooperation on the higher international level. The alternative construction would not allow for the balkanization of the Balkans.

By no means do we want to suggest that the international activities culminating in the Dayton agreement caused the belligerent behavior of the countries involved. Everybody knows that the agreement brought peace. What we contend, however, is that it also created a situation and produced a structure that has blocked access to a better possible outcome.[3]

The complete picture is then composed of an area of antagonism circumscribed by an area of co-operation. We should not conceive the situation upon the model of those Chinese boxes where a larger box contains a smaller one. Rather, we should regard as primary the non-antagonistic contradiction between regional antagonism and international cooperation: The structure of the situation is whatever crystallizes around this contradiction as the outcome of conjunctural over-determinations.

This means that the matrix of the prisoners' dilemma is over-determined by its specific exterior. The players, caught within the scheme, are determined by a double articulation, and it is this double determination that imprisons them within the dilemma. This is important because it shows the mutual dependency of the two contradictory levels of action, the level of antagonism and the level of cooperation.

We can illustrate this structure with the help of Roman Jakobson's concept of the "two axes of language," which stipulates an axis of oppositions and an axis of contiguity.[4] This scheme is particularly convenient in our case: If we conceive the post-Dayton situation as a model[5] of Jakobson's concept, it immediately appears that the two axes are not symmetrical, and that the axis of oppositions dominates the axis of contiguity.

The opposition is the (paradigmatic and contradictory) opposition around which the structure organizes itself—the field of cooperation versus the field of antagonism. This opposition can ideologically be conceived as the opposition "Europe/the Balkans."

The relations of contiguity are those established among the elements situated inside the double space created by the paradigmatic opposition. These are the relations of co-operation within the "international community" (ideologically conceived as, for example, Europe, the democratic community, the civilized world, and so on); and the relations of antagonism within the area of the prisoner's dilemma (ideologically conceived as, for example, the Balkans). It is of utmost importance that neither of the two types of relations can be conceived, established, reproduced, or acted out without the reference to the constitutive contradictory opposition, "Europe/the Balkans."

This reference is constitutive not only for the relations among the elements, that is, the countries involved, but it is also constitutive of the elements themselves, that is, of the concrete socio-ideological structure of the countries in question.[6]

A piece of ideological discourse from a well-authorized source will best illustrate our point:

(1) "There exists an objective danger that Europe, 'safe' and stable, encloses itself in order to defend itself against unpleasant surprises coming from politically, economically, militarily and socially unstable countries. . . . We are certainly interested that the Schengen-border does not run north of us. . . . Will Slovenia be in the position to choose on which of its borders, northern or southern, the Schengen-border will run? We will do everything to secure that it runs on our southern borders. . . . If Slovenia is forced, we will act without altruism. . . ." (Milan Kucan, president of the Republic of Slovenia, in an interview published in *Globus*, Zagreb, July 25, 1997.)[7]

It is with reference to the "Europe/non-Europe" opposition that the (antagonistic) relation to one's neighbor is conceived: This seems to be a definite indication that Slovenia is a country that belongs to the Balkans, since its hegemonic ideology[8] reproduces the pattern that is constitutive of the Balkans as a symbolic region. The president's discourse is evidently not only a discourse deployed within the domain of antagonism between the countries, it is also a discourse that belongs to the country's internal political scene and that is intended to trigger internal ideological and political effects—that is, it aims to reproduce the relations that constitute one of the antagonistic terms, namely, the element "Slovenia."[9]

Before we consider how the representation of the border operates within the internal reproduction of ideological and political relations among the countries involved, we should first comment briefly upon the interconnection between the representation of the Balkans and that of Europe.

"The Balkans" and "Europe" are two representations that each define an area of relations, actions, and operations and that possess contrary codes of behavior: cooperation in "Europe," antagonism in "the Balkans."[10] Instead of two representations, we should therefore speak of two sets of beliefs (including principles of practical action) with different domains of application. Although discourses and actions, performed against the background of one or the other belief-set, determine their context all by themselves and without any further guarantee, there is no ambiguity about the moment in which one or the other belief-background is activated, precisely because the syntagmation in one or the other domain (co-operation or antagonism, "Europe" or "the Balkans") is always dominated by the same paradigmatic opposition that distributes between the two domains. From the point of view of this ideology, it could almost be said that antagonism is the specific mode in which co-operation is performed in the Balkans (as opposed to Europe). It is the reference to the dominating paradigm, "*Europe/the Balkans,*" that, in this case, secures the decisive feature of socially operative beliefs, their "reflexivity."[11] This dominating paradigm provides the native theory of the operativeness of the two sets of beliefs, and assigns them their domain of operation: antagonism in "the Balkans," co-operation in "Europe."

Agents interpellated within this ideology act according to the prisoner's dilemma matrix. They do not act in this way because they know the matrix: their actions are motivated by the belief that this is the right or appropriate way of doing things within one of the particular domains (the Balkans) set up by the great divide "Europe/the Balkans." The limits of this belief (it "holds" for a particular region) make it an operational belief, both in the sense of its locus of application ("the Balkans") and of its modus operandi (antagonistic behavior). These limits articulate the operational belief within the dominating paradigm, "Europe/the Balkans."

In this light, the native theory, although enclosed within the area of belief, seems both more sophisticated and more complete than knowledge as expressed, for example, by the prisoner's dilemma. We can infer from this the structural condition of knowledge, *le savoir* in the Foucaultian sense, as opposed to belief in the sense of ideology. Knowledge, then, is a set of beliefs, described and/or formalized according to some institutional (academic) criteria, but excluding the ideological conditions that could possibly make this set of beliefs operative.[12] Within the field described by the prisoner's dilemma, natives' operations depend upon identification with a believing subject; on the other hand, the ideal agent of rational choice, as the knowing subject, is the believing subject *minus* the ideological conditions that would make it possible to identify with those beliefs. These conditions are inscribed into ideological structures, but are excluded from the field of knowledge.

II.   Who Are "the Balkan People"?

The "Balkan people," here metonymically representing the the natives of any ideological conjuncture, are those who move freely and safely among different sets of beliefs, mythic or otherwise, plugging in one belief-background when appropriate, and then discarding it in favor of another. The Balkan people need neither compass nor guidance; all the operational theory required is already contained within each package of beliefs, in the form of its particular limitations, borders, and articulations toward other belief-bundles.

The people of the Balkans, like other agents who deal with the region, are natives of a sort—but only in certain situations, such as those defined by reference to the Dayton Agreement. The theory here presented does not rest on the notion of the interiorization of imperial representations; the people of the Orient interiorise Orientalist fiction no more than so-called Westerners do. Rather, that fiction is a universal Baedeker, cherished and used for its practicality, not because it represents some mysterious colonization of the mind. Ever since the West fell for the political-correctness craze, the manual actually sells better in the region itself.

One embarrassing detail remains, however: The agents of the prisoner's dilemma are countries, not individuals. The countries have to be constructed as *collective agents* of rational choice. We said that the collective agent holds together through its double articulation, which links it to the matrix on one side, and to the specific exterior of the matrix on the other. Without much simplification, we can say that the same Orientalist ideology that downgrades and holds down the Balkan region as a whole also holds up the ruling position of local political classes, which in turn act (actually or *in spe*) as the local agents of the international system of domination.

The Orientalist representation of the Balkans functions simultaneously in two dimensions:

1. In the international dimension, this ideology defines the Balkans as a particular region with specific codes of behavior, which are opposed to the universal code of co-operation. It defines Balkan countries as collective agents due to their capacity to shift from co-operation to antagonism and *vice versa*—that is, by their ability to move between the levels of "Europe" and "the Balkans." We see that the practical effect of the ideology contradicts its explicit contents: *Balkanism* is not what

separates these countries from "Europe;" rather, it is their means of integration into the international system. Nevertheless, this illusion of separation supports and reproduces the essential feature of this integration: It keeps the Balkan countries in an inferior position. The Orientalist view of the Balkans is thus a mechanism of international domination.

2. However—and this is what makes it both possible and necessary to reject any mystique of "interiorization"—this same Orientalist ideology also functions as a mechanism of domination within the Balkan countries themselves.

We now have to explain how this ideology holds the countries themselves together, and how it constructs Balkan countries as collective subjects. In other words, we have to explain how and why this is the hegemonic ideology of the countries concerned, and what role it plays in the ideological (and, consequently, class) struggles within the countries themselves. Therefore, our next topic will be:

III. *Balkanism* as a State Ideology

We will start the discussion with what, at first sight, may seem to be a diversion from the main topic: with the self-image of "*young democracies,*" which the Balkan countries share with the rest of the post-communist states.

This self-representation is one of the mechanisms by which relations of economic oppression and exploitation are introduced by *political means*. Its limit-effect would be the installation of conditions where economic exploitation would appear normal and would, classically, be performed without recourse to extra-economic pressures. One can be reasonably skeptical that the limit-effect will ever be achieved, which also means that one can be optimistic with regard to the future of the ideological mechanisms of capitalist reproduction, whether democratic, Orientalist, or otherwise. Specifically, the "young democracies" aim to break down the strong egalitarian ideology of social solidarity, which is solidly implanted across the social spectrum of the countries concerned. For our inquiry, though, the most important feature of this ideology is its individualism. In the ideological dimension, this means freedom of consciousness, freedom of expression, the right to embrace any opinion, to shift from one belief to the other, and so on. This is what is commonly called ideological modernization; it does away with all relics of the status-societies of the past, and with "traditionalist" structures in general. Karl Marx was one of the first thinkers to lament this historical novelty of capitalism. He did not consider it modernization. Rather, he wrote about the liquidation of "*naturwuechsige*" ties of personal dependence, replaced in capitalism by civil liberties, freedom, juridical "equality," and de-personalized relations of economic dependence, domination, and exploitation.

In the broadest terms, the liquidation of status-society with its personalized relations means the disappearance of any *naturwuechsig*, or any link between the position an individual occupies socially and the thoughts and utterances he or she produces; this also implies the absence of any link that would tie an individual to his or her position, or status, in society. The idea of freedom of consciousness thus presupposes a free individual in the bourgeois sense, that is, a historical situation where there is no easily conceivable relation between the position an individual happens to occupy and the thoughts and utterances he or she happens to think and to utter.[13]

If an individual is to be free to embrace any set of beliefs socially available, the belief-packages, in their turn, have to be free of any indication of the situation where they may rightfully be activated. The beliefs no longer point to the domain of their application. In other words, their limitations are no longer an inherent part of their structure.[14] The simple native situation no longer applies.[15]

Instead of the tightly structured, multiply articulated social space typical of "status societies," modern political society presents an atomized field of free and equal, equally abstract individuals, who entertain shifting packages of beliefs, and who manifest no evident social anchorage. Without mutual articulation and socio-structural relativation, the belief-sets have to be stabilized in some other way: One possible solution is to stabilize them relative to the border of the universe within which they operate. Instead of being mutually articulated by their internal borders, as in a simple native situation, the belief-sets are individually articulated by the outer border that embraces them all. Needless to say, this articulation of beliefs in individualist societies actually *determines* the outer border of the discursive social universe—the universe of the nation.[16]

IV.   A Theory of Nation

We need a theory of nation to underpin the present analysis of Balkanist ideology. Let me briefly trace the outlines of such a theory.[17]

In a 1956 article,[18] Claude Levi-Strauss developed the thesis that dualist social organizations spontaneously develop into ternary organizations. Without elaborating on its possible relevance for the main idea of the text, he also suggested that in every society, there exists an apparently non-functional *zero-institution*, which makes a society possible to exist. Starting from an appropriate definition of a dualist

Table 4.2

Winnebago village according to the informants of the upper moiety	Winnebago village according to the informants of the lower moiety

society, we can show that introducing a third component is structurally necessary, and that this component is the zero-institution.

Levi-Strauss offers the example of the dualistically organized Winnebago village, noting that informants from different moieties give different accounts of the way the village is organized. Although both representations are dualistic, one rests upon a diametric conception of dualism, the other upon a concentric conception. (See table 4.2.)

The discrepancy between the two representations—one diametric and the other concentric—supports the historical materialist contention that the notion of the social totality depends on the structural position from which that totality is conceived. It also radicalizes the question of how such a society can produce the effect of totality at all, and how it can reproduce itself: Under these conditions, social integration and reproduction seem impossible, for they appear to be blocked by two radically different, mutually exclusive, ideological schemes that cannot inter-communicate.

This apparent explanatory dead end is actually a theoretical overture. It offers a good starting position for a stricter definition of a "dualist" (or any other) social organization, for it introduces the necessity for such a definition to take account of the ideological mediation of the reproduction of social relations.[19] A dualist social organization can then be defined as the kind of organization that allows for two different dualistic conceptions of the social whole.[20]

Such an organization faces a structural break-down of communication that can (only) be resolved by the introduction of a third ideological conception of society that is "neutral" with respect to the other two, and in reference to which the two constitutive ideologies can define and situate each other, thus inter-communicating.

Let us present a simplified model of this solution. Assume that a small social world, consisting of objects defined by three distinctive features in coupled oppositions, is initially organized in a dualistic way. One side of the initial dualism organizes this world along the opposition circular/not circular (o/v), and the other along the opposition bold/not bold (o/o). Conceiving the social world in two different dualistic ways, members of this society cannot communicate directly, unless the two groups find a common solution. The solution proceeds from the introduction of a

Table 4.3

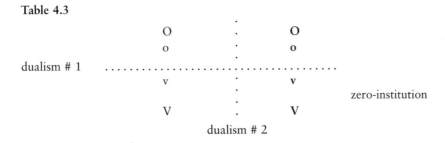

third type of conceptual scheme, based on a non-pertinent distinctive feature. The process can be broken down into two steps: 1. The perception and the definition of misunderstanding (misunderstanding appears as a positive moment in social integration): "Your conception of the social world is based on a feature that is not pertinent to my conception."—"My way to organize the world proceeds from a distinction that is not pertinent to your way of organizing it." This step introduces the notion of the non-pertinent distinctive feature. 2. At the second stage, both groups agree upon a common scheme of world organization, based upon a distinctive opposition that is non-pertinent within their respective specific ideological conceptions, for example, "large/not-large" (O/o). This "third" conceptual scheme is the zero-institution. The zero-institution functions as the common reference of the two mutually exclusive conceptual schemes (they can both be generated from it), and thus secures their inter-communication, imposing itself as a neutral, mediating instance. The zero-institution produces the totalizing effect "Society." (See table 4.3.)

Our hypothesis is that the nation functions as a zero-institution. Intuitively, the idea seems persuasive: 1. Whereas other institutions, divisions, etc., seem to be functional in a modern society, the nation seems to lack a function; 2. In nationally organized societies, all functional institutions refer to, and are conceived with respect to, the nation. It would therefore seem plausible that the nation has no other function than to enable a certain type of society to exist, that is, to reproduce itself as a whole. Then again, this type of society already possesses a mechanism for overall social reproduction: the state. The nation would then seem to duplicate an existing institution. Other difficulties arise when we consider how the zero-institution operates in stateless societies, as opposed to the way the nation operates:

1. While the standard zero-institution divides a society from within, the nation unifies a modern society and defines its outward border. While the zero-institution divides a society into exclusive segments, the nation totalizes a society into an inclusive whole.

2. While the standard zero-institution defines itself in relation to other (functional) institutions of the same society—the nation defines itself in relation to the same institution (the nation) of other societies.

The nation is inwardly inclusive and outwardly exclusive, while the standard zero-institution is inwardly exclusive and has no outward dimension. Or, in more exact terms:

• *The nation is inclusive in the heterogeneous dimension* (it includes other heterogeneous institutions of the same society) *and exclusive in the homogeneous dimension* (it excludes institutions of the same kind, that is, other nations).

• *The standard zero-institution is exclusive in the heterogeneous dimension* (it "cuts across" other institutions of different, heterogeneous kinds) *and inclusive in the homogeneous dimension* (it distributes individuals in a unified way).

Important consequences follow from these differences. While a standard zero-institution defines itself in relation to other (functional) institutions and divides the social field into exclusive partitions, the nation defines itself in relation to other nations, first to those with whom it shares its borders, and in relation to individuals within those borders; it unifies the social field into an inwardly inclusive and outwardly exclusive "whole."

Translated into our idiom of belief-sets, these features indicate that the nation, as a zero-institution, is a solution to the problem of social integration under the conditions of mutually independent beliefs. In Levi-Strauss's example, he links conceptual schemes to social position. Neither situational nor social relativization is anywhere linked to the abstract political constitution of individualist societies.

The only opposition the nation introduces into the social field it defines is the opposition between the individual and the collectivity. This structural opposition functions as, or is conceived or experienced as, a cultural identification. It is identification with the structural instance of the subject ascribed to the national zero-institution. Contrary to the instance of the subject motivated by beliefs, which supports the belief-sets,[21] this is a subject motivated by knowledge, for the identification with this instance correlates with the occultation of the conditions that make such an identification possible.

And yet, the knowledge that allows the subject to identify with the national zero-institution is void: It exhausts itself in its function, which is to permit the subject to shift among otherwise unconnected belief-sets. Hence, that knowledge is open to investment by some *particular* belief-set, by some *particular ideology* that operates within the space circumscribed by the national zero-institution. The ideology that invests this otherwise void field of knowledge becomes the *hegemonic ideology*. The hegemonic ideology can claim to be supported by the authority of the knowing subject. In nationally organized societies, the ideological struggle is fought around the question *which* ideology will (temporarily) invest the knowledge ascribed to the subject of the national zero-institution, which will in turn support the national identity. Balkanist ideologies are particularly well suited to this task: Since they are ideologies of a border, they fit well with the imperfect ideological skeleton of the national border; what is more, by taking over the zero-institution, these ideologies support it in its function of maintaining the outer borders of a nation.

V. How *Balkanism* Works

(2) "The Croat armed force has changed strategic relations in this part of the Balkans." (Franjo Tudjman, president of the Republic of Croatia, at the celebration of the "Day of Patriotic Thanksgiving," at the Zemunik air-base; *Vjesnik*, Zagreb, 5. 8. 1996)

(3) "...those who want to push Croatia into the Balkans...." (Tudjman, in the same speech, transmitted by Croatian TV, 4. 8. 1996)

It seems that between (2) and (3), the speaker has shifted from one belief-background to another; or at least, that the referent of the term "the Balkans" has changed. If it is the referent that has changed, then the Croatian president appears to have formed the poetic trope Pierre Fontanier calls "*syllepse de metonymie,*" or syllepsis of metonymy[22]: Croatia is not in the Balkans, but the Balkans are where its armed forces are. The literal sense of the expression "the Balkans" pertains to the military context, while its figurative, metonymic sense figures in the statesman-ship context. This certainly is a possible interpretation, but it actually rejoins the first proposed possibility: For with the change of context also comes a change in the relevant belief-background.

How can such a shift occur so naturally? It is because the belief-sets in question are already mutually articulated and structurally refer to each other. The difference in the sense of the two occurrences of "the Balkans" is *not* a difference between the literal and the figurative sense; it is the difference between two modes of operation of the same term within two different dimensions. *The clue to the mystery of the double meaning of "the Balkans" is the structural position of the term "Croatia."* The term "Croatia" is *doubly articulated*: vertically to the area of cooperation (which is *not* the Balkans), and horizontally to the area of antagonism, where its armed forces are active.[23] Utterances (2) and (3) thus reproduce the Balkanist scheme where an area of antagonism is circumscribed by an area of cooperation. Far from being contradictory, only *together* do they deploy the complete ideological scheme.

The same quasi-natural shift from one belief-background to the other occurs in the following more entertaining utterance:

(4) "The spirit of the Balkans" was hovering over the sports hall of Lucija. Not so much for the performance of the renowned players, though, but rather by virtue of their coaches Svetislav Pesić (Alba) and Miroslav Nikolić (Partizan). (*Dnevnik*, Ljubljana, 19. 8. 1996)

"The spirit of the Balkans" is invoked first in the sense of the basketball mythology: Basketball is of high quality in the Balkans: The same expression is then transferred into the domain of the moral (or political) belief-background: The two coaches, both Serbs, were quarrelling with the judges.

The same scheme underlies the following headline from the Ljubljana daily *Slovenec*: THE BALKAN METHODS OF CROATIAN CLIENTS referred to a demonstration in front of the Slovene Parliament, organized by clients from Croatia whose deposits in the leading Slovene bank had been frozen since the separation of the two countries. Here the simultaneous inscription of the adjective into the two registers of the factual and the moral geography produces a nice racist innuendo: It insinuates that the presumably objectionable methods have something to do with the country of origin of the protesters.

This last example shows yet another important feature of Balkan *Orientalism*: No special indication is needed to trigger the second (imaginary, moral) meaning of the terms "Balkan" and "the Balkans." For its very triviality, the following example may confirm this impression[24]:

(5) *The reporter*: "The management of the team does not trust Balkan cuisine: the team will take its own food along with it." *The sports program anchor*: "Yeah, there might be unpleasant ingredients in the Balkan cuisine."[25]

The automatic activation of the derogatory connotations may lead one to suppose that they have to some extent entered the lexical meaning of the terms pertaining to the Balkans. Our theory, though, permits us to avoid such a conclusion, which would unduly place the linguistic lexicon at the mercy of politics; we prefer to explain the same phenomenon through the pressure of usage. According to this explanation, it is usage which, under particular conditions, transfers the *locus* where the shifting between belief-backgrounds occurs from the believing subject to the knowing subject. Instead of functioning as *possible* connotations, which are only activated relative to certain belief-backgrounds, the derogatory semantic elements then assume a quasi-universal value, active in *every* context. This is a decisive development: *As soon as support for the articulation of different belief-sets within which terms pertaining to the paradigm of "the Balkans" function starts to be secured by the knowing subject, the Balkan-Orientalism scheme has taken over the national zero-institution.* The contamination of the term "Balkan" with derogatory ideological connotations is the effect of the Greek ideological scheme having over-determined the abstract individualist one.

This means that the outer border of the national zero-institution is defined with the reference to the Balkan-Orientalist dichotomy. This may have quite agonizing effects, as shown in this series of titles in the Split daily *Slobodna Dalmacija*:

(6) 19. 7. 1996: ZAGREB DOES NOT NEED THE BALKAN CONNECTION FOR THE COUNCIL OF EUROPE (pp. 1 and 6–7)

20. 7. 1996: IS CROATIA BEING PUSHED INTO AN ALLIANCE WITH THE BALKANS AND AFRICA? (pp. 1 and 5)

21. 7. 1996: THE BALKANS RESPECT ONLY AMERICA (p. 10)

We said that the dualist schemes, in the "native" model, pertain to dualist social structures: Typically, a dualist scheme entails the possibility of another dualist scheme, and only the two together complete the dualist structure of the social space. Here, things may be different. Consider the following type of utterance:

(7) "This path leads Croatia towards Balkan waters and not toward Europe, *say many observers* . . ." (*Dnevnik*, Ljubljana, 22. 8. 1996, italics ours)

The reference to "observers" may well be a stylistic alibi; still, this is the particular alibi that has been chosen.

(8) "Croatia had to fight a tough diplomatic battle against those who have been trying (and still attempt) to situate it on the Balkans." (*Vjesnik*, Zagreb, 6. 8. 1996)

The Balkan-*Orientalism* scheme is traumatic because it is ascribed to the perspective of the other. The location of the outer border of the national zero-institution therefore depends upon *recognition by the other*.[26]

(9) "We have been assured by the unreserved support of the United States that Croatia belongs to Central Europe and not to the Balkan region." (President Tudjman upon his return from Washington, 3. 8. 1996, Croatian TV)

The Balkanist scheme is immanently conceived as pertaining to the "view of the other":

(10) "Any appeal to international arbitration to settle the Slovene-Croat border controversy would justify *distant observers* in their belief that in the Balkans and in their vicinity live bellicose tribes, incapable of solving their problems themselves." (*Delo*, Ljubljana, 22. 8. 1996, italics ours)

The scheme may be the object of parody, where the spirit has survived:

(11) "The international community occupies itself more with mad cows than with crazy Balkanites." (*Svijet*, Sarajevo, 27. 6. 1996)

It may also justify morbid self-degradation:

(12) "I thank the Minister for having come to our dark Balkans." (President Tudjman, at a joint press conference with French Foreign Minister Alain Juppe, 10. 2. 1994; Croatian *TV*)

Still, what may appear to be a discourse of self-degradation actually operates as a discourse of domination. The reasons are structural. We have maintained[27] that a "dualist social organization" is a structure that reproduces itself with the support of *two dualist self-conceptions*. In order to survive, such an organization has to appeal to a third scheme that is neutral with regard to the two others. By extrapolation, we have construed the nation as such a zero-institution. In the Balkanist scheme, the zero-institution supports itself by appealing to a dualistic scheme, where the structural function of the third and neutral dualism is performed when those who should develop a vision of their own (and do not develop it) instead submissively acquiesce *to a dualistic scheme ascribed to a privileged "other."*[28] The dualist scheme "*Europe/the Balkans*" is ascribed to a hegemonic other, to "the international community," the United States, et cetera.

We can now appreciate the *tour de force* whereby this scheme is reflexively turned back and addressed to the "balkanized" public mind:

(13) "This is the choice between Europe and the Balkans." (Slovene Prime Minister Janez Drnovšek, *Dnevnik*, Ljubljana, 3. 6. 1995)

The underlying rhetorical enthymeme may well be: "You have to make a choice. Still, the premises of the choice can only be understood from the point of view from which I address you, from the point of view of Europe. It is only as Europeans that you can choose. *Ergo*: If you want to have a choice, you must always already have chosen." The Prime Minister speaks in the name of the distinction "Europe/the Balkans," and he conveys that the distinction can only be drawn from the point of view of Europe. But how can the "slash" of the distinction be located? It can only be located by making *the knowledge possessed*, the knowledge of the border *defined by the zero-institution*,[29] coincide with the *knowledge to be acquired*, the border between "Europe" and "the Balkans."[30] It is by *recognizing* themselves as members of the Slovene nation that the addressees of the message posit themselves as "Europeans." And *this* is the real effect of the ethymematic conclusion. In this way, the "young democracies" organize their social field with the help of differentialist racism.[31]

VI. The Mechanisms

According to Edward Said, *Orientalism* is a conceptual scheme, which ideologically mediates the domination of the West upon the Orient.[32] The Orientalist hegemony affirms itself when "Orientals" can no longer conceive of themselves except in Orientalist terms. This reflexive moment completes the constitution of the Orient and the Orientals as objects of western domination. It is the *subjectification* within the symbolic field of *Orientalism* that finally transforms "the Orient" into the *object* of domination.

Balkanism appears as an even more radical mechanism. Contrary to *Orientalism*, where the logic of domination is imposed by colonial rule, in Balkanism, it is the immanent logic of self-constitution itself that generates the incapacity to conceive of oneself in other terms than from the point of view of the dominating other.[33]

Let us briefly review the features of *Balkanism* we have so far detected:

1. It is an ideology of *the domination within* the nation-state, strongly and efficiently articulated to the mechanisms of *international domination*.

2. It does not intervene in the argumentational discourse by providing the premises of the argument, but rather *sets up the frame within which the argumentation is to be carried out*. *Balkanism* is not so much a content-component as a para-logical device, which provides the horizon of a specific rationality.

In order to grasp the ideological mechanisms that *Balkanism* sets in motion, it may be appropriate to start by viewing the Balkans theme as a simple rhetorical *topos*. This is how the theme usually occurs: as a *stenographic* indication, a piece of discourse that refers to background knowledge the speaker and audience share. This background knowledge is supposed to be, and is offered as, *shared, trivial, and true*[34]: It is a common place, *lieu commun, koinos topos*. This "place" offers the speakers the advantage of situating themselves upon a privileged border-line, in a limitrophic position at the point where the national and international dimension articulate each other (feature no. 1), or where the general frame of the argumentation touches upon the particular arguments offered (feature no. 2).[35]

Investigations that approach the Balkans theme from an angle different from ours, concentrating on its contents,[36] can shed an interesting light upon the capacity of the theme to articulate the explicit argument with its implicit background, and to function as a particularly powerful discursive operator. Maria Todorova[37] proposes that *Balkanism* is not just another variant of Said's *Orientalism*, but has a specificity of its own:

Contrary to the Orient, the Balkans have a concrete historical existence. . . . Not only did part of southeastern Europe acquire a new name—Balkans—during the Ottoman period, it has been chiefly the Ottoman elements or the ones perceived as such that have mostly invoked the current stereotypes. . . . It seems that the conclusion that the Balkans are the Ottoman legacy is not an overstatement. . . . It may well be that what we are witnessing today, wrongly attributed to some Balkan essence, is the ultimate Europeanization of the Balkans. If the Balkans are, as I think they are, tantamount to their Ottoman legacy, this is an advanced stage of the end of the Balkans.[38]

It may be productive to carry Todorova's point a little further: The Balkans would then be the perception, from the point of view of "Europeanization," "Westernization," or "modernization," of what is assumed to be "the Ottoman legacy."[39] Under this hypothesis, "the Balkans" would be the myth of Europe read twice: first *recto*, as a myth of progress and modernization, then *verso*, as the myth of "non-European" backwardness and the like. "The Balkans" arise at the point where the *recto* and the *verso* readings come together.

The particular efficiency of the Balkanist ideology would then stem from the very features that distinguish *Balkanism* from different *Orientalisms*.[40] Not only does the Balkanist ideology presuppose a "European" point of view, and thus partake of the mechanisms of domination; it is also structured along a *teleological* axis (Westernization as normalization, modernization as the course of History, etc.), which endows it with a particular mobilizing power.[41]

The Balkans is thus a particular type of *Grenzbegriff*. It operates along two different axes, and produces two types of complementary effects:

1. Upon the "horizontal" axis of the discourse, it produces a (semantic) effect of *disjunction*:

2. Either a *spatial* disjunction upon the imaginary map (the Balkans as opposed to Europe, the West, the Euro-Atlantic civilization, et cetera);

3. Or a *temporal* disjunction upon the line of teleological time (Europeanization, Westernization, modernization, transition etc.).

Here, the Balkans is a border-line concept, because it is *the concept of a border*. As such, it provides the co-ordinates, which support the "logical" coherence of the discourse.

4. Upon the "vertical" axis that links the discourse with its background, it produces a (pragmatic) effect of *conjunction*:

1. Both the conjunction between the "subject of uttering" (*sujet de l'enonciation*) and the "subject of utterance" (*sujet de l'enonce*);

2. And the conjunction between the explicit elements of discourse and the implicit "belief-background" upon which the utterance acquires meaning. Here, "the Balkans" is a border-line concept because it reaches *across* a border, or rather, is *doubly inscribed*—both on the surface of the manifest content of discourse and within the specific exterior of discourse, within the non-explicit belief-background, or the latent thoughts upon which the discourse acquires its coherence and its meaning.

Whereas the semantic effects of the first type are relatively easy to analyze, and have been the object of our discussion so far, the analysis of the second-type pragmatic effects requires a stronger apparatus, especially since this type of effect supports the installation of the relations of domination and, correlatively, establishes the horizon of rationality wherein the discourse appears to be meaningful. One could even say that the facade of rationality and coherence, established by the first type of effect, serves as the vehicle for the pragmatic effects of the second type.

At this point, we need to strengthen our conceptual apparatus. As our wording has already suggested, the structural *locus* of the signifying element "the Balkans" is formally analogous to the paradoxical position occupied by what Freud calls "the dream's nucleus," which both figures within the "dream-thoughts," and operates as the pivotal element around which the "labor of, as it were, building up a facade of the dream"[42] organizes itself.

I am in the habit of describing this element of dream-thoughts as a "fantasy" (*Phantasie*).[43]

The signifying element "the Balkans" thus functions like what Lacan calls the *point de capiton*, the quilting point, or an element common both to the facade of coherence and rationality and to what this facade conceals. We can already anticipate that such an element may have the capacity to function as a genuine fantasy within the circuit of communication. It then acts like a structural element, which diverts the addressee's demand for sense towards the mediating loop of the unconscious desire.[44] In this case, what may normally be just the addressee's *conditional identification with the believing subject* transforms itself into an *unconditional identification with the knowing subject*, whereby the addressee of the message is *interpellated as a subject* and succumbs to the ideological mechanism.[45]

Still, we should not be too quick to enter the Freudian conceptual apparatus: The Freudian *Phantasie* is an idiosyncratic element of the individual unconscious, whereas "the Balkans" are a Durkheimian *collective representation* that leaves wide open the question of its eventual articulation to idiosyncratic mechanisms of the individual unconscious—that is, the question of its theoretical status *tout court*. We should proceed carefully: Without speculating upon the eventual *Phantasie*-potential of the term "the Balkans," we will first consider its *formal* properties and invoke the more modest concept of the "*pre-construct*," which has been elaborated within the theory of discourse.[46] For this tactical move, we can borrow some justification from Freud:

In the erection of a dream-facade, use is not infrequently made of wishful fantasies, which are present in the dream-thoughts *in a pre-constructed form* . . . thus, in some cases, the facade of the dream directly reveals the dream's actual nucleus. . . .[47]

Two qualifications should be added to Freud's optimistic statement: The facade "directly reveals" the dream-nucleus only through the process of analysis; grasping the dream's nucleus is only a first step toward analyzing the dream's mechanisms. Without these qualifications, one might miss Freud's main point: The coherence of the facade masks the unconscious mechanisms at work in the background of the latent dream-thoughts. The *intelligibility* of the facade prevents *understanding* the unconscious process. Fantasy may be used as a privileged alley to reach dream-thoughts starting from the facade, because it belongs to both dimensions, for it is incorporated into the facade in the pre-constructed form, produced by inconspicuous mechanisms.

In an analogous way, the Balkanist stereotype helps organize the discourse in its horizontal semantic function presented under point 1 above; it thus helps to achieve discursive coherence while masking its vertical pragmatic function, presented under point 2 above. In Balkanist discourse, its specific rationality, its intelligibility, masks ideological mechanisms the Balkanist stereotype helps to trigger.

VII.   The Balkanist Stereotype as a "Pre-construct"

As an example of the preconstruct, Pecheux quotes a joke from Freud's *Witz*[48]: "Is this the place where the Duke of Wellington pronounced the famous words?—Yes, this is the place, but he never pronounced those words."[49] Pecheux notes that the effect of this kind of joke comes from the fact that it explicitly discloses how *identity* ("of a subject, of a thing or an event," as he specifies) is constituted "somewhere else, in an *hors-lieu*," and that for this reason the effect-of-identity is not hurt *regardless of what happens within the utterance proffered*.[50] Pecheux then jumps to the conclusion that "the effect of preconstruct can be taken as the discursive modality of the interval from which the individual is interpellated into subject . . . being simultaneously 'always-already' a subject."

We should carry Pecheux's reflection further and introduce some further distinctions. We can agree that the identity of discourse-items is constituted somewhere else, that is, within the conceptual schemes that are a part of the *belief-background* upon which an utterance makes sense. The question then arises of how the addressee of an utterance (or, for that matter, the speaker him or herself) *assumes* the belief-background upon which she or he is to interpret (or to proffer) the utterance. This question itself suffices to suggest that the constitution of the subject (the speaker, the hearer, the communicational community of subjects) *differs from* the constitution of discourse-items (referential expressions, predicates, etc.[51]). We should further be able to explain how a speaker-hearer is able to *shift* from one belief-background to the other, including to those she or he does not believe in.[52]

The mechanism of subjectivation (or, should we say, the production of the effect "subject") should then secure that the discourse-items function, and be treated, *as if* they were not constituted "somewhere else," within the belief-background. *As if* their occurrence within the utterance were self-sufficient. The effect-subject should secure the invisibility of Pecheux's "interval," it must be able to *saturate* the utterance to make it meaningful.[53] Taking Lacan's circular definition of the signifier[54] as a determination of the effect-subject, we could then say: The subject is what the discursive *interval* within the utterance, *taken as a signifier*, represents for some other signifier within the belief-background.[55]

Coming back to our topic, we can now say that in our example:

3. "This is a choice between Europe and the Balkans."

The effect-subject takes place between the (bizarre, nonsensical, counter-factual) *interval* created by the opposition "Europe/the Balkans," and the signifier "the Balkans" as it figures in the belief-background which supports the meaning of (13). The (Althusserian) subject (of ideology) is, so to say, the relation between the paradigmatic ("ideal") entity, constructed in the background-alibi, and its actualization as an occurrence in an utterance.

The "background," of course, is nothing more than the relations among discourse-items, which have to be assumed, presumed, taken as pre-conceived, in order for the utterance to make sense—and which can be expressed in the form of the complement to a prepositional attitude.[56] The background is, therefore, no less a retroactive, *nachtraeglich*, effect than the subject. That is why the background is constituted by the very utterances where it occurs as a preconstruct. This is also why individuals can be led to assume such backgrounds merely by being exposed to them and by pronouncing them.[57]

Only some items qualify for this subjectivating function, though. "The Balkans" do: Why? Because "the Balkans," like other similarly privileged ideological elements, can *organize* the belief-background upon which the discourse makes sense. Under the threat of communication break-down, and the consequent loss of intersubjectivity, communication partners (or social individuals in general) need anchoring elements upon which they can suspend the network of their intersubjective (and, generally, social) relations.

"The Balkans," and similar elements, provide such a suspension-hook because they support, from the outside, as it were, the constitution of the "zero-institution"[58] that is itself the absolute guarantee of the possibility for communication in individualist societies. By tracing an additional distinction which either coincides, or is teleologically designed to someday coincide, with the outer rim of the zero-institution, "the Balkans" and similar segregational devices *supplement* the immanent instability and non-saturation of the (national) zero-institution.[59]

Since the zero-institution provides for the possibility of shifting among different belief-backgrounds, its maintenance is an absolute condition for the reproduction of a "communicational community." Since such a zero-institution is a pure form, it cannot sustain itself without being, at any given moment, overdetermined by some particular ideological scheme. This scheme is the familiar hegemonic ideology. In democratic individualist societies, the more formal an ideology is, and the less it is "content-bound," the better it qualifies for the hegemonic role. *Balkanism* is precisely such an ideology: After all, it traces only a distinction, leaving wide open the secondary question of how its two separate compartments will be semantically filled.

In order to be able to shift from one belief-background to the other, which is a precondition for communication[60] and generally for social interaction in modern democratic societies,[61] the social individual has to be able to accede to the identification with the knowing subject ascribed to the national zero-institution. Unconditional identification with this subject is a condition for the possibility of conditional identification with the believing subject, which in turn supports everyday communication. The individual is immediately confronted only with possible beliefs and their belief-subjects. But she or he cannot accede to them without having first performed the preliminary identification with the subject of knowledge, the identification that opens the field of possible beliefs and the access to belief-subjects ascribed to them. In other words, it is not possible to understand or communicate without having first identified oneself with the knowing subject of the zero-institution, without *having become a subject*, that is, without *having been interpellated into some (particular) ideology*.

Ideologies whose belief-schemata can be made, in one way or the other, to coincide with the underlying scheme of the zero-institution, and whose believing subject can thus *be blurred with the knowing subject of the zero institution*, are therefore *la voie royale* toward securing the absolute preliminary condition for all communication and social interaction. *Balkanism* is one such ideology.

VIII.   Stereotype as "Program Manager"

We have dealt with two different cases in which we attempted to seize the Balkanist ideology "in action":

1. We construed the first case as a matrix of rational choice, which guides practical action and practical reasoning. *Balkanism* there operates as a formal distinction which either does not need to be lexicalised in the familiar Balkanist vocabulary, or is eventually only secondarily so expressed. In this case, what we can only analytically recognize as *Balkanism* functions on the level of *common sense*, which sets the horizon of rationality to different everyday practices and lubricates the mechanisms of different apparatuses by which and within which these practices are carried out.

2. In the second case, we were concerned with a series of historical utterances in which the Balkanist vocabulary explicitly occurred, and did so in a way that might disturb the common sense shared by the communicational community to which the utterances were proffered.

The two different and even contradictory modes apparently do not exclude each other; in fact, they operate simultaneously within the same communicational community. How can we account for this?

In the first case, the ideological horizon is divided into two domains where two different sets of practical regulative principles apply. It should be noted that, already in the first case, the stereotype of "the Balkans" performs a double function: It is the name of one of the two domains, but it is also *the operator of dichotomization*. The ideological map is broken into two unequal parts *because* there is something we call "the Balkans."

By its very nature, this is not a symmetrical scheme. On the imaginary map, "the Balkans" figures as an *enclave*; if the dynamism of asymmetry gathers momentum, it can assume the figure of an *exception*. Given what we have called the double function of the stereotype, the development from enclave toward exception produces an important consequence: with the shrinking of the domain "the Balkans" denote comes the expansion of the operational capacity of the stereotype.

We have already noted the teleological structure of the Balkanist stereotype: Spatially, "the Balkans" are something to be pushed southward; temporally, they are something to be left in the past. We have explained this teleological component as an incidence of popular ideologies of modernization, Europeanization, and the like. We can now see that, even before this secondary, external support, the teleological bias pertains to the immanent logic of the Balkanist scheme. The more evanescent "the Balkans" becomes as a domain within the imaginary geography, the more powerful it is as a premise of practical reasoning and as a principle within legitimization procedures. Since even as a geographical domain, "the Balkans" is nothing but a pragmatic *alibi* and a justification *topos*, the logic of the scheme pushes the stereotype from its denotational dimension toward the operational function.

Invocation of "the Balkans" can then justify exceptional actions, ill-fitted to the prevailing frame of common sense—as it does in the utterances we have grouped under the "second case" (*vide supra*).

3. "Slovenia favors a solution in political terms; but we will understand the use of force, since this seems to be the only language which this part of the world understands."[62]

The stereotype then functions as *a shifter* between the normal and the exceptional. At its limit, it can become a device that justifies *any* course of action.[63] It is also a strong mechanism in the discourse of authority, that is, of legitimized power, for it both creates the situation of exception and offers a ready-made solution to such a situation.

Generally speaking, this kind of stereotype helps us shift from one conceptual scheme to another, one belief-background to another, one set of pragmatic guidelines and justification principles to another. Such a stereotype then functions in the same way as what, in the PC-culture, we call the program manager: It is a device by means of which it is possible to close down and to open up different "programs" available in a given culture.[64]

IX. Stereotype as a Mechanism of Ideological Hegemony

We have assigned a similar role to the national zero-institution: It contains and holds together all the ideological schemes within a national culture, and assures shifting among them in terms of understanding. We have pointed out that the national zero-institution, as a void and purely formal scheme, does not exercise ideological interpellation on its own account. Correlatively, successful ideological interpellation under the conditions of a nationalist ideological constitution depends upon the capacity of a particular ideology to promote its believing subject upon the structural place of the knowing subject of the national zero-institution.

It now appears that a stereotype of the Balkanist kind may serve as a privileged instrument that enables a particular ideology, capable of incorporating such a stereotype into its own discourse, to invest, and eventually to appropriate, the position of the knowing subject of the national zero-institution. Balkanist stereotypes, and others like them, can work as shifting devices: What's more, the shifting the stereotype supports does not limit itself to the relatively benign interpretational effects of understanding—the stereotype *incorporates* different ideological backgrounds into the prevailing framework of common sense. It may serve as the royal road toward *the ideological hegemony*.

X. Some Conclusions

From the above, we can draw certain theoretical and practical conclusions:

1. An ideology that is hegemonic at a given moment is not one that succeeds in persuading the majority of the population. It is the ideology that can provide a means of shifting among the different conceptual schemes, belief backgrounds, or ideological programs that exist in a given culture. Since the existence of a plurality of such programs is a necessity in any society, *a fortiori* in any complex and *modern*[65] society; and since shifting among different ideological backgrounds, among different sets of practical principles, et cetera, is an existential necessity of the human condition, the function performed by the hegemonic ideology is of vital importance for the survival of a community and of the individuals who live in it. The question of hegemony is not a question of persuasiveness, of public relations, or of propagandistic campaigns—it is a question of survival.

2. Enlightened attempts to demystify stereotypes systematically miss the point: Stereotypes do not function within the semantic dimension, they are a *pragmatic* discursive device.

3. Balkanist stereotypes, and others like them, additionally provide a precious tool that helps nationally constituted communities to manage their external relations: Since the national zero-institution is exclusive in its homogeneous dimension (that is, in its relation to other analogously constituted communities), it is at pains to design its inter-communal relations. A dichotomous stereotype of the Balkanist kind offers a useful regulatory principle by which to resolve this difficulty. In contexts densely populated and heavily burdened with nationalist ideologies, Balkanist or other similar stereotypes are almost bound to appear. This is our tragic modern enactment of the old anthropological adage that people have to be divided for their communities to hold together.[66]

Appendix: The Scheme of Ideological Interpellation

Table 4.4

				F			
I	d	D		I	I	d	D
	T				T		
Lacan's scheme				Ideological interpellation			

D   demand (of sense)
I   identification
T   point of transference (subject supposed to believe/know)
F   (individual) fantasy
I   ideological interpellation

Notes

1. Etienne Balibar and Immanuel Wallerstein, *Race, Classe, Nation* (Paris: Decouverte, 1988).

2. The problem should be viewed within the larger frame of the world economy. (See Gyorgy Wiener, "The Change of Epochs in World History and the Changes of Eastern Europe," in *The Anti-Capitalist Left on the Eve of the 21st Century* [Budapest: Eszmelet Books, Liberter], 1996).

3. A "theory of Dayton" is not the subject of this article. If one is to be devised some day, we would suggest that it proceed in the style of "*le matérialisme de la rencontre,*" or materialism of the encounter, of the last Althusserian manuscripts (cf. "Le courant souterrain du materialisme de la rencontre," in *Ecrits philosophiques et politiques*, vol. 1, ed. F. Matheron (Paris: Stock/IMEC, 1994), and that it consider the attempt to freeze the post-Yugoslav situation in terms of an *encounter* between the class-struggles within the region and the contradictions of the capitalist world-system. As for analysis of the latter, we have no particular proposals (although we would suggest starting from the theses proposed by Gyorgy Wiener (*The Anti-Capitalist Left on the Eve of the 21st Century*). For the former, our hypothesis would be roughly as follows: International relations are essential to the establishment of capitalism in the countries that formerly practised state socialism; in certain respects, the role of these relations today is *inversely symmetrical* to the one they performed in the establishment of the early class-societies. While class-organization historically occurs when the relations of domination and exploitation expand beyond the scope where they can be regulated by kinship structures—that is, when alliances and oppositions (typically through processes of trade and conquest) cease to be ones between kin-groups and turn into relations between classes. In the case of the "transitional" societies, international relations (again "by trade and war") help establish *intermediary* local bureaucrats and managerial elites which then rule over populations that are for this purpose organised into pseudo-kinship mega-groups, that is, into ethnic nations. While the first states emerged from the *expansion* of the relations of domination and exploitation and from the *limitation* of kinship-based regulation, the present

the process of its institution: "You look like XY." "I *am* XY." "No wonder you look like him.")

50. "The effect of the preconstruct is founded upon the interval through which an element intrudes into the utterance, as if it were thought 'before, somewhere else, independently.'" (Michel Pecheux, ibid.)

51. For simplicity of exposition, we are here assuming the "substantialist bias" of Pecheux's discussion; the same questions would arise in a much sharper and better differentiated form if, instead of debating referential expressions and predicates, we focused on speech acts: How are speech acts happily performed and taken up if, as is usually the case, they are not performed by way of an explicit performative? This approach immediately leads to questions of intersubjectivity and of the formation of a "communicational situation."

52. Marxist theories of ideology tend frequently to underestimate the *plurality* of ideologies at play in every society. More precisely, most Marxisms tend to view that pluralism almost exclusively from the angle of "ideological struggle," which is then conceived in overly agonistic terms. To be fair, this remains a thorny and unresolved issue in other traditions as well, for example, that of British anthropology (cf. Raymond Firth, Edmund Leach, Maurice Bloch). Paul Veyne made an important development when he introduced the concept of truth-programs (*programmes de vérité*) (*Les Grecs ont-ils cru en leurs mythes?* [Paris: Seuil, 1983.]) The general picture behind the above discussion is roughly this: Every social situation can be described in different (ideological) idioms; the description chosen by a particular social agent defines the scope of actions open to him or her; before engaging in the Aristotelian practical syllogism, agents negotiate descriptive idioms that determine its premises; this means that, even as they attempt to grasp their situations, agents *shift* among different descriptive idioms. It would be naive to suppose that the agents' shifting is controlled, and their final choice determined, by their "interests," since those too depend upon the idiom within which they are conceived. Rather, most of this shifting and negotiating may go undetected by the agent involved: A background "pattern" of shifting and a mechanism of negotiating make the process largely "invisible," quasi-automatic, or "*natural*." It is for these mechanisms of situational "*collages*," for the "*naturwuechsige*" processes of everyday pragmatic "*bricolage*" that I here want to reserve the concept of "ideology."

53. We could apply to the subject the formula Lacan uses for "sense": It does not exist in any of the discourse-items, but it insists on all of them. We could also play with the etymology: In the relation to the utterance, the subject ex-sists.

54. "Le signifiant est ce qui représente le sujet pour un autre signifiant." The signifier is that which represents the subject for another signifier.

55. Less cryptically, we could say: The Althusserian "subject of ideology" is a certain modality of the relation between the linguistic *sujet de l'énonciation* and *sujet de l'énoncé*, the modality which makes the two "instances of subject" become undifferentiated. By treating "the interval," "*l'écart*," as a signifier, we only extend an old structuralist idea ("zero-value" features, non-markedness as a particular marker, etc.), which Marcel Mauss introduced into the social sciences in two essays ("Les parentes a plaisanteries," 1926; "La cohésion sociale dans les sociétés polysegmentaires," 1931). Mauss argues for the structural relevance of the "negative fact." A generation later, and under the additional influence of Kojève's

Hegelianism, "negativity" became the obsession of a generation (Georges Bataille, "College de sociologie"; also Claude Lévi-Strauss, Jean-Paul Sartre, Jacques Lacan, Maurice Merleau-Ponty, etc.).

56. That is, like *p* in the utterances of the type: "I believe (know, doubt, assume, etc.) that *p*."

57. The reader does not need to be reminded of the connection with Blaise Pascal's idea of "the habit, pushing the automaton which induces the spirit, without the spirit being aware of this" (cf. *Pensées*, nos. 250, 252).

58. As developed in section 4, "A Theory of Nation," supra.

59. In his article on "joking relationships," Radcliffe-Brown offered the first lucid formulation of this *necessity of supplementation, which is immanent to institutionalization*: the "normal" functioning of institutionalised social relations *by itself* produces contradictory situations, such as those in which social disjunction and social conjunction coincide, or those in which it is necessary both to keep a distance and to draw closer. This type of situation is regulated by its *supplementary institutionalization*, by the rituals of avoidance or those of "joking." (Alfred Reginald Radcliffe-Brown, "On Joking Relationships," *Africa* 13, no. 3 (1940). Reprinted in *Structure and Function in Primitive Society* (London: Routledge & Kegan Paul, 1952.)

60. For an outline of our background theory of "communication" (i.e., of ideology), see note 21, supra.

61. It is a condition also in other types of society, but there it is secured in different ways; the general problem is approached by Maurice Bloch; specifically for ancient Greece, *v.* Paul Veyne, op. cit.

62. This utterance is a reconstruction; it was reported in *oratio obliqua* by *Dnevnik* (Ljubljana, 26. 9. 1998) as a statement Slovenia's minister of foreign affairs made at a UN press conference in New York. The "use of force" refers to the threat of NATO strikes against the Federal Republic of Yugoslavia (FRY). "This part of the world" is obviously a euphemism.

63. No wonder stereotypes flourish in situations of crisis, or when insufficient arguments are available to support decisions already made, and actions already performed; after NATO began air strikes against FRY, and Slovenia participated by opening its air space, there was an outburst of *Balkanism* in Slovenia's pro-government media. For example: "taking into account 'the Balkan particularities' " (*Delo*, Ljubljana, 2. 4. 1999); "air strikes are not enough for the Balkans" (*Delo*, 6. 4. 1999); etc.

64. In a theoretical afterword to Paul Veyne's book *Les Grecs ont-ils cru en leurs mythes?* (translation into Slovene, /*cf., Ljubljana, 1998) I tried to show that, in the classical and Hellenistic periods, this was the function assumed by mythological references. Such references served as pragmatic devices that allowed the Greeks to believe in the different and not necessarily compatible beckgrounds among which their discourses shifted. Paul Veyne introduces a convenient, though strong, term for such backgrounds: *"programme de vérité,"* or, truth-program.

65. On these grounds, one could eventually conceptualize Immanuel Wallerstein's argument in "Three ideologies or one? The pseudo-battle of Modernity," in *Social Theory and Sociology*, ed. Stephen P. Turner (Oxford: Blackwell, 1996).

66. Marcel Mauss formulated the principle in his article, "La cohésion sociale dans les sociétés polisegmentaires" (1931), in Marcel Mauss, *Oeuvres III* (Paris: Minuit, 1969). Radcliffe-Brown further developed it in two articles on "joking relationships" (1940 and 1949); see Alfred Reginald Radcliffe-Brown, *Structure and Function in Primitive Society* (London: Routledge & Keagan Paul, 1952).

5

Carl Schmitt on Kosovo, or, Taking War Seriously

Grigoris Ananiadis

"There are plausible enough arguments for the use of violence on the grounds that it is in the best interests of the world as a whole. . . . But all these supposedly good intentions cannot wash away the stain of injustice from the means which are used to implement them."

Immanuel Kant[1]

"The discrimination of the enemy into a criminal and the invocation of a justa causa go hand in hand with the perfection of the means of annihilation and the dislocation of the theater of war. The perfection of the technical means of destruction deepens the chasm of a legal and moral discrimination that is already devastating."

Carl Schmitt[2]

"The unconditionality of thought, of a thought that should find its topos and its example in the university, is recognized where it can, in the name of freedom, call in question the principle of sovereignty as a principle of power."

Jacques Derrida[3]

1. Carl Schmitt and Kosovo I

The thoughts on the relation of air warfare to the concept of just war with which Carl Schmitt concludes his *Der Nomos der Erde*,[4] an important but usually under-valued work of his maturity, could have been written as a reaction to NATO's bombing of Slobodan Milošević's Yugoslavia. Instead, they were written over half a century ago. Of its own, this fact seems to attest to Schmitt's disquieting *actuality*. His *actuality*, however, extends to every aspect of the Yugoslav drama. Indeed—given his reduction of the concept of the political to the friend/enemy opposition and his insistence on the homogeneity of the state—Schmitt could safely be considered the theorist *par excellence* of the ethnic cleansing policies that, following Milošević's lead, all nationalisms that clashed on Yugoslav soil pursued.

We know, however, since at least Niccolo Machiavelli's *Discourses*, that the "actuality" of a political thought is never given, self-evident, or unambiguous. The relation of a past political thought to the present is always the product of a complex mediation. Strictly speaking, in such cases we are dealing not with the self-imposing actuality of a work, but with its *actualization*.

Such an actualization of Schmitt was attempted by two of the many prominent European thinkers who voiced publicly their endorsement of the NATO war, on the ground that it ultimately promoted international justice. Both Jürgen Habermas[5] and Myriam Revault d' Alonnes[6] saw fit to buttress their position by attacking Schmitt's anti-humanism and anti-universalism, turning him into a figure emblematic of all the possible objections to this self-styled "humanitarian intervention." "Schmitt," however, would not have functioned as an effective synecdoche were it not for a widely accepted parallelism: the presentation of the conflicts, atrocities, and crimes of the Yugoslav crisis through the prism of Nazi expansionism and the Holocaust.[7] The choice of Schmitt as a privileged adversary was obviously meant to underscore the liberal democracy/totalitarianism opposition at the level of theory, in order to denigrate in advance any alternative approach as politically affiliated to the notorious German jurist. This schema was in many instances further reinforced by the highly problematic fusion of discourses that opposed the NATO bombings. One need not share Revault d' Allonnes' position on the military intervention to be alarmed at the undiscriminating convergence between anti-imperialists of the left and nationalist sovereigntists of the right that she denounces.

Is this, however, the only way that Schmitt can be actualized? I think not. The fact that his answers are objectionable does not annul the questions he dealt with, and these questions are to a great extent still with us. By that I don't mean that we could possibly separate Schmitt's "theory" from his political positions. Any attempt to set Schmittianism, thus "purified," to a "good cause" must be categorically rejected. Such an appropriation of Schmitt would be not only fruitless but also highly dangerous. Nonetheless, if it is true, as Derrida supposes, that Schmitt is "the last great representative of the European metaphysics of politics,"[8] a reconsideration of the aporias that traverse his work could help us rethink the categories through which the wars on and against Yugoslavia were thought, to rethink, more generally, the *modi* and *loci* of politics in conditions of globalization. The reading of the *Nomos der Erde* I propose here is undertaken in this spirit.[9]

2.   "Nomos" and Decision

Schmitt is the polemical thinker *par excellence* of the twentieth century. His pre-1945 texts are permeated by a sense of decisive confrontation—be it political,

ized twentieth century, for the unitary spatialized order of the *respublica christiana* rested on a specific configuration between *imperium* and *sacerdotium*. According to Schmitt, central to the cohesion of this spatialized order was the eschatological notion of the "catechon" as expounded by Apostle Paul in his *Second Epistle to the Thessalonians*.[31] The *catechon* is the historical force that can check the coming of the Antichrist, of the "*anomos,*" thereby deferring the end of time. It was precisely this capacity that Rome recognized in the figure of the Emperor, and for this reason the imperial title was neither exclusive, nor did it entail absolute power. On this interpretation, the medieval Christian order dissolved, and lost its sanctity, when the idea of the *catechon* ceased to be effective.

According to Schmitt, the *nomos* of western Christianity, the distinction, that is, of the territory of the Christian princes, was clearly reflected in the then prevalent notions of the conduct of war and the gradations of the concept of the enemy. Feudal wars had the character of legal contests that were conducted under the pretext either of the realization of law or of the exercise of an entrenched right to resistance or retribution; in neither case did any of the warring parties dispute the framework of the shared order. Hence, in accordance with the *jus gentium* of the time, they were, or were expected to be, contained wars. The question, furthermore, of whether such a war was "just" or "unjust" constituted an acute theological and juridical issue. In contrast, wars against non-Christian princes or peoples were considered *a priori* to be just wars. The Pope could grant such territories to Christian princes for missionary expansion or for conquest following a crusade. And since such opponents were regarded as absolute enemies, the war could be conducted with no limitations, to the point of annihilation. A just war, Schmitt emphasizes, always tends toward total war. Similar views were entertained in the Islamic world, where *dar-el-islam*, or the house of peace, was distinguished from *dar-el-harb*, or the house of war extending beyond its confines.

Pre-modern conceptions of "international" relations were in Schmitt's view profoundly affected by the "spatial revolution" that took place in the fifteenth and sixteenth centuries. The circumnavigation of the earth and the discovery of America changed "not just the measurements and the scales, not just the external horizon of people, but also the very structure of the concept of space."[32] As the spherical dimension of the earth acquired for the first time practical and political significance, the foundations were laid for a global spatial order that was to last for about four centuries.

Successor to the Christian commonwealth, this "planetary" order was from the very outset Eurocentric, which is why Schmitt designates the juridical tradition to which it gave rise *jus publicum europaeum*, or European public law. At its very centre lay modern Europe's newly constructed state, whose territorial and political "sovereignty" were shaped in reaction to the religious civil wars of the sixteenth and seventeenth centuries. The European state was forged as a unitary public power occupying a clearly demarcated segment of the European surface and personified in the figure of the absolute monarch conceived as a *"persona moralis."* The latter asserted his absolute power or sovereignty by prevailing over the "supra-territorial" religious parties (*cujus regio, ejus religio*) and disengaging from the ecclesiastic and feudal dependencies of the medieval order. After the Treaty of Westphalia (1648), the state emerged as a subject of law and as the basic unit of the new juridico-political order, which developed into a system of balance between sovereigns that were equal in status, but not necessarily in power.

Back in the 1920s, this process had furnished Schmitt with the historical raw material upon which to elaborate the basic concepts of his decisionist political philosophy.[33] In Schmitt's analysis, the *arché*—in the sense of both starting point and *principium*[34]—of the unitary and homogeneous state was the sovereign political decision that put an end to the crisis of the premodern order by neutralizing the conflicting parties and eliminating particularist powers. The order thus inaugurated was henceforth to be the effective legitimizing presupposition breathing life into any legality. The unity and homogeneity of the state precede any specific institutional articulation. This *arcanum* of the political is obscured by legal positivism and liberal political theory, which, in the midst of the interwar crisis, Schmitt set out to obviate in order to restore dictatorship as a necessary state tool.

Considered now from the angle of the spatial revolution and the concept of *nomos*, this process acquires in Schmitt's eyes a global dimension. In this connection, he rejects the idea that the cohesion of the European system can be reduced to the concept of sovereignty, to the notion, that is, of the self-restraint and contractual arrangements among the autonomous sovereigns, as encapsulated in the principle *pacta sunt servanda* and as supposed by classical liberalism. Schmitt realizes that the concept of sovereignty itself needs to be "spatialized," or reconsidered in the context of the broader *raumordentlich* parameters that made it possible.

In this light, the decisive historical event for the configuration of the European space into an "inter-state" order, into a "family of nations," was the perception of the New World not as a hostile entity but as a "free space," namely, as a space open to conquest and exploitation. The European powers scrambled to lay claim to the "free" lands and to control the "free" or open seas. European public law developed

in this context primarily as an attempt to justify and rationalize these novel acquisitions. "The meaning and the core of the Christian-European international law
[*Völkerrecht*], its ground order," Schmitt argues, "lies precisely in the distribution
of the new land."[35] Europe was thus transformed into the measure and centre of
the world in an entirely new sense. The European peoples—as Christians initially,
as the bearers of civilization subsequently—became the subjects of the new world
order, while the non-European peoples—as non-Christians or as "uncivilized"
respectively—were condemned to be its objects. In other words, European modernity, "civilized" Europe and its spatial *status*, emerged out of a constitutive violence
that determined non-European ground as colonial ground. As Giorgio Agamben
appositely puts it,[36] connecting implicitly the logic of the early Schmitt to that of
the later, the newly forged *nomos* of the earth, the background of the *jus publicum
europaeum*, as indeed of every *nomos*, is literally an *Aus-nahme*: the taking of the
outside.

However, as is the case with every *Ausnahme*, or exception, this relation between
the "inside" and the "outside" is anything but simple. Schmitt examines its complexity through an analysis of "global linear thought," which governed the distribution of the New World in both its continental and oceanic components.
Specifically, he considers how geography was politicized immediately following the
discovery of America by means of drawing demarcation lines. The first such demar-
cations, the *rayas* that separated Spanish from Portuguese acquisitions, were agreed
upon in the context of a still premodern juridical and spiritual order, as the Catholic
rulers of the Iberian peninsula acknowledged the Pope's arbitration in the appor-
tionment among those of non-Christian territories. Of an entirely different character were the *amity lines*, the drawing of which was a decisive factor in the shaping
of the modern order. A product of the era of the religious wars between Protestant
and Catholic sea powers, of the dissolution, that is, of the Christian commonwealth,
these lines demarcated no dominions; on the contrary, they defined an arena of conflict for their acquisition. This side of the amity lines extended the Old World, where,
despite the not infrequent confrontations, the memory of past unity was preserved
and European public law applied, viz. "conventions, peace, and friendship."
"Beyond the line" commenced an indeterminate overseas space of "freedom," where
violence prevailed and the justice of the strongest was in force. By consent, whatever happened that side of the line "remained outside the legal, moral and political
valuations" that were recognized this side.[37] As Schmitt saw it, the emblematic figure
of this distinction was the notorious *privateer* who, as opposed to the outlaw pirate,
was granted the *right* to plunder, being exempted from the rules that formally

applied in Europe.[38] In other words, from a juridical point of view, the privateer was the very personification of the exception.[39]

Thus, according to Schmitt's analytical schema, we are not dealing with simple geopolitical expansion; the "inside" was not extended to include an "outside." On the contrary, we are dealing with a historical movement that constituted their very difference: The normalization of the *jus publicum europaeum* presupposed the "localization" of its exception; in other words, it presupposed the suspension of all law in the New World. The inter-state order of Europe was erected on the foundation of a clearly fenced off disorder. The global *nomos* of Europe embraced its negation; it was, we might say, constitutively antinomic.

According to Schmitt, this ethical and political "catastrophe," which lies at the root of the *nomos* of the earth, leaves its traces in the political philosophy of early modernity, and the traces are visible to whoever takes into account the parameters of the new spatial order and the new linear thinking. For instance, Pascal's famous dictum "*Un meridien décide de la vérité*" should be read not as a relativist banality but as a thinking person's reaction to "the shocking fact that Christian rulers and peoples had agreed to consider the distinction between right and wrong non-existent for determinate spaces."[40] Pascal's meridian, in other words, pointed directly to the amity lines of his time, to the fact that political geography defined moral geography as well. The same, Schmitt maintains, is true of the concept of the state of nature in Hobbes and Locke. Despite its rationalist construction in their work, the historical referent of this concept lies "beyond the line." Hobbes's "*homo homini lupus*" and Locke's "*In the beginning all the world was America*" equally echo the demarcation of "freedom" beyond Europe, in the New World.[41]

A similar tension, Schmitt points out, runs through the humanist ideology of modern Europe. The fact, for example, that as late as the sixteenth century, a humanist philosopher like Bacon could come up with the "inhuman" argument that the Indians, being cannibals, "are proscribed by nature itself," attests to the "often unexpected dialectics" of the notion of humanness (*Humanität*). Despite its apparent universality, Schmitt argues, this notion always contains the specifically political possibility of division and exclusion. That Schmitt's "suspicion" sounds today familiarly Foucauldian should come as no surprise considering the two theorists' common debt to Nietzsche. "Only with the appearance [in the eighteenth century] of man [*Mensch*] in the sense of absolute humanness (*Humanität*)," Schmitt writes, "there appears, as the obverse side of the same concept, his specific new enemy, the *inhuman* [*Unmensch*]. The distinction between human and inhuman was followed in the history of men in the nineteenth century by the still deeper division between the *superhuman* and the *subhuman*. Just as man entails non-man, superman too brings to the history of humanity, from the very outset and by dialectical necessity, the underman as his twin enemy."[42]

4. *Jus publicum europaeum* and the "De-theologization" of War

In Schmitt's approach, precisely because law presupposes the exception, *nomos*, and division, the core of any international legal order consists of the way in which it spatially concretizes the relation between war and peace: "international law is the law of war and peace, *jus belli ac pacis.*"[43] In this regard, the historically significant achievement of the *jus publicum europaum* was the renunciation, this side of the line, of the "discriminating war" and the institutionalization of its containment. The atrocities of the religious and civil wars of the sixteenth and seventeenth centuries had brought home the close connection obtaining between a just war, a war waged in the name of a dogmatic certainty or absolute value, and a total war. A war deemed "just" in this sense entails a moral and legal discrimination of the enemy that in turn increases the intensity of conflict and induces the enemy's annihilation. It is for this reason that the "rationalization" and "humanization" of war emerged as central components of the broader process of secularization of public life.[44] This was made possible by the juridical formalization of war into a legal institution of the new inter-state order. The slogan of the humanist jurist Albericus Gentilis, "*Silete theologi in muniere alieno!*" (Be silent theologians in foreign matters!) is, according to Schmitt, emblematic of the arduous efforts expended to shift the problematic of war from an ethical and theological context to a juridical and political one.[45]

The starting point for the determination of the just war, of the *bellum justum*, was no longer the theological authority of the Church, but the equal sovereignty of the newly fashioned states. The decisive step was the dissociation of the concept of just war from the concept of *justa causa*, of the just or right cause. The just war, understood as the legally acceptable war, hinges now on the concept of the *justus hostis*, or the legally recognized external enemy, who is no longer morally or juridically diminished and who is clearly distinguished from the internal enemy (the rebel, the criminal, or the pirate). To avoid a war of extermination presupposes recognizing "the opponent as an enemy at the same level."[46] Henceforth, "just" war is exclusively inter-state war, namely war among sovereigns conceived as *magni homines*, for only they are rated as *hostes aequaliter justi*, as equally "just" enemies. Given the lack of a commonly accepted, overarching spiritual authority, what interests the emerging public law of Europe is the *agent* of war, whether he is a legitimate holder of the *jus ad bellum* or the right to war, and not the *reasons* leading to war, whether and to what extent they are intrinsically just or unjust. In any case, each one of the warring sides claims its cause to be just. This is the point, Schmitt observes, at which the tradition of humanist skepticism and the decisionist problematic inaugurated by Jean Bodin converge: "[I]n international law as in domestic law, over the endless self-righteous bickering entailed by the claims of a *justa causa* prevailed the simple question, 'Who decides?'—the great: *Quis judicabit?* Domestically as well as internationally this could only be the sovereign."[47] In other words, "each sovereign decides on his own account what is a just cause" (*auctoritas non veritas facit legem*), as Schmitt's teacher, Hobbes, put it. It is this logic of sovereignty that makes possible the transition from the axiologically undecidable, and hence destructive, religious war, the war of *veritates*, to the "pure state war," the *guerre en forme* of the age of baroque.[48]

As an exclusive prerogative of the state, war was rationalized and contained: It was henceforth conducted as a duel between sovereigns of equal legal standing in a limited theater of operations and in accordance with all the forms and rules of a commonly accepted *jus in bello* (distinction between combatants and non-combatants, between military and civil or economic targets, respect for the prisoners of war, etc.). Furthermore, it was precisely the logic of sovereignty that made possible the conclusion of peace between the warring parties and allowed for the neutrality of third parties, a most important provision for the limitation of war. It is wrong, therefore, to consider war coterminous with the disorder of a state of nature, as the enduring stereotype of classical political theory would have it; as an inter-state institution, Schmitt concludes, war was a constitutive component of the European order that should not be confused with the conjunctural territorial *status quo*. Territorial readjustments in the context of the broader balance of power were often inescapable, and "partial" or contained war was accepted as a legitimate means for their realization, provided that neither the system as a whole nor the existence of its individual members were questioned or jeopardized. This new state of affairs may well be characterized as "anarchic" but never as "anomic."[49] It is thanks to this institutionalization of war—Schmitt calls it an "artwork of human reason"[50]—that over a period of two centuries, no war of extermination took place on European soil.

Schmitt, of course, keeps reminding us that this "normality" was founded on its exception, on the consciousness of the difference separating Europeans from the rest of the world. War is conducted differently between Europeans and non-Europeans, as indeed among Europeans outside continental Europe. The very term *Hegung* (literally: enclosure) that denotes the limitation or containment of war is among the archetypal words that preserve the memory of the spatial determination of law and peace. In this respect, Schmitt attributes special significance to the distinction between land and naval warfare. This in turn reflects the great opposition between land and sea which, having for the first time acquired global dimensions, marks the *nomos* of the earth from the very outset.

5.   Land and Sea

Expanding on an insight of Hegel's,[51] Schmitt considers the opposition between land and sea the key to modern history, indeed, its long disregarded *arcanum*.[52] This opposition arose from the fact that the open seas could not be subjected to the continental state order and in this sense remained "free," *staatsfrei*, even after the peace of Utrecht (1713) which solidified the state character of international relations and outlawed piracy. The designation of the seas as *mare liberum* was part and parcel of the English thalassocracy or, in Schmitt's terms, *Seenahme*: "Solid land belongs now to a dozen sovereign states, the sea belongs to no one, or rather to every one; in reality it belongs finally to one: England."[53] Having taken the world-historical decision to turn to the "element" of the sea, to "become" an island, England occupied a nodal point in the new global order midway between land and sea, "of Europe, but not in Europe."[54] While the order of continental Europe was premised on a balance of forces between sovereign states which acknowledged the role of "great powers," no such balance between naval forces obtained in the open sea. The uncontested naval superiority of England was, on the contrary, decisive for the very maintainance of the continental equilibrium. According to Schmitt, the upshot of this configuration was the development of two distinct and opposing worlds, two incommensurate worldviews, and two concrete "universal and global orders which cannot be reduced to a relation of universal and particular law. Each one of them is universal. Each one has its own concept of the enemy, of war and plunder, even of freedom."[55]

In what way are the concepts of war and freedom related? In Schmitt's view, one does not notice the tension-ridden coexistence of these two orders in the context of the global *nomos* as long as the law of peace is considered separately from the law of war. The specific feature of the freedom of the seas is that it applies equally to global trade and to the conduct of war. Hence, the freedom of sea trade cannot be grasped independently of the means that imposed it or of the conditions that annul it. In this vein, Schmitt stresses that, contrary to the limited land war, war at sea has neither a localizable theatre of operations, nor does it distinguish between combatants and non-combatants, or between military and civil targets (e.g., naval blockade, indiscriminate bombardments of the coast, deployment of mines, economic warfare), nor still does it recognize neutral navigation (right of plunder). In other words, from the viewpoint of the sea, the enemy is *de facto* a "total" enemy, and naval warfare is intrinsically uncontainable.[56] It was precisely by means of this type of war that England came to control the sea routes and to build its essentially economic empire. As a consequense, there is a close relationship between the international law of free trade and of the free economy, on the one hand, and the freedom of the sea, as it was interpreted and imposed by the dominant naval power, on the other.

Ultimately, Schmitt reduces the difference of the orders of land and sea to the fact that England was never formed into a "state" on the Continental model—to the fact, that is, that it never turned absolutist. The concept of sovereignty was never applied in England in its "pure" form. Hobbes, Schmitt observes, got it wrong with his mythical references. Hobbes made Leviathan, the great sea-monster, his symbol of the territorially enclosed and centralized Continental state, whereas Behemoth, the biblical beast of the land, stood for the anti-absolutist forces that rallied to the parliament in the English Revolution, and which, paradoxically, would ultimately push England toward the openness of the sea.[57] According to Schmitt, this is where the specificity of English expansion lies: It was not the outcome of state policy, nor was it organized along state lines; on the contrary, it was carried through by *social forces*, which is why the British Empire adopted "indirect rule" as its method of domination. The distinction between state and society, the development of "mixed" government, the separation of political and economic power characteristic of the Anglo-Saxon conception of the state, all, Schmitt stresses, stem from this historical reality.[58]

Thus spatially determinate or "concrete," the freedoms of trade and the sea functioned as vehicles for the penetration of "Anglo-Saxon" ideas and practices (liberal constitutionalism, individual freedoms, universalism) into continental Europe, where they undermined the continental tradition of sovereignty and relativized the classical dualism between inter-state and domestic law.[59] The constitutional distinction between public and private law reflects the demarcation of a "free" world economy from the strictly state-based international law. It can, therefore, be seen as a sort of modern-day "amity line."[60] Inside every constitutional state, this line defines the economy and the press as a private sphere, exempt from state interference, creating thereby a supra-state "community" of interests and ideas. According to Schmitt, the broader historical and political significance of the liberal movements of continental Europe, irrespective of the motives and self-understanding of their protagonists, can be assessed only in the context of the global aspirations of British policy.[61]

6.   Crisis of the *Jus publicum europaeum*

This new dialectic between the "inside" and the "outside" was destined eventually to remove the opposition between land and sea and to dismantle the spatialized order of modernity. Crucial in this respect were the consequences of the industrial revolution. The English rule of the seas was its necessary condition, and England's industrial dominance solidified British world hegemony for a long stretch of time. The dynamics of industrial expansion, however, brought about a profound redistribution of economic and political might. New powers came to the fore: the United States, Germany, Japan, Russia. According to Schmitt, these trends must be seen as part of a broader transformation. The radical technological advances in the means of production, communication, and war changed once more "the measures and the scales," and "the possibilities of man's domination over nature and other men was raised to unforeseen dimensions."[62] Technology made it now possible for the air, too, to become politicized, thereby changing the configuration of land and sea, as neither radio waves nor airforces have any limits. In effect, these developments comprise a "second spatial revolution," which affected profoundly the current perceptions of space. While since the sixteenth and seventeenth centuries, space was understood as a "void" and neutral framework within which objects were arranged mathematically, in the twentieth century space was increasingly conceived "as a dynamic field of energy, activity, and productivity." Without this second spatial revolution, Schmitt characteristically remarks, Martin Heidegger's subversion of Kantianism as encapsulated in the proposition: *"the world is not in space, on the contrary, space is in the world"* would have been unthinkable.[63] Thus, once more the conditions were ripe for a new, global, spatialized order.

At this historical juncture, however, and under the sway of liberal ideology and legal positivism, Europe had already lost consciousness of its spatio-cultural specificity; it had forgotten its historically concrete *nomos*, the political starting point and principle that informed the *jus publicum europaeum* and maintained the cohesion of its state order. As a consequence, it was unable to think the pressing question of a new world order in spatial terms. The upshot was that the European *Völkerrecht*, the *jus inter gentes europaeas* was thoughtlessly transformed into the "spaceless" universalist *International Law.* As Schmmitt sees it, this could only be "a series of generalizations of dubious precedent, which referred for the most part to entirely obsolete or entirely heterogeneous situations; generalizations combined with norms generally recognized to a greater or lesser extent, and whose application to a concretely contested case was the more disputable the wider and intenser their 'recognition.' "[64] Having unlearned the lesson of Gentilis, legal thought henceforth resigned from dealing with the important juridico-political questions, considering them to be "extra-legal."

Schmitt analyzes two events that prefigure this development at the end of the nineteenth century. The first is the admission into the Eurocentric state order of Asian powers such as Japan. International lawyers had naively welcomed this universalizing trend as a triumph of European public law, not realizing that such an expansion undermined the very conditions of reception, namely the concrete spatialized order of Europe, whether "good or bad," and its cultural homogeneity.[65] The second, to which Schmitt attributes even greater significance, is the colonization of Africa. At first sight, Schmitt observes, this process appears as a replica of the *Landnahme* of the New World. The European powers distributed among themselves the land of Africa, being conscious of the ties that joined them as bearers of "progress" and "civilization." However, this civilizing worldview was now only a "caricature" of the European cohesion at a time when Europe was truly the "sacred centre of the World."[66] This can be seen in the fact that, whereas originally the legal status of European soil was clearly distinguished from that of colonies, this distinction was soon annulled as, starting with the Belgian Congo, colonies were gradually recognized as extensions of metropolitan territories. "When a colony," Schmitt concludes, "becomes an undifferentiated state territory, then in effect no colony exists any longer and the difference in 'constitution' [67] between metropolis and colony is transformed to the merely intra-state question of the field of validity of various legislative norms. Similarly, toward the end of the nineteenth century, the distinction between civilized, semi-civilized (barbaric) and uncivilized (wild) peoples dissolves in the undifferentiated 'international community.' "[68]

According to Schmitt, a major blow against the *jus publicum europaeum* was the international legal order—or "disorder," as he was inclined to think about it—imposed by the victors of the First World War. The Treaty of Versailles and the legal framework of the League of Nations had been subjected to Schmitt's critical scrutiny in a number of highly polemical works, including his famous *Concept of the Political*, published in the 1920s and 1930s. Schmitt's main contention was that, under the guise of universalist and pacifist principles, the League of Nations in effect legitimized the political exploitation by the Western allies of the Central powers' defeat. The *status quo* that the new international institutions guaranteed was only nominally peace; in reality, it was "something worse than war, namely the juridification of a state between war and peace in which the politically mighty robs the politically weak not only of his life, but also of his right and honour."[69] In Schmitt's view this "Janus-like two-facedness"[70] expressed the deeper antinomy marking the League of Nations. Its creation was seen as a step toward a "universal society" and a "world state." Such a unification of humanity, Schmitt argued, would result "in a total depoliticization and, as a consequence, in the elimination of statehood [*Staatslosigkeit*]," because without enemies, "humanity as such cannot wage any war."[71] But the League of Nations never ceased to be an "organization of states." It sought to regulate *their* relations and to guarantee *their* existence. Hence, it fully preserved its political character as well as the *jus belli*. Far from being a realization of world unity, it was a coalition of states promoting a set of particular interests against others. Schmitt's concern was not only to denounce the partisan abuse of universalism and the idea of humanity but also, implicitly, to urge his compatriots to reject Germany's legal banishment from the "sphere of the political" and the Versailles' *status quo*.

7. Revival of the Just War

In *Nomos der Erde*, Schmitt revisits this subject from the point of view of his macroscopical spatial analysis. His style is no longer polemical, though he does not explicitly revise his previous positions. As he sees it, the final collapse of the *jus publicum europaeum* in the aftermath of the First World War is marked by two interconnected developments: the emergence in the international political scene of the Western Hemisphere and the revival of the idea of the just war.

Schmitt points out that the Versailles Treaty introduced in two highly controversial articles a most important change in the classical conception of war. Article 227 charged the Kaiser, in his capacity of head of state, as a war criminal. The novelty here consisted in the fact that the Kaiser was not accused of the violation of the commonly accepted *jus in bello*, but for committing the crime of war as such. War of aggression was named a crime, indeed a "crime against humanity," not on the grounds of the then valid international law, but with reference to morality and politics. Equally lacking in legal footing was article 231 of the treaty, which imputed to the defeated powers "guilt" for the war and, accordingly, gave war reparations a penal character. Aggressive war was outlawed for the first time in the ineffectual

Geneva Protocol of 1924, in which aggressor states were designated perpetrators of the new international crime and sanctions were specified. However, the resistance of the classical state logic was still strong, for, despite the curtailment of the *jus ad bellum*—which Schmitt deemed essential to sovereignty—the Protocol called for the respect of the sovereignty and political independence of the unlawful states, "the primary obstacle to the criminalization of war."[72] Such contradictions, Schmitt observes, were of no consequence for the exponents of universalist law who, concerned as they were with the idea of progress, judged the present from the viewpoint of the future and law on the basis of morality. This moralization of law resulted in the rearticulation of the notion of the just war to the concept of the *justa causa*, and in the concomitant distinction between admissible or just war and inadmissible or unjust war. It further implied the abandonment of the idea of the morally and legally equal enemy, of the *justus hostis*, in favour of a "quasi-theological" concept of the enemy.[73]

According to Schmitt, it was not at all accidental that, in this ideological climate, the exponents of universalism in international law often drew their arguments from the just-war doctrines of premodern scholastic theology.[74] To consider, however, Catholic theologians of the sixteenth century such as Francisco de Vitoria[75] the harbingers of a modern universal law and morality represents for Schmitt an unacceptable historical anachronism. Detached from its concrete spatial and historical context and inserted in a modern problematic, the notion of the just war acquires an entirely different meaning, the two settings being incommensurable. The difference has to do not only with the absence today of an overarching spiritual authority, but also with the fact that in the Middle Ages, in the absence of a centralized state enjoying an institutionally entrenched monopoly of force, unjust war was still deemed to be war, which entailed an elementary equality among the opponents. In contrast, modern theories of just war aim at the abolition of war. From the moment that a supra-state international entity is entitled to decide, in a manner that is binding for its member states, which war is just and which unjust, war is indeed abolished as an institution of international law. Such an abolition, however, is only virtual, because it is achieved by dint of a mere resignification of the concept of the enemy. International law turns into criminal law, and the armed action of one side is regarded as coterminous with law enforcement entitled to use "all the means of modern technology" to achieve its aim, including "police bombing,"[76] whereas the action of the other is likened to resisting authority, rebellion, or crime.[77] Such a criminalization of the enemy does away with the limitations that made possible the contained war of the *jus publicum europaeum*; the existence of a "total" enemy, of an enemy that is determined by invoking "supra-state" and "supra-national" criteria, justifies the conduct of an unrestrained, "total" war.[78] What is more, when war is waged in the name of humanity, the enemy is placed not only *"hors la loi,"* but also *"hors l' humanité,"* which pushes conflict to an "extreme inhumanity."[79]

The revival in international law of this discriminating concept of the enemy goes, Schmitt maintains, hand in hand with the abandonment of the classical idea of neutrality. Previously a "symbol of peace," inasmuch as it contributed to the containment of war, it now becomes a "symbol of war."[80] According to European public law, the right to neutrality entailed that in case of war, a third state could determine its conduct autonomously: It could either enter the war on one of the warring sides, without its choice affecting in any way the legal equality of the opponents, or it could opt for a neutral stance in accordance with the principle of equal friendship. But following the revival of the just war doctrine, states are instead obliged to join forces against those considered to be "perturbers" of international law. This results in a further intensification of the conflict, for it now assumes the character of an international crusade or a world-wide civil war.

8.   The Predominance of the Western Hemisphere

According to Schmitt, the die for the eventual prevalence of these ideas was essentially cast on April 2, 1917, at the moment when the United States decided to abandon its carefully maintained neutrality and to declare war against Germany, thereby transforming an "old-style" European war to a world war. What is more, after the war, the United States continued to interfere in European affairs, putting an end to the spatial autonomy of Europe. "Whereas in the past centuries," Schmitt sarcastically notes, "it was the European conferences that determined the spatialized order of the earth, in the winter 1918/19 Paris peace conferences the opposite occured for the first time: the spatialized order of Europe was shaped by the world,"[81] and especially by the Western Hemisphere. The United States, caught in the dilemma between isolationism and universalism, did not ratify the Versailles Treaty and refused to join the League of Nations; it was, in other words, formally absent from the international institutions of post-war Geneva. However, eighteen other American states joined the league, making up one third of its total membership. It was through these states, which, though nominally independent, were in effect variously dependent on the United States, that the latter secured its indirect but effective presence in the affairs of Europe. At the same time, the United States succeeded in having Article 21 of the League of Nations Charter explicitly recognize the superior legal validity of the Monroe Doctrine, that is to say, the specific spatialized order of the Western Hemisphere. On the basis of this asymmetry, the United States could henceforth have a say in the affairs of the League and, by implication, of Europe, while the latter had consented to its exclusion from the sphere of American hegemony. Article 21, Schmitt concludes, "was the symbol of the Western Hemisphere's triumph over Europe. . . . With it [the League of Nations] resigned from basing its own spatial system, whether specifically European or consequently universal, on a clear spatialized order."[82] In Schmitt's analysis, the demarcation of the Western Hemisphere by the Monroe Doctrine of 1823 represents the most important application of modernity's "global linear thinking" since the *rayas* and the amity lines. In contrast to these, the American line of demarcation had originally a clearly defensive character. Its aim was to secure the independence of American states, to prohibit the colonization of American territories and to raise a barrier against the interference of non-American forces in the continent's affairs. The political idea that animated the drawing of this line was opposition to the monarchical-dynastic principle of legitimation of the Old World, which justified the intervention of European powers within and without Europe. However, America's self-delimitation vis-à-vis the Europe of the Holy Alliance did not entail its exit from the still Eurocentric "international community," or the renunciation of European civilization. On the contrary, ever since the end of the eighteenth century, Americans have entertained the conviction that America has come to represent the true Europe, and that, as the cradle of civilization, the West had moved further West. The Puritan idea of the chosen people entrusted with a special mission, combined with the civilizational merits accorded to America by the French Enlightenment, turned the Western Hemisphere into a space of "freedom" (in the positive sense this time), of peace, and of the rights of man. This American self-image was to receive an extra boost from waves of disenchanted European refugees in the wake of the abortive 1848 revolutions. The refugees fled a reactionary Europe that was naively suppressing the questions raised by socialism, anarchism, and "nihilism." The distinction between "old" and "new," Schmitt notes, became the standard not only for the condemnation (*Verurteilung*) of a decadent and corrupt monarchical Europe, but also for a new distribution (*Verteilung*), a new articulation, or rather disarticulation, of order and localization that was to be of global significance. Indeed, as far as Schmitt is concerned, America's conviction that it represented the haven of freedom, morality and justice condensed "true political energy," that is to say, "a first rate war potential,"[83] which was to be unleashed with the country's imperialist turn, starting with the war against colonial Spain in 1898.

Schmitt's interest in the "international principles of legitimacy and the legal forms" of "American imperialism" goes back to the early 1930s.[84] His perspective, it should be stressed, was neither "anti-imperialist" nor anti-American. The aim of his analysis was not to criticize American imperialism in general, *qua* imperialism, but only those of its aspects which, in his view, constituted its "universalist" deviation. More generally, the formation of American hegemony furnishes Schmitt with material for a reflection on the novel, the post-modern we might say, crystallizations of the political.

Schmitt notes that the Monroe Doctrine proved to be extremely elastic in its logic and in the scope of its application. Although it had been adopted as as a means of deterring foreign interventions in the Western Hemisphere, it gradually developed into an instrument for the submission of the entire continent to U.S. hegemony, as well as into a springboard for the global expansion of the United States as an "arbiter of the world."[85] The very same doctrine could sustain a policy of isolationism and strict neutrality as effectively as a policy of active intervention in global politics. As a consequence, the question arose in international law whether the doctrine represented a legal principle or a mere maxim of action. For Schmitt, of course, such a question is totally inappropriate: "International law, as indeed constitutional law, is an absolutely political law."[86] In fact, it was precisely the positivist approach to the matter, which strictly distinguished law from politics, that had obscured its spatial-political dimension for over a century. For his part, Schmitt regarded the juridico-political indeterminacy of the Monroe Doctrine as an indication of "a genuine and great imperialism." "It is inconceivable," he wrote in 1932, "that a great power, indeed a global imperialist power, be legally nailed down to a code of fixed norms and concepts which any foreigner could turn against it."[87]

In Schmitt's interpretation, the key to American imperialism, the "most modern imperialism," is the liberal separation of economics from politics. Washington's maxim, "as much commerce as possible, as little politics as possible," formulated in 1796, summarized the aim of U.S. foreign policy from the very outset. On the basis of this distinction, American economic expansion and exploitation could appear to be essentially "apolitical" and "peaceful." As opposed to older forms of colonialism, American ascendancy was founded not on hierarchical value distinctions such as Christians/non-Christians or civilized/uncivilized, but on the economic distinction between "creditor" and "debtor" peoples.[88] Free trade and the free market were established as constitutional standards in international law through which the United States pursued its economic expansion ("open door" policy, distinction of "most favoured" states, etc.) The United States, however, always maintained the right independently to decide when economic transactions acquired political character and to act accordingly. The country's central position in the world capitalist system pushed it also to become an "island," to develop its naval forces and, reapproaching the British Empire, to pursue an international politics of global intervention. "It is impossible in the long run," Schmitt generalizes, rejecting economistic approaches to globalization, "for world trade to exist without world politics."[89]

Schmitt pays particular attention to the methods by which the United States consolidated its hegemony in South America and, especially, in Central America and the Carribean. He points out that the United States introduced an important novelty into the established colonial practice of the nineteenth century: It did not question the territorial integrity of its client states, nor did it impose fixed and direct methods of control that would interfere with their formal equality under international law. Its political influence was established by means of "intervention agreements," whereby the client states granted the United States the right unilaterally to decide whether there were grounds for intervention in their internal affairs. Such grounds could be the protection of independence or of property, the restoration of order, the defense of a government's legality, or the control of its democratic legitimacy. Practically, this right to intervention was granted by ceding to the United States forts, naval bases, refuelling depos, and the like. The territories of the dependent states were thus integrated into the sphere of the "special interests" and the "spatial ascendancy" (*Raumhoheit*) of the hegemonic power.

In these developments Schmitt saw the rupture of the unity between order and localization that had characterized the classical form of state sovereignty. Territorial sovereignty turns into an "empty space," deprived of any substantive content. A state that is subject to such limitations can no longer decide within its territory "on the concrete realization of concepts such as *independence, public order, legality*, and *legitimacy*," as it cannot autonomously determine its economic and property regime.[90] In the conditions of the globalized economy of late modernity, the fundamental principle of sovereignty "*cujus regio ejus economia*"[91] is reversed to "*cujus economia ejus regio*."[92]

Schmitt did not confine his analysis to the factors of economic and military might, for he considered that the success of American imperialism, as of any "historically significant imperialism," was premised on its ideological clout, that is, on its capacity to invent, interpret, and define political and legal concepts, making them broadly acceptable. "*Caesar dominus et supra grammaticam*: Caesar dominates also over the grammar." This is how Schmitt sums up his position, stressing that this is the most insidious aspect of imperialism: "A people is only then primarily defeated, when it is subjected to a foreign vocabulary, to a foreign conception regarding what is right, especially what is international right."[93] To this issue I shall return later; for the moment it is sufficient to note that Schmitt's "struggle against Weimar, Geneva, and Versailles"[94] was conceived precisely as a struggle against the "foreign vocabulary" of liberalism and universalism.

Schmitt originally opposed "Anglo-Saxon" universalism in the name of state autonomy and cultural diversity.[95] However, after the end of the 1930s he reckoned that, "as a time-bound, historically determinate, concrete, and specific organizational form of political unity,"[96] the state had exhausted its possibilities. The "age of statehood," according to the "spatial" problematic that he had just started to explore, was coextensive with the age of the *jus publicum europaeum*. The dissolution of the European spatialized order, the generalization of the state as the basic norm of international law, irrespective of spatial context and content, and the globalization of the economy contributed to the crisis of the state form and posed anew the question of the form of the political—the question, in other words, of "pluralism" on the global level. According to Schmitt, the new principle of political unity that international law should register was, or should be, the principle of *Grossraum* (great space), as expressed for the first time in the original and "authentic" version of the Monroe Doctrine.

9.   *Grossraum*

Schmitt introduced the concept of *Grossraum* in 1939, immediately after Nazi Germany's invasion in Czechoslovakia and the creation of the protectorates of Bohemia and Moravia. In other words, in its original conception, Schmitt's problematic was intended to provide Hitler's "New Order" with a foundation in international law. *Grossraum*, as Schmitt understands it, constitutes the broader space, extending beyond state borders, over which the political, cultural, and economic influence of a hegemonic power is exercised. Schmitt calls that hegemonic power *Reich*, in order to distinguish it both from the now obsolete state form and from the concept of empire, which he hesitates to adopt because of its universalist historical connotations. Schmitt's position does not entail the total disppearance of the state: He expected states to continue existing in the *Grossraum* as subordinate forms of political organization; he also expected Reichs themselves to preserve certain elements of "statehood." Schmitt's point was that, as dynamic centers of spatial influence, only the Reichs and not the states could function as "bearers and makers" of the new international legal order,[97] a position that implied, of course, "a genuine hierarchical ranking" of the subjects of international law.[98]

Grossraum, Schmitt further explains, should not be conceived as a linear extension of the "micro-spatiality" (*Kleinräumigkeit*) of the spatially enclosed state. The two concepts are incommensurable, because they belong to different conceptual fields. The notion of *Grossraum* condenses the changes that the "second spatial revolution" brought about in the domain of international politics. Hence, the adjective "*gross*" refers not to the general, neutral, and quantitative determinations of space associated with the classical concept of the state (space as a necessary "ground" or as the clearly demarcated "theatre" of power), but to a new, qualitative, and dynamic magnitude, determined, as we have seen, by "man's planning, organization and activity."[99]

If, however, the formation of a *Grossraum* presupposes the integrating trends generated in the fields of economy and technology, its substance, according to Schmitt, can only be political: "Considered from the viewpoint of the science of international law, space and political idea cannot be separated. For us there are no spaceless political ideas, nor, conversely, idea-less spaces or spatial principles. It is, moreover, characteristic of a determinate political idea that it is borne by a concrete people and that it is directed against a concrete enemy, whereby it acquires the quality of the political."[100] In Schmitt's view, the Reich signifies precisely the rearticulation of order and localization, the "connection of *Grossraum*, people, and political idea,"[101] which is why he considers it to be the primary receptacle of the political. Reich and *Grossraum* can be seen as the ultimate refuge for Schmitt's notion of sovereignty.

In the period 1939–1942, Schmitt deemed the construction of a Central and Eastern European *Grossraum* lead by the German Reich to be a necessary condition for the supercession of the "Balkanization" to which Anglo-Saxon universalism had condemned Europe. Seen in this light, the Second World War was precisely a war about the spatialized order of Europe, a *Raumordnungskrieg par excellence*.[102] Defined by a "German Monroe Doctrine," this *Grossraum* was meant to check the corrosive effects of globalization, restoring on a continental level the principle *cujus regio ejus economia*. Above all, however, it was expected to raise a barrier to the intervention of "extra-spatial" forces. A major issue in this regard was the protection of minorities established by the "Versailles system." Construed on the principles of "liberal individualism and supra-national (*übervölkisch*) universalism," minority rights served the Western powers, which considered such rights by definition democratic, and which eyed them as a lever for the control of a Central and Eastern Europe that had fragmented into weak and ineffectual states.[103] The strengthened German Reich, Schmitt expected, would subvert this order, replacing the liberal-democratic principle of legitimation with its own "great" political idea of respecting "each people as a living reality determined by birth and origin, blood and soil"[104] and by establishing in lieu of a "merely inter-state order" a "genuine law of the peoples."[105] In other words, Schmitt ascribed to the Reich the role of a contemporary *catechon* capable of containing the disintegrating forces of modernity. In his view, it was only on the basis of a "meaningful" coexistence of similar spatial hegemonies that an enduring global order could be secured.

10. The "Peacemaker's" Aporia

Schmitt preserves the idea of *Grossraum* in his *Nomos der Erde*, although it no longer occupies center-stage: "Global development [has] for a long time been leading to a clear dilemma between *universum* and *pluriversum*, between monopoly and polypoly, in other words, to the question of whether the planet is ripe for the world monopoly of a single power, or whether the new international law [*Völkerrecht*] will be determined by a pluralist coexistence of independently ordered *Grossräume*, spheres of intervention and cultural cycles."[106] Nonetheless, the restatement now of this position is no more than an empty gesture, theoretically disconcerted and devoid of any programmatic content. Having lived through the destructive effects of yet another world war, Schmitt, on his own admission, writes no longer as a "prophet" of a new world order, but as a "Christian Epimetheus," as "the last conscious exponent of the *jus publicum europaeum*."[107] As we have seen, he analyses *ex post* the spatial parameters of the Eurocentric world order, the modern *nomos* of the earth, and on this basis proceeds to offer a "diagnosis" of the causes that brought about its dissolution in the age of "nihilism" and "technology." Despite the fact that he does not conceal his nostalgia for the "classic" state system of Europe, he entertains no illusions as to the possibility of its restoration. He emphasizes from the outset that the dissolved *nomos* of modernity was the product of a unique conjuncture, as it was made possible "by the unexpected discovery of a New World, by an unparalleled historical event." It should be stressed, however, that Schmitt does not dissect this historical *unicum* from the viewpoint of geopolitics; he does so as a jurist or a *Rechtsphilosoph* seeking the "sense" or the *Sinnreich* of the earth, seeking, that is, a "rooted" principle capable of sustaining the restructuring of international law. What is more, Schmitt hinges this principle on his concept of *nomos*. He may not be in a position to specify the content of a new international order, but he is convinced that it will be rational or "meaningful" only if it is grounded in a new *nomos* of the earth. "The thought of men must once again turn towards the elementary orders of their terrestrial existence [*Dasein*]."[108] This is the lesson that

Schmitt draws from his historical narrative and this is precisely where we can locate the aporetic character of his enterprise.

More specifically, we observe that in Schmitt's schema the concept of *nomos* performs a double function. It operates as a tool of analysis and critique, but also as a springboard for recomposition, as an instrument of orientation. On the one hand, the concept of *nomos* allows him to dissect the rationalist self-consciousness of liberal modernity; it helps him disclose, "render spatially visible," the violence, the discriminations, and the exclusions—in one word, the exception—that lies at its root. On the other hand, however, it is through this very same concept of *nomos* that Schmitt seeks the meaning of a new world order. The problem with this configuration becomes obvious if we consider how Schmitt treats the beginning and the end of the *jus publicum europaeum*. As we have seen, Schmitt expresses in Pascal's words his abhorrence of the ethico-political catastrophe and the global discriminations caused by drawing the amity lines that constitute the modern *nomos* of the earth. However, at the other end of his historical parabola, Schmitt's attitude is diametrically opposite. He censures European consciousness for having lost its sense of difference, its sense of spatial and cultural specificity with all the "good or bad" that it entailed—as, for example, in the distinction between metropolitan and colonial territory, between "civilized" and "uncivilized" peoples. While in the first instance he laments the exception, in the second he deplores its having fallen into oblivion. We are dealing here with something more than a mere inconsistency or an inconsequential moral occasionalism. The problem points to the heart of Schmitt's decisionism, and of its reception as well.

That decisionism in general has incurred a bad name in political theory, being identified for the most part with irrationalism, amoralism, and fascism, is due primarily to Schmitt himself and his legacy. Starting with Karl Löwith's classical critique,[109] Schmitt's political positions and engagements have been considered to be necessary extensions of his decisionism, and this despite the fact that he was explicit in denouncing decisionism precisely during the period of his Nazi involvement.[110] Nonetheless, the anti-foundational turn of currents of contemporary thought[111] has once again brought the question of decision to the fore in a manner that makes it possible to reassess the *necessity* of this correlation.

Briefly, in light of these theoretical developments, it can be argued that a decision, if it is to be a genuine decision and not a prejudged and calculable application of the rules of an already decided normative order, is always characterized by an element of indeterminacy or contingency. This is the case because, by its very nature, decision is a movement that distances itself from the universality of the rule and is directed towards the singularity of the case in question. It is, in other words, coterminous with the break or separation (*krisis, de-cisio, Ent-scheidung*) whereby one possibility is realized at the expense of others. In this sense, it is precisely its lack of foundation that grants decision its tragic freedom—a freedom to inaugurate, to found, and to open up new horizons. Such an anti-foundationalist approach poses the question of ethics, politics, and the relations between them in new terms because it rejects the subsumption of the latter to the former. This rejection in no way entails moral unaccountability, as the routine rationalist objection would have it, for it politicizes ethics no more than it ethicizes politics. If, on the one hand, it regards antagonism as a constitutive and uneliminable element of the social, thus underscoring the potentially political dimension of every moral judgment, on the other hand it equally emphasizes that every political decision bears a particularly heavy burden of responsibility precisely for lack of any binding, reassuring, or consoling foundation.

Schmitt's work is permeated by anxiety about the "nihilism" that, in his view, marks modernity and its crisis. However, his attitude toward nihilism is quite peculiar, in that he fights it at the same time as he adopts it: "We live indeed in an age of theogony when we accept the concept of nihilism and refuse to be pinned down to it," he characteristically writes in his *Glossarium* at the time he was working on the *Nomos der Erde*.[112] As I see it, this sentence condenses Schmitt's entire philosophy. It is therefore suitable to unpack the antinomies that traverse it.

Here I shall restrict myself to a few remarks that are pertinent to our subject. If in the past, Schmitt saw nihilism as the epigone of Nietzsche and Weber, coterminous with the dangerous inflation of "truths" that followed when the theocratic premodern order dissolved, in *Nomos der Erde* he defines nihilism more strictly as an outcome of law's "dislocation." "For nihilism not to end up as yet another empty word, one must be aware of the specific negativity whereby nihilism occupies its historical place, its *topos*. . . . It is precisely in the conjunction of *utopia* and *nihilism* that it becomes obvious that only the final and radical separation between order and localization can be called nihilism in a concrete historical sense."[113]

In Schmitt's eyes, then, nihilism is coterminous with the dissolution of the *nomos* of the earth, with the levelling and "spaceless" uniformity of the age of technology and programming. This is the reason why Schmitt places his hopes for a future overcoming of nihilism in a new *nomos* of the earth, in a global re-localization or re-rooting of law. And yet, it is Schmitt who has demonstrated the inherent antinomy of *nomos*, the fact, that is, that there is no grounding that is not simultaneously an un-grounding, no localization of law that does not entail a dislocation, no order that

does not embrace disorder or the exception. As we have seen, the "specific negativity" of nihilism marks the *nomos* of modernity, as it does every *nomos*, from the very
first moment: Nihilism and *ou*-topia characterize *both* the sovereign decision which,
detaching itself from the theological order and passing judgment on the exception,
founds the modern European state, *and* the "unmediated" acquisition of land and
sea that formed the state's broader spatial context. Construed on a double void—the
theological void created by the dissolution of the Christian commonwealth and the
spatial void of the New World—the global order of *jus publicum europaeum* was *ab
initio* fragile and precarious because it was artificial or contrived. Moreover, its "con-
cretization" rested upon the very aqueous forces that were to cause its eventual
implosion (naval power, overseas *Landnahme*, industrialization, and globalization).
"Liquidity" has been a mark of modern existence all along.[114] It is therefore on
Schmitt's own premises that his expectation of a nihilism-free re-foundation of a
nomos of the earth proves groundless. Such a re-foundation can only be the result of
a political act, of a decision, of an assertion of sovereignty, or domination, which will
be the more authoritarian and violent the more it conceals the "nihil" of its origins
and claims "roots" of sense and legitimization. It is far from accidental that the micro-
universes of Schmitt's *Grossräume* reproduce, albeit on a different scale and intensity,
the very problems that he imputes to universalism, whereas, conversely, his expectation of a "meaningful" coexistence among *Grossräume* reintroduces surreptitiously
no less than the shunned question of universality. Schmitt states: "I hear: critique and
critic and I know and hear: crisis, crisis. . . . There is a universum and a pluriversum,
but no duo-ambiversum. Binarius numerus infamis; whoever says: ambiguity, antinomy, aporia, already says nuclear fission, i.e., civil war, i.e., friend and foe."[115]

11.   The "Theologian," the Enemy, and the Sovereign

In the preceding paragraphs I employed the concept of "nihilism" as self-evident
and non-problematic; it is nonetheless a concept that makes sense only within a
foundational discourse such as theology. Schmitt's treatment of the question of
nihilism can therefore offer us access to the contested interpretative problem of the
place that theology occupies in his work; it can help us determine what exactly the
theologico-political dimension of his thought consists of.

As we have seen, Schmitt considers the "de-theologization" of war a major
achievement of modernity; he furthermore sees in the revival of the concept of just
war a dangerous return of the "theological" conception of the enemy. In his *Ex
Captivitate Salus*, an account of his life and work written in prison[116] and published

the same year as the *Nomos der Erde*, he repeats his position in a personal, quasi confessional, tone: "Theologians tend to define the enemy as something that has to be annihilated. But I am a jurist and not a theologian."[117] How is this Schmitt compatible with the Schmitt of *Political Theology*, who declared explicitly that "all important concepts of the modern theory of the state are secularized theological concepts,"[118] considering that we are dealing here not with a mere observation, but with a deeply held position?

Schmitt provides the answer in *Ex Captivitate Salus* where, referring to his heroes, the *jurisconsulti* that carried through the separation of law from theology, he writes: "On their way out [from the Church], the jurists brought along with them, openly or secretly, certain sacred relics. The state was adorned with certain *simulacri* of ecclesiastical descent. The power of the secular Princes raises through symbols and arguments of religious origin."[119] On Schmitt's own admission, then, neither the state, nor its founding decision, issued *ex nihilo*. How could they? *Ex nihilo*, however, was *made to appear* the *simulacrum* par excellence of state power, namely the sovereign, Hobbes's "mortal God," whose "trancendence" in relation to the state is, according to Schmitt, analogous to "the transcendence of God in relation to the world."[120] It was this *simulacrum* and this trancendence that Schmitt served, or would have liked to have served, throughout his life, because he was convinced—*pace* Revault d' Allonnes—that a "re-enchantment" of the world is impossible, which explains why his "I am a jurist and not a theologian" in *Glossarium* can be restated easily as "I am a theologian of *Jurisprudenz*."[121] This is where Schmitt's "realism" both draws its strength and hits its limits.[122]

These limits become visible in the distinction between the external and the internal enemy that supports Schmitt's entire edifice. In this respect, Habermas is absolutely right when he points out that, while Schmitt denounces the moralization of international relations for entailing a moral and legal discrimination of the enemy, he doesn't show the slightest compunction regarding the criminalization and elimination of the internal enemy.[123] He is wrong, though, when he attributes this "asymmetry" to a warlike "*Lebensphilosophie*."[124] Habermas believes that Schmitt's interest in the containment of war is misleading and that his true concern was the restoration of war as a legitimate means by which to affirm a political entity in the international arena. The elimination of the domestic enemy, or internal pacification, is, on this account, no more than a necessary preparation for revitalizing external conflict.

It is certainly true that in his pre-1945 combative texts, Schmitt considered the recourse to the *jus ad bellum* indispensable in order that Germany recover its forfeited sovereignty and shake off the yoke of Versailles. In *Nomos der Erde*, too, Schmitt's tenor, when dealing with this question, is clearly apologetic.[125] It is also true that in the interwar period, Schmitt's language was influenced by the then prevalent "aesthetics of the *Stahlgewitter*," or storm of steel. The existentialist terms in which he couches enmity and war in *The Concept of the Political* are a case in point. Yet, to reduce Schmitt's entire problematic to war lust or to a celebration of violence is, in my view, highly questionable. If this interpretation were true, we could get rid of Schmitt as easily as Habermas does. We would, however, be missing the key question, the blind spot of political theory,[126] namely, the intractable problem of sovereignty.

It is wildly held by critics and followers of Schmitt alike that at the epicentre of his theory lies his concept of the "political," in other words, that his views on the state, the constitution, and international law are determined by his affirmation of the ever present possibility of war and the corresponding friend/enemy opposition. Such an interpretation is certainly not implausible; yet it can be put forward only at the cost of turning Schmitt into a mere "sociologist" of *Machtpolitik* or an enthusiast of violence, and both of these views miss the mark. As I see it, the opposite is true: Schmitt's concept of the political, far from being self-luminous, is in effect *derivative* of the logic of sovereignty and its specific transcendence. (It should be noted in this regard that Schmitt had erected the scaffolding of the concept of sovereignty long before he articulated it with "democracy" or the "nation.") I have developed this position elsewhere[127] and shall not repeat my arguments here. I will only point out that the polemical quality of the Schmittian concept of the political derives from the fact that Schmitt is incapable of thinking the subjects of politics without the insignia of sovereignty. For him, an agent of politics can only be the sovereign or the potential (anti-)sovereign. This is why Schmitt's sovereign, in the attempt to affirm the fullness of its presence, refuses to recognize the internal enemy "at the same level" and reduces him morally and legally to a "rebel," a "villain," or a "criminal," in short, to an extra-political, "total" enemy. The negotiation of the relation between identity and difference through the prism of sovereignty nurtures an "ethics of exclusion"[128] and inclines to the elimination of difference. However, the opposite is also true, because the existence of a difference to be eliminated, of heterogeneity or the exception, is, at the limit, the very *raison d'être* of sovereignty.

Schmitt comes very close to superceding this logic in his "Cell wisdom," the most pensive of the essays included in his *Ex Captivitate Salus*, in which he revisits the concept of the enemy in general without pausing to distinguish between the internal and the external enemy. Of particular interest in this respect is the fact that at the starting point of his reflection lies the subject of modernity in two of its characteristic instances: Descartes and the philosopher of singularity, Max Stirner. Schmitt notes that, in his search for certainty, Descartes is possessed by the fear of being deceived by the *spiritus malignus*, and that this fear is "the more terrifying, the more it is transformed into a source of new doubts." In order to ward off this fear, Descartes puts on a mask, he becomes "*l' homme au masque.*" And yet, Schmitt comments, "[w]hoever doesn't think but how to avoid deceit, falls directly on it."[129] How, we might at this point ask, does the "mask" of the Cartesian subject differ from the *simulacrum* of that other classical subject of the age of baroque, the sovereign? The isomorphism of the two subjects is, I think, the key to deciphering Schmitt's entire meditation.[130]

It is also as a case of deception, indeed of delusion, that Schmitt approaches the subject of "poor" Max Stirner,[131] whose "self-armouring [*Selbstverpanzerung*] is the highest form of self-deception." The self-affirmation of this subject, Schmitt specifies, consists in the fact that, "[a]s everyone who is crazy [of or] with himself [*Ich-Verrückte*], it sees its enemy in the non-I [*Nicht Ich*]," thereby transforming "the entire world" into its enemy. This egomaniac or ego-crazed subject thinks that it will manage to elude the menacing world and preserve its independence by offering the world a "brotherly kiss."[132] In reality, however, it can deceive no one but itself. The enemy, Schmitt says, "is an objective force" that nobody is capable of escaping from: The genuine enemy does not allow to be deceived."[133]

How are we to interpret this cryptic formulation? Of what does the "objectivity" of the enemy consist? I think that it would be a mistake to understand the formulation in "realist" terms. In my view, what Schmitt wants to underline is that the enemy, *qua* subject, has his own substance, irrespective of how Stirner's subject "imagines" him. The subject, in other words, cannot be self-(de-)limited; the limits to its presence and action are posed by the presence of the other, or the potential enemy. It should be stressed, though, that this is not merely a case of collision or mutual limitation of opposite entities or monads. Schmitt takes a step that distances him decisively from his mentor Hobbes: he realizes now that, despite the deceptive effect of the mask, the subject is far from unitary and complete. If Stirner's subject deceives itself, it is mainly because, in its attempt to armor itself, it "hides from the dialectical splitting force [*Aufspaltungskraft*] of the ego."[134]

Having in this way cleared the ground, Schmitt proceeds to the crucial question: "I therefore ask myself: In this case, who can be my enemy in general? And, what is more, in a way that I recognize him as enemy; in a way that I am, indeed, obliged to recognize that he too recognizes me as enemy?" It is clear from the way Schmitt formulates it that the question of recognition here has nothing to do with the protocol of relations between fully constituted, self-contained, or sovereign subjects. It is, on the contrary, a question pertaining to the *mutual lack* that constitutes their relation.

I can recognize as my enemy, Schmitt answers, "obviously only he who can call me in question. To the extent that I recognize him as my enemy, I recognize that he can call me in question. And who can call me in question? Only myself. Or my brother. That's it. The other is my brother. The other emerges as my brother, and my brother emerges as my enemy."[135] In other words, the other as the enemy emerges as the *internal limit* of the subject, which, always incomplete and constitutively split, strives in vain to affirm its fullness or sovereignty. As a consequence, the greatest deception or, rather, self-deception of the subject consists in the idea that its self-affirmation can be achieved through the annihilation of the other. Given the dialectics of the split ego, Schmitt now stresses, "any annihilation cannot be but self-annihilation."[136]

The recognition of this insuperable partiality of the subject, the recognition of the other in one's self, could have served Schmitt as an opening for a radical revision of his answer to "nihilism," for an inquiry into the possibility of a different "decision" and a different "nomos." Schmitt, however, sticks to his guns. This is a step that he will never take, as he will never apologize for his Nazi complicity. His obsessive, indeed his "terrifying," fear of "ambiguity, antinomy and aporia" prevails and nails him to his mask to the end.

Self-contained air war does have its own space, but it has neither a theatre, nor spectators. Air-fights apart, self-contained air war is no longer conducted as a horizontal confrontation in which the belligerents oppose each other on the same plane. . . . At this decisive point, all metaphors, analogies and parallelisms which could otherwise be extended from land or naval war to air war are rendered null and void. This is also the point where all institutions and principles which until now made possible a law of war, i.e., the containment of war, are annulled.[137]

Man as the rational being of the Age of Enlightenment is no less a subject than the man who defines himself as a nation, who wills himself as a people, who reproduces himself as a race, and who finally empowers himself as the master of the globe.[138]

Freedom would be not to choose between black and white but to abjure such prescribed choices.[139]

12.   Carl Schmitt and Kosovo II

"Human rights" are today the *lingua franca* of politics. Only few would consider this language "foreign," imported, or threatening, as Schmitt did. Irrespective of

5. Jürgen Habermas, "Bestialität und Humanität: Ein Krieg zwischen Moralität und Moral," *Die Zeit*, 29 April 1999. Habermas deals more systematically with Schmitt's positions on international law in his *Die Einbeziehung des Anderen* [1996] (Frankfurt: Suhrkamp, 1999). See also his "The horrors of autonomy: Carl Schmitt in English," in Schmitt, *The New Conservatism* (Cambridge, Mass.: The MIT Press, 1989) and "Continuités allemandes," in *Liber*, no. 18 (June 1994).

6. M. Revault d' Allonnes, *Le deperérissement de la politique* (Paris: Aubier, 1999).

7. On the misleading character of this parallelism, see J. Rosenthal, "Kosovo and the 'Jewish question,'" *Monthly Review* 51, no. 9 (February 2000).

8. J. Derrida, *Politiques de l' amitié* (Paris: Galilée, 1994), 227.

9. In *Nomos der Erde*, Schmitt draws from a large number of articles, essays, and monographs, which he published in the 1930s on questions of international law and politics. Most of these texts are concentrated in three volumes: *Positionen und Begriffe im Kampf mit Weimar—Genf—Versailles: 1923–1939* [1940] (Berlin: Duncker & Humblot, 1985)—henceforth PuB; *Verfassungsrechtliche Aufsätze aus den Jahren 1924–1954* [1958] (Berlin: Duncker & Humblot, 1985)—henceforth VA; *Staat, Grossraum, Nomos: Arbeiten aus den Jahren 1916–1969*, ed., intro., and annot. G. Mashke) (Berlin: Duncker & Humblot), henceforth SGN. Although my primary focus is on the *Nomos der Erde*, I shall be referring to these works whenever necessary to flesh out Schmitt's argument.

10. Schmitt, "Die andere Hegel-Linie. Hans Freyer zum 70. Geburtstag," *Christ und Welt* 10, no. 30 (26 July 1957): 3.

11. On Schmitt's biography see J. W. Bendersky, *Carl Schmitt: Theorist for the Reich* (Princeton: Princeton University Press, 1983) and A. Koenen, *Der Fall Carl Schmitt: Sein Aufstieg zum "Kronjuristen des Dritten Reiches"* (Darmstadt: Wissenschaftliche Buchgesellschaft, 1995).

12. See, among others, Schmitt, *Die Diktatur* [1921] (Berlin: Duncker & Humblot, 1978); Schmitt, *Politische Theologie* [1922] (Berlin: Duncker & Humblot, 1985); Schmitt, *Verfassungslehre* [1927] (Berlin: Dunker & Humblot, 1989).

13. See in particular his *Über drei Arten des Rechtswissenschaftlichen Denkens* [1934] (Berlin: Duncker & Humblot, 1993), where Schmitt contraposes to both the normativist and decisionist juridical traditions the *"konkretes Ordnungs- und Gestaltungsdenken"* considered to be a specifically German tradition. Pure decisionism presupposes "disorder" and "conflict" and, as a consequence, is indifferent to the concrete content of the order instituted by the decision. From the viewpoint of decisionism, "every juridical argument is but a potential ground for decision which lies in wait for conflict" (25). However, this antifoundationalism of the logic of decision, apart from accommodating unpalatable outcomes such as the dictatorship of the proletariat, is obviously incompatible with the basic tenet of Nazi theory that the Führer and the Reich restore and express a primary German *Substanz*. Schmitt adapts his propositions accordingly and replaces "decision" with "command": "The new public and administrative law has confirmed the Führer-principle and with it concepts such as loyalty, devotion, discipline and honour, which can be comprehended only in the context of a concrete order." See also Schmitt's "Der Führer scützt das Recht," PuB, 217–227.

14. Schmitt, *Der Nomos*, 6.

15. On Schmitt's method see, among others, Meier, "Zu Carl Schmitts Begriffsbildung— Das Politische und der Nomos" in *Complexio Oppositorum: Über Carl Schmitt*, ed.

H. Quaritsch (Berlin: Duncker & Humblot, 1988) and J. Miller, "Carl Schmitt's Method: Between ideology, demonology and myth," *Journal of Political Ideologies* 4, no. 1 (February 1999).

16. Schmitt, *Der Nomos*, 41.

17. A few words are in order here regarding the question of Schmitt's antisemitism. Apologists of Schmitt, such as G. Schwab (*The Challenge of the Exception* [Westport, Conn.: Greenwood Press, 1989]) and J. Bendersky maintain that Schmitt's anti-Semitism was of an "intellectual" or "metaphysical," but not "racial," variety, and that most of his antisemitic outbursts should be seen as public manifestations of conformity deemed necessary for his survival, as they can be dated to the period in which he had fallen out of favour with the SS. This interpretation is convincingly refuted by D. Dyzenhaus (*Legality and Legitimacy: Carl Schmitt, Hans Kelsen, and Hermann Heller in Weimar* [Oxford: Clarendon Press, 1997], 98–101). Monumental in this respect is Schmitt's article "Die Deutsche Rechtswissenschaft gegen den jüdischen Geist," *Deutsche Juristen Zeitung*, no. 41 (1936). Schmitt's theory is not essentially racial, but it can certainly "host" racism.

18. The proposition belongs to the Romanist Alvaro d' Ors (*De la Guerra y de la Paz* [Madrid: Ediciónes Rialp, 1950], 160). Schmitt cites it in his "Die Lage der europäischen Rechtswissenschaft" [1943–1944], VA, 427.

19. Schmitt, "Nehmen/Teilen/Weiden" [1953], SGN, 572–591.

20. Schmitt, *Der Nomos*, 30–40.

21. Ibid., 13.

22. Literally "characterless," that is, incapable of being carved or engraved upon (*charassein*). NdE: 14.

23. The concept of *Lebensraum* was first developed by General Haushofer [1869–1946] and his group at the Institute of Geopolitics in Munich, but owed its wide popularization to Hitler's *Mein Kampf*. Hitler transformed it from a theory of power-political hegemony into a doctrine of expansion to the East, invoking the demographic requirements and the racial superiority of the Germans. Schmitt was careful to keep his distance from this concept as far back as the early 1940s, when he put forward his own concept of *Grossraum* (see below, section 9). Indeed, Nazi theorists took him to task for disregarding the "biological" factor. On this, see Bendersky, *Carl Schmitt*, 259–260.

24. Schmitt, *Der Nomos*, 44.

25. Ibid., 42, 50.

26. Ibid., 16.

27. Ibid., 67.

28. Galli, *Genealogia della politica: Carl Schmitt e la crisi del pensiero politico moderno* (Bolgna: Il Mulino, 1996), 881. Galli's voluminous monograph is one of the most penetrating analyses of Schmitt's oeuvre.

29. Derrida defines *ontotopology* as "an axiomatics linking indissociably the ontological value of present-being [*on*] to its *situation*, to the stable and presentable determination of a locality, the *topos* of territory, native soil, city, body in general." J. Derrida, *Specters of Marx*, trans. P. Kamuf (London: Routledge, 1994), 82.

30. Schmitt, *Der Nomos*, 48.

31. *Thessalonians II*, chapter 2, verses 6–7. On the historical trajectory of the concept of the "catechon" in Christian theology and on Schmitt's use of it, see F. Grossheutschi, *Schmitt und die Lehre vom Katechon* (Berlin: Duncker & Humblot, 1996).

32. Schmitt, *Land und Meer: Ein Weltgeschichtliche Betrachtung* [1942] (Stuttgart: Klett-Cotta, 1993), 57.

33. See above, note 12.

34. For this formulation see Schmitt, *Ex Captivitate Salus* (Cologne: Greven Verlag, 1950), 62.

35. Schmitt, *Land und Meer*, 74.

36. G. Agamben, *Homo Sacer: Sovereign Power and Bare Life* (Stanford: Stanford University Press, 1998), 18.

37. Schmitt, *Der Nomos*, 62.

38. Ibid., 14–15, 61.

39. On the question of piracy see also his *Land und Meer*, 40–50 and "Der Begriff der Piraterie" [1937], PuB, 274–277.

40. Schmitt, *Der Nomos*, 64.

41. Ibid., 64–66.

42. Schmitt, *Der Nomos*, 72–73. This idea was further developed by Reinhart Koselleck in his "Zur historisch Semantik asymmetrischer Gegenbegriffe" in *Vergangene Zukunft* (Frankfurt: Suhrkamp Verlag, 1979).

43. Schmitt, "Völkerrechtliche Grossraumordnung" [1941], SGN, 311.

44. Schmitt, *Der Nomos*, 91, 113.

45. Apart from Gentilis, Schmitt also examines the works of Balthasar Ayala, Grotius, Richard Zouch, Pufendorf, Cornelis van Bynkershoek, and Vattel. In this vein, he goes on to contrapose the concept of the *hostis justus* of the *jurisconsulti* to Kant's *hostis injustus* (NdE: 124–143).

46. Schmitt, *Der Nomos*, 159.

47. Ibid., 128.

48. Ibid., 113.

49. Ibid., 119.

50. Ibid., 123.

51. "Just as the earth, as solid ground, is a condition for the principle of family life, so is the sea the natural element that breaths life into industry by turning it outwards." (*Grundlinien der Philosophie des Rechts*, 247). In a 1981 postscript to his *Land und Meer* (108), Schmitt specifies that his *nomos* project should be regarded as an attempt to expand on this *Grundlinien* paragraph in a manner similar to the way Marxism had built on the paragraphs 243–246.

52. Schmitt, *Der Nomos*, 20.

53. Schmitt, *Land und Meer*, 86.

54. Schmitt, *Der Nomos*, 145.

55. Ibid., 144.

56. See, among others, Schmitt, "Über das Verhältnis der Begriffe Krieg und Feind" [1938], PuB, 278–285.

57. Schmitt, *Der Leviathan in der Staatslehre des Thomas Hobbes* [1938] (Stuttgart: Klett-Cotta, 1982), 120.

58. Schmitt, "Völkerrechtliche Grossraum," SGN, 420–421.

59. Schmitt, *Der Nomos*, 229.

60. Ibid., 209.

61. Schmitt, "Raum und Grossraum im Völkerrecht [1940]," SGN, 249.

62. Schmitt, *Land und Meer*, 104.

63. Ibid., 106. Schmitt does not name Heidegger. The sentence he cites is from *Being and Time* [1927]. In the original, the relevant passage is as follows: "*Space is not in the subject, nor is the world in space.* Space is rather 'in' the world in so far as space has been disclosed by that being-in-the-world which is constitutive for Dasein." (Translated by J. Macquarrie and E. Robinson [Oxford: Blackwell, 1985], 24, 146 [111].)

64. Schmitt, *Der Nomos*, 212.

65. Ibid., 206–207.

66. Ibid., 190.

67. It is obvious in this context that Schmitt uses the term "constitution" [*Verfassung*] not in the normative sense of constitutional law, but in the ontological sense denoting the mode the political unity of a people is constituted. The ought-constitution presupposes the being-constitution. On this distinction, see Schmitt, *Verfassungslehre* (Berlin: Duncker & Humblot, 1989).

68. Schmitt, "Raum und Grossraum im Völkerrecht," SGN, 245.

69. Schmitt, "Der Status quo und der Friede" [1925], PuB, 45. As is well known, this assessment was shared by many commentators on the "other side," from Keynes to Lenin.

70. Schmitt, "Der Doppelgesicht des Genfer Völkerbundes" [1926], PuB, 48.

71. Schmitt, "Der Begriff des Politischen" [1927], PuB, 82.

72. Schmitt, *Der Nomos*, 247.

73. Ibid., 95.

74. Schmitt mentions, with great respect for their scholarly work on the medieval and pre-modern sources of international law, the Belgian international jurist Ernest Nys and the American James Brown Scott, founder and chairman of the American Institute for International Law and secretary of the Carnegie Foundation for International Peace (NdE: 89–90). Both championed the criminalization of war of aggression.

75. Francisco de Vitoria was a prominent Thomist political thinker of the Counter-reformation. A Domenican monk and professor at the University of Salamanca, he wrote extensively on secular and ecclesiastic power, but is mainly known for his *De Indis* and *De Indis Relectio Posterior, sive de jure belli*, in which he defends the natives of the New World on the basis of natural law. Vitoria not only refuted the discriminatory arguments that justified the conquistadores' inhuman treatment of the Indians, but he also challenged the

arguments that legitimized the very titles of the Crown of Castille to its overseas possessions. (Francisco de Vitoria, *Political Writings* [Cambridge: Cambridge University Press, 1991].) In his *Nomos der Erde* (pp. 69–96), Schmitt analyses extensively Vitoria's positions in order to demonstrate that those who consider him a harbinger of international law and universalist morality lack in historical spirit.

76. The idea of "police bombing" developed in the interwar period in the context of proposals to provide the League of Nations, conceived as a world state, with a standing military branch capable of enforcing international law. Many military analysts at the time saw in air force the ideal weapon for international policing. Schmitt includes air force, as the "spatial weapon" *par excellence* (*Land und Meer*, 104), among the main factors that effectively undermine the classical concept of sovereignty. What is more, he correlates the *unlimited* technical possibilities of the new weapon to the universalist ideology of the Western powers. In corroboration of his position, he cites, among others, the British analyst and air force promoter J. M. Spaight: "Air power will clear the way of the acceptance of the new ideas" (*An International Air Force*, London 1932). See Schmitt, "Völkerrechtliche Grossraumordnung," SGN, 304. See also note 51 of Mashke, *Staat, Grossraum, Nomos*, 338–339.

77. Schmitt, *Der Nomos*, 95.

78. Schmitt, *Die Wendung zum diskriminierenden Kriegsbegriff* [1938] (Berlin: Duncker & Humblot, 1988), 2.

79. Schmitt, *Der Begriff des Politischen* [1932] (Berlin: Duncker & Humblot, 1979), 55.

80. Schmitt, *Der Nomos*, 272.

81. Ibid., 213.

82. Ibid., 227.

83. Ibid., 266.

84. Schmitt, "Völkerrechtliche Formen des modernen Imperialismus" [1932], PuB, 185. For a factually "enriched" presentation of Schmitt's analysis of imperialism see G. L. Ulmen, "American Imperialism and International Law: Carl Schmitt on the US in World Affairs," *Telos*, no. 72 (summer 1987). The recently published book by Michael Hardt and Antanio Negri, *Empire* (Cambridge, Mass.: Harvard University Press, 2000) is also indebted to Schmitt's approach.

85. Ibid., 192.

86. Ibid., 190.

87. Ibid., 191.

88. Ibid., 184–185.

89. Schmitt, "Beschleuniger wider Willen"[1942], SGN, 434.

90. Schmitt, *Der Nomos,* 226.

91. In Schmitt's view, this is the principle that defines sovereignty in an age in which the "central domain" of public and "spiritual" life is taken up by the economy as opposed to religion. "Neutralization" of the economy cannot but entail a "depoliticization" of the state. See his 1929 essay "Das Zeitalter der Neutralisierungen und Entpolitisierungen" in Schmitt, *Der Begriff des Politischen*, 87.

92. Schmitt, *Der Nomos*, 285.

93. Schmitt, "Völkerrechtlichen Formen des modernen Imperialismus," PuB, 202. A similar position was expressed on the eve of the Second World War by E. H. Carr: "Theories of international morality are . . . the product of dominant nations or groups of nations. For the past hundred years, and more especially since 1918, the English-speaking peoples have formed the dominant group in the world; and current theories of international morality have been designed to perpetuate their supremacy and expressed in the idiom peculiar to them. . . . Both the view that the English-speaking peoples are monopolists of international morality and the view that they are consummate international hypocrites may be reduced to the plain fact the current canons of international virtue have, by a natural and inevitable process, been mainly created by them." (*The Twenty Years Crisis: 1919–1939* [London: Macmillan, 1939], 101–102.)

94. From the subtitle of *Positionen und Begriffe*.

95. See Schmitt, *Der Begriff des Politischen*, 54 and Schmitt, "Staatsethik und pluralistischer Staat" [1930], PuB, 160: "the world of the objective spirit is a pluralist world: a pluralism of races and peoples, of religions and cultures, of languages and legal systems. . . . The political world is also essentially pluralist. Bearers, of course, of this pluralism are the political unities as such, namely the states."

96. Schmitt, "Staatliche Souveränität und freies Meer" [1941], SGN, 402. See also idem, "Staat als ein konkreter, an eine geschichtliche Epoche gebundener Begriff" [1941], VA.

97. Schmitt, "Völkerrechtliche Grossraumordnung," SGN, 297.

98. Ibid., 299.

99. Schmitt borrows the term *Grossraum* from economic thought: After the First World War, the term *Grossraumwirtschaft* was coined in Germany to denote the large-scale planification and rationalization of industrial sectors and networks ("Raum und Grossraum im Völkerrecht," SGN, 235–237). Schmitt points out that, whereas jurists typically ignored the problem of the new global spatialized order, German "exponents of *Nationalökonomie*," such as Gustav von Schmoller, Werner Sombart and Heinrich Dietze, posed "the question universalism or pluralism in world economy" as early as the turn of the century (NdE: 207). It is interesting in this respect to compare the determination "*gross*," as Schmitt understands it, to the concept of "magnitude" [*Grösse*] developed by Heidegger in his "Die Zeit des Weltbildes," *Holzwege* [1950] (Frankfurt: Klostermann, 1994), 95 [88].

100. Schmitt, "Völkerrechtliche Grossraumordnung," SGN, 282.

101. Ibid., 297.

102. Schmitt, "Die Raumrevolution. Durch den totalen Krieg zu einen totalen Frieden" [1940], SGN, 389.

103. Schmitt, "Völkerrechtliche Grossraumordnung," SGN, 292–293.

104. Ibid., 306. Schmitt makes the hair-raising qualification that this great political idea applies to all nations and ethnic groups of Central and Eastern Europe, "*von den Juden abgesehen*," with the exception of the Jews, considered as "*Artfremde*" or essentially foreign. Ibid., 294.

105. Ibid., 302.

106. Schmitt, *Der Nomos*, 216.

107. Schmitt, *Ex Captivitate Salus*, 12, 75.

108. Schmitt, *Der Nomos*, 6.

109. K. Löwith, "The Occasional Decisionism of Carl Schmitt" [1935], in *idem*, *Martin Heidegger and European Nihilism*, ed. Richard Wolin (New York: Columbia University Press, 1995).

110. See supra, note 13.

111. One thinks of Wittgenstein's treatment of the "rule" in the *Philosophical Investigations*; of Derrida's "undecidability"; of Lyotard's "différend"; of Vattimo's "war of interpretations"; of Bauman's "post-modern ethics"; of Laclau and Mouffe's "hegemony."

112. Schmitt, *Glossarium* [1947–1951] (Berlin: Duncker & Humblot, 1991), 66.

113. Schmitt, *Der Nomos,* 36.

114. Cf. Zygmunt Bauman's *Liquid Modernity* (Cambridge: Blackwell, 2000).

115. Schmitt, *Der Nomos*, 17.

116. In the context of de-Nazification and a few months before the Nuremberg trials, Schmitt was arrested by the American occupation authorities and placed in an internment camp, pending the determination of his degree of participation in the Nazi regime and the extent of his responsibility. He was kept in prison for over a year, but was released with no charges having been brought against him. The minutes of his discussions with his interrogator, Robert Kempner, as well as his written replies to questions that were posed to him are published by J. W. Bendersky under the title "Carl Schmitt at Nuremberg," in *Telos*, no. 72 (summer 1987): 91–121.

117. Schmitt, *Ex Captivitate Salus*, 89.

118. Schmitt, *Politische Theologie*, 49.

119. Schmitt, *Ex Captivitate Salus*, 70.

120. Schmitt, *Politische Theologie*, 63.

121. Schmitt, *Glossarium*, 23.

122. This is why Schmitt's work remains "classic," that is to say, potentially productive, even (or rather, especially) against the intentions of its author, which cannot be said of the banalities of textbook realism.

123. J. Habermas, *Die Einbeziehung des Anderen*, 234.

124. Ibid., 231.

125. *In Nomos der Erde*, Schmitt's analysis implies that Germany was forced into the Second World War. What is more, the war itself remains deliberately outside Schmitt's field of vision, which allows him to be silent about the way in which Nazi Germany treated its enemies, both "external" and "internal." This is why "discriminating" war remains in his eyes to the end associated with "universalism."

126. And especially of the philosophy of law which, in the liberal tradition, passes as *political* philosophy.

127. G. Ananiadis, "Carl Schmitt and Max Adler: The Irreconcilability of Politics and Democracy," in Mouffe (ed.), *The Challenge of Carl Schmitt* (Verso, London, 1999).

128. The felicitous phrase is Rob Walker's; see his *Inside/outside: International Relations as Political Theory* (Cambridge University Press, Cambridge, 1993), 60 ff.

129. Schmitt, *Ex Captivitate Salus*, 87–88.

130. On the "family resemblances" between the concept of sovereignty and that of the classical subject, see, among others, J. Edkins et al. (eds.), *Sovereignty and Subjectivity*, Lynne Rienner, Boulder, Colorado 1999, and Etienne Balibar, "Citizen Subject," in E. Cadava et al. (eds.), *Who Comes After The Subject?* (Routledge, London, 1991).

131. M. Stirner, *Der Einzige und sein Eigene* [*The One and his Own*, 1845] (Stuttgart: Reklam, 1981). Schmitt considers this "the most beautiful or, at any rate, the most German among the book titles of the entire German literature" (*Ex Captivitate Salus*, 81.)

132. Schmitt, *Ex Captivitate Salus*, 88.

133. Ibid., 89.

134. Ibid., 88.

135. Ibid., 89.

136. Ibid., 90. Schmitt here is implicitly departing from his original understanding of the friend/enemy relation. Compare with the following formula taken from *Der Begriff des Politischen* (33): "War issues out of enmity, for enmity is an existential negation of another being." Schmitt, however, shrinks from developing the full implications of his move from the "existential negation" of the sovereign subject to the "calling in question" of the split subject.

137. Schmitt, *Der Nomos der Erde . . .* , 296–297.

138. M. Heidegger, "Die Zeit des Weltbildes," in Heidegger, *Holzwege*, 103 [111].

139. T. Adorno, *Minima Moralia* (London: New Left Books, 1978), 85, 132.

140. We are dealing here with an instance of a broader cultural phenomenon. Despite the fact that war has been in every respect a determining factor in the formation of liberal modernity, it has been effectively suppressed from public consciousness. As a consequence, liberalism is unable to think its own brand of militarism. On this see P. K. Lawrence, "Enlightenment, modernity and war," *History of the Human Sciences* 12, no. 1 (1999). See also Paul Virilio and S. Lotringer, *Pure War* (New York: Semiotext(e), 1983); Virilio, *Speed and Politics* (New York: Semiotext(e), 1986; H. Gray, *Postmodern War* (London: Routledge, 1997). A similar point is made by Dan Diner in a recent historical work that makes fruitful use of Schmittian analytical categories (*Das Jahrhundert verstehen: Eine universalhistorische Deutung* (Frankfurt: Fischer Verlag, 2000). Diner contrasts the political cultures characteristic of the continental and the maritime powers respectively and relates them to the different modalities of war they engaged. In the case of the continental powers, the exigencies of territorial conflict and the proximity of violence it entailed contributed decisively to the centralization and militarization of domestic life. The Anglo-Saxon powers, on the other hand, shielded as they were by geography against an immediate military threat, were in a position to reduce the levels of force applied internally. The growth of "civil" society was thus in direct proportion to those states' capacity to wage war at a safe distance by means of naval or air power and long range weapons. With land war kept at bay, Diner points out, "the internal political culture of civil society was spared from the mental fallout of the outwardly directed use of force" (p. 55).

141. S. Avineri, letter to the *International Herald Tribune*, 13 April 1999.

142. P. Virilio, interview in *L' Humanité*, 13 January 2000.

143. Schmitt, *Politische Theologie*, 11.

6

The Dark Intimacy: Maps, Identities, Acts of Identification

Alexander Kiossev

The label "The Balkans" shares with other clichés a kind of automatic essentialism—it is a geographic metonym that presupposes the existence of a nongeographical referent. In political debates, journalistic essays, and everyday conversations this is a self-evident, unquestionable presumption: The name's usage indicates that the Balkans exists as a region with a certain identity established by certain common features. One can ask what exactly these relevant features are—are they historical? cultural? political?—and this will be one possible "politics of questioning." Unfortunately, it shares the presumptions of the cliches.

It is also possible to ask different questions, ones that don't take these presumptions for granted. For instance, one can ask about the uncertain and dynamic relations between names, territorial spans, borders, social groups, individuals, and identities.

The presupposed referent of "the Balkans" is ambivalent. First it claims that there is some cultural and political entity, localized within a certain territory, that can be described by a list of common predicates, following the logical model "X is determined by the possession of the qualities a, b, c, d, ... x, y, z." For instance, the inhabitants of X are a clear, homogeneous group because they share a common religion, language, historical narrative, and pattern of behavior, as well as everyday practices and rituals, political and economic traditions, canons of art and literature, et cetera.[1]

Some researchers claim, however, that the determination of collective identity using such a list of predicates is a logical mistake, because it invokes an unjustifiably essentialist core of qualities while excluding those considered to be nonessential. The German scholar Lutz Niethammer claims that: "Strictly speaking, a collective statement is always a false statement. It distinguishes itself from the simple collective significators—for instance, 'the Romans' or 'the women'—by the fact that it isn't a simple, shortened linguistic expression, but pretends (confronted with the self-evident internal difference), that the common features are based on a certain essential core and ascribes to these common features a special meaning."

Other authors indicate that, from a logical and pragmatic standpoint, there are several types of identities: logical (where two terms are mutually substitutable in all possible contexts, that is, they share the same "full and close" list of predicates), "numeric" (where the list of predicates does not fully coincide, but an observer could verify that the spatio-temporal continuity of the object in question was not interrupted), and "personal identity" (where self-consciousness, memory, and narration indicate that "I" is the same "I").[2]

Collective cultural identity is a fourth, different type, where numeric identity (spatio-temporal continuity plus the incomplete list of shared predicates) is intensified by the political medium. In the case of collective identity, "shared predicates" are not only a question of cognition but also a question of (political) recognition. "I recognize that 'we' (you, I, he . . .) share the same essential qualities, you recognize the same for me and the others, he recognizes the same, et cetera." Here the "essentialist reduction" is not a matter of the observer's cognitive illusion, but a question of internal self-recognition and of the self-proclamation of the group "itself" (the illusion, being essentialist from a cognitive point of view, is nevertheless constitutive for the group itself). These mutual and multiple acts of recognition are often accompanied by the feeling of "belonging."

Therefore, to claim that group X is determined by its cultural identity (as the Balkan cliché implicitly does) can be quite an ambivalent claim. Does this claim point to a numerical identity fixed by an external observer, or does it designate a feeling of similarity shared by the members of the observed community? Does it imply "belonging"? Or does it do all of the above?

Things get even harder when we reflect on the fact that the "feeling of belonging" is different in the case of the group than in the case of the individual. In fact, the group cannot "feel," but can only produce the institutional, ritual, or discursive preconditions for feelings, which will then be shared by individuals. The group declares its "belonging to itself" (i.e., its recognition of its own identity) through publicly understood and institutionally reproducible symbols and norms: It maintains (invents, creates, et cetera) tradition, worships a pantheon of heroes and martyrs, fulfills missions, tells narratives, envisages imaginary "homelands," and so on.

The individual has a flexible relationship to the symbolic and institutional identity of the group. In the process of socialization as well as later, in his or her mature life, the individual is caught in peculiar dialectics. At least two alternatives are open to the group member. He or she can either internalize the group symbols or distance him or herself from them; the latter option alienates the individual from the collective "belonging."

Thus, along with questioning the numeric identity of the Balkans, one should also ask whether or not there are groups or individuals who feel that they belong to the Balkans. The first question is, "What are the Balkans?" (Its more sophisticated version might be, "can we describe the Balkans in a satisfactory way?") The second question is then, "Who is *Homo balkanicus*?" In other words, what collective, and what individual, recognizes itself as Balkan? These questions might further lead us to several others: Does *Homo balkanicus* exist at all? What nuances distinguish the feeling of belonging, or non-belonging, to the Balkans?

Two Suspicious Examples

Let us approach the subject by means of a very typical personal/collective experience, which is not documented (and remains therefore unproven) but is nevertheless quite common. Every Bulgarian, Greek, or Serb who has spent a long time elsewhere in Europe knows that if he or she craves a dear old "manja" (meal), he had best go to a Greek restaurant or a Turkish shop. The Bulgarian might order his meals in the Greek restaurant using unfamiliar names—tatsiki, suvlaki, giros—but the taste will be much like that of tarator and shish-kebab, whilst the sarmi and musaka stand a good chance of being just like my mother's sarmi and musaka. The Turkish shop will sell white brine cheese, vine leaves, khalva, kashkaval, and boza, as well as the beloved gherkins—real sour ones, unlike the sterilised insipidness they sell in German, French, or Czech supermarkets. Kebabcheta (čevapčići in Serbia and in Macedonia) are obviously a common Balkan phenomenon as are "sljivovica" ("slivova" in Bulgarian, "cuika" in Romanian) and sturdy grape brandy ("loza" in Serbian, "lozova" in Macedonian, "grozdanka" in Bulgarian), to say nothing of shopska salad and emblematic spices like mint, savory, basil, et cetera, which set the overall profile of the Balkan taste.

And then there is another experience—similar, yet different. Each of us Balkan guys who have been abroad knows that we can recognize another Balkan guy by his or her gait, by other mannerisms, by the inimitable mechanics of the body on the street, by the way he or she gets on and off the subway, jay-walks at crossroads, approaches an unknown individual, by his or her behavior at the table, et cetera. It is a kind of spontaneous and abrupt recognition, an "a-ha" experience of momentous (maybe a little bit joyful, a little bit shameful) identification—*But isn't he or she just like me?*

Identities versus Acts of Identification

In his famous essay *The Mirror Stage as Formative in the Function of the I*, Lacan wrote the following concerning the identification process in a six month old baby: "Unable yet to walk, or even to stand up . . . he (the nursling in front of the mirror) nevertheless surmounts in a flutter of jubilant activity, the obstructions of his support in order to fix his attitude in a more or less leaning forward position, and bring back an instantaneous aspect of the image to hold it in its gaze."[3] He speaks further about the "problematic libidinal dynamism" of this moment, describing the mirror phase as an act of "identification in the full sense which analysis gives to this term: the transformation which occurs with the subject when he assumes an image."

What is of interest for us here is a kind of structural homology between acts of individual mirror identification and acts of spontaneous cultural identification (self-recognition in the mirror, or mirrors, of culturally similar others). In the latter case the *a-ha experience* and the *"libidinal investment"* are definitely there; present also is the interdependence between "Innenwelt" and "Umwelt" (although all these relations are essentially transformed). And as we will see further, the strange dialectic between dynamism and stillness (the jubilant *activity*, the desire to interact versus the attempt *to behold*, *to hold* in the gaze) is present too. In fact, one can claim that this dialectic is repeated and transformed on every level that separates the nursling from the mature member of society, and hence at every stage of the psychic and social development of the individual and/or the group. It persists in the opposition between the dynamic mirror stage and the static "symbolic" stage (Lacan describes this transition in metaphors expressive of this opposition: He labels the symbolic identity of the individual as "objectification,"[4] an "armour of alienating identity," "rigidity," "structure,"[5] et cetera). But elsewhere he points out that the static forms of symbolic "identity" are not permanently fixed, that signifiers (identity models) float and change, libidinal investments and acts of identification continue and, as he puts it, "to break out of the circle from the Innenwelt into Umwelt generates the endless quadrature of the inventorying of the ego."[6]

So, could we assume that this endless dialectic between flux and fix, between identities and acts of identification, persists in the sphere of culture as well? Society and culture create a lot of possible mirrors for the individual or group, a lot of opportunities for identification. At the same time they try in various ways to force the individual and/or the group to assume a certain "stable" identity, a rigid structure, a fixed and stable totality. Therefore the play between the *"a-ha* experience" and the "armor," between the libidinal dynamism of spontaneous self-recognition and the "objectification in stable identities," seems infinite in the social and cultural realms.

Everyday Practices and the Maps of Anthropological Similarities

All of the above "examples"—cuisine, eating habits, interpersonal communication, social etiquette—belong to the realm of customary practices. They are a part of the practical and symbolic universe of culture, which is the object of anthropological study. In brief, one is dealing here with "forms of life" (Wittgenstein). Following these "uncertain" examples, could we take a risk and presume a certain common Balkan anthropological type—a "numeric identity" of a deeply embedded "form of life," shared by these ethnic groups and nations that so aggressively pretend to be different from one another? It would be even riskier to presume that this is *the form of life*, the ultimate and deep Balkan communality, which typically remains invisible because it is repressed by the "armors" and "structures" of the dominant national, confessional, and linguistic identities. But its ultimate reality is so strong that in spite of all repression (or because of it, as in "the return of the repressed"), it always bursts out suddenly, becoming visible and forcing the individual into an overwhelming, unintended act of identification: *Isn't he or she just like me?* One might even be tempted to see, in this occasional and unexpected "*a-ha* experience" of identification, a regression to a certain Balkan mirror-stage: an abrupt and non-voluntary self-recognition in the Balkan Other, a stigmatized label that all emancipated Romanians, Serbs, Greeks, Bulgarians, Croats, et cetera, are eager to avoid.

What might this common Balkan anthropological type be like? Is it feasible to go beyond the random and provisional personal identifications and describe it in an explicit and analytically disciplined manner? Let us attempt such a description—and see whether it is possible at all.

A hypothetical "objective observer" (i.e., a positivistic historian or anthropologist), could easily demonstrate that in previous centuries, the rural communities of the Balkans shared a lot of common features in their forms of life. Besides the similarities born of common natural and social conditions (climate, specifics of geography and agriculture, traditional types of livelihood, patterns of settlement and trade, underdeveloped infrastructure, pre-modern kinship and family codes, demographics), and besides the shared "heroic forms of life" or the "common cultural heritage" (shared myths, fairy tales, jokes and rituals, wandering "folklore" motifs, etc.), the fictitious observer will probably also point to the underlying reason for these similarities. The entire region shares a common macro-social frame which originated in the Byzantine and Ottoman legacies and resulted in a lack of Christian aristocracy, a relatively free peasantry, small estates, a specific position of the church, et cetera.[7]

On _____ xtend the list of similarities, drawi _____ Balkan ethnicities or areas. Ethnc _____ Romanian Danube corridor has cl _____ on both sides of the Danube. The s _____ nd nomadic forms of life, condu _____ hibit functional similarities in clot _____ [8] The cult of bread is very popula _____ dress are also shared (long, homes _____ lals, fur coats, skirts, breast pieces, _____ r holidays and rituals. The most c _____ (Christmas back-slapping and we _____ many overlapping pagan holiday _____ _____ngumes), which is called Tsvetnitsa in Bulgarian and Florille in Rumanian; St. Lazar's fertility rituals overlap with the Rousal gangs (which are in Rumanian called Calus or Calusari); the rain-making rituals—like Skaloyan in Bulgarian, Kaloyani in German, and Caloianul, or Scaloianul, or Ene in Rumanian—overlap with butterfly rituals—Paparuda in Rumanian—and with Bulgarian Eniovden and Rumanian, Dragaica, Cununa, and Sinziene.[10]

One could abandon this narrower perspective and compare more distant Balkan areas and broader territories. The list could be extended to other cross-border similarities, for example, among Romanian, Dobrudjan, Macedonian, and Greek costumes; among Bulgarian or Macedonian ring-dances (horo), Serbian dances (kolo), Romanian dances (hora), and the Greek sirtaki, et cetera. Later, parallels could be sought not only on a broad transnational scale but from a micro-perspective in urban environments and architecture. For instance, there are many cultural and architectural similarities among multiethnic villages, and among cities that share the multicultural Ottoman legacy. The famous Plovdiv houses (celebrated in Bulgarian national historiography as the paragon of Bulgarian Renaissance architecture) have often belonged to rich Greek or Armenian merchants. The semi-Ottoman, semi-European style of their architecture and interior design and furniture can hardly be described as "purely Bulgarian."

Another set of similarities will surface if we focus on cuisine. Take, for example, the Bulgarian, Greek, Romanian, Armenian, Macedonian national dishes. The Romanian anthropologists Vintila Mihailescu and Radu Anton Roman begin their article "How National Is 'the National Cuisine'" with the following:

Whoever visits the Romanian restaurants in Montreal may savour some of the "typically Romanian" dishes which are like "home made"—*sarmale, mija, chiftele, pilaf, musaca, etc., sarmale, mija, chiftele, pilaf, musaca, etc.* Then if one fancies going to a Bulgarian restaurant, one may have the pleasure of relishing some of the "typically Bulgarian" dishes: *sarmale, mija, chiftele, pilaf, musaca, etc.* Finally, one can check in at a very good Serb restaurant, where a band of Gypsies play Serb music (quite familiar to us, too) and where the chief offers a "typically Serb" menu: *sarmale, mija, chiftele, pilaf, musaca, etc.*[11]

Other similarities also exist—in architecture and manners, celebrations, attitudes, and household organization.

Differences and Alternative Mappings

The problem with such descriptions, however, is that the list of similarities (which from a logical point of view should amount to a complete description—a full list of predicates, determining and delimiting a certain identity) could never be complete. It remains open—changing, heterogeneous, "multileveled," and infinite. What's more, it could be easily paralleled by another list: In addition to the infinite and heterogeneous enumeration of similarities, one could come up with an infinite and no less heterogeneous enumeration of differences.

Let us once again provide some examples. Historians speak of the great regional differences within the Ottoman empire (especially among Bosnia, Rumelia, and Northern Africa in the area of agriculture or in the way the "Ottoman legacy" was appropriated by the young national states[12]). Perhaps the single most important differences, however, are confessional[13]: The Eastern Orthodox, Muslim, Catholic, and even Evangelical communities comprise a quaint internal patchwork, a differentiated mosaic of borders and crossings. Not only do their official doctrines differ, but they underlie differing practises that include feasts, bans, rituals, costume, cuisine, and sexual mores. No less significant are the variances among the highland, lowland, Mediterranean, and Black Sea regions of the peninsula, which engage in diverse types of trade and cultural communication with the rest of the world, as well as varying patterns of commerce and migration. All this may have (and it did have) a powerful bearing on the differences among everyday life forms, on wealth and poverty, on the openness or hermetism of these relatively autonomous islands of everyday culture.

If we look also to Balkan nomads and seminomads (groups such as the Kazalbash, the Yurucks, and the Gagaouz),[14] we can enumerate yet another array of differences and nuances within this Balkan panorama. Furthermore, if we account for the degree of regional involvement in the civilizational orbits of the Great Empires, or in wars, revolutions, modernization processes, and the like,[15] the variances among the peninsula's regions and provinces will change their territorial contours several times

more. The invisible (and often politically instrumental) border between the Habsburg
and Ottoman Empires divides the peninsula even today. It does so not only in terms
of politics and religion, but also in everyday life. But the Habsburg-Ottoman border
hardly coincides either with contemporary state borders, or with the chaotic multitude of overlapping borders that divide local rural communities. The imperial division is a relative one, too. Cuisine, for example, is definitely influenced and "mapped
out" by the empires as well as by the great religions, "minor" cultural influences,
random historical fusion, distant contacts, and "long durée" legacies. Experts claim
that Balkan cuisine descends from the Arab or Ottoman versions of Persian cuisine.
Its "natural" borders (which coincide neither with the former empires nor with the
contemporary nation states) can be drawn somewhere around Zagreb, where it abuts
the mid-European front of chocolate cakes, sugary salads, and milky potages, while
to the South, at Rijeka, it shades into the Dalmatian/Mediterranean cuisine of frutti
di mare, pizzas, and spaghetti. But the poor highlanders' cuisine, as well as the cuisine
of various religious minorities and nomads, remain outside this map; and the various
national "cultivations," appropriations, and emblematisations of traditional cuisine
demand a different history, different maps.[16]

We can observe the unresolved and multidimensional interplay of similarities
and differences even through the example of a single cultural phenomenon. In the
article quoted above, Mihăilesku and Roman praise the "common" Balkan dishes—
sarmale, chiftale, pilaf, et cetera—but they also write:

In the above story, the description of "sarmale" as a "typically" Romanian, Bulgarian, as well
as Serb dish was obviously suggestive of the existence of a common Balkan background, but
at the same time it demonstrated the differences: it almost never was the same kind of food.
Even when referring to the Romanian *sarmale*, can we speak of the same type of meal in case
of, on the one hand the sarmalute, wrapped in vine leaves, which Moldavian housewives take
great lengths to make "as small as a fingernail" and serve with a spoonful of sour cream, and,
on the other hand, the Oltenian sarmale which are folded in cabbage leaves and are "as large
as a palm"?[17]

The Romanian anthropologists further point out that there is always great regional
diversity, "which makes it possible for the same dish to be utterly different from one
region to another."[18]

Thus, we have learned a simple and well-known Nietzschean lesson: that the cognitive "mapping" of a field (in this case, the field of everyday practices in a certain
region) is always pluralistic and can be viewed from a variety of perspectives. A perspective, free from all possible ideological premises, cannot describe an "essential"
Balkan anthropological type. It can simply articulate and re-articulate this field in

alternative ways, producing a series of similarities and/or differences from a multitude of possible points of view. The various acts of cognition draw "borders" between given (actually cognitively constructed) identities, grafting sets of commonalties onto the "territory" in a controversial and manifold way. But the very projection of these similarities or differences onto the given area (i.e., "region," "peninsula," "the Balkans") is unreliable, too. Couldn't we assume that the "peninsula" is itself a construct—that it is just a part of this relativistic mapping? (One could further compare Albanians in Albania with Albanians and Italians in Southern Italy, popular culture in Thrace with the popular culture in Anatolia, et cetera, and thus demonstrate that the interaction of differences and similarities neither begins nor ends at the borders of the area called "the Balkans").

Maps of Identities

This seeming relativism is obstructed by the fact that the "territory" is anything but empty for arbitrary cognitive projections. Today, just like centuries ago, it is full of people who clearly recognize their shared characteristics and stable belonging. For centuries, various ethnic, linguistic, confessional, cultural, and other groups have drawn and redrawn borders through this territory (using various forms of military, economic, and cultural power), and in one way or another they have tried to impose rigid models of identity on their members.

It is well known that the Ottoman Empire, although a strong imperial state, allowed some cultural, religious, and administrative autonomy to its vassal communities. As a consequence, these local communities (especially in their predominant, rural variant) became hermetic, autarchic, self-reproducing, and isolated from one another. (Non-intensive trade and bad infrastructure also contributed to that isolation.) Their strong, internal, patriarchal orders subjected the individual to a fixed religious identity. The strength and rigidity of those identities can be illustrated by the fact that in Medieval Ottoman cities, ethnic groups and religious communities lived in close proximity for centuries without mixing or fusing their identities. They lived in different neighborhoods, celebrated different holidays, performed different rituals, wore different clothes,[19] and often—in spite of the everyday communication—labeled one another in a pejorative way and even hated one another. Under these circumstances ethnonymes, destined later to become national names, didn't designate inclusive, great, homogeneous "imagined communities," but instead referred to the rigid internal divisions among small local communities. In the city of Plovdiv, for instance, until the middle of the nineteenth century, the contemporary "national" ethnonymes articulated the social hierarchy between town and village: "Greek" meant "a citizen of Plovdiv" and "Bulgarian" meant "a simple peasant."[20] Even today, examples of this multicultural separatism and isolationism persist. There are still areas in Northeastern Bulgaria where neighboring Bulgarian (Orthodox), Turkish, and Pavlikyan (Catholic) villages lead separate and relatively isolated economic, religious, and cultural lives.

In fact, the play of cognitive perspectives (the changeable recognition of similarities and differences, and their use for delineating certain identical entities) was never free of the historically, politically, and culturally superimposed constraints of the existing identities. Nor was it free from their multiple overlapping tensions, conflicts, competitions, and struggles. The link was always dialectical: The politics of a certain group's identity secretly determined the reception and cognition of "the similar and the different." Inversely, the "recognized" similarities or differences then strengthened and stabilized the initial identities, inscribing them into the group's narrative. The alternative perspective of another community could, in its turn, contest the status quo, highlight other similarities and differences, narrate other stories, and try to re-articulate the mapping of identities. Such, for example was (still is, in some religious communities) the religious regulation of food symbolism in the Ottoman Empire. In spite of all the similarities in eating habits, in spite of the solid penetration of Turkish-Persian cuisine throughout the peninsula, there was a widespread prohibition against members of one religious community eating together with members of other confessions.[21] The similarities, the influences, and even the fusion of the cuisines were usually not mentioned at all; what mattered was that Christians ate pork and Muslims didn't. Against the backdrop of this archaic attitude (the food of others was deemed "dirty" and repellent[22]; in popular folklore, the image of unclean, alien food is a stable, repetitive stereotype[23]) the emblematic food differences delineating religious identities were much more important than the similarities.

Does that mean that the figure of the observer, free of any conflicting politics of identity or politically burdened acts of (re)cognition, is a mere fiction?

What about the great army of scholars (historians, ethnographers, anthropologists, et cetera) who have been trying to play this role for the last 150 years?

Politics of Cognition

Let us distinguish several types of such "observers." Needless to say, these are "ideal types"; reality offers various "deviations" and admixtures.

rise to centripetal movements among neighbors and former cultural cooperators. During the period between 1850 and 1912, the nation states in the region developed—slowly but relentlessly—relatively isolated national economies underpinned by hostile cultural codification (mutually antagonistic educational systems, linguistic standards, art canons, etc.). During this period, after several military and cultural wars and a whole series of ideological rivalries, the Balkan nations chose to foster their mutual non-communication, to develop and even to transform into institutions their various political struggles and ideological hostilities, and aggressively to segregate from their neighbors. This differentiation was a complex process that had a deep impact on the constitutive patterns of each nation's high culture. At a certain phase of the nation's building (with some chronological variations, for the Balkan nations it took place between 1850 and 1912), the anthropological similarities and differences were reshaped and re-mapped. They were, in fact, transformed into separate and "authentic" national "folklores" (with the claim that they express the metaphysical depths of this or that National Soul). The different national folklores suspiciously coincided territorially with national borders and imagined homelands (a modern territorialization entirely alien to the local ancient oral tradition). During the same period, the characteristics of the new national high cultures—the structure of historical time and geopolitical space, national heroes, martyrs, leaders, teleological narratives, deeds, and sacrifices that structure the axis of historical time, values, and authorities—distanced themselves to the point of incompatibility. The ever growing isolation from one another, combined with the war traumas (1885, 1912, 1913, 1914–1918), gave birth to the image of the opaque, adversely deviant, and actively hostile neighbor (upon whom the stigmatizing label of being "Balkan" was usually projected).[39]

These efforts at differentiation and at producing distinct national politics of representation (institutional, political, and even military ones) clashed with the stubbornness of Western *Balkanism*, which was unwilling to see any differences and perceived the region from a macro-colonial perspective. Despite the availability of good, expert, diplomatic, and journalistic knowledge about the differences, the Western mass media repeatedly reproduced the image of an obscure geopolitical and cultural whole, senselessly fragmented, where unrecognizably small tribes and aggressive micro-states staged long forgotten European dramas in miniature: mutual hatred, uncivilized wars under the banner of hysterical and idiosyncratic nationalisms, cultural oppression, ethnic cleansing.

In such a situation, the national high cultures had no chance to create a positive image of the peninsula. Its inevitable but amorphous geographic space was always perceived as a threat to the national elite's longing for authenticity, a fatal obstacle in the way of achieving clear distinguishability and "moral personality" (Kant). As a trope, presupposing a common cultural, historical and political referent, it threatens to shake up not only the anthropological, but the national borders and differences as well. Thus, for the national ideologies of the Balkan countries, different as they were, the Balkans also had a hidden, dark, mythological aura. It is the non-variable, constantly repeated sign of unsuccessful self-differentiation and self-determination; it signifies the melting and disappearance of the national subjectivity before the gaze of the "Significant Other." In short, for them it always symbolized the lack of "genuine" cultural recognition hidden behind the surface of Western official acts: diplomatic, political, and juridical recognition of the region's independent national states. A detailed discursive analysis of the Balkan trope in the public discourse could demonstrate that it has absorbed all negative energies, accommodating in its semantic vagueness the quasi-mythical image of everything Oriental, everything Ottoman, and everything "anti-progressive." Being a traumatic mirror-discourse, the "native" *Balkanism* seems to share the same stigmatizing series of predicates as the Western one[40] but associates them with different emotional nuances: at times, with anger and aggression against the Significant Other; at times, with failure and shame, even self-disgust.[41]

The Dominant Strategies of (Dis)identification

The force field of competing identity models seems to be constricted between the Scila of the Balkans, seen as the label of external condemnation, and the Haridba of the Balkans, seen as the name of the internal, "native," fear and shame.

This gives birth to two major forms of identification, each escaping one of the Balkan ghosts.

The first option is to leave, to escape, to cast off the unbearable "armor" of the imposed identities: a radical emigration, close to cultural amnesia.

In the last ten years, more than two million people left the former Yugoslavia (there is a lack of firm statistical data; some estimates show only 700,000 emigrés, the rest being internal refugees who moved inside the ex-Yugoslavian borders; other observers estimate that as many as three to four million people left ex-Yugoslavia altogether). Croatian emigration during this period has been estimated at 300,000. During the period 1993–1998 alone, Romania exported more than 120,000 emigrants. The sad story of the unsuccessful emigration of thousands of Albanians to Italy, and their brutal expulsion, is well known.

Unlike Yugoslavia, Bulgaria did not experience war or ethnic cleansing. But despite the country's relative peacefulness, stability, and moderate economic success, more than 600,000 people fled, more than 300,000 of them in the period 1989–1992.

To speculate about "common regional reasons" for emigration against a background of diverse national situations and a variety of centripetal social factors is a risky task. Nevertheless, one is surprised by the proportionally consistent number of emigrants despite the quite different conditions among the Balkan countries. It is as though there are reasons beyond the collapse of communism and the wars, beyond the economic crises and ethnic conflicts. It is as though the wars and the political chaos, the embargo and the bankruptcy of Albanian, Romanian, and Bulgarian banks unlocked another catastrophe. A large number of people experienced it as "bankruptcy" of the symbolic national capital, as an identity crisis. Emigrants' letters, oral accounts, and unofficial reports radiate the irrational fear of belonging to a "fatal" place, haunted by the demons of civilization. The political and economic motives behind this mass emigration are probably also mixed with a spasm of disgust: the wish (or rather the compulsion) to leave definitely, at all costs, despite the unpredictability and misery emigration entails.

Isn't it possible to propose that all these people fleeing war crimes, mass poverty, unemployment, and so on were also running from the stigma?

The escape in the opposite direction—into passionate nationalism and hyperbolic (Serb, Bulgarian, Albanian, Rumanian) pride—is well known and does not need a detailed description. What is difficult is to recognize, behind the face of traditional and official state patriotism, the hysterical attempt to compensate for the stigma. The political instrumentalization of the Kosovo myth, and Slobodan Milošević's successful propaganda manipulation of "heavenly Serbia" to mobilize millions of ordinary people, offer a provocative case study. What is worth mentioning, however, is that these nationalist reactions were also—not surprisingly—anti-Balkan. They were hysterical forms of differentiation, in which the neighboring nation, ethnicity, or confession was perceived as embodying the Balkan "Gestalt"—of the "Turks," "Ustasha," "Gypsies," or, in the last resort, "the same Balkan shit as us."[42]

The Balkans as Tricksterlike Field of Counteridentifications

The situation is still more complex. Groups and individuals can choose among these dominant identity models, secretly charging the two extremes (citizen of the [better] world versus national patriot; nomadic versus settled, et cetera) with traumatic

ene ...   nentioned cognitive dynamics
also ...   The old rural and local com-
mu ...   more; the "national" and the
"un ...   but the contemporary everyday ...   new plethora of pre-modern,
mo ...   The field, which is structured
thro ...   d discourse, often blocks the
dom ...   pected opportunities for multiple ...   :ounter-identifications. Placed
amic ...   l paradigms, individuals and
grou ...   h" way, and to escape for a
whil ...   :igma. These are momentous
posit ...   of identification—exploding
a-ha ...   :al forms.

Th ...   eeling of belonging, in which
the i ...   of them could develop into
relati ...

In ...   the "Mystery of Bulgarian
Voice ...   the variants of this Balkan
image ...   ounter) culture was born in
all the ...   belly dance developed, new-
old sr ...   f arrogant Balkan intimacy
haunt ... most important symptom of this process was the lack of
popular will to be Westernlike (a rejection not only of the current political slogan
"on the way to Europe," but also of the old Balkan perception of the West as a
kind of secular transcendence[43]). Marketing agents and managers immediately
smelled the new demand on the cultural market, and they hurried to satisfy it with
a new Balkan cultural industry: an aggressive and arrogant, yet "democratic" and
"intimate," mass media, new types of amusements, a new-old type of music.

Popular music and its various metamorphoses are especially interesting: turbo
folk and yugo-rock in Yugoslavia, chalga and folk music in Bulgaria, "manale" in
Romania. In Bulgarian cities and villages, chalga music not only killed the old socialist popular amusements but also successfully replaced English and American rock
and disco music in clubs and pubs. It represented a culture of enjoyment that
opposed both the "post-protestant," globalist ethos of entering capitalism and the
hollow slogans of official nationalism. It took elements from traditional "orgiastic"
Balkan festivities, from obscene folklore, from Turkish and Gypsy music, and from

the newborn semi-criminal subculture and combined them with postmodern electronic synthesizers and rhythm-boxes. The result is less a music of protest and
trauma (although some parallels to Afro-American rap music are here possible)
than a tricksterlike, comic, and aggressive transformation. It turns the lowermost[44]
picture of the Balkans upside down and converts the stigma into a joyful consumption of pleasures forbidden by European norms and taste. Contrary to the traditional dark image, this popular culture arrogantly celebrates the Balkans as they
are: backward and Oriental, corporeal and semi-rural, rude, funny, but intimate. As
an act of counter-identification, it scandalizes what Norbert Elias called the "civilizational standards" and the "borders of taste, shame, and uneasiness," combining
into a controversial structure warmth, familiarity, and "Oriental" epatage. It is a
kind of willing regression into a great, scandalous, Balkan "neighborhood," away
from both Europe and the annoying official homelands.[45]

Surprisingly enough, nostalgia for such counter-models of identification (they
are by far not only musical) is especially strong where the familiar "sarmale,"
"mousaka," and other quasi-Oriental amusements are missing, such as in the steril-
ity of the Dutch or German cultural landscapes. The Balkan cultural diaspora is
worth studying from that point of view—for its nostalgic and intimate cooking,
celebrating, and chatting.

A Story Instead of an Ending

Unable here to initiate such a study, I would like to finish with a personal story.

In 1993, I taught Bulgarian language and literature as a lecturer at the University
of Goettingen in Germany. One day I was invited to a student party together with
a friend of mine, a Yugoslavian PhD student who during the siege of Sarajevo realized that she was Bosnian and Muslim, and so became an anti-war activist. We
decided to have a bite before the party. Confronted with the difficult choice between
Italian, German, Chinese, and French restaurants, we chose—with a slight twinge
of shame—to go to a Greek tavern and enjoy native culinary pleasures. As we ate
our "moussaka" and "souvlaki" (not at all different from the Bulgarian-Serbian-
Macedonian-Turkish "shish kebab"), we watched the weather forecast for Europe
on the restaurant's TV. International borders were delineated with white contours.
For no apparent reason, Romania and Bulgaria appeared as a common state with
Bucharest as its capital. At the end of our dinner, we asked the Greek waiter for
Turkish coffee. He said, however, that at this restaurant they only offered Greek
coffee. We ordered it, and it was the same "Ottoman" type: sweet and thick,

inappropriate to the German taste for filtered coffee, known in Bulgaria, Romania, Albania, Bosnia, and Turkey as Turkish coffee. Later on, at the party, I was introduced to a nice German girl who, noticing my accent, immediately asked me "Woher sind Sie?" "Aus Bulgarien" I answered, worried about my Bosnian friend, who had meanwhile gotten involved in another verbal war with a bunch of Serbs, Slovenes, and Albanians. I observed the arguing group, their energetic gestures, loud voices, the way they patted one another's shoulders, and I felt a strange feeling of closeness and intimacy. Now I realized what a German student had in mind when she insisted that I demonstrated "Balkan movements" ("eine balkanesische Motorik," she said).[46]

The party went on. Some Germans asked a Turkish girl to do a belly dance for them, which she refused. "Sie sind also ein Rumaener?" the German girl sought to confirm fifteen minutes later. "Nein, ich bin ein Bulgare, aber es ist egal," I replied.

She looked embarrassed.

Notes

1. Paper presented to the Sofia conference *Istoriyata pred predizvikatelstvata na promenite*, October 27–28, 2000. My point here is, however, that such "Kolektivbezeichnungen" (collective significations) are not in principle different from the "collective statement." In their automatic usage, they presuppose the collective statements in question.

2. Jean-Marc Tetaz, "Personale Identitaet, Errinerung—kollektive Identitaet," Paper, presented to the Sofia conference *Istoriyata pred predizvikatelstvata na promenite*, October 27–28, 2000.

3. First English translation in *New Left Review* 51 (September/October 1968), reprinted in Jacques Lacan, *Ecrits*, A Selection (London: Travistok/Routledge, 1989).

4. ". . . before the *I* is objectified the dialectic of identification with the other." Ibid., 94.

5. "Armor of alienating identity which stamps with the *rigidity of its structure* the whole subject mental development." Ibid., 96.

6. Ibid., 96.

7. Maria Todorova, *Imagining the Balkans* (Oxford: Oxford University Press, 1997), 161–184.

8. See Antonina Kuzmanova, *Roumyana Atancheva and Vassilka Alexandrova, Roumaniya* (Sofia: Otvoreno obshtestvo, 1999), 105–135.

9. Ibid., 35–40.

10. Ibid.

11. In *Reflection on Differences: Focus on Romania*, by Irina Culic, Istvan Horvat (Cluj: Christian Stan, ed., Limes, 1999), 125.

12. Todorova, *Imagining the Balkans*, 180–183.

13. About the division of the Ottoman Empire in "non-nationalistic" confessional categories see Stavrianos, L. S. *The Balkans since 1453*, (London, 1958, 2000), 222.

14. Kalyonski, Alexei, "Kazulbashki eyud," *Nova publichnost*, (Sofia, 1998).

15. See Stavrianos, ibid., 178–413. See especially 212–213.

16. Mihăilesku and Roman, ibid., 125–136.

17. Ibid., 126.

18. Ibid., 134.

19. For more details see the book *Predstavata za "drugiya" na Blaknaite* (Sofia: Marin Drinov, 1995).

20. See for example the programmatic article of the founding father of Bulgarian ethnography—Prof. Ivan Shishmanov "Predmet I zadachi na nashata ethnographiya" (Sofia: *SBNU*, 1889).

21. See Mihăilesku and Roman, ibid., 127.

22. Inna Peleva Botev, *Tyaloto na nacionalisma* (Sofia: Mab, 1998), 22–172.

23. See Mihăilesku and Roman, ibid., 127, see also Peleva, ibid., 49–58.

24. See "Slavic Weimar/Jena" by Gabriella Schubert and Miro Masek, forthcoming in *Junctions and Disjunctures: East European Literary Culture*, edited by John Nedubauer and Marcel Cornis-Pope (Oxford University Press). The authors stress the importance of the University of Jena, with its Protestant/Romantic cultural spirit, for awakening interest in "folklore" among the South Slavs. Besides the personal contacts that developed among the Grimm brothers, Wilhelm von Humboldt, L. Ranke, J. S. Vater, J. Kopitar, and Vuk Karadžić, the ideological reception of "Humanitaets Briefe" by J. G. Herder, the celebrated promoter of the Slavs, was here of special importance. His ideas about language as the "immortal property" and genuine expression of the nation, about the "creative people's soul" (*schaffende Volksseele*) and the specific "Volkston" of each popular national "poetry" as the true representation of the people's nature, about the natural, simple-minded "song" as spontaneous "Urpoesie," were very influential in the Balkans during the whole nineteenth century.

25. Ibid.

26. About the influence of Czech, Slovak, and Russian scholars on intellectuals in the Balkans, see I. V. Yagic, *Istoriya slaviyanskoi filologii* (St. Peterburg, 1910).

27. See the symptomatic metaphors of the authentic people's self-expression in Herder's famous title *Stimmen der Voelker in Liedern* (Voices of the Nations in Songs, 1807), or in J. Grimm' s expression "Atem jeder Sprache" (the breath of each language), quoted in Schubert and Masek, ibid. Variants of these metaphors are reproduced by all Balkan folklorists. See for example the preface of the Miladinov brothers' song collection (contested by Bulgarians and Macedonians): "Folk songs are an indicator of the mental stage of the nation and a mirror of its spiritual life. The People pours out its feeling in songs" (*Bulgarski narodni pesni, sobrani ot bratya Miladinovci, Dimitar ∂ Konstantin i izdani ot Konstantina* [Zagreb, 1861].)

28. The first Bulgarian academic textbook in literary history (Balan, A., *Bulgarian literature: A Brief Manual for Secondary and Specialised Schools.* [Plovdiv, 1896]), is a good example of this unified "philological complex." The author, in spite of the fact that his

textbook was the first one in the young Bulgarian university context, structured it according to firm and prestigious models, which came from the established practice of international Slavistics and philology. Without any hesitation, he united in his textbook structure the history of popular oral culture (folklore), the history of medieval religious manuscripts, and modern Bulgarian literature. The argument was a traditional one: According to Balan, (who simply follows Herder and Humboldt, as did the whole of international Slavic philology), national language is the most significant work of the national spirit. Therefore, literature and folklore are akin because they are *verbal*, they are *expressions of the soul* (collective or individual, naïve or reflexive), and they are both *ours*. So the textbook secured in an unproblematic way both discursive and institutional continuity between "popular" and "elitist" culture.

29. Unpublished manuscript of V. Mihăilesku.

30. For more details see Yagic, *Istoriya slaviyanskoi filologii.*

31. Gesemann, Gerhard, *Heroische Lebensform, Zur Literatur und Wesenkunde der Balkanischen Patriarchalitaet* (Berlin: Wicking Verlag, 1942).

32. Gerhard Gesemann, "Der Paristaere Balkaner," *Slavusche Rundschau*, 1933, 1–16.

33. For more details see my articles "The Debate about the Problematic Bulgarian," in *National Character and National Ideology in Interwar Eastern Europe*, ed. Ivo Banac, Katharine Verdery (New Haven: Yale Center for International and Eastern Studies, 1995) and "Racism in Potentia?" in *Usvoyavane I emancipaciya*, ed. Atanas Natev (Sofia, SU, 1997).

34. See Benedict Anderson, *Imagined Communities*, revised edition (London: Verso. 1991), pp. 163–187.

35. One can find interesting insights into the nature of *Balkanism* in the books and articles of Larry Wolf, Eli Skopetea, Milica Bakić-Hyden, Maria Todorova, Alexander Kiossev, Dimitar Kambourov, and many others.

36. Todorova, *Imagining the Balkans*, 17.

37. Ibid., 18.

38. Of course, one should distinguish the intellectually subtle and invisible Balkanism of Western institutions of knowledge (anthropology, sociology, history, philology, etc.) from the *Balkanism* of the mass media, which reproduces the cliches in a much more brutal way.

39. See Diana Mishkova, "Friends Turned Foes: Bulgarian National Attitude toward Neighbors" in *Pride and Prejudice*, Working Paper Series 2, Central European University History Department (Budapest: CEU, 1995), 163–186; Nadezda Danova, "Vzaimnata predstava na bulgari i garci," XV–XIX vek, in *Predstavata za drugia na Blakanite* (Sofia: Marin Drinov, 1995), 77; Velichko Todorov, *"Znam gi az tyach," Serbia I serbite v bulgarskata literatura* (Sofia: Kritika, 2000).

40. This needs further research; the rhetorical differences between the two could be of great importance.

41. A relevant symptom of this *self-stigmatization* is so-called "nesting *Balkanism*" ("nesting *Orientalism*"), a phenomenon by which one projects negative emotions upon one's neighbors and shifts the image of the shameful peninsula eastward (recently explored by Milica Bakić-Hyden, Maria Todorova, Marko Živković). Slavoj Žižek puts it this way: "For

Austrians, the Slovenes are wild hordes they have to protect themselves from by an imaginary wall; the Slovenes erect walls before the onslaught of the "uncivilized" Croats; the Croats are walling themselves up against their neighbors, the "wild" Serbs; the Serbs think of themselves as the last shield of Christendom that protects them (but also Europe!) from the Islamic invasion. Four times, therefore, the culturological borders are shifted and the walls erected—all justified by the protection of Christendom against the onslaught of the wild hordes" ("Uživanje u pokornosti i sluganstvu," *Naša Borba*, January 5, 1997).

In his unpublished dissertation, M. Živković describes the mental mapping of the Serbs as follows: "Neither close to the West like the Czechs, nor at the extreme end of the East like Russians, neither affiliated with Central Europe like the Croats, nor positioned as 'the Balkans of the Balkans' like Macedonians, Serbs find it hard both to pass the negative valuations further down and to exploit the exotic potential of the extremes. The stigma they bear combines the stigmas of the South and of the East, both Slavdom and Turkish taint, of congenital communism and Balkan violence. They don't have the option of claiming descent from one of the cultures that the West sees as ancestral to itself like Greeks and Romanians do. Accepting this largely negative stigma, their responses oscillate between playing it back in exaggerated form as 'minstrelization' and various shades of ambivalent self-exoticization as, for instance, in 'magic realism.'" (Živković, manuscript)

Both his and Žižek's analyses share a deficiency: They are made from an ex-Yugoslavian point of view and, in fact, secretly reproduce the "nesting." They interpret the phenomenon in clear recent national and political categories, creating a new implicit eastern border; besides, they exclude from consideration not only Bulgarians and Turks, but also Roma, Armenians, Jews, and other minorities, which (or the mixture of which) can also provide a focus for the Balkan bogeyman who once again muddles the clear national borders.

Especially appropriate for this Balkan projection were the "tyrants," the Turks, who not only embodied for all national ideologies the "sick" medieval imperial power but carried the centuries-old, sinister aura of the demonic foe of Christianity and Europe, and of the scandalous presence of the Other "in our very midst"—of the Orient in the Occident, of Asia in Europe (See, Larry Wolf, *Inventing Eastern Europe, The Map of Civilization and the Mind of the Enlightenment* [Stanford: Stanford University Press, 1994] p. 167.)

Another sign of the stigmatization of the Balkans by national discourses is the frequent shameful associations bound to its image: the "dark Balkan," Oriental idleness. Neighboring nations often labeled each other as "gypsies," "Balkan shit," et cetera.

42. In *Warrior's Honor: Ethnic War and Modern Consciousness* (Vintage: London, 1999) Michael Ignatieff describes the efforts of a Serbian soldier to formulate the difference between Serbs and Croats. The peculiar use of the Balkan trope here is worth quoting. "But the question I've asked bothered him, so a couple of minutes later he tosses the weapon on the bunk between us and says '*Look, here's how it is. Those Croats, they think they are better than us. They want to be the gentlemen. They think they are fancy Europeans. I'll tell you something. We're all just Balkan shit*'" (36).

43. See my article "The Self-Colonizing Cultures," in *Bulgariaavangarda* (Sofia: Salon Verlag, 1998).

44. Todorova, ibid., 18.

45. There is much in common between this Balkan culture of familiarity and Michael Herzfeld's concept of "cultural intimacy." See Michael Herzfeld, *Cultural Intimacy: Social Poetics in the Nation-State* (New York: Routledge, 1997), 1–37. Much like Herzfeld's

"cultural intimacy," Balkan popular culture domesticates the official codes of national representation and auto-representation through the multiple uses, misuses, and flexible appropriations performed by social actors in everyday life. Popular amusements in the Balkans produce ironic self-images and display them in semi-public spaces of insiders' "collective privacy" (thus creating embarrassment and uneasiness when observed by outsiders). Manifesting skeptical self-knowledge of collective defects, it also often scandalously perverts these negative auto-stereotypes into positive ones, still with a peculiar emotional ambivalence: between pleasure, shame, and joyful misuse of the official pomp, between familiarity and aggression against the West, between embarrassment and laughter.

An important difference, however, is the fact that in the situation, described above, the agency in power is multiplied: popular Balkan culture is engaged in discursive interactions (or rather battles) with more then two combatants. On this battle field, relics of pre-modern identities still question the ultimate power of national "high" cultures, while the national high cultures passionately reject the apparent Balkan similarities (cultivating simultaneously nesting Balkanisms). These high cultures are still engaged—each for its own sake—in a vain struggle against the arrogance of Western Balkanism. In turn Balkanism, as a variant of a colonial discourse, has to cope with the new discourses in power: cultural globalism, postcolonialism, and multiculturalism. The trained ear can still perceive discursive fights under the current—like *basso contionuo* in baroque music—echoing the battle between Occident and Orient, Christianity and Islam.

In a historically unresolved competition like this one, where the agencies of cultural authority continue to challenge each other, the symbolic economy is not limited to the interaction between the "official idiom" of a single national state and the multiple everyday uses (as Herzfield suggests). It rather resembles: a struggle among a multitude of official ideologies, cognitive strategies, and competing idioms on a contested field. Therefore the field itself is vague, full of alternative niches and fissures.

Accordingly, the intimate interaction between Balkan pop culture and all these cultural authorities resembles a multi-screen trickster performance more than it does a calm, everyday use and appropriation. The main difference between it and Herzfield's "cultural intimacy" consists in the fact that the popular culture in question scandalizes the official idioms (both high national culture and Western civilizational standards), rather than using and appropriating them. In its extremes, its regional intimacy joyfully breaches national borders, norms of politeness, and archaic taboos, aping a kind of momentous "Balkan identity," which is just a form of anarchic protest against any kind of identity and any kind of symbolic order.

46. Several years later I read the following lines in an internet journal: "People here talk with their whole bodies. They lean forward and touch their colleagues. When they meet or depart, they kiss each other on the cheeks and hug passionately." ("The Phlegm and the Anima" by Dr. Sam Vaknin, *Central Europe Review*, no. 4 [July 1999].)

7

The South Slav Identity and the Ultimate War-Reality

Ugo Vlaisavljević

We should not be misled by the paradox that nationalists claim their nations are rooted in antiquity and self-evidently natural, when they are in fact quite recent and novel constructs.[1]

In one of his last interviews, which he gave to Giancarlo Bosetti (1993), Karl Popper argued for intervention in Bosnia and for applying the "war on war" principle to the terrorism that had started to spread in the former Yugoslav region after the collapse of communism. To the question, "Why has this happened?" Popper responded by pointing out that nationalism has no solid ground:

Communism has been replaced by this ridiculous nationalism. I say ridiculous, because it sets against each other peoples who are virtually all Slav. The Serbs are Slavs, the Croats are Slavs. And the Bosnians are also Slavs, converted to Islam.[2]

But ground had been given to this ridiculous nationalism:

The terrible thing is that we in the West have caved in by allowing things to develop as they have done in the last two years—with massacres, murders, heinous acts. We have given up the key elements of a Western policy and abandoned our own principles, starting with the principle of peace itself. We should not have done that; we should not have surrendered. It was a terrible mistake that exposes us to a huge danger, because the weapons and means of destruction have increased.[3]

By "a huge danger" Popper has in mind "Sakharov's hydrogen bombs" which are "circulating in the world." He thinks that Western peoples should be aware of the situation: "A nuclear threat to us all may come out of the Balkans." His memories of Sarajevo in 1914, and of the event that triggered the First World War, are apparently still vivid. He cherishes no illusion that "after what has happened" there is any "compromise which can lead to peace." The most important principle of peace, and in this case, the only effective one, is the "war on war" principle. Popper refers to Kant and his famous "Perpetual Peace" essay in which "the idea of war fought against war"[4] can already be found, but also to the First World War, when, "even during the years of fighting," this idea "had made its appearance."

At that moment, in the second year of the Bosnian war, the conflict seemed irreversible, leading far beyond any possibility of compromise that might bring peace to the country. "That is absolutely impossible," affirmed Popper. To that the interviewer insisted: "What with the attempts to reach a political agreement about the map of Bosnia?" Popper's reply was categorical: "You could never get peace inside a country by reaching a compromise with the criminals."[5]

Peace should be imposed by Western countries in their own interest. It must be established with weapons. Popper reminds us of the lesson of the twentieth century: "Peace on earth (at least until it has been established once and for all) needs to be backed up with weapons." Yet he did not forget the painful lesson the Americans learned in Vietnam: "It is a mistake to fight for difficult terrain in a foreign country. You can do that in the desert but not in the Balkans."[6] Popper was right: Bosnia has an extremely difficult terrain. For that reason, he suggested withdrawing all ground troops and intervening militarily from the air. Because Bosnia is no desert, peace could come to its people only from the sky! Obsessed with their ridiculous nationalism, the Serbs, Croats, and Bosnians will "go on massacring each other as long as we allow them to do it. They will stop only if we seriously discourage them."[7]

Popper had a clear picture of the proposed action:

Anyway aid, medicines—even doctors, if necessary—can be parachuted in. People can be carried to safety by helicopter. And a lot more can be done from the air, such as hitting armored cars and any kind of heavy weapon.[8]

Subsequent events proved him right. Although the ground troops were never withdrawn, permanent air-lifts were established in some towns in Bosnia, bringing food, medicine, heavy weapons, and from time to time even doctors and politicians. Finally, after several long years, an air intervention, though limited and doubtlessly belated, successfully lifted the siege of Sarajevo. The new political map of Bosnia all sides signed in Dayton was partly the outcome of this "aerial survey."

Now we have set the stage for the purpose of our inquiry. However, it lacks one important element: television. On several different occasions, Popper highlighted the role of television in the Bosnian conflict. In the interview with Bosetti, he accused television of contributing to what he called surrender in Western countries; that is to say, "the key elements of Western policy," most importantly the principle of peace, was abandoned. In reply to the question of how this surrender came about, Popper pointed to television:

The only explanation I find is that what we do not manage to see in the real world by means of television, it appears not to exist for us. The massacres have been out of sight for us during these years, and so it is as if they had not taken place.[9]

Television kept the Western public from viewing the cruelties of war. This amounted to the annihilation of the war itself. In his article devoted to the dangerous box of images, published in France a few years later under the title "Une loi pour la télé-vision," Popper stresses television's "colossal power," and its pretense of replacing even "the voice of God."[10]

The Bosnian conflict was much more present on television in the following years, but Popper would no doubt claim that it remained "out of sight" for the Western public despite or even due to its televisual presentation. Because it constantly pro-duces violence on an enormous scale, while making fiction reality in a fascinating manner, as Popper understands it television cannot "transmit" to us any violence taking place in the real world without making it fictitious, customary, and all-too-human. When shown on television, any real event suffers a sort of distortion, since it is fiction that has recently become so vivid and real that all reality has been absorbed into it. Its power is colossal and godlike because it creates and annihilates wars.

In Bosseti's book, the interview on Bosnia is directly followed by one on tele-vision. These interviews are actually two parts of the same conversation, and both argue for what Popper has confessed at the beginning of his talk:

There are two things I have at heart: one is Bosnia, and the risk that international relations will degenerate into nuclear catastrophe; the other is television and its consequences, which are hastening the moral corruption of mankind.[11]

The leitmotif of the second piece, titled "Television Corrupts Mankind. It Is Like War," is that television plays today the same role war played yesterday: it intro-duces violence into society. While yesterday "crime was a sensational exception," today it is something "we constantly have before our sight and our mind."[12] Tele-vision makes people blind and insensitive to the world's tragedies. Its incompara-ble seductive power is out of control even in the democratic world, where all powers should be brought under control. As television has reached its full impact only recently, few people are aware that it threatens their lives. Children are most exposed to television, as are those living in underdeveloped and undemocratic parts of the world. In such countries, television has become the principal tool of rule, and tele-vised propaganda has a tremendous impact on people's lives.

Was it not Popper who actually suggested that the ridiculous Balkan nationalisms were in a way the product of local television? What else but such a powerful tool, given over to irresponsible politicians and criminals, could turn fiction into reality? Moreover, Western television has made things even worse: It has allowed things to happen by making them not happen at all. The first television has turned fiction into reality, and the second has reversed the process. It is difficult to say which is worse. By intermingling reality and fiction, they both have helped evil do its business.

Nonetheless, Popper seems to share the widespread opinion that *nationalism should be attacked primarily as a fiction*. Like so many analysts, Popper sees in present-day Balkan ethno-nationalism illusions, fascinations, and seductions to which many local people have succumbed. The imaginary, to use a Lacanian term, is thus considered to offer a *via regia* to this kind of "perverted reality." Consequently, television is regarded as a principal instrument of mass manipulation, and its critique becomes the focus of any serious attempt at explanation. No wonder nationalist politics flourish today, when television and war appear to be such close relatives. It is perhaps *this peculiar politics of images* that explains the increasingly evident interdependence of war and television. If television represents a *locus of fictitious reality*, and war represents a *locus of the reality of fiction*, then nationalism might be considered the point of transgression and transformation between the two.

This popular approach seems to run the risk of intermingling two mutually irreducible realities: the Western reality and the Balkan reality. However, it is very important not to confuse the reality of television, which is a famously virtual reality, with the war reality that is so characteristic of the Balkans.[13] The present-day Balkan ethno-nationalism possesses a particular *realism* that deserves our attention. However, to reveal that ethno-nationalism's sense and logic, to understand why the majority of the people who suffered from the last Balkan wars viewed it as justified and legitimate, requires a *symbolic analysis*. Lacan has argued against reducing psychoanalysis to the imaginary order, pleading that instead of fixating on deceptive surface appearances, psychoanalysis should restore its symbolic character. In the end, all analysis is symbolic, and the imaginary is available for such analysis, since it is not chaotic but always already structured by the symbolic order. Images must be translated into words if they are to be interpreted. Lacan warned analysts: "The imaginary is decipherable only if it is rendered into symbols."[14]

The symbolic analysis we are proposing here, within an anthropological rather than a psychoanalytical framework—although we should be placed at the *locus* characteristic of psychoanalysis, at its "place opened to the Real"[15]—detects a different reality, diametrically opposed to the Western one and produced within a different semiotic regimen. The typical Western reality is the product of a regimen of metaphors, of the Sign reduced to the Signifier, as well as of a developed and expansionist semiotic economy. The typical Balkan reality is the outcome of a regimen of proper names, of the sign in good "metaphysical" condition, as well as of an underdeveloped, limited economy. In contrast to the Western reality, quite convincingly depicted by Baudrillard,[16] we will outline the Balkan, notably the Bosnian, war reality. Baudrillard's grand tableau of the new, *orbital ere* that has recently begun, in which "the man, with his Earth, with his territory, with his body"[17] are now being satellized, in which a society of proliferation is created, with a trans-economy and an infinite semiologization, will stand in the background of the analysis.

Popper, speaking of the war in Bosnia, gave us a Baudrillard-like portrait of the encounter between two realities, or two semiotic universes, one of which seems to be settled in the sky, and the other on the earth. From his "down to earth" account, we have borrowed our two basic leitmotifs: South Slav identity and the lack of reality. It is South Slav identity that reveals the lack of reality in the raging ethnonationalism.

As we are going to speak of Balkan *ethnie*, and particularly of South Slav *ethnie*, we need first to define *the typical Balkan ethnic format*. Following Anthony D. Smith's general classifications of all ethnic communities, the subject of Balkan reality could be described primarily as an *incorporated ethnie* or as an *ethnic "minority."* Smith includes in this particular set, "various subjugated Eastern European ethnic communities like the Serbs, Croats, Bulgarians, Greeks, Czechs, and Slovaks."[18] What is most characteristic of these *ethnie* is their guiding ideal of "ethnic homeland or territory of belonging," which has replaced the notion of a "political kingdom and dynastic state." Smith has thus suggested that the prolonged subjugation of Balkan peoples territorialized an ideal that was initially more political.

Secondly, the Balkan *ethnie* are designated *vertical-demotic communities* rather than *lateral-aristocratic* ones. They are characterized by the "ability to mobilize powerful sentiments of attachment and self-sacrificing action on behalf of the community."[19] This is due to the fact that frequent wars have helped cement strong social ties.

Thirdly, the Balkan *ethnie* may be classed as *"frontier" ethnie* whose "frontier" position is partly *geopolitical* and partly *strategic-economic*.[20] Their difficult geopolitical position forces them into constant popular mobilization and "mass conscript" military engagements,[21] which distinguish them from *lateral-aristocratic ethnie* whose engagement remains "elite professional."[22]

We could also note other important traits (for example, the predominance of the Little Tradition, combined with the absence of strong cultural homogeneity).

But these few parameters hopefully suffice for our purposes. According to the first parameter, that of incorporation, which seems to imply the greatest number of habitual traits, we might conclude that the smaller a Balkan community is, the more typical it appears. Consequently, in this context, we will treat the small South Slav nations as the most typical Balkan nations.

What seems to have decisively molded the typical character of these *ethnie* is their pre-modern condition. This is a long-lasting condition that results from being incorporated into an alien political, social, and cultural universe after an invasion. We can describe it roughly as follows: The war has already taken place; the gravest *external* threat belongs to the past, and it ended in defeat. The majority of the population has survived the conqueror's military campaign; the traumatic events of the war presented a turning point in the communal history. These events are vividly present in the collective memory of subjugated people; their narrative elaboration started during or immediately after the war, mainly through the oral traditions characteristic of vernacular cultures, including epic poems, ballads, legends, and the like.

To the imperial power of the conqueror corresponds an immense seductive power of his culture. To write a history of a Balkan community, especially at the moment when this community regards its history mainly as an ethnogenesis, is to fabricate a narrative in which the greatest danger is not war but its long-term consequence. For the Balkan *ethnie*, especially smaller ones, peace was often more perilous than war. Cultural assimilation brings about the symbolic death of the whole community. This death takes its time, for it comes after a lengthy and scrupulous *cultural preparation*. During the time of peace, the threat of extermination becomes increasingly imperceptible, and to that extent it is reinforced. Consequently, the habitual pre-modern condition of Balkan *ethnie* is treacherous insofar as ethnic incorporation may end in an extinct language, an abjured religion, and lost proper names. There is a sense of impending doom: the worst is yet to come.

The semiotic analysis of the contemporary Balkan ethno-nationalism, into which we would like to make some inroads here, assigns to war the role of main cause or, more precisely, of principle of explanation. When one speaks about the Balkan region, no matter what kind of story one tells, one always refers, in one way or another, to a war or wars and their consequences. However, when one looks for a principle by which to explain current reality, one rarely takes war itself as a point of reference. Each war has one or more causes, which may stretch deep into the past and which may claim the war as their result. On the one hand, war is always an effect; in a sense, it is the effect of all effects. On the other hand, war can also

be seen as the cause of all causes. It might be said, at the price of oversimplification, that when we try to explain war as an effect of numerous causes, we tend
to look at it from the perspective of a large nation involved in the war, that is,
an "imperialist aggressor." Conversely, when we try to explain war as a cause of
numerous effects, we look at it from the perspective of a small nation that has been
victimized by a sudden campaign.

Viewed from this second perspective, war appears to be the event that constitutes
small nations, especially their social, cultural, and political beings, or their collective selves. Balkan ethnic cultures are *epic cultures*, that is, cultures narratively constituted by war. Moreover, the historical, cultural, and political reality of small
nations is markedly a war reality. War usually brings about a shift in the dominant
cultural code of small nations, serving as a trigger for a lasting constitution, or, more
precisely, for a whole series of reconstitutions that affect the culture and reality of
the collective self.

War constitutes small nations in two ways: First, war forces one to face its reality
(and this appears to the defeated party as an ultimate reality); second, it incorporates the small *ethnie* into the large one. In fact, these events are one and the same,
and the result is that one faces reality at the very moment when it is to the smallest extent one's own cultural reality. The collective trauma of the last battle,[23] as
well as the resulting military occupation, is reinforced by the inscription of the
victor's symbolic order on the lost territory. Battles made the earth tremble, while
foreign culture moved away much of the solid ground. Ethnic space no longer
corresponds to inherited territory, or, to put it more cautiously, these correspond
less than before.

War is not just a military clash but an experience of cultural deprivation as well.[24]
This deprivation, suffered by the defeated *ethnie*, opens up a gap in that nation's
symbolic universe, or a wound in its spiritual body. After the Real intrudes, the
small *ethnie* begins to be exposed to an irresistible symbolic intrusion, and this
happens at a time when it is in a fragile condition and requires all its symbolic tools
to be recovered, that is, to elaborate the first intrusion. War describes a point
of transgression between two cultural patterns, a lacuna that will attract intensive
symbolization within at least one of them.

No one has explored *the characteristic war reality of the Balkans by focusing on
the constitution of a collective self and its own world*. This may be because the
event of war has never been taken into consideration as such. This event, in turn,
has been ignored because the process of self-constitution was overlooked. It seems
that the periodic re-constitutions of an *ethnie* can be explained properly only

through a war event, and war becomes noticeable as the event *par excellence* only if we pay attention to the condition of the self in question. The war event reveals that the ethnic self has an imaginary and a symbolic body (cultural corpus) that make up its (subjective) reality. This double body and its real world reveal, in turn, that the war is an event of self-metamorphosis.

The defeated ethnic community experiences the loss of its territory as the loss of its grip on reality. At no price must it completely lose its territory. Nationalism, as a collective movement of ethnic resistance and cultural restoration,[25] is also the way to maintain and regain the lost reality, collectively perceived as unquestionable and concrete. It is a struggle against the illusion that the enemy's imposed culture, and most of all his language, cover over reality. Ethnic resistance has the task of turning the reality of that enemy culture into fiction, and turning illusion, that is, the cultural reality that is threatened by disappearance, into reality.

Intensive post-war narrative production, which constructs the war reality as the reality of all realities, seeks not only to preserve the memory of an age when the territory belonged to the ethnic community, but also to maintain its symbolic force by recovering its lost reality. Its whole language is subordinated to the function of naming the ethnic community's proper land.

The post-war period in small Balkan nations—and on this peninsula, each historical period is, in a certain essential way, a post-war, if not a war period—is marked by a vigorous process of re-territorialization.[26] This is an attempt to regain control of lost territory and to prevent the disappearance of reality. It is a semiotic, mainly narrative production or re-production of ethnic culture, which is governed, at least in the case of Balkan *ethnie*, by proper names, owing to their unquestionable referential force. The ethnic character of proper names—all proper names are the property of an ethnic community—reveals that they are toponyms, that is, proper names of a territory.

Re-territorialization at its height is a condition in which a given language almost exclusively refers to a territory. This means that every sentence, at least if it is forged in the predominant narrative genre and its phrase regimens, quotes or implies a proper name—an ethnic name of a threatened ethnic community.[27] The language that is threatened by disappearance is markedly referential.

The toponymization or landing (Baudrillard's famous *"aterrissage"*) of the language on its territory is marked by a strong tendency toward transforming all words into proper names and all proper names into toponyms. The language then sticks to the reality, leaning heavily on its territory. Only small ethnic cultures, on the verge of disappearance, reveal that their languages are rooted in the earth. These are languages whose speakers experienced the *postwar, postinvasion* appearance of other languages on their territory, confronting the whole family of ethnic names with the imminent danger of eradication. There is nothing strange in the fact that powerful cultures are expanding, that their influences are growing, and that their languages are penetrating into new lands. However, a small language cannot prevent, at least in the long run, the semiotic invasion and expropriation of its territory. The language of the conqueror, and his cultural idiom more generally, not only enters the land of the defeated minority but seeks to occupy the very *place of the conquered language*. In other words, the language of the intruder has a *strong toponymical claim*.

The referential function is reinforced through the incorporation of small ethnic communities into the larger one, establishing a bilingual situation in which two languages are in "exterior contact" and meet each other as two disparate cultural patterns or *myth-symbol complexes*.[28] In this situation, where the natural language appears as a stock of proper names, the small *ethnie* must obstruct translatability or symbolic exchangeability in order to survive. Attempts at translation trip over proper names, which are the words that most obstinately preserve the *ethnie's* reality. The collective linguistic experience of subjugation causes each word pronounced in the universe where the Other Language reigns to become emphatically "our word," "our name," or "our proper name" of *exclusively our reality*. Each encounter between the two languages occurs as a clash between two different proper names for the same referent.

Furthermore, if its use is brutally restricted, the minority language becomes ritualized and thus unveils its symbolic body. The natural language is so reduced to the myth-symbol complex that (most successfully) protects it. The language of a minority becomes literally *minor*. Owing to limited or lost cultural freedom, this language is semi-public or, at worst, no longer public. It becomes oppressively localized in its practice and its diffusion; its *locus* is to be found in shadows, shelters, and enclaves; at any moment it must be ready to give up its place to a "major" language; it obeys rigid rules about when and where it should be used; its edges and ramifications appear through the inexorable process of its suppression and extinction. It is in this process that toponyms proved to be the most stubborn stains of ethnic resistance.

The most proper names are the names of war heroes. By celebrating the names of its heroes who died in battle, the defeated *ethnie* not only preserves its past from oblivion but continues to defend its most precious ethnic territory. Each Balkan *ethnie* has its sacred territory, and it is usually a territory on which decisive battles took place. There, an indissoluble tie joins the symbolic universe of an *ethnie* to its territory. The place where the famous soldier was killed, where he *fell*, is a *place* where *a proper name* was inscribed *in the earth*.

The "beautiful death"[29] of a hero is a monumental historical event in the ethnic symbolization of a territory. On the symbolic map of an *ethnie*, battlefields lie at the heart of its territory, which is, in turn, completely marked by the graves of ances-tors.[30] In the mythical history of an enslaved people, all ancestors, even those who did not take part in famous battles, die a beautiful death and charge their sons with continuing the struggle to re-appropriate the territory where they fell. The whole territory is thus sacrosanct, as it belongs to an *ethnie*; and it belongs to that *ethnie* as an extended and multiplied battlefield. The battlefield contains a privileged semiotic agriculture: *It is the place where the most proper of all proper names are planted*. It is there that the remarkable referential power of ethnic symbolization should be demonstrated.

The earth appears to be the most protective shelter from invaders. Names planted in the earth assure that the *ethnie* is real, because they mark its property. Since the whole community depends for its survival on the preservation of that property, all future generations are assigned the task of erecting monuments and transmitting the names engraved in stones. Conversely, circulating proper names is a way to preserve the territory. Thus, the transmission of ethnic names inherently includes territory (because of the cruel war reality, anthroponyms are territorialized in the conscience of the people). This process naturalizes ethnic culture—to say nothing of an *ethnic imaginary* permeated with agricultural and geo-mythologies, which include geological, botanical, and animal families of metaphors—so that the trans-mission of names and territory looks like the hydrologic cycle in nature. The referential potential of the battlefield is particularly impressive because territory prevents the *referent* from disappearing under the *signified*, or the former from being reduced by the latter. For a whole symbolic universe, the battlefield repre-sents the place of intrusion of the Real. That is why Balkan ethnic cultures are so mythical. The greatest historical events mark places of feverish mending: Numer-ous coats of collective imagination and a dense texture of symbolisation conceal a deep wound.

Recent Balkan history has shown that the battlefield can resurrect the reality of a mythical world and restore the ethnic form of quite modernized communities. Owing to their continuing epic tradition, or to their perpetually reproduced war reality, or, most likely, to their *topologic cycle*, the small Balkan communities still live in the regimen of the *sign in good condition*.[31] If Lyotard is right that moder-nity is the age of "withdrawal of the reality"[32] because it lacks "a solid anchorage of language in the referent,"[33] then these communities still live in a pre-modern reality. They owe the striking ethnic character of their cultures to the preserved referential capacity of their languages.

By keeping alive the memory of the most recent war reality, the community preserves its ethnic name. As long as this reality is alive, the ethnic name is not interchangeable with a foreign ethnic name of an enemy. In long-lasting ethnic incorporations, the injunction not to lose one's proper name, not to allow it to disappear, is considered an injunction not to die. An *ethnie* may survive even if its members have accepted a foreign language into their proper names (as it happens in the case of religious conversions), under the condition that their mother language is not forgotten. In that case, it is the whole language that becomes an invaluable stock of ethnonyms no matter what its words designate. Owing to chronic pressure to assimilate, ethnic continuity is gradually reduced to the continuity of name-transmission. The increasing impoverishment and weakening of the "myth-symbol" complex makes the already slight tread of the patronymic all the more fragile. Actually, the resistance of a symbolic cultural body depends on the totality of previous assimilations it has absorbed. A former enemy's reality is never as alien as that of the present-day enemy. The *ethnie* survives through a strategy of belated adoption: what was unacceptable in a previous incorporation, today is built into the ethnic culture as its most genuine content, under the condition that the enemy is not the same. Premodern wars are inscribed in Balkan ethnic histories as pompous introductions to a series of acculturations, which in turn form numerous layers of cultural sediment. We recognize these wars as the scars that mark the numerous, vertiginous, metamorphoses of a collective self. Ethnic identity is to be considered permanent and imperishable only if it has poor content or lacks content altogether, that is, if it is to be reduced to the continuity of ethnic names. In reality, ethnic identity is an abstract axis around which the collective self, which incessantly metamorphosizes, turns. Proper names retain their referents in all possible worlds.

The modern age has made even more manifest this struggle for self-preservation through constant changes, imparting to the process a fascinating dynamism and vigor. The continuity of the collective self depends on its ability to adapt to new circumstances. The self re-constitutes and reproduces itself because of suddenly changed circumstances. Each reconstitution is an attempt to escape extinction.

It is only upon the "final liberation" of the South Slav *ethnie*—the smallest Balkan *ethnie* that presumably had the most difficult past—that we realize that its symbolic struggle to survive and to preserve the basic, distinctive features of its inherited cultures did not consist in obstinately preserving cultural remnants allegedly produced at the beginning of the time. We have still not, however, reached the end of the illusion of the complete ethnic self that resists all historical changes for millennia. After all, the war reality persists in the triangular heart of the former Yugoslavia; in fact, it is more vigorous than ever.

Given the frequent wars, the modern history of this region does not differ significantly from its tumultuous past. Present-day ethno-nationalism owes all its power and attraction to the war, which broke out after socialism began to crumble. The reign of communism was the result of mass suffering and partisan victory in the Second World War. The so-called first Yugoslavia, which had the beginnings of a capitalist mode of production, was created after the First World War through the dissolution of Great empires. Bosnia and Herzegovina entered modernity when Austro-Hungarian troops entered its territory. Perhaps the most noticeable fact concerning the modern age in the Balkans is that *pre-modern, mostly lost wars* have been replaced by *victorious "national liberation wars."* Owing to these wars, small nations have become, for the first time, the genuine creators of their own histories and realities. Most people understand this to be the time of a final, long-sought affirmation of their collective Being, which once, at the beginning of history, had been free and sovereign. For these people, the modern political idea of emancipation has become inseparable from the striking historical notion of the violent upheaval of a subjugated people.

Let us put aside, for a moment, the complex local context of modern times and notice that almost all recent liberations, whether political, economic, social, cultural, or sexual, were *ethnic* in the final analysis because they took place through war or owing to war. Numerous pre-modern wars created a reality in which the most insistent demand for liberation comes from ethnic communities. The legitimacy of any other demand was proven on the basis of this millennial demand that was handed down through the chain of generations.

In this respect, it is instructive to consider Tito's communist ideology—today so often discredited on account of its modernistic antitraditionalism—of *ethnicism* during and after the Great National Liberation War. Even superficial analysis shows that almost all of Titoism's key concepts, figures, and symbols were actually couplets, in which the modern political reality was associated with the ancient ethnic one. It seems that the "political psychology" (per Bertrand Russell) of Yugoslav communism, its popular appeal, consisted in turning now *recto* side, now *verso* side of these ideological couplets. It was important that any modern political vocabulary or activity be able to present itself as a sort of *translation* of traditional ethnic survival practices, particularly their way of making sense of reality. The fusion of the two discourses, two vocabularies, two worlds of symbols, was based on triple denotative pairing:

1) the last war was conceived at once as "communist revolution" and "national (i.e., ethnic) liberation war";

2) the subject of current history is at once "the working class/all working people" and "our nations" (i.e., our ethnic communities); and

3) the postwar reality is an example of both "free communist society" and "cohabitation in brotherhood and unity."

A hypothesis might be advanced that in all of Eastern Europe, the adoption of communism after the Second World War bore a strong ethnic mark. The majority of people warmly welcomed the idea of revolution, at least in the beginning, not only because of the strong ideological pressure or the lure of industrialization and electrification, but also because of the collective "ethnic experience" of the replacement of cultural paradigms through war. These two revolutions, industrial and cultural, provided the semblance of social/proletarian revolution. Fraternization during the war even furnished abundant evidence of one. For a long time, communism successfully prevented society from feeling the major effects of modernization: *individualization*, *disenchantment* and *the reign of instrumental reason*. To that extent communism, at least in this part of the world, might be characterized as a modern strategy against modernity, a strategy at the bottom of which *ethnic resistance* is to be found.

Today, South Slav ethno-nationalism (a declared politics of ethnic resistance) more or less directly opposes modernity,[34] but in reality it builds upon the achievements of its predecessor,[35] being obliged to be even more radical. Essentially, both are regimes of defense against the perilous impact of modernity on the ethnic community, and against that community's perfidious individualization.[36] What differentiates them most is the metamorphosis in the understanding of the ethnic that has occurred in the meantime.

Tito's communism and present day ethno-nationalism both promised the end of pre-modern incorporation and the release of the ethnic self after its long incubation. Contrary to the accusations of the ethno-nationalists, the Tito regime did not neglect or reject the demand for final ethnic liberation, but rather radicalized it by identifying it with the communist demand for social liberation from exploitation. To adopt proletarian anti-imperialism as a revolutionary theory of ethnic resistance was at last to return to the most original culture beneath all sediments of assimilation, and to release the oldest ethnic Self. The identity of this ethnic proto-Self, according to the testimony of the preserved axis of ethnic names, is *South Slav*. All of the region's ethnic communities belong to a large ethnic community of South Slavs and, therefore, should live in "brotherhood and unity." However, this injunction of the communists in power did not have *ethnic substance*, and so it was *gradually reduced to an abstract political demand*. Actually, the proto-Self was found to have but bare bones, since no proto-culture remained historically operative. The urn containing the ashes of ancient pagan cultures, opened after the last liberation war, turned out not to contain any truly vivid flame. The discrepancy between such an archaic ethnic identity and the existing ethnic cultures *prevented the development of any South Slav ethnicism*. Given their shared, axial identity, the preserved ethnic cultures are belated, behind the time that counts for ethnic constitution, and on that basis, they were at least to a certain degree marginalized. A tendency to paganize the existing ethnic cultures and to reduce them to folklore was strongly marked during the communist era. To privilege traditional customs and rites over religious culture was part of a strategy aimed not to efface inherited ethnic differences but to bunch them up tightly, because the ethnic communities were falling apart precisely in their religious capacities. Initially, the dominant ideology's militant atheism actually protected the proto-ethnic identity from its subsequent inscription on the ethnic culture, an inscription that would conceal its delay.

The modern process of liberation did not lead to the harmonization of major ethnic differences, and still less to their absorption. Instead, the pale proto-ethnic identity was inexorably dissolved in the far more real identities professed to be derivative or *sub-ethnic*. South Slav ethnicism never appeared. The successful Yugoslav *national construction* could be only a poly-ethnic, by no means mono-ethnic one. Still, the Yugoslav Federation was considered, at least in its heroic days, to be something more than a *political community* or a *defense alliance* of threatened ethnic communities. It was a unity in brotherhood, or the unity of a big family built on allegedly common ethnic origins. However, it was *inter-ethnic union*, but not *ethnic community*, strictly speaking. Tito's slogan "brotherhood and unity" meant in the first place the brotherhood and unity of already recognized ethnic communities: Croats, Serbs, Slovenes, et cetera. Only then, on the basis of this communitarian mediation, did it address the individual members of the Yugoslav society.

The main political assumption here was that the people already lived in brotherhood, but within historically limited communities that should be enlarged. The slogan contained an injunction: "Be brothers to others who appear to be your distant relatives!" And at the same time it was a warning: "Don't forget the solidarity forged in the last war!" It was thus suggested that the brotherhood from the time of war should be maintained, and that the inherited ethnic brotherhood should be enlarged, which is to say that the interethnic brotherhood germinated in the war should be completed so as to encompass all the people. Global ethnic solidarity was associated with the solidarity of soldiers in the Second World War, while the future was associated with the past. To fulfill the promise of the revolution, to build the classless society, was to work on *the reconstitution of a primordial ethnic community*, subsequently divided through numerous invasions and a long history of foreign governance. The project of political democratization of the society did not actually differ from the project of ethnic resocialization. The free human society was conceived as an organic community after the model of ethnic community. Tito's politics were essentially *ethno-politics* of the *large semi-ethnic community*, that is, of the South Slav community affected by a certain *ethnic lack*. At the time, such a community seemed, from the point of view of the already constituted communities, to be *supra-ethnic*, and, from the point of view of their members, *sub-ethnic*. The term *ethno-politics* should indicate that the communist politics were a supplement to the absent South Slav ethnicism, while the ethnicism of the constituted ethnic communities was a supplement to a communism that lacked a proletariat (and in fact addressed peasants). The attempt to amalgamate the ethnic communities was an undertaking of which only an ethno-politics was capable, and it implied the involvement of a pure political instance that had no reality. The communist ideology provided such an instance, one that transcended the boundaries of any particular *ethnie*. To detect it, simply ask where leaders and party officials spoke from when they addressed the Yugoslav *ethnie*. Their discursive appropriation of the proletariat principally obstructed their identification by proper names, rendering them Yugoslav in the ethnic, and not only the political, sense of the word. It is exactly at the symbolic axis of the proto-ethnic name that the discursive locus of the most important political designation was placed. The public discourse, for all the existing *ethnie*, almost exclusively used the expression "*naši narodi*" (our *ethnie*), a formula that could be used only from the non-ethnic, trans-territorial, orbital perspective of the proletariat.

It seems that South Slav unity could not outlast the vivid memories of the last world war, or the hope of creating a *proletarian culture* that would be a true common culture for all Yugoslav people, replacing the lost proto-culture. In reality, this union has lasted as long as the *ethnic illusion* of a radical liberation from the colonial past; as long as the interethnic brotherhood forged in war; and as long as the geopolitical need for a defensive alliance among the smallest Balkan nations.

The basically ethnic character of Tito's communism comes from the narrative and magical nature of its *constitutive political myth*. The great narrative of the Second World War, the so-called National Liberation epoche, was actually a myth that encompassed the myth-symbol complexes of all the fraternal *ethnie*. Tito's *political religion* owed its popularity in the first place to the spell cast by the cherished war stories that were constantly retold in public speeches.

Present day ethno-nationalism, which pretends to recapitulate the whole history of liberation, especially its teleology and eschatology, as the last re-birth of the ethnic community, reveals a strange tendency: *Modernity ethnologizes*, bringing about ever more archaic and authentic cultures.[37] The new regime exposes the *ethnic illusion* of its predecessor as a gigantic fraud, depicting the famous brotherhood as treason, communist ideology as a disguised imperial culture, the reality of the World War as a fiction, and so on. Ethno-nationalism became more attractive to the masses as it proved to be just as capable as its predecessor of drawing on the strongest cards: the axis of the ethnic name, *mithomoteurs* of the ethnic tradition, and the reality of the last interethnic war. It will be a long time before this interpretation of the war-reality becomes fiction. To conclude with Popper: Bosnia has an extremely difficult terrain.

Notes

1. Anthony D. Smith, *Nationalism and Modernism* (London: Routledge, 1998), 120.

2. Giancarlo Bosetti, *The Lesson of This Century: With Two Talks on Freedom and the Democratic State* (London: Routledge, 1997), 53.

3. Ibid., 53, 54.

4. Ibid., 51.

5. Ibid., 54, 55.

6. Ibid., 54.

7. Ibid.

8. Ibid.

9. Ibid.

10. Karl Popper, *La télévision: un danger pour la démocratie* (Paris: Anatolia Editions, 1994), 36.

11. Bosetti, 56.

12. Ibid., 58.

13. Reda Bensmaïa, "La guerre du Golf a bien eu lieu: Lettre ouverte à J. Baudrillard," *Intersignes*, automne 1992, nos. 4–5. Paris, 71–87, 77.

14. Ibid.; Jacques Lacan (with W. Granoff), "Fetishism: the symbolic, the imaginary and the real" in *Perversions: Psychodynamics and Therapy*, ed. M. Balint (New York: Random House; London: Tavistock, 1956), 265–276.

15. Serge Leclaire, *Démasquer le réel: Un essai sur l'objet en psychanalyse* (Paris: Editions du Seuil, 1971), 32.

16. Jean Baudrillard, *La Transparence du Mal* (Paris: Editions Galilée, 1990).

17. Ibid., 37.

18. Anthony D. Smith, *The Ethnic Origins of Nations* (Oxford: Blackwell 1986), 44.

19. Ibid., 83.

20. Ibid., 84.

21. Ibid., 74.

22. Ibid., 76.

23. Claude Romano, *L'événment et le monde* (Paris: Presses universitaires de France, 1998), 150–155.

24. Jean-Luc Nancy, "La surprise de l'événment," *Dialogue*, international issue 1–2, Sarajevo, 1995.

25. Smith, *The Ethnic Origins of Nations*, 50.

26. Gilles Deleuze and Felix Guattari, *What Is Philosophy?* (London: Verso, 1994), chap. 4 "Geophilosophy," 85–113.

27. Jean-François Lyotard, *The Differend: Phrases in Dispute*, translated by G. van den Abbeele (Minneapolis: University of Minnesota Press, 1988), 137.

28. Smith, *The Ethnic Origins of Nations*, 57–68.

29. Lyotard, *The Differend*, 99.

30. Ivan Čolović, "L'éspace ethnique et la mort: Essai de la thanatologie politique," *Ethnologia Balkanica*, vol. 1 (Sofia: Prof. Marin Drinov Academic Publishing House, and Muenster: Waxmann Verlag, 1997), 178–182.

31. Jean Baudrillard, *Pour une critique de l'économie politique du signe* (Paris: Gallimard, 1972), 194–199.

32. Jean-François Lyotard, *Le postmoderne expliqué aux enfants: Correspondance 1982–1985* (Paris: Editions Galilée, 1988), 24.

33. Ibid., 10.

34. Jocelyne Philippe and Streiff-Fenart Poutignat, *Théories de l'ethnicité* (Paris: Presses Universitaires de France, 1995), 28–30.

35. Olivier Ladislav Kubli, *Du nationalisme yougoslave aux nationalismes post-yougoslaves* (Paris and Montréal: L'Harmattan, 1998).

36. Pierre Clermont, *Le Communisme à contre-modernité* (Paris: Presses Universitaires de Vincennes, 1993), 175.

37. Clifford Geertz, *The Interpretation of Cultures* (London: Fontana Press, 1993), 260.

8

The Impossible Escape: Romanians and the Balkans

Adrian Cioroianu

It seems that the harder life is in the Balkans, the stronger the desire to live some-where else—as far from the Balkans and as close to the West as possible, away from this politically, economically, and mentally stigmatized region. To put it in a less rhetorical manner, this has been the Romanians' collective drama for the last 150 years; it is as much the drama of those Romanians who pretend to be concerned about the real or possible destiny of their people, as of those who show indifference toward abstract collective dramas but at the same time seek historical alibis for their eternal lamentations.

Atlas, Sisyphus, or *Hero in a Comedy of Humors*

Are Romanians the only Balkan people in this situation? Certainly not. And yet, instead of making things easier, this simple finding complicates them. It is my belief that the Romanians are but one of many Southeast European peoples who endeavor, sometimes tragically and sometimes comically, to escape their geographical condition, or in other words, to shake off this cliché. I think that the Balkan person is not some mythological hero like Atlas or Sisyphus; he does not carry his own world on his shoulders, nor is he quite willing to push it up the slope of history. The first image that usually comes to the Romanian intellectual's mind when he wants to visualize his Balkan destiny is one that pertains rather to animated cartoons or silent comedy films from the golden age: a convict with an iron ball implacably chained to his leg.[1] I believe that this iron ball affixed to the Romanian ankle is the Balkan location itself. Although this experience may be common throughout Southeastern Europe, for obvious reasons, my concern here is the Romanian variant of the seemingly eternal escape from, and return to, the Balkans.

The Balkans or the Geographical (and Mental) Indecision

In order to escape, it is first advisable to explore and become acquainted with the space from which one seeks to be freed. This essential condition, even after two thousand years of more or less scientific geography, appears hard to fulfill. The boundaries of the Balkan region are still very unclear, and as a consequence, those who reside just inside the boundaries are left in an unenviable condition. They are concomitantly *inside* and *outside*, actors *in* and audience *at* a play; owing to this ambiguity, they neither perform nor watch very well.

Even today, those who popularize geography do not seem to have agreed upon the boundaries of the Balkans. According to a French variant (*Le Petit Larousse Illustré*, 1993), the Balkan Peninsula is limited in the north by the Sava river and the Danube; by this definition, the Balkans include such states as Albania, Bulgaria, Croatia, Greece, Slovenia, Turkey (the European portion), and Yugoslavia. Romania is not on the list of *these* Balkan countries. Since she is not a prisoner here, she does not need to escape.

And yet, in a venerable English variant with a generally unimpeachable reputation (*Encyclopaedia Britannica CD*, 1998), the Balkan peninsula has a slightly different composition: "In contemporary usage the term Balkans signifies the territory of the states of Albania, Bosnia and Herzegovina, Bulgaria, Croatia, Greece, Macedonia, Moldova, Romania, Slovenia, and Yugoslavia (Montenegro and Serbia); further the Balkan states are for the purposes of this article . . . the states of Slovenia, Croatia, Bosnia and Herzegovina, Yugoslavia (Serbia and Montenegro), Macedonia, Albania, Bulgaria, Romania, and Moldova," states "containing more than 60 million people, occupy an area of 257,400 square miles (666,700 square kilometers)." Therefore the difference between the Balkan peninsula and the Balkan region in the English perspective is Greece. The difference between the *French* Balkans and the *English* Balkans consists mainly of (including or excluding) two states: Turkey and Romania. Turkey is accepted by the French but not mentioned by the English, while Romania remains invisible in the Balkans for the French but is included by the English. True, the authors of the "Balkans" article in the *Encyclopedia Britannica* do not forget to mention that "there is considerable doubt as to whether Slovenia and Romanian Transylvania are Balkan in any meaningful sense," and they eventually admit that "the term also includes the European portion of Turkey, although Turkey is not a Balkan state").

All this is already complicated enough to fuel endless debates. However, in the United States (*Compton's Interactive Encyclopedia CD*, 1998) the Balkans "are generally understood to include Albania, Bulgaria, Greece, Turkey in Europe, Slovenia, Croatia, Bosnia and Herzegovina, Yugoslavia, Macedonia, and Romania." According to this American view "the Balkans cover an area of about 243,000 square miles (629,000 square kilometers) that is divided into many countries. . . . More than 75 million people live on the Balkan Peninsula."

In other words, the *American* Balkans are sensibly smaller than the *English* Balkans, excluding the lilliputian Republic of Moldavia, yet they are populated by an additional 15 million people. Certainly, these differences between *different Balkans* are not scandalous in themselves; however it is strange enough that, despite their being mentioned in international political discourses throughout this century, the Balkans still remain under the sign of indecision, prisoners of an incoherent geography.

"Frailty, Thy Name Is Balkans"

The problem is not the Balkans but so-called *Balkanism*. I think we should say it loud and clear: The real problem is not the indecision about the geographic location of the Balkans, but the stubborn persistence in overwhelming the term "Balkan" with more stereotypes than it can actually accommodate. Though the discourse on the Balkans suffers from a worrisome linearity, today's Balkans are not exactly the same Balkans of yesterday, and they will probably not be the Balkans of tomorrow, even if anyone thinks he knows them like the back of his hand. This place is merely a product of constant construction and reconstruction, in which process clichés are at least as important as concrete facts. The inhabitants of the Balkan states do not live within a mere geographic area, but within a space that undergoes intense ideological reconstruction. Approaching the Balkans from a cognitive perspective, you first encounter the *Balkan forest of symbols*,[2] which is, as Vintila Mihǎilescu puts it, the main obstacle and biggest challenge for whoever chooses this path. The *forest of symbols* is nothing other than the main referent in the ideological construction of the Balkans.

It is generally accepted that this uninterrupted (re)construction of the region has undergone several stages, which Maria Todorova outlines in *Imagining the Balkans:*[3] i) An *innocent error*, resulting from an inexact knowledge of this space, was taken over by tradition and perpetuated; ii) this purely geographical denomination, *The Balkans*, derived from the Turkish word for "mountain," then acquired what Mihǎilescu calls a number of "political, social, cultural and ideological supralicitations which at the centuries crossroads will give pejorative implications" to the word itself; iii) finally, the term "Balkan" became dissociated from the object it initially designed, which resulted in a rapid evolution of the term's pejorative meaning.

The developments of the twentieth century have favored the poly-semantic evolution of "the Balkans," and the dissociation between the term and the object it designates has led a word family to develop: "Balkans" and "Balkan" (i.e., "from the Balkans," pertaining to the Balkans, but also *primitive*, with strong reminiscences of *tribalism*, lagging *behind civilized Europe*); and also "Balkanization," a peculiar term for the fragmentation of ethnic groups (particularly by violent, almost "tribal" wars). Some of the modern encyclopedias (such as *Britannica*'s) claim that this fragmentation derives in part from the geography of the place. These terms, with their cluster of meanings, in a sense imply one another: the Balkan people seem by definition condemned to *Balkanization*. Moreover, with this virus of ethnic primitivism, they are able to contaminate all of Europe or even the entire world: "Apparently this is how things stand. All studies dealing with this subject offer enough examples of intellectual and political assertions and comments, which approximate *Balkanism* and *tribalism* to such an extent that they almost identify with each other. At a closer look, it seems that lately we have been in a 'post-evolutionist' stage: Balkan tribalism seems to tend to *barbarian* rather than *primitive*, which is entirely different."[4]

Two Thousand Years of Continuous Escape

Romanians do not easily accept their location on this map. Obviously, it is not the location itself that causes *historical migraines*, but the stereotypes with which it is associated. With its Orthodox majority, Romania has strong ties to the Christian East; but its Latinate language and ethnic roots also tie it to the Roman West. This is a dilemma with no apparent escape. One of the leitmotifs of Romanians' self-descriptions renders the country *as a Latin island in a Slavic ocean*. This nostalgia of origins has always produced an inexhaustible desire to escape geographic determinism.

We will see that this desire to escape the Balkans was and remains an early stage in the desire to escape Eastern Europe.

The First Attempt

One of the dominant theses in Romanian historiography is that the Romanian people were born north of the Danube. It's a thesis some neighboring historians contest, which is to be expected considering the ethnic and geographic indecision and suspicion that govern the area. Born north of the Danube, *at the foot of the Carpathian Mountains*, the archetypal Romanian is not Balkan, or at least he should not be considered so. Two thousand years ago, on the north-Danubian territory inhabited by Romanians today, there were Dacians, inhabitants of Dacia. Frankly speaking, the Romanians know very little about the Dacians, but their tender feelings toward them are remarkable—the more so as, according to historical tradition, the Dacians are considered Romanians' very first ancestors and Dacia, a sort of Romania *avant la lettre*. (If you meet a Romanian, don't tell him right away he is a son of Dracula; tell him he is the son of a Dacian-Roman. He'll appreciate the compliment much more.)

Historical reason leads us to believe that the Dacians were subsumed in the common Thracian background of the Southeastern European area. It is well known that we live under the imperialism of the imagination[5] and of the imaginary[6] as well. So if we accept a *north-Danubian Romania* preceding the *real Romania*, we have to accept south-Danubian Balkans preceding the Balkans of today; once we accept these *proto-Balkans*, we are to accept the proto-stereotypes tagging them as well. The spirit of the places seem always to have been stronger than the people of the places, so no matter how many qualities the Dacians might have in contrast to other Thracians,[7] the Balkan contamination of the inhabitants of Dacia had already been effected.

Fortunately, opportunity came soon enough—in the year 106 AD, when the Roman emperor Trajan finally defeated the Dacian King Decebal (about 87–106 AD) after his legionaries waged two tough wars against the Dacians in the Carpathians. Here are some technical details that will be useful later: The Roman army crossed the Danube on a bridge specially built by Apollodorus of Damascus, a famous architect of antiquity; Trajan established his headquarters at Drobeta, the city of Turnu Severin of today, in the southwest of the country. After the Romans' victory and Decebal's death (by suicide), Dacia became a province of the Roman Empire. "The Birth Certificate" of the Romanians is Trajan's Column commemorating his victory over the Dacians, which still can be seen in Rome. The vigorous colonists from the Empire and the veterans of the Roman army married—according to mythical history—beautiful Dacian women. The sons of these families were obviously the very seeds of the future Romania. Trajan's victory and the Roman colonists' settlement in Dacia were, according to the cliché, the West's very first civilizing arrival on the territory that would become Romania. Fire is known to be the favorite purifier in the imaginary world. Following the *fire* of the two wars between Dacia and Rome, the Romanian people were obviously *cleansed* of any Balkan memory.

With Trajan, the proto-Romanians had made their first successful attempt to escape proto-*Balkanism*.

King Carol the First, or, the Second Escape

And yet, the purity of origins has gradually been lost. In 271–275 AD, Emperor Aurelian decided to withdraw the Roman army and administration from Dacia and move it south of the Danube. The Romanians (that is, their ancestors, then proto-Romanians) were abandoned by the West—for the first but not the last time in their history!

The following more than 1600 years of domination by migratory peoples—Turks, Phanariots, and Russians—threatened the presumed *purity* of the Romanian Dacian-Roman origin. A new attempt to escape the Balkans became more necessary than ever.

The second—imaginary—de-Balkanization of the Romanians took place in the latter half of the nineteenth century, with, naturally, the second arrival of the West on Romanian territory. By a stratagem both brilliant and surprising, Moldavia and Wallachia were united under ruling prince Alexandru Ioan Cuza in January 1859. In 1862, the United (Independent) Principalities officially became Romania. The reformist attempts of united Romania's first ruler were remarkable, as were his privileged relations with his Balkan neighbors, especially the Serbian prince Mihailo Obrenović. But over the next few years, the sympathy he initially enjoyed diminished considerably, and there was nothing left to guarantee the survival of the 1859 Union past that of Cuza himself.

The political elite of the country understood that to guarantee its durability, it had to forge an alliance with an important European ruling family. That is why the Prussian prince Carol of Hohenzollern-Siegmaringen became Romania's ruler as Prince Carol I. Without knowing exactly where Romania was located on the map, and without ever getting a good command of the Romanian language, Carol I became the most efficient ruler Romania ever had, making important contributions to the modernization (i.e., *Westernization*) of the country.

The Balkans and *Balkanism* were once more yesterday's news; but the prince's foreign policy inevitably developed around the Balkans. More precisely, Romania found new allies in the "Balkan League," which reunited states like Serbia, Montenegro, Greece, and a Bulgarian revolutionary society; along with Romania, they coordinated a rebellion against the Ottoman Empire.

The assassination of Mihailo Obrenović in June 1869 put an end to the short-lived "Balkan League," but not to the endemic Oriental crisis. During the last

Russo-Turkish war (1877), Carol I's Romania sided with Russia and gained its independence (like Serbia and Montenegro), though the two Peace Congresses that followed (San Stefano in March and Berlin in July 1878) decided the fate of the Balkans in the usual manner: *over the heads of the Balkan peoples. Independent Romania* also becomes *bigger Romania*, by including Dobrudja. The *Bridge of Cernavodă*, which links Romania with this Southeastern province, was built by engineer Anghel Saligny and inaugurated in 1885; it would be the longest bridge in Europe for some time.

From this point onward, the *imaginary king* Carol I became as important as the real king. Leading his armed forces in the Independence War, the non-Romanian king of the Romanians joined the gallery of medieval Romanian princes and rulers who fought *for the Cross* against the Turks. Under the rule of this icy man, who was always smartly dressed and never seen laughing heartily, Romania became a kingdom in 1881. This time, the stakes were different: Every step toward modernization was perceived as a step away from the Balkans.

For anyone who embarks upon the study of the historical imaginary, the year 1906 represents a moment of tremendous importance in Romanian history.[8] By a chronological artifice—historians have always been good at this—the Roman emperor Trajan (the "father of the Romanian people") and the Romanian king Carol I shake hands across the centuries. The year 1906 was a year of anniversaries: On the one hand, two jubilees related to the royal house (forty years since the arrival of King Carol in the country on May 10, 1866, and twenty-five years since Romania became a kingdom on May 10, 1881); on the other hand, a jubilee related to "integral Romanianness" (eighteen hundred years since the Roman conquest of Dacia, or *the very first escape*). The most important leaders of opinion at that time univocally asserted that King Carol I had concluded masterfully a historical epoch initiated by Trajan, the archetypal founder.

The commemorative parchment document of May 1906 is imbued with these historical references: Emperor Trajan and King Carol are portrayed close together, surrounded by the most prominent Romanian medieval rulers; on the right side, one can see Trajan's Column, *the Romanians' birth certificate*, while at the bottom of the parchment a Roman legionary and the bridge over the Danube from Turnu Severin (in the southwest) are presented close to a *dorobantz* (a Romanian soldier from the war of 1877–78) and the bridge over the Danube from Cernavodă. The symbolic connotation of this last detail—the bridge—is crystal clear and the parallel is perfect: While in ancient times the bridge built by Apollodorus of Damascus linked the Roman Empire with Dacia under *romanization*, the bridge of Saligny linked Romania with Dobrudja under *romanianization*.

For those willing to accept this game of imaginary—and there are many—the similarity between Trajan and Carol is still perfect:

i) They both come from the West, the direction from which the light of civilization breaks.

ii) They both traveled on the Danube. Trajan arrived in Dacia after having crossed the above-mentioned bridge, while King Carol reached Romania from Germany by traveling on the Danube. This fact further certifies the perfect brotherhood between Romanians and the surrounding nature ("The woods are the Romanian's brother," we used to say, but this is a folk motif common to all the peoples in this area).

iii) Both Trajan and Carol reached the Dacian/Romanian land on the same spot: Drobeta, the future city of Turnu Severin.

iv) By birth, Trajan was provincial, that is, *peripheral* (he was born in the Spanish province of the Roman Empire); so was Carol I, originating in the Rhenan region of southern Germany. Understandably, their provincialism came as manna for the Romanians, especially considering that the most excruciating of the national complexes (and a continuing cause of lamentation) originated in this feeling of belonging to the outskirts of the West, of a provincial Latin-ness (that is, impure, always in jeopardy, abandoned by their fortunate cousins). This complex seems to have become part of what Fernand Braudel called "*la longue durée de l'histoire*": Tormented by the complex about their origin, the Romanians remain easy to convince that the Balkans to which they feel related by history represent the outskirts of the *civilized world*.

v) Finally, both Trajan and Carol turned up at times when the local situation was intolerable, as it was for the Dacians at the beginning of the second century and for the Romanians at the end of nineteenth century. Looking more carefully into this last parallel as presented in about 1900, we will easily notice that all the flaws attributed to Dacians/Romanians before their being civilized by an Occidental implant are those usually associated with *Balkanism*. The Dacians of the year 106, before they were *saved* by the arrival of Trajan, were as "Balkan" as the Romanians were in 1866, before they were *rescued* by Carol I.

1. The Dacians before Trajan

According to a volume of historical vulgarization published at the beginning of the century, "As all primitive people, they (i.e., the Dacians) had extremely cruel habits."[9] The author of a textbook from the 1920s adds details: "the Dacians loved freedom, but they did not have written laws and, many times, would take justice in their own hands, by sword or by knife, like savages. They had yet another bad habit, that they seldom refrained from wine and would make contest as to who is a harder drinker. They used to refrain from work, but would gladly go to war."[10]

2. Romania before Carol I

In one of the homage volumes of the jubilee year 1906, historian Dimitrie Onciul recalls a detail of an immensely symbolic power: The spring of 1866 had been a long dry one; suddenly it started raining in the very instant Carol arrived in Bucharest on the tenth of May.[11] The detail, despite its suggestive power, appears insignificant—but it gains a different value if we recall that Trajan did not succeed in defeating the Dacians of King Decebal until he had their water supply cut.

Whether or not it had suffered a long drought, Romania before Carol was in a miserable situation, particularly from the moral point of view. Here is how an occasional poet depicts Romania before 1866: "Our poor country was/A slave of cruel pagans."[12] The royal court physician recalls the time of Carol's arrival: The king was received by "a Romanian milieu motley in terms of race, feelings and aspirations, a milieu where intrigue speaks all Oriental languages."[13] Finally, the author who best describes King Carol's civilizing role sees the latter entering "a country whipped by the winds of the strongest influences . . . a country of waste . . . where the irresponsible imitation of strangeness had imported the most extravagantly democratic forms of government, . . . where older or younger boyars had been influenced by Levantine touches."[14]

I think that if one summed up the situation of the Dacians/Romanians before being saved by civilization (that is, Trajan and Carol I), he will easily obtain a *top ten* of their possible sins: i) a desire for liberty coupled with cruelty; ii) the rush to enforce their own justice for lack of written laws; iii) drinking; iv) unwillingness to work; v) war-like qualities; vi) a motley ethnic landscape; vii) servitude to *pagans*; viii) inhabiting a space where "intrigue speaks all Oriental languages"; ix) inhabiting a crossroads of all kinds of influences and interests, but especially x) inhabiting a space contaminated by "Levantine touches."

Are these the Balkans, or what?

I think the Romanians of today want to identify, at least from one point of view, with King Carol I: They want to have his detachment from the geographic condition of the country. That is, they wish to be Westerners all their lives and to get the best things out of the Balkans. Carol I was an illustrative example. Though a temperate man who ate frugal meals, the king became fond of Romanian traditional cuisine, including fish broth (*borsch*) and grilled carp. He is said to have sent his chef to the villages of the Danube Delta to get recipes from the locals.[15] However, King Carol was in the end a symbol of a "Westerner" immune to even the most charming Balkan temptations: On the night of September 27, 1914, he died with a glass of water and a biscuit on his night table.

From the Balkan Wars to Balkan Impurity

For the Romanians, this flight from the Balkans is but a stage in their flight from an East that is unpredictable by definition. After centuries of apparent reconciliation with the geographical location, things changed deeply in the nineteenth century. "The break with the East, decided by the country's elite, translated into a serious devaluation and blaming of peoples and cultures which previously had offered the Romanians models rather than reasons for lamentation."[16]

Lucian Boia makes an inventory of the "victims" of this flight.[17] The first, was the generic *Greek*: the revolution of 1848 in Moldavia and Wallachia (less in Transylvania, under the imperial influence of the House of Habsburg) coincides with "virulent, almost obsessive anti-Greek feelings. . . . The Greeks were the symbol of the East and of a few centuries of Eastern culture which were to be given up in favor of the beneficial Western trend." The second victim was the *Turk*, former generic master and enemy in the fight for liberty through the late Middle Ages. Like the Greek, the Turk may be—if necessary—a quintessence of Levantinism, of the Orient we wish to escape. At the beginning of the nineteenth century, a Romanian author opined that "each and every Turkish custom and fashion adopted inseminated our ethnic soul with corruption and idleness. . . ."[18] Even today, after a hundred years, this sentence remains present and active in the Romanian collective memory, though in the meantime the Turk and the Greek have merged into the more comprising and suggestive formula, *"the Balkan."*

Strange as it may seem, this country so persistent in its efforts to escape the Balkans improved its status and emerged as a power due to the same Balkans— more precisely, the Balkan Wars of 1912–1913. In October 1912, Romania was already engaged in a secret 1883 agreement with Germany and Austria-Hungary— an agreement seen as a step toward Central Europe (a nice first move toward *escape*). Under these circumstances, the Romanians did not rush to enter this Balkan War, started by Serbia, Bulgaria, Greece, and Montenegro (backed by Russia) against the Ottoman Empire. Romania entered the conflict only in its second phase, in 1913, after Bulgaria turned on its former allies. Romania's war adventures were remarkable, from a certain point of view: The army crossed the Danube, entered Bulgaria and, although no shot was fired, suffered many casualties from typhus. The nation's pride was reestablished by hosting the postwar conference in Bucharest, in August 1913; and Romania's flight from the region did not stop it from winning back Southern Dobrudja, a former Bulgarian territory.

After war, everybody seemed pleased: Greece occupied southern Macedonia and Crete, Serbia occupied Kosovo and central Macedonia, and Albania gained its independence. Everybody seemed pleased except Bulgaria. It is as though some unwritten law proclaims that the Balkan countries can be happy only by turns and never all at the same time.

Romania entered the First World War very late by attacking Austria-Hungary in August 1916, after having been persistently courted by both sides in the conflict. It was for the Romanians a bittersweet experience. Bitter, because by the end of November the German General Mackensen had Bucharest occupied, while the royal family, government, and armed forces withdrew to Iaşi in the northeast, where the most dreaded enemy was again to be typhus. One cause of this rapid failure, acknowledged today in all history textbooks, came from the Balkans: the troops of the *Entente* (at Salonika, under the command of General Sarrail), were supposed to launch an offensive concomitant with the Romanian attack against Austria-Hungary—but they did not. Bulgaria entered the war on the side of the Central Powers—the same Bulgaria that still had scores to settle with its neighbors from the previous Balkan War—and, at the end of August 1916, Romania suffered at Turtucaia one of the most crushing defeats in its whole history.[19]

But *la Grande Guerre* also had a favorable outcome. The Romanians fulfilled "their dream": Romania recovered the old, legendary, and often disputed Transylvania—the province where the Dacian king Decebal had opposed the Roman armies, do not forget![20] Transylvania opened Romania to Central Europe and, for two decades, put some distance between her and the Balkans. Even today, some of us nostalgically remember the old days when Romania was called the *Belgium of the Orient* and Bucharest (with exaggeration, but not irony) was *the Little Paris* (ignoring the fact that Romania was still a member of the Balkan Pact[21]). Selective oblivion has an explanation. As Nicolae Iorga—the most notorious Romanian historian—put it once, "a country does not belong to the place where it lies, but to the target it looks at." Iorga wrote this in 1940, the last year of his life, and there must be some truth in his words. However, it is equally true that 1940 was the year when old Romania died: After having lost that summer the eastern, northeastern, and northwestern provinces (Bassarabia, Bukovina, and Transylvania) to Stalin's Russia and Horthy's Hungary, King Carol II abdicated and left Romania in the hands of his nineteen-year-old son, Mihai; or more accurately, in the hands of the red-haired, strong-willed general Ion Antonescu who, in September 1940, would form a government with the "legionaries" of the Iron Guard, Romania's Fascist party. It is no surprise that one of the legionaries' most ardent wishes was to *purify* Romania—that is, to remove the Jews but also the "Balkan disease," for which they blamed the traditional and democratic political parties.

The Communist Takeover of the Balkans

Let's admit it: during the Cold War, Europe was simplified, as it had been divided with great precision into the East and the West. After imposing the first pro-Soviet government (March 6, 1945), the Romanian communists (numbering eight hundred members in August 1944 and four million in December 1989) might be said to have *really* taken Romania out of the Balkans for the first time, because the word "Balkan" had been erased from their vocabulary. Having escaped the Balkans, Romania was instead locked into the Soviet sphere of influence, as geopolitics—and the Balkans—dictated. On October 9, 1944, in Moscow, Winston Churchill and Josef Stalin delineated on a paper napkin the spheres of influence in Southeastern Europe. In his memoirs, Churchill reveals that he offered the Russians 90 percent influence in Romania in exchange for 90 percent influence in Greece. This is how Romanian communism began. Constricted between Churchill's cigar and Stalin's pipe, the Balkans took revenge on Romania.

At the end of the 1940s, as a result of Stalin's refusal of the Balkan Federation project,[22] "Balkan" became a banned word. It seemed that Romania was anyway following another track, with its back to the Balkans, its face to the East. The salutary solution was soon to be found: Mitiță Constantinescu, one of the most renowned financiers and economists of the country, had a revelation which finally led the Balkans out of the vernacular Romanian language.[23] He discovered that the Soviet Union was not only a state, but also a *continent*; and that the Russians were not to be blamed for what geographers had failed to understand. Constantinescu claims that the USSR is actually a continent as it covers a large area of the globe. This new continental entity, accepted and consecrated as such by the general opinion of the world, expects to be acknowledged in geography books as a non-integrated part of Asia, reconsidering by that the outdated notion of the Asian continent. The obsolescence of these geographical concepts made it possible for Romania to enter the open arms of the Soviet continent. The Balkans seemed lost somewhere behind. The cards of the world political game had been dealt between the East and the West, and all former landmarks were gone.

Gheorghe Gheorghiu-Dej, the Romanian leader in the gallery of Soviet satellites (general secretary of the Romanian Communist Party, 1945–1965) apparently had no feeling for the Balkans or *Balkanism*, and he discouraged the use of these terms. Despite his ability to recruit his own clients and supporters, and to brutally eliminate his enemies in a manner reminiscent of the golden age of political Byzantinism, despite his Levantine delight in long chats over nice meals and good drinks, it might be said that for twenty years Dej and the Balkans did not meet at all.[24] Dej's evolution from the minor Stalinist dictator of the early 1950s, who spoke dichotomously about the irreversible break between the East and the West, to the *national leader* of the early 1960s who spoke of "independence" and "sovereignty," was perfectly linear, without any Balkan twists.

The rediscovery of the Balkans is, from this perspective, the achievement of Nicolae Ceauşescu, Dej's follower and disciple (1965–1989). Should someone today undertake an analysis of Ceauşescu's foreign policy toward the Balkans, he would see a silent clash between two incompatible goals: the desire *to remain in* (enjoying all political advantages involved) and *escape from*, at the same time. The Romanian leader wanted to avoid and yet conquer the Balkans.

Under Ceauşescu, the Balkans became present in Romanian diplomatic language.[25] In September 1967, Suleyman Demirel (the prime minister of Turkey) visited Ceauşescu in Bucharest; during their meeting, according to the press release, the two leaders "express their common wish to develop bilateral relationship, and their mutual interest in improving the climate *in the Balkans and Europe*."[26] One year later, in March 1968, when the Bulgarian leader Todor Zhivkov paid a visit to Ankara, Bucharest interpreted this event as underlining "the decision of the two countries to join forces for the implementation of collaboration in the *Balkans*."[27] Then, following the meeting between Ceauşescu and Zhivkov in September 1970, a communiqué says that the two leaders "reiterated the common determination to contribute to an atmosphere of collaboration and security *in the Balkans, in Europe, and in the whole world*."[28] In other words, when it comes to Ceauşescu, any Balkan matter becomes a European matter (if not an international one!).

It appears very clear to me that to Ceauşescu, the Balkans were never a purpose as such, but rather a step on the ladder leading to a policy at a planetary level. By the beginning of the 1970s, the Balkans shrank to the dimensions of a backyard for a Romanian leader who started to feel very uncomfortable there. I think that Ceauşescu had a superiority complex toward the Balkans—for reasons I will not analyze here—and it sometimes showed. Bulgaria's Zhivkov was undoubtedly no rival for him. But things were different with Tito—Yugoslavia's man and legend—as he was a rival in the battle for Western sympathy. Ceauşescu understood very early that the *fight for peace* could bring legitimacy to himself and his regime. The

United Nations General Assembly agreed, approving, on December 16, 1969, Romania's proposal to declare the decade 1971–1980 the "decade of disarmament."[29] However, relations between Romania and the Warsaw Pact had been shaky since August 1968,[30] which is why Ceauşescu—perceived by the Western press as a *maverick*, a *thorn* in the Soviet Union's side, and thus encouraged—could afford to call for the simultaneous dissolution of both the Warsaw Pact and NATO.

The first step toward this "disarmament decade" could be taken in the Balkans. Before becoming a *world champion of peace*, Ceauşescu was to play for a while the role of a fighter for peace in the region; in June 1973, he proposed a "meeting of the Balkan states to discuss the ways to transform the Balkans into a zone of peace, free of nuclear weapons and foreign military bases"[31]; but by the beginning of the 1980s, the demilitarization of the Balkans had become too small a game for a Romanian leader eager to play his trump card of world peace.

Ceauşescu left the Balkans without too much regret, eager to become the person of planetary importance mentioned again and again by the propaganda of Bucharest. The death of Josip Broz Tito on May 4, 1980, left Ceauşescu without his rival in the Balkan region; having gotten rid of any competition, Ceauşescu launched after 1980 an unprecedented peace campaign, turning the increasingly bleak streets of Bucharest into settings for huge human processions ardently calling for the cessation of the arms race. I have no doubt his ultimate goal was to acquire the Nobel Prize for Peace, which would have given perfect legitimacy to his regime and sufficient credit to him.

A *Historic* Rejection of the Balkans

Running away from the Balkans, Ceauşescu was again accompanied by his subjects, including several thousand of the country's historians.

Even before Romania entered the First World War, the historian Nicolae Iorga founded in Bucharest, in 1913, the Institute for Southeastern European Studies. The institute reflected Iorga's scientific preoccupations and philosophical thoughts about the relationship between the local and the regional. Although fond of Balkan history, Iorga constantly advocated the idea that Romania did not belong in the Balkan region[32]; he claimed that Romania was rather a part of Southeastern Europe.[33] Iorga's Institute (another symbol of the Romanian escape) had a very interesting history.[34] In 1948, when Romania entered the Stalinist orbit, the Institute was closed. It was to be reactivated in 1963, when—as Georgescu put it—"Romanian foreign policy opened to the Balkans and to the world." Today, the situation remains the same: the Institute of Bucharest publishes the *Revue des études sud-est européennes* ("Review of Southeastern European Studies"), while 150 kilometers south, in Sofia, Bulgaria, the Institute for Balkan Studies publishes the *Revue des études balkaniques* ("Review of Balkan Studies"). At first sight, it appears to be a mere lexical problem; but if you look behind it, you'll see the eternal Romanian dream of escape from the region.

Nonetheless, under Ceaușescu *Southeastern European studies* had never been a real priority. After a relatively promising beginning (Ceaușescu himself made the opening address to the Third International Congress of Southeastern European Studies, held in Bucharest in September 1974), the Communist regime became fascinated by another cultural idea: the *protocronism*,[35] translated in history by a real "thracomania."[36] (As mentioned earlier, Thrace was the ancient term for the Southeastern European region and the Thracians were the common ancestors of the area's peoples). In September 1976, Bucharest hosted the Second International Congress of Thracology (held under the high patronage of Nicolae Ceaușescu). But the regime was aiming another target which would become obvious only after a few years: The goal was not to study history thoroughly, but to immortalize the image of the regime led by the *Conducator* (that is, Leader).

Once again, a *politically correct past* was to be re-created, in order to legitimate the present. On October 26–27, 1977, the Plenary Session (specially summoned!) of the Romanian Communist Party's Central Committee decided to celebrate (in 1980) 2050 years since "the first centralized and independent state" was established under the rule of the Dacian king Burebista on the territory of the former Dacia (82–44 BC). To put it in a nutshell, thracomania had distilled into a finer essence: Ceaușescu's *dacomania*, converted into party and state policy.[37] The resolution was put in practice, the more so as on May 28, 1980, Ceaușescu attended a workshop meeting with "scientists of history" to prepare down to the finest detail what we might call *Operation Burebista—2050*. The art galleries of Bucharest were to have Dacian exhibitions, the publishing houses were to issue literature on the same theme, reviews and newspapers were to feature this great celebration. The cultural manifestations gathered momentum and culminated on the evening of Saturday, July 5, 1980, in Bucharest's *Republicii* Stadium, under spotlights and torches carried by young men and women dressed in *Dacian* costume. At the end of this manipulative audio-visual performance, King Burebista himself turns up on a huge shield carried by these young people and oversees a symbolic relay race to his *descendent*, Ceaușescu.

Needless to say, this model—Burebista's Dacian state—was, according to official propaganda, the very seed that had grown into Ceaușescu's *centralized and independent* state; Burebista's Dacia was nothing but the historic precedent of Ceauşescu's Romania. Besides, there was a good explanation for going all the way back to Burebista, rather than Decebal: Whereas Decebal was defeated by the Romans, Burebista had been a victorious king when he confronted them. Caesar himself had wanted to face Burebista, but unfortunately he was slain in the Senate before bringing his army to Dacia. And Burebista, like his descendant Ceauşescu, developed a foreign policy with global implications: In 48 BC he got involved in the conflict between Caesar and Pompey the Great, entering into an alliance with the latter.

From the perspective of my concern here, the key to this historical allegory lies neither in the fraudulent merge between a Dacian king and a Communist secretary general, nor in the Communist regime's preference for the Dacian root of the Romanian people over its Latin one[38]; rather, the key is to be found beyond the borders of Burebista's state. It is symbolic that Burebista's kingdom had the Balkan Mountains as its south border, while its north-west border reached the river Morava. As if aware of his Romanian descendants' desire *to escape*, Burebista had been the first to push, by successive conquests or diplomatic alliances, this imaginary *proto-Romania* deeply into the heart of Central Europe. Like Ceauşescu's Romania later on, Burebista's ancient Dacia had stood with its face to *Europe*, its back to the Balkans.

The Post–Cold War Balkans as a Steep Road

In 1989, the formerly monolithic block of Eastern Europe broke into pieces: One of them—the Balkan region—once again became a worldwide front page subject. The Balkans might be said to have erupted violently immediately after the fall of communism; the metaphoric hidden magma, rather frozen during the communist era, sprang out of the reborn democracy, hotter than ever in the last forty years. Once again, like in 1914 (the criminal attempt of Sarajevo) or 1947 (the Balkan Federation plan), the Yugoslavian space was the detonator of the bomb.

From a certain point of view, Romania was already used to the idea of reborn *Balkanism* it experienced in recent years. Romanians seemed to have reconciled themselves to the idea that, although geographically located outside the Balkans, they had been ruled by a leader who could be described as "Balkan" (or "Byzantine"[39]); a leader who, most Romanians agree, was removed by some sort of mixture of popular revolution and Byzantine *coup de palais*.

One of the most popular Romanian novels published at the end of the 1980s had as a leitmotif a very comforting phrase: "*les Roumains sont des européens mal placés.*"[40] But was Ceauşescu's the only *Balkan* in a country with 23 million *Europeans*? Certainly not; and here we get to the strictly contemporary avatars of Romanian *Balkanism* with all their moral and political implications. Once again, clichés and stereotypes vanquished geography; so should you intend to offend someone in Romania, tell him he behaves *like a Balkan*, and nine of ten chances, he will get angry.[41]

But this offense is nothing strictly Romanian. Because after 1989, in the imaginary cartography of Europe, the Balkans have again become that "step," less modest than doubtful, just like they were for ages in the European imaginary.[42] This route *Europe—Eastern Europe—Balkans* is a route with steps; thanks particularly to our projection onto the real world certain ideological antagonisms, one does not simply go from Europe toward the Balkans, but descends, like traveling downhill toward a valley. And the countries in the area—Romania *y compris*—would like to ascend, not to descend. Therefore, this more or less acknowledged flight from the Balkans toward Europe is the secret dream cherished by all of them. If the Balkans "are portrayed in the liberal Western media as a vortex of ethnic passion—a multiculturalist dream turned into a nightmare," they always begin—says Slavoj Žižek—with our neighbors: "If you ask 'Where do the Balkans begin?' you will always be told that they begin down there, toward the southeast."[43]

It is not only the countries proper that want to escape from the Balkans, but historical regions within the borders of those countries seem to have the same desire. The Romanian case is perhaps illustrative from this perspective, the more so as the five provinces of today's Romania (Banat, Transylvania, Moldova, Dobrudja, and Wallachia) initiated the union process only in the middle of the nineteenth century. In the electoral year 1996 (when, for the first time in postwar Romania, pro-Western political parties came to power), a role in the propagandistic campaign of the ethnocentric nationalists was unintentionally played by Samuel P. Huntington's book *The Clash of Civilizations*,[44] particularly its division of Europe into "Occidental Christianity" and "Orthodox Christianity and Islam." This map—where the line separating the West from the East crosses the Romanian Carpathians Mountains and separates Transylvania from the rest of Romania—became an electoral trump card in the hands of those Romanians who (backed by the often inflammatory declarations of Magyar extremists) complain about the danger threatening the unity of the Romanian state. In the fall of 1998, this fear was to be confirmed: Sabin Gherman, a young Romanian from the Transylvanian city of Cluj, released, in the name of a Foundation called "Pro Transylvania," a manifesto titled *I'm tired of Romania*, which could be summarized as follows: Tired of that Balkan Romania on the other side of the Carpathians, Gherman wants his Transylvania back. This rhetorical cry brought him celebrity. Previously an anonymous reporter for the local branch of Romanian Television, Gherman became public enemy Number One. Rumors explaining this gesture—and which he partially confirmed—spread as quickly as rumors do in the Balkans. While a student in Craiova (a city in the south-west of the country, three hundred kilometers closer to the Balkans than Cluj), young Sabin fell in love with a young Balkan girl from the town, but she was colder than ice. And so, *I'm tired of Romania* would be a belated gesture of revenge. However, his destiny was, for some, predictable: In the beginning of January 2000, the most important Romanian newspaper reported that Gherman would be invited to Budapest's Karoly Gaspar University to deliver a course on Balkanology.[45]

Perhaps such accidents are inevitable in the escape from the Balkans.

Yet, I don't think that two entirely opposite perspectives on *Balkanism* (in general, and Romanian *Balkanism* in particular) coexist by pure coincidence in the Romanian intellectual field. On the one side, there is the effort to increase the intellectual value of *Balkanism*. It is sustained by understanding and tolerating this little, harmless "Balkan weakness," considering both the memory of the past and the charm of the Oriental/Balkan life. On the other side, there is a strong rejection of *Balkanism*—particularly *Romanian Balkanism*, considered a contradiction of terms.

Alexandru Paleologu and Alexandru George, two representative personalities of the Romanian *intelligentsia*, are the embodiment of these two opposite ideas. Though from different social backgrounds, they shared the destiny of intellectuals forced to live most of their lives under a totalitarian regime. Moreover, they are considered today two distinct voices of Romanian liberal thought.[46]

This is how differently the Balkans can be seen through liberal lenses.

Alexandru Paleologu has no doubt about it. From Europe to the Balkans one always *ascends*, not *descends*: "Europe is a creation of the Balkans. . . . Moreover, . . . let's remember that Socrates, Plato, and Aristotle were Balkan and it was they who created Europe as a vision of world, philosophy, and wisdom. To the extent that it got Balkanized, Europe became Europe." To him, the characteristics of the Balkans are mostly positive: "vivid and intelligent cynicism, relativism, high spirits, great flavor, a special taste for existence, for the concrete, the voluptuous, and the most terrible risk.[47] To reject the Balkans, says Paleologu, is stupid: "Out of snobbery, the word Balkan was given a disgusting connotation: 'Balkan savagery,' 'Balkan lack of civilization. . . .' We, the Romanians, are not actually Balkan for the good reason that we are North Danubian. Fortunately, we have a strong old Balkan induction which provides us with savor, subtlety, liveliness, and this extraordinary power of intellectual metabolism."[48]

To Alexandru George, things are entirely different. In December 1999, in a critical note dedicated to Andrei Pleşu (Minister of Foreign Affairs at that time), the writer wrote: "I think that is an insult to say Romania is situated in the Balkans"; to be fully understood, he added, "this term (which is disgraceful, fabricated in the old times by the Chancellery of Vienna) should be excluded, under the penalty of law, from the vocabulary of the employees of the Ministry."[49] When it comes to Balkan characteristics, George is extremely severe: "compared to the Serbs' and Turks' cruelty . . . , Bulgarians' dull earnestness, Greeks' craziness, and Russians' cruel fanaticism, we are a white spot on the map of Europe, not only of the Balkans, where the Austrian diplomats contemptuously introduced us."[50]

A War and an Epilogue (or *All—Kissed—Independence—Square*)

Many Romanians suddenly rediscovered their Balkan roots when Serbia was bombed by NATO—that NATO into which Romania had been making every effort to integrate. It is no paradox. Surveys of public opinion say that more than 80 percent of Romanians are in favor of their country's integration into NATO; yet perhaps the same percentage of Romanians strongly disagree with NATO's manner of solving the Yugoslavian crisis. Officially, Romania endorsed the intervention by the Western Alliance at any risk. It implied obvious political risks assumed by the pro-West forces ruling Romania after 1996,[51] economic risks (the blockage of the Danube and the embargo on Yugoslavia brought considerable losses to the already fragile Romanian economy), and moral risks (most Romanians believe that their most friendly neighbor throughout history has been the Black Sea, followed by ex-Yugoslavia).

The Romanians' tender feelings toward ex-Yugoslavia have at least three explanations:

i) During the last centuries, Romania has had no disputes with Yugoslavia, as compared with the rest of its neighbors;

ii) Most Romanians have vivid recollections of Yugoslavia under the communist regime. While Ceauşescu's Romania grew more and more self-sufficient in its own autarchy, Yugoslavia opened (like a window) to the West. It was from there that the blue jeans, chewing gum, and *Vegeta* cooking spices came, as well as Yugoslavian TV shows. In the late 1980s, Romanian television broadcast only two hours a day (hours dedicated to Ceauşescu anyway), and the Romanians in the southwest of

Table 8.1

Adoption		Rejection
106 (Trajan)	**versus**	271–275 (Aurelian)
1866 (Carol the 1st)		1945 (Yalta)
1968 (Prague)		1997 (Madrid)

the country (cities such as Timişoara) watched on *TV Beograd* or *TV Zagreb* Orwell's *1984*, rock concerts (like *Live Aid in 1985*), football games, or beauty contests (today, in the age of cable television, it is almost incredible to recall the popularity that Lepa Brena, a beautiful *Miss Yugoslavia*, enjoyed in Romania, or how familiar the Romanian children were with the meaning of *crtani film*—cartoons).

iii) Romanians' sympathy for the Serbs during the Kosovo war was a result of their old fear of being abandoned by the West. On the imaginary level, the Romanians were *adopted* and *rejected* three times by the West. Historical landmarks, characters, legends, and real facts mingle in the collective memory and the story of their adoption/rejection could be highlighted as shown in table 8.1.

In other words, today Romanians believe they were adopted by the West when the Roman emperor Trajan conquered and Romanized Dacia, when King Carol I saved the union of the Principalities, and when Ceauşescu became a political star in the western mass-media with his denunciation of the Soviet invasion in Czechoslovakia. The Romanians felt betrayed by the Roman emperor Aurelian when he withdrew his administration and army from Dacia, by the Yalta post-war arrangement, and when Romania was not admitted to NATO after the Madrid Summit in the summer of 1997. As I said, escape from the Balkans is but a stage in Romania's hotly desired escape from the East; the more persistently the Romanians are pushed back into the Balkans and to the East, the more difficult their endeavor.

Under these circumstances, the conflict in Kosovo functioned like a chemical reaction. Many Ceauşescu-type nationalists, as well as former genuine anti-Communists, sympathized immediately with Serbia's cause. Many Romanians thought the Romanian fate itself was at stake in Kosovo: Romania was to become the next target and Transylvania the next Kosovo. Other Romanians (like the Greeks and Bulgarians) abruptly rediscovered their Orthodoxy and their solidarity with the Balkan Orthodox peoples, against this combined *Protestant/Catholic/Muslim* coalition. Others remembered their Serbian relatives and friends—like Cornel Dinu, the charming coach of Bucharest's Dinamo football team (the best team at present, leader of the 1999/2000 national championship), who made public his friendship with Arkan. After all, the notorious paramilitary commander was also the owner of Belgrade's football team Obilić (let it be said that for many Romanians, there was no need to have Serbian friends to wonder why Yugoslavian football teams had been banned).

The most important playwright in Romanian literature is Ion Luca Caragiale; the *theater of absurd* made famous by the Romanian-born Eugene Ionesco goes back to the comedies of this nineteenth century author. Caragiale was Balkan not only by his name (he was the descendent of a Greek family settled in Romania), but also by the bittersweet jocularity of his plays. In one of his comedies, *A Lost Letter*, a satire on provincial political life in Romania at the end of the nineteenth century, there is a witty remark frequently used by Romanians today with regard to their Balkan conduct. After heated political disputes, a few characters sent a telegram saying "*All—Kissed—Independence—Square*"; it is not clear whether they kissed each other in Independence Square or actually kissed the pavement of the square. It is behind this ambivalence that the moral of the story hides.

However, it is a fact that Caragiale (himself imbued with *Balkanism*) went into exile in Germany without any knowledge of the language. He eventually died in Berlin.

I personally doubt that the German Manfred Wörner, former secretary general of NATO, or any of his successors read Caragiale. Yet, on April 4, 2000, in Bucharest, in the presence of the former secretary general's wife, the *Manfred Wörner Foundation* granted awards to persons and institutions which had made an "important contribution to the plan of integrating Romania into Euro-Atlantic structures." Among the prize-winners were open supporters of the 1999 NATO campaign as well as opponents. Thanks to the *Manfred Wörner Foundation*, Romanians might be said to have kissed Independence Square once more.

One of the winners was Andrei Pleşu, Romanian Minister of Foreign Affairs at the time of the conflict. Pleşu is the very incarnation of the Romanian Balkan. An esteemed philosopher, irremediably fond of Caragiale, founder of *Dilema* magazine (the most popular weekly of intellectual debate in Bucharest), Pleşu is able to speak with the same charm and self-assurance about *the missing groom* in a Bruegel painting as about his regrets for the missing *braga*, a 100 percent south-Danubian (i.e., Balkan) soft drink.

Shortly after having received the award, Pleşu returned it with the following explanation, which I find wonderful as a conclusion to my essay: "If Mrs. Wörner hadn't been there," he wrote to the foundation, "on 4th April I would have done what I feel obliged to do now; that is to return the 'Award for Excellence' with which your Foundation honored me. It couldn't have possibly occurred to me that I was invited to participate in a bluff. Under a noble patronage, you organized an embarrassing *kermesse*, Balkan in the saddest meaning of the word."[52]

After all, the Balkan Pleşu refused to *kiss Independence Square*.

As I said, Romanians want to run away from the Balkans; yet the Balkans keep on their heels, always rising from nowhere, when we expect them least.

The Romanians don't believe in the *end of the history*. And so the race to escape is still going on.

Notes

1. "We, the Romanians, consider ourselves Balkan without actually being and deny our *Balkanism* as we consider it the iron ball chained to our leg, pulling us down, preventing us from being 'an integral part' of Europe"—Alexandru Paleologu, "Balkan Socrates and Socratic Caragiale," *Secolul* 20, nos. 7–9 (1997): 20.

2. Vintilă Mihăilescu, "The Balkans, 'anthropologically correct,'" in *Secolul* 20, nos. 7–9 (1997): 101.

3. Maria Todorova, *Imagining the Balkans* (New York: Oxford University Press, 1997).

4. Mihăilescu, "The Balkans . . . ," 102.

5. See Vesna Goldsworthy, *Inventing Ruritania: The Imperialism of the Imagination* (New Haven: Yale University Press, 1998).

6. See Lucian Boia, *Pour une histoire de l'imaginaire* (Paris: Les Belles Lettres, 1998).

7. A paragraph in Herodotus' *Histories* saying that, despite the limitations of their behavior, the Dacians however were "the most valiant and most honest of the Thracians" has been frequently used by Romanian historians during the past decades, entering the collective memory.

8. See my "*Ante mare, undae*. History and Politics: *Conducator*'s Strategies of Legitimization," in *In Honorem Dinu C. Giurescu. Le Temps de l'Histoire II, Mémoire et Patrimoine* (Bucharest: Universitatea Bucureşti, 1998), 359–388.

9. *Istoria Populară a Românilor*, vol. 1 (Bucharest: Minerva, 1900), 9.

10. N. A. Constantinescu, *Istoria Patriei. Lecturi pentru clasa I-a elementară de comerţ* (Bucharest, 1929), 8–9.

11. *Amintiri despre jubileul de 40 de ani de domnie a M. S. Regelui Carol I, 1866–1906* (Bucharest: Imprimeria Statului, 1906).

12. George Bengescu Dadija, *Majestăţii Sale Carol I Regele României la 10 mai 1891, la serbarea celui de-al 25-lea an al întrănării sale* (Bucharest, 1891).

13. Ion Mamulea, *Din amintirile Medicului Curții* (Bucharest: Imprimeria Națională, 1939), 7.

14. Constantin Chirițescu, *O mare personalitate morală, Carol I, Regele Întemeietor* (Bucharest: Cartea Românească, 1941), 13–14.

15. Grigore Antipa, "Cîteva amintiri despre regele Carol I," in *Din viața regelui Carol I* (Bucharest: Editura Fundației Regale, 1939), 15.

16. Lucian Boia, *Istorie și mit în conștiința românească* (Bucharest: Humanitas, 1997), 183.

17. Boia mentions three "victims"—Greek, Turk, and Russian—and the role played by the "French myth" and the "German counter-myth" in the configuration of the Romanian elite during the last 150 years.

18. Boia, *Istorie si mit* . . . , 183, 184.

19. See Constantin Kiritescu, *La Roumanie dans la guerre mondiale, 1916–1919* (Paris: Payot, 1934).

20. The actual National Day of Romania, the 1st of December, commemorates the 1st of December 1918, that Sunday when a large number of Romanians of Transylvania gathered at Alba Iulia and decided to unite with their "mother country."

21. Or *Balkan Entente*, defensive alliance formed in February 1934 by Greece, Romania, Turkey, and Yugoslavia, against the state which had refused to become the fifth partner: Bulgaria.

22. "Tito's Balkan federation project envisioned 8 federal units (the five Yugoslav republics, plus Albania (with Kosovo), Bulgaria, and Big Macedonia (Yugoslav Macedonia plus Northern Greece), with Belgrade as the center. . . . In fact, the federation project was officially proposed only to Bulgaria": Nebojša Bjelaković, "Comrades and Adversaries: Yugoslav-Soviet Conflict in 1948, A Reappraisal," in *East European Quarterly* 33, no. 1 (March 1999): 104. See also Milovan Djilas, *Conversations with Stalin* (New York: Harcourt, Brace & World, 1962).

23. Mitiță Constantinescu, *Continentul URSS. Sinteză geo-economică* (Bucharest: Imprimeriile Independența, 1944), 14–15. Advocate of the Romanian separation from the Balkans, Constantinescu had a Balkan destiny *par excellence*: An ex-liberal minister, he betrayed his party so as to join the elite of King Carol II, whom he served as a minister of finance and governor of the National Bank. After the war, Constantinescu becomes in 1945 president of the Publishing House *Cartea Rusa* ("Russian Book") and one of the leaders of the *Romanian Association for Tighter Relationship with the Soviet Union* (ARLUS). His premature death (in 1946, at the age of 56) saved him from bigger compromises or—worse—from communist prisons.

24. Consider the relationship between Gheorghiu-Dej and Josip Broz Tito, a "Balkan" story in itself: In 1949, prompted by Stalin, Dej was one of the wild accusers who pointed the finger at Tito during Cominform meetings, while the Romanian bank of the Danube was covered by huge placards showing the Yugoslavian leader as an executioner with a blood-stained hatchet in his hand. Fifteen years later, after having gotten rid of Stalin and involuntarily returned to the Balkans, the two leaders, now good friends, inaugurated the hydrocentral power plant on the Danube on September 7, 1964, at *The Iron Gates*—almost the same spot covered before by placards!

25. See Nicolae Ecobescu, ed., *Relațiile internaționale postbelice. Cronologie diplomatică,* vol. 1: 1945–1964; vol. 2: 1965–1980 (Bucharest: Editura Politică, 1983). In the first volume, dedicated to Dej's period, the term "Balkan" is never mentioned, while in the second one (dedicated to Ceaușescu's epoch) the term appears eight times.

26. Ecobescu, *Relațiile,* 2:90.

27. Ecobescu, *Relațiile,* 103.

28. Ibid., 170.

29. Ibid., 145.

30. "Romania's finest hour in its communist history came on 21 August 1968 when its state and party leader, Nicolae Ceaușescu, denounced the Soviet-led invasion of Czechoslovakia that had just taken place." J. F. Brown, *Eastern Europe and Communist Rule* (Durham, Duke University Press, 1988), p. 263.

31. Ecobescu, *Relațiile,* 2:225.

32. In his travels, Iorga was a strong advocate of this idea. See his lectures delivered in the United States, particularly the one explicitly titled "Is Romania a Balkan State?" in the volume *My American Lectures* (Bucharest: State Printing Office, 1932).

33. See his brochure, *What Is the European Southeast?* (Bucharest, 1940), which includes a phrase that is still very close to the Romanian intellectual's mind: "A country does not belong to the place it lies, but to the target it looks at."

34. See Vlad Georgescu, *România anilor '80* (Munich: Jon Dumitru Verlag, 1994), 36.

35. For the best approach, see Katherine Verdery, *National Ideology under Socialism. Identity and Cultural politics in Ceaușescu's Romania* (Berkeley: University of California Press, 1991).

36. See Iosif Constantin Drăgan, *We, the Thracians, and our multimillenary history* (Milan: Nagard, 1976).

37. For details, see Florentin Dragoș Necula, "Communism in Dacia. Burebista—our Contemporary," in *Analele Universității București—seria Istorie,* XLII–XLIII (1993–1994): 37–51.

38. Another detail: In the same stadium, in September 1983 the Romanian soccer team beat Italy 1 to 0; the main sports newspaper in the country printed the headline, THE DACIANS BEAT THE ROMANS (ignoring the technical detail that the victory goal had been scored by the *Dacian* Ladislau Bölöni, Romanian player of Magyar nationality).

39. See Vladimir Tismăneanu, "Byzantine Rites, Stalinist Follies. The Twilight of Dynastic Socialism in Romania," *Orbis* 30 no. 1 (spring 1986): 65–90, or the declaration of 12 May 1989 made by the president of the Hungarian National Assembly, M. Szuros, according to which Romania was ruled by a "nepotist and dictatorial" system, tainted with "Byzantinism and Balkanism." Edith Lhomel, "La Roumanie en 1989," in *Notes et etudes documentaires,* nos. 4920–4921 (1990): 225.

40. Constantin Țoiu, *Căderea în lume* (Bucharest: Cartea Românească, 1987).

41. "Balkan" is a political insult: "If they imagine they can do whatever they want by pulling Balkan strings, well, they are wrong" said the Romanian Minister of Transportation, Traian Basescu, referring to the president, Emil Constantinescu, and some of his partners in the government coalition, *Adevărul,* February 23, 2000, 1.

42. See my "Eastern Europe between the Cold War and the Imaginary Cartography," in *Lettre Internationale* (Romanian edition), no. 31 (fall 1999): 19–22.

43. Here are the Balkan steps as described by Žižek: for a Slovene, "the Balkans begin in Croatia or in Bosnia. . . . For Serbs, they begin in Kosovo or in Bosnia. . . . For the Croats, the Balkans begin in Orthodox, despotic and Byzantine Serbia. . . . For many Italians and Austrians, they begin in Slovenia. . . . For many Germans, Austria is tainted with Balkan corruption and innefficiency; for many Northern Germans, Catholic Bavaria is not free of Balkan contamination. Many arrogant Frenchmen associate Germany with Eastern Balkan brutality. . . . Finally, to some British opponents of the European Union, Continental Europe is a new version of the Turkish Empire with Brussels as the new Istanbul." Slavoj Žizek, *"You May!,"* in *London Review of Books*, no. 6, March 18, 1999.

44. Samuel P. Huntington, *The Clash of Civilizations and the Remaking of World Order* (New York: Simon and Schuster, 1996).

45. C.M. Chiş, "Gherman pleacă la Budapesta să predea balcanologie" (*Gherman goes to Budapest to teach Balkanology*), in *Adevărul*, January 5, 2000.

46. Alexandru Paleologu—or *Conul* Paleologu for friends, that is boyar in the noblest-*Balkan* meaning of the word—is a writer; descendent of an old phanariot family and political convict in the 1950s, he was appointed ambassador of Romania to Paris in the early 1990s. Alexandru George is a novelist, translator and essayist, one of the most active and polemic spirits of the Romanian cultural press.

47. Interview with Alexandru Paleologu in the magazine *22 Literary Supplement*, no. 13, in *22*, no. 10, March 7, 2000.

48. Alexandru Paleologu, "Între Balcani şi Europa," in *Cuvîntul*, no. 1 (237), January 1997.

49. Alexandru George, "Compromiterea istoriei," in *Adevărul literar şi artistic*, December 7, 1999.

50. Alexandru George, "Cei care n-au muncit, dar ne-au ţinut," in *Adevărul literar şi artistic*, March 28, 2000.

51. In the evening of his sixtieth birthday, president Emil Constantinescu recognized, in a TV show, that "during the conflict between NATO and Yugoslavia, I was perfectly aware that I was moving against the current popular trend in Romania." (PRO TV, November 19, 1999). His firm position in favor of NATO's intervention was undoubtedly one of the causes that led to the internal popularity decrease of the center-right regime in Romania.

52. See the letter in *Adevărul*, April 22, 2000.

9

The Eros of Identity

Ivaylo Ditchev

A Bosnian applied for a job.
"Aren't you Bosnians too lazy?" asked the employer.
"Oh, no" said the Bosnian, "It is the Montenegrins who are lazy. We are the stupid ones."

The Balkan imaginary reemerged suddenly after the end of the Cold war. Before, the region had been divided between different types of phantasms. Some saw it as confirmation of the communist theories of miraculous industrialization and urbanization of backward rural societies. Others projected on the south of the peninsula the noble defense of the free world against Soviet barbarism. Still others saw in Yugoslav self-management and nonaligned politics some third way between Stalinism and capitalism. Even tiny Albania had its fans: a dissident faction of Maoists, who ran a bookstore in the Latin Quarter and claimed that Enver Hoxha was the only leader who had remained true to the communist ideal.

Encouraged by the attention (often accompanied by substantial economic and military aid from the respective geopolitical sponsors), the Balkan countries raced to occupy the place of some big Other's desire. Thus Romania, expecting Western loans, exalted its supposed Latin origins; Bulgaria noisily affirmed that it was the most faithful Slav brother of Russia and silently re-exported Soviet oil; Greece, applying for European Community membership, posed solemnly as the cradle of European civilization.

With the end of the ideological era, the Balkans slipped back to what they had been before the war, that is, a periphery of Europe: at best, a virgin frontier land to civilize, at worst, a ghetto to contain unwanted populations from emigrating to the West.[1] The Balkans responded quickly by internalizing this new status quo of the imaginary. Thus the new identity debate in the 1990s was largely dominated by the question of whether to be or not be Balkan.

It has become commonplace in the last decades to say that Oriental identities are constructed by the gaze of the Western other.[2] The internalization of that prestigious other becomes the "content" of the local self-representation strategies, which aim to both seduce and defy this same other. In fact, identity is always a negotiation between assigned and accepted attributes.[3] The erotic tension—or shall we say, the structural discrepancy[4]—between those is an essential part of intercommunity relationship. Misapprehension of the other, voluntary or not, is part of the interaction: Too much hermeneutics risks undermining identity formations and the human relations they imply.[5] Consider the child who is told that he or she is nice in order to make him or her be nice; consider the use of stereotypes and clichés in the "war of the sexes."

In the case of semi-independant states like those in the Balkans, national actors are constantly torn between the need, on the one hand, to fit into the schemes of the geopolitical sponsors, abiding by general keywords, norms, and narratives, and the need on the other, to differentiate themselves and acquire an existence of their own in the universal imaginary of modernity. The balance between those is rather delicate, as too much compliance with rules blurs the image of the country and makes it difficult to "sell" it internationally, but too much identity risks making it drop out of the system of world exchange. In the 1990s, as the "good pupil of transition," Bulgaria was an example of the first tendency, while Serbia, having challenged the West to a real war, embodied the second.

In fact, the technology of identity-building was constructed by the end of the nineteenth century and has been since at the disposal of every nation-state wishing to affirm itself, since "there is nothing more international than national identities."[6] Those include not only the establishment of institutions of sovereignty[7] like parliaments, schools, and armies, but also imaginary productions like great ancestors and myths of origins, literary heritage and museums, centralized folklore, and typical national landscapes. The dimension of imitation is thus one of the most striking characteristics of modernity.[8] To put it in Lacanian terms, identification runs on two levels: On the level of the imaginary, you identify with a specific object you want to be, whereas on the level of the symbolic, you also identify with the gaze (or the subject of the gaze, the rule this gaze imposes), creating the field in which identification takes place.[9]

On the first level, the group identifies with the object of desire produced by the universalized modern cultural scene. The object is desired not for its own qualities, but because others desire it, and this accounts for the mimetic violence that necessarily accompanies the process.[10] Identity building under the conditions of delayed modernization will thus imply ferocious competition over minor differences, over-investing one's own attributes, and aggressively ignoring those of one's competitors.[11] On the second level, which we might call the level of meta- or framework identity, the group identifies with the (international) field itself where national identities are produced, and with the rules of the game that characterize it.

The situation becomes even more confused because both levels of identification are subject to historical change where older figures of self-image do not disappear, but persist and enter strange constellations with the new ones. Thus imaginary interaction becomes extremely complex and the very notion of identity, problematic, because different identity strategies coexist, contradict one another, and enter into complex interrelations. In this sense, it is not sufficient to criticize "essentialist" usage of identity, but we should rather interpret complex situations of imaginary interaction. In general, I prefer not to use the term "essentializing," as it supposes that there is some type of iconicity that would *not* be essentialist, that some sort of playful feeling of arbitrariness of the sign could protect us from taking too seriously the attributes assigned to the other or ourselves. It seems to me that every time we assign an image to someone we do the same thing: We reduce his or her or our existential richness, imprisoning him or her or ourselves in the eternal ideality of the sign. The effect of arbitrariness—of irony, of relativization—seems to be a secondary effect of the multiplication of contradictory attributes, of mastering the subtleties of the language of identity.[12] Essentialization and de-essentialization appear thus to be situated on rather different levels: The first is basically linked to the way the sign operates, while the second is a sophisticated cultural strategy, limited in time and space. One way to relativize (or de-essentialize, if one wishes) is simply to juxtapose concrete identity-constructions in time and space.

In the classical century of nation building, the fundamental attribute of the national myth was its eternity. Being ancient was considered the most prestigious attribute of the imagined community, legitimizing among other things the possession of territories and the rule over people.

The race toward ancientness, in the Balkans, was certainly launched by the Greek national movement, which captured the desire of romantic Europe and privatized the classical heritage of Antiquity. No Balkan country would resist the temptation to dig up some obscure ancestors that would be at least as ancient as the ancient Greeks—Illyrians, Thracians, Dacians, et cetera. One of the paradoxes of community sentiment is that historical truth is of secondary importance: The symbolic war over ancestors itself makes nationals stick together, exclude traitors, and recognize who "we" and "the others" are.[13]

Nevertheless, the effort to represent the Balkan nations as eternal substances encountered one major difficulty, which was the gap separating modern states from the supposed glory of their ancestors. Thus the major problem confronting identity builders was *continuity*. Konstantinos Paparigopoulos, a professor of history at Athens University, was the first to develop, in the middle of the nineteenth century, the interpretation of Greek history as a single continuum encompassing ancient, medieval, and modern. Nevertheless, the practice of "progomoplexia" (worship of ancestors) and "arkhaiolatria" (adoration of antiquity) was not simple in a culture where the Orthodox Church had already once broken away from pagan practices. It had now to swallow the introduction, by patriots, of ancient names (like Achilles) that started to replace the Christian ones.

Establishing historical continuity would be particularly difficult in a country like Bulgaria, the existence of which was suspended by five centuries of Ottoman rule. The founding text of the national revival is the "Slav-Bulgarian History," written in 1762 by the Athon monk Paisii, which begins with Adam and proceeds to piece together the scattered accounts of the "very glorious deeds of the first in our race."[14] His principal enemies are not the Ottomans, but rather the Greeks, and to some extent the Serbs, who are said to mock Bulgarians for not having a history of their own. But one should not be ashamed to be Bulgarian and to speak our native tongue, because we too have had our glorious kings, and even Greeks came to pay them tribute. Things were even more difficult for the intellectuals in Macedonia, which appeared on the map as late as 1945; they undertook the difficult task of bridging the gaps between the ancient kingdom of Alexander the Great in the fourth century BC, the short rule of the Bulgarian king Samuel of the tenth and eleventh centuries, and their contemporary Socialist Yugoslav Republic.

The Greek national revival set another trend that would be followed throughout the Balkans, which was the invention, in the nineteenth century, of an artificial language, purified of foreign imports and rather difficult to understand by the common man, that was supposed to prove the direct link between the prestigious antiquity and the poor modern Balkan nation. The obstinacy in imposing the "katharevousa" reached its climax during the dictatorship of the colonels (1967–1974), which finally discredited the undertaking and brought about the officialization of the "demotiki" ("popular") as late as 1976.

Language reform was equally important to Romanian intellectuals and political elites who, in the nineteenth century, discovered their roots in the Roman empire that had occupied Dacia for as short a period as a century and a half. In fact the only link they had to it was the Romanized language they spoke, so they changed their alphabet from Cyrillic to Roman script, replacing Slavonic in the Church service with Latin and purging Slav words (the reform officially took place in 1859). The emblematic national historian Nicolae Iorga would argue in the 1920s that Slav influences were "superficial," that you could easily speak Romanian using hardly any Slavic words.[15] The ideological meaning of this creation of an "Oriental Latinity" is to fully distinguish the not-quite-consolidated national identity from those of Balkan competitors.

Late differentiation through language from above is a common pattern in the region. Let us note that when the new Bulgarian state adopted its official language in 1879, it chose the Eastern dialects that are the most removed from Serbian; when the official Macedonian was established in 1945, it was based on the most "autochthonous" Western dialects, rather than the northern ones, similar to the neighboring Serbian, or the eastern ones, gradually shading into Bulgarian.[16] With the remarkable exception of Serbo-Croatian, promoted by the artisans of Yugoslavism, centrifugal linguistic forces have always been stronger than centripetal ones. (Let us note that one of the first results of the breakup of Yugoslavia was the publication, in Croatia, of a "Dictionary of differences," helping patriots to use the words and expressions that would differentiate them from their Eastern neighbors.)

Let us also note that the Ottoman Empire itself replicated the pattern of nation inventing modeled by its former provinces, but it did so at what might seem an accelerated pace. The Kemalist revolution, which aimed to transform the remnants of the Ottoman empire into a modern nation-state, would not miss the opportunity to develop, in the 1930s, the "Turkish history thesis," arguing that Turks had contributed to civilization long before Ottoman times, as well as to embark on a search for ancient ancestors among peoples like the Hittites. This imaginary activity was accompanied by the break away from Arabic script and the introduction of a Latin alphabet, adapted to the Turkish language. A linguistic theory was developed about the so-called sun-language, a kind of pure Turkish, close to the contemporary vernacular and free of all Arabic and Persian imports, which was said to be an ancient language that had played a central role in the development of civilization.

A number of similarities in this regional pattern of identity-construction seem worth considering—for instance, the tendency to "privatize" historic heritage and fight over it with neighbors. National identity becomes a kind of competition, as differentiation takes place on the universal scene of desire established by modernity. On the other hand, young nations without uninterrupted traditions tend to consider heritage a conspicuous source of prestige rather than a cultural effort and self-limitation. This makes the competition even more ferocious, as everyone is in a similar position (political will, state institutions, intellectual activity . . .) with respect to identity emblems, the content of which is of lesser interest. The Balkans have become notorious for symbolic wars over heritage. Alexander the Great is disputed between Macedonia and Greece,[17] Cyril and Methodius between Greece, Bulgaria, Macedonia, and Serbia, the Thracian culture between Bulgaria and Romania, et cetera.

Most of these emblems of identity have but little relation to the present local cultural practices and are the product of the big Western Other's desire. We can illustrate this through the story of the reinvention of the Olympic games. The German professor Curtius delivered a passionate lecture on this question, and it came to the attention of the rich merchant Zappas, who thought it was a good idea to try to revive the games. King Otto I was also interested in doing something about the image of the poor country in which he found himself. But there was no real tradition of modern sport and competition in Greece in the middle of the nineteenth century, and the first couple of games were a disaster. When the baron Cubertin started to work toward establishing modern international Olympic games, he nevertheless faced stubborn resistance on the part of the Greeks, who saw the trademark of the games as their property. Finally the event was negotiated in the format we have it today: Greece has a particular place in the symbolic arrangement (fire comes from Olympus, Greek athletes march in first), but the organization, financing, and participation is international.

Similarly, one could ask in what way modern Romania is influenced by its Dacian ancestors, what links the ancient Hittites and the nation-state of Mustafa Kemal Atatürk, or where in modern Albania one can see traces of the noble Illyrians. Troy would not have been discovered by the Turks, who did not give a damn about it; nevertheless, it has since become a powerful symbolic resource for the country. In a way, antiquity is like oil: A western company discovers it, then young nation-states nationalize it and start selling it back to the West.

The superficial character of the production of national "identity kits" is of course a universal phenomenon. As Michael Herzfeld puts it (interpreting Benedict Anderson), national identity is iconic: It presupposes the passage from social relation to icon, from something more complex to something simpler.[18] In fact, simplification is an essential aspect of identification. In order to "handle," through metonym and metaphor, the complex other, the ego reduces him or her to what Freud called the unique trait (*einziger Zug*), much the way his patient Dora identified unconsciously with her father by imitating his cough.[19] The other aspect of this is the well-known paradox of memory: You have to forget in order to remember,[20] because memory is necessarily a rearrangement of the past, an introduction of hierarchies, of repression and glorification. In the Balkans, those two universal aspects of identity-formation are enforced by a very speedy "catch-up-with-Europe" modernization from above, as well as by the traumatic character of nation-building itself, which had to cope with several centuries of stateless, survival-oriented existence under the Ottomans and with the foreign interventions that were necessary to create practically all the modern states in the region. The result is the substitution of proximity by remoteness. The immediate past, the centuries inside the Ottoman Empire that profoundly shaped the entire life and culture of the region, is repressed, and the icon of a distant age of glory is invested with national pride[21] even if its link to the present is often problematic. This same psychosocial pattern is repeated each time a "shameful" period of history is left behind and new political elites enter the public scene. For instance, decommunization in Bulgaria started by banishing forty-five years of cultural production and returning to the prewar "golden" years.

The other particularity already hinted at is what we might call the Byronic complex: the predominant role of foreign gaze and approval in the construction of identities. The complex of indebtedness to the West is being constantly turned upside-down, so that there is no nation in the region that has not, at one point, produced some idea of what it has *given* to the world and civilization. This is due to the ambiguous character of the gift itself,[22] which is not only an object of desire but also a menace. Gifts have to be returned, as debt is one of the accessories of power. Nevertheless, some of them—like the gift of life from parents to children—are impossible to return, and so they become the backbone of the traditional ideology of domination. By the same token, the gift of national sovereignty from the Great powers to the Balkan peoples—even before they constituted themselves as subjects of their own history!—becomes a symbolic burden. Paying back those geopolitical benefactors by obedience only prolongs this state of symbolic submission. A radical way to escape from it and nullify the debt is to invent a *preceding* gift that reduces the generous foreign gesture to mere payback. Thus, if Greece was the cradle of civilization, Europe merely pays back its duty by helping it recreate its state. If Russia was civilized and Christianized through the gift of the Cyrillic alphabet and writings, it was simply obliged to liberate the Slav nations in the Balkans.[23]

The strategy of debt-invention, launched by the Greek national revival when philhellene committees for the support of the Greek national cause were disseminated throughout Europe, has thrived ever since. Its usefulness can be illustrated by the debate over Greek accession to the European Community in 1980, when in the

British Parliament an official of Foreign office said that Greek entry would be "fitting repayment by Europe of today of the cultural and political debt we all owe to Greek heritage almost three thousand years old."[24] In the same vein, post-communist discourse underlines the obligation of the West to help Eastern Europe because it abandoned it at Yalta. ("Nice restores the historical injustice of Yalta," declared the Bulgarian prime minister after the November 12, 2000, summit affirmed European Union [EU] enlargement). After NATO's bombardment of Serbia, it has become a common place to say that the West is obligated to reconstruct the country; all future help is thus anticipated as payback, rather than as a gift.

Geopolitical dependence makes foreign approval the basic factor for legitimizing internal political, economic, and cultural positions. The consequence is a general split of attitudes toward the West and the division of the intelligentsia into Indigenists and Westerners,[25] a phenomenon that has been best observed in Russia, the first state to be modernized by force from above. One less obvious effect of this split on the level of the imaginary is a strange coexistence of a deadly seriousness about national heritage and its reification into cheap mass products for quick consumption by tourists.[26] This schizophrenic state of affairs is to be seen, for instance, with respect to Orthodox Christianity: On the one hand, it is being cherished even by nonbelievers and ferociously defended against all criticism and comparison; on the other, monasteries are transformed into hotels and souvenir shops.[27]

But the split runs through all relations to heritage. Throughout the Balkans, you have two completely separate itineraries for tourism: one for foreigners, the other for nationals.[28] Thus in Istanbul, Turkish groups of schoolchildren, soldiers, and retirees pay tribute to the neobaroque Dolmabahçe palace, symbol of modern statehood, whereas foreign tourists line up to see the harem of the ancient Topkapi; in Athens, the Parthenon attracts pilgrims from all around the world, whereas the patriotic war-museum is of interest mainly to local visitors. In this division between the "convertible" value of ancient heritage and the use of modern history only for the purpose of national education, a third point is about to develop regarding Orthodox and Byzantine heritage. Being of less interest to western tourists (Byzantium also seems to have a slightly negative connotation in Catholic cultures), such sites hold enormous interest for visitors from Orthodox countries, especially the rich "new Russians" in search of cultural origins. The industry of "religious tourism" seeks alternative strategies to occupy the place of the other's desire.

Modernity can be defined as a culture that allows itself to *choose* among ancestors: Plato or the fathers of the Church? Imitate the ancients or the moderns? Follow

Germanic or classical mythology? The more distant the ancestors are, the easier it is to use them in the present. In the Balkans, it was again the Greeks who set the example in playing upon the different keyboards of the past: Athens when it came to legitimizing democracy, Sparta when military rule or dictatorship was looking for roots in the past; antiquity when seducing the West, Byzantium when addressing Russia. Similarly, the Romanian intelligentsia since the nineteenth century has been divided between the Latinist and the Dacianist tendencies, that is between emphasizing the supposed Roman or Dacian origins of the Romanian nation. For example, the growing isolation of Ceauşescu's regime was accompanied by a rise of Dacian indigenist tendencies.[29]

In Bulgaria the official pillars of identity are three. The proto-Bulgarians are warriors, having defeated the superpower Byzantium and established a state on its land in the seventh century. Their singularity makes them a perfect emblem for nationalists, irredentists, and the like. The national pantheon represents the Slavs as industrious, egalitarian, freedom-loving people, useful in times of pro-Russian orientation or in the construction of socialism.[30] The Thracian ancestors (ancient, wise, peaceful) were canonized as late as the 1970s, maybe not without some relation to the new orientation toward peaceful coexistence and the need for recognition from the West.[31] This heritage is imaginary, as it is difficult to see what influence on modern Bulgarian culture has been produced by the proto-Bulgarian khans. Its ideological function is to break the continuity of the real cultural tradition, inherited from the Byzantine and Ottoman empires.[32] Such a break, essentially political in its nature, seems to be at the core of collective identities[33] (it is difference that founds identity).

The eroticism of identity is most obvious in national stereotype jokes, quite developed in such a multicultural area as the Balkans. And if communism transposed national stereotyping onto the Comecon space,[34] within the Yugoslav federation it never lost its impact. There was also a more somber, "political" (or shall we say politico-paranoid) dimension to this. The loudly promoted brotherly relations between the republics were unofficially interpreted in terms of who-owes-what and who-exploits-whom: Was it the rich (like Slovenia) who helped the poor (like Macedonia) by the redistribution of national product, or were the undeveloped exploited by the industrialized through an unequal exchange? The pseudo-dissident Memorandum of the Serbian Academy of Sciences and Arts (1986), a milestone in the rise of nationalism, was a testament to this "we-give-more-than-we-take" phantasm.[35]

National identities are closely linked to what Goffman calls "team-performance."[36] In the Balkans, a very high level of solidarity is expected in front of foreigners when questions of symbolic importance to the imagined community are approached. Under communism and the different Balkan dictatorships, the act of "presenting a bad image of the country" was often considered to be a crime and could be punished by prison or "re-education." After the change in the 1980s, the pressure on the individual was obviously diminished, but it did not disappear. It can best be observed through the sacred taboos that each Balkan national culture has imposed upon itself and that produce the linguistic rituals of belonging or not-belonging. The name "Republic of Macedonia" cannot be pronounced by a real Greek, a Bulgarian should deny the existence of a Macedonian language, a Turk should never admit the occurrence of the Armenian genocide,[37] et cetera.

Pushing the other into a presumptive identity is not only an aesthetic activity; in the Balkans, it has a political pretension. In declaring one's eastern neighbor hopelessly Balkan, Orthodox, or Moslem, the national ideologue seems to throw away ballast and come closer to the heavens of modernity, currently called "Europe." Thus the dissolution of former Yugoslavia has often been seen as motivated by the promise of "entering" Europe. Seeing Euro-modernity as a *telos*, nations interpret identity-construction as a kind of competition, expressing thus the deep ambivalence of the process of identification.[38] The tacit resistance to regional cooperation, stated as a prerequisite for foreign aid in the 1990s, is another example of such ambivalent identification. On one hand, the individual countries are afraid to be tucked away in a Balkan identity,[39] but on the other, they seem to see modernization as a zero sum game that has winners and losers. Along with numerous examples from the age of classical nation-statehood, the rivalry between Bulgaria and Romania, two candidate countries for EU membership, has been astonishing: The Bulgarian government invested all of its energy into dissociating itself from such coupling. In December 2000, when the council of ministers announced the future abolition of visas for Bulgarians, no one tried to hide their joy over the fact that "we are ahead of Bucharest." On the other hand, the democratic turn in Serbia was met in Sofia with some anguish: "They will get now all the attention from the West." Some observers suggested that Serbia would now be added to our Balkan package, and that "we shall have to move on together with it."

We could say that the surest sign of Balkan identity is the resistance to Balkan identity. The nation-builders of the region devote themselves to breaking away from regional culture; thus Iorga affirms that "The Romanians are more neighbors to Paris than to Belgrade and Sofia."[40] The more distant and imaginary the ancestors (Illyrians,

Dacians, Hittites), the easier it is to create a myth of absolute authochtony and to dissociate oneself from the regional context.[41] In fact, the markers of national identity are produced as if mainly to be presented to the big western Other, who is supposed to adjudge your country better than the rest. If borders are drawn by foreign politicians and generals, it will be foreign public opinion that will appreciate the "progress" made by the individual countries and draw lines between national cultures.

In other words, the intentional self-invention is directed towards "catching up with historical delay" in the process of modernization; since the nineteenth century, the Balkan countries have been trying desperately to negotiate an image of rapid change, compliance with standards, and the acquisition of all attributes of European nation-states. (This could explain Todorova's accurate observation that, if the Orient has been constructed as the irreducible Other, the Balkans have internalized the position of bridge, crossroads, region condemned to eternal transition.[42])

The strategic goal of national high cultural productions[43] is to create discontinuity and sharply to distinguish each national culture from its neighbors. (In the Balkans, more than anywhere else, comparison is a political engagement!) As elsewhere in the world, this contrasts with the relative homogeneity of everyday culture, which does not stop at state frontiers. Throughout the region one will find the same way of making coffee or burek, of playing music or belly-dancing, of swearing or of carrying oneself. This dramatic clash between what has been called "identity-from-above" and "identity-from-below"[44] is maybe the most distinguishing characteristic of the region. In fact, high culture is constructed precisely by repressing all traces of local culture considered degrading, Oriental, body-centered, amorphous, et cetera. Such is the self-discipline that national elites prefer to offer the gaze of the western Other. Through this binary tension between the presentable and the shameful, we can best understand the construction of identity.[45] The official high culture is to be understood in dynamic tension with what it represses; norm and transgression form one system and presuppose each other.

What makes the erotics of identity even more complicated is that the standards imposed by that foreign gaze are changeable. Thus, quite apart from the different *objects* of national desire, there are also periodic changes in the *rules of the game* that produce those objects. Those changes could be classified into three major waves of modernization.

The first wave was the desire to catch up with the rest of the *civilized peoples* by founding national institutions: real, like parliaments, armies, opera houses, and museums; imaginary, like prestigious ancestors, national literatures (possibly including an internationally recognized Nobel laureate); and linguistic and folkloristic homogeneity. After the First World War, the world changed. It was now the *developed states* that produced a model of industrialization, urbanization, and mass culture, but also of ideological purity. The latter generated a whole range of regimes, starting from the extreme right of Metaxas and Antonescu and ending with Hoxha's orthodox Stalinism. The third wave came in the 1980s, with the conservativism of Thatcher and Reagan, and culminated with the fall of the Berlin wall. All of a sudden the poor Balkan nations had to take one more turn: Development and smoking factories had become obsolete, and national homogeneity sat poorly with international institutions concerned about things like human rights. The aspiration toward the standards of the *normal countries* was no longer motivated by the wish to be free or to produce like them, but to consume like them.[46]

In this new world, the binary tension producing the effect of identity tends to be reversed; the universal and the particular seem to have changed places, so that the culture of chronic deficit of modern universality[47] is replaced by one of chronic demand of the local and particular. The shameful multiethnic character of the region, inherited from the Ottoman millet system, has curiously become a symbolic resource.[48] Cities like Istanbul, Thessaloniki, Sarajevo, or Plovdiv host international institutions, conferences, or simply tourists by staging their multicultural tradition; on the Web site for Bucharest, the metaphor of "rhapsody" is used to suggest the free intermingling of peoples, cultures, and traditions. Multiculturalism is pushed to what Goffman called the "front" as Western sponsors and protectors have started to see it as something authentic and valuable; national homogeneity is repressed into the "back" of identity, as it is seen as linked to arbitrary violence and selfishness. Strategies of self-representation start to change directions: Identity is no longer based on the universal breaking away from the particular, but on the aestheticized local resisting the impersonal global. The change that has affected the entire planet is again felt most strongly in the Balkans, where identity is conceived as a natural resource attracting foreign geopolitical "investors." Capitals of victimhood (postcommunist countries, then Bosnia and Kosovo) are financed on the media market; thus it was the bloody succession of wars in former Yugoslavia that changed international attitudes toward the region, obliging the EU to adopt a quicker procedure for integrating it, to develop the Stability pact for financial aid, et cetera. Modernist figures of universalism who come from the region, such as dramatist Eugene Ionesco, literary theorist Julia Kristeva, or director Theo Angelopoulos, are replaced by exclusive resellers of local color such as writer Ismail Kadare, musician Goran Bregović, or director Emir Kusturica. As for the economy, the brief foray into industrialization was rapidly abandoned in the postmodern era, consigning the region to develop the sectors of leisure, cuisine, and exoticism. Heroic modernization, which sacrificed the particular to the universal, no longer interests anyone: Instead, the foreign gaze privileges all that was repressed before, namely, specificity. And if that did not exist, we would have to invent it.

Notes

1. The last example of this attitude was the hasty creation of the Kosovo protectorate (or whatever we decide to call it), done, among other reasons, in order to have somewhere to return the Albanian refugees who had settled in Western Europe.

2. Edward Said's *construction* of the Orient, Larry Wolff's *invention* of Eastern Europe, Maria Todorova's *imagining* of the Balkans.

3. "My identity crucially depends on my dialogical relations with others," Charles Taylor, *The Malaise of Modernity* (Toronto, Ont.: Anasi, 1991), 48.

4. Melucci underlines the "gap," the "unresolved tension," between self-definitions and definitions imposed by others (Alberto Melucci, *The Playing Self: Person and Meaning in the Planetary Society* [Cambridge: Cambridge University Press, 1996], 32). Cf. also Robert G. Dunn, *Identity Crises: A Social Critique of Postmodernity* (Minneapolis: University of Minnesota Press, 1998).

5. This does not mean that mutual understanding between men and groups is impossible, but rather that such understanding necessarily goes beyond identity.

6. Anne-Marie Thiesse, *La création des identités nationales: Europe 18e–20e siecle* (Paris: Seuil, 1999).

7. The reason for such uniformity is the need for mutual recognition in a world-system that is ever more closely interrelated. The nineteenth century is, among other things, the century of diplomacy.

8. In fact, it has been often pointed out that, on the level of collective as well as individual identities, European culture privileges opposition and challenge as a paradoxical way of integrating into the norm: You become like the others by pursuing your own "authentic" particularity.

9. This distinction proceeds from Lacan's juxtaposition of the *Idealich* (the mirror image of the I invested by an essentially narcissistic libido), and *Ichideal* (the Ego ideal, constructed through the symbolic function of language and situated to the side of castration, renouncement, and the rule that Freud developed into the Superego). (Jacques Lacan, *Le stade du miroir comme formateur de la fonction du Je, telle qu'elle nous est revelée dans l'expérience psychanalytique* (1936), and *Remarque sur le rapport de Daniel Lagache: "Psychanalyse et structure de la personalité,"* in *Écrits* (Paris: Seuil, 1966); *Seminaire, livre I. Les écrits techniques de Freud* (Paris: Seuil, 1975). Cf. also Slavoj Žižek, *The Jouissance of One's Nation* (Sofia: Lettre Internationale, winter 1993); *The Sublime Object of Ideology* (chapter 3, "*Che Vuoi?*") (London: Verso, 1989).

10. According to René Girard's theory, the more equal the positions that aspire toward the same object, the greater the violence resulting from the competition. The relative similarity of the Balkan countries makes it tempting to apply this contested model (René Girard, *La violence et le sacré*, [Paris: Grasset, 1972]).

11. Michael Ignatieff, developing Freud's notion of "narcissism of minor differences," underlines the incapacity of nationalists in the post-Yugoslav space to see or hear anything but their own sufferings in a sort of narcissism of pain (Michael Ignatieff, *Blood and Belonging: Journeys into the New Nationalism* [London: Vintage, 1994]).

12. What should happen could be compared to the passage from the literary "work," conceived as having a *telos*, center, privileged interpretation, and author, to the "text," a space where different meanings and voices coexist and intermingle (Roland Barthes, *De l'oeuvre au texte*, in *Oeuvres completes*, vol. 2 [Paris: Seuil, 1994]). The "civilization process" in the sphere of identity would imply overcoming hierarchies and establishing a dialogical space where identity strategies can coexist.

13. For instance, it is not important to know whether ancient Macedonia has anything to do with modern Greeks or Macedonians. But the emotions this question provokes and the linguistic rituals that surround it (for example, the taboos, the apparent disgust, and the obligatory indignation) are certainly essential parts of those two national identities.

14. Paisii Hilendarski, *Slav-Bulgarian History* (Sofia: Bulgarski Pisatel, 1972), 12.

15. Nicolae Iorga, *Etudes Roumaines: Influences étrangères sur la nation roumaine. Leçons faites à la Sorbonne* (1922) (Paris: Librairie universitaire J Gamber, 1923), 23.

16. The imaginary part of the operation consisted in the claim that modern Macedonian was the legitimate heir of the old Slavonic dialect that had been spoken around Thessaloniki and that was supposed to be the language of the saint brothers Cyril and Methodius, on which the Slavonic Church service would be based.

17. As well as the name of Macedonia itself, considered by Greeks to be an essential part of their identity foundation.

18. Michael Herzfeld, *Cultural Intimacy: Social Poetics in the Nation-state* (New York: Routledge, 1997); *The Social Production of Indifference: Exploring the Symbolic Roots of Western Bureaucracy* (Oxford: Berg, 1992); Benedict Anderson, *Imagined Communities: Reflections of the Origin and Spread of Nationalism* (London: Verso, 1983.).

19. Sigmund Freud, *The Ego and the Id* (1923) (Chapter 3, "Ego and Superego: The Ego-Ideal"), in *The Standard Edition of the Complete Psychological Works of Sigmund Freud* (London: Hogarth Press, 1953–1966), vol. 19; *Dora: An Analysis of a Case of Hysteria* (London: Simon & Schuster, 1997).

20. Cf. for instance Marc Augé, *Les formes de l'oubli* (Payot, 1998).

21. In Greek, *ethnikos eghoismos*.

22. Cf. Ivaylo Ditchev, *The Gift in the Age of Its Technical Reproducibility* (Sofia: LIK, 1999). Ivaylo Ditchev, Sonia Combe, eds., *Albanie utopie: Huit-clos dans les Balkans* (Paris: Autrement, 1995).

23. After the Russo-Turkish War of 1828–1829, Serbia became an internationally recognized autonomous principality under Turkish suzerainty and Russian protection. Bulgaria acquired the same status after the Russo-Turkish war of 1877–1878. Consider the following schoolbook verse by the nineteenth century national poet of Bulgaria, Ivan Vazov: "We too have given something to the world, to all Slavs, an alphabet so that they could read." All terms of this proposition are obviously ideological constructions: who are *we*? (the Bulgarian nation is projected back into the ninth century), what means "given"? (the creation of the alphabet was commissioned by the Byzantine authorities), et cetera.

24. Richard Clogg, *Concise History of Greece* (Cambridge: Cambridge University Press, 1992), 2.

25. For Romania, see Katherine Verdery, *National Ideology Under Socialism* (Berkeley: University of California Press, 1991).

26. All countries in the region started to develop their tourist industries in the 60s, the only exception being Albania, which started opening up to the world as late as 1992.

27. On the road from Sofia down to Greece, you pass a big billboard "icon" of Christ the Redeemer, with an arrow underneath him pointing to the temple behind him and announcing in Bulgarian and Greek: "Church souvenirs, Fifty meters."

28. In most of these countries, admittance to museums is different for locals and foreigners, the latter being asked to pay several times more.

29. Ceauşescu's anti-Slav nationalism, which backed his political declarations and ensured him great popular support, was generously rewarded by the West. Romania was admitted to GATT in 1971, to the IMF in 1972, obtained trade preferences from the EC and the status of most favored nation from the United States in 1973. (Cf. Katherine Verdery, *What Was Socialism and What Comes Next?* [Princeton: Princeton University Press, 1996]; Verdery 1991).

30. A couple of decades before the liberation of the country, in the nineteenth century the Russian Slavophile Iuri Venelin encouraged the Bulgarians to gather historical and ethnographic evidence for their Slav origin, as at that time Russian public opinion was modeled by Nikolai Karamzin, who thought they were Tatars; and this would certainly not favor a Russian intervention on their behalf. (Iuri Venelin, "Two Letters to Vassil Aprilov" [Sofia: n.p., 1942].)

31. Ilia Iliev, "The Proper Use of Ancestors," *Balkan Ethnology*, vol. 2, December 1998.

32. The Byzantine heritage accounts for the Christian-Orthodox tradition, while the Ottoman one has deeply marked all aspects of everyday life.

33. Ernesto Laclau, ed., *The Making of Political Identities (Introduction)* (Verso: London, 1994).

34. It was after the breakup of the Comecon Balkan that stereotyping began to reappear.

35. Serbs are said to be exposed to "genocide" in Kosovo, to be unjustly accused of being "oppressors, centralists, and policemen" even though "they had borne the greatest sacrifices," and Serbia's economy was allegedly subjected to unfair terms of trade" (Memorandum of the Serbian Academy of Sciences and Arts [1986] [Beograd: GIP Kultura, 1995], 119, 120, 122, 123).

36. Even if he does not actually use the term identity, Goffman could be useful understanding the complex way in which one's social "character" is the result of the interaction of fact, cultural convention, conscious and unconscious performance, and reception or interpretation on the part of the other. One's socio-cultural mask is permanently negotiated; it is part of one's relations to others.

37. A couple of years ago, a Turkish patriot designed a virus that destroyed your hard disk whenever you typed the expression "Armenian genocide" on your computer.

38. Freud wrote in 1923 that "the identification with the father then takes on a hostile coloring and changes into a wish to get rid of his father in order to take his place with his

mother." Thus identification, essentially ambivalent in its character, is a further development of the oral organization of the libido that assimilates the object in destroying it (*The Ego and the Id*, in *The Standard Edition of the Complete Psychological Works of Sigmund Freud*, translated by James Strachey [London: The Hogarth Press, 1953–1966], 32).

39. Two examples of refusing to be part of the Balkans can be seen in presidents Tujman and Constantinescu, of Croatia and Romania respectively.

40. Iorga, *Etudes Roumaines*, 10.

41. One aspect of this is the voluntary neglect of the other. "Nationalism is the transformation of identity into narcissism. . . . Nationalist language—speaking about oneself rather than the others. . . . The problem, to use H. M. Enzensberger's useful term, is *autism*: groups so enclosed in their own circle of self-righteous victimhood, or so locked into their own myths or rituals of violence, that they can't listen, can't hear, can't learn from anybody outside themselves. [What is frightening is the] 'you don't understand' aspect of identity politics" (Ignatieff, *Blood and Belonging*, 69, 97).

42. Todorova, *Imagining the Balkans* (Oxford and New York: Oxford University Press, 1997).

43. Even folklore, largely used under communism, can be considered a part of high national culture, because it was the result of a rigorous politics of observation, filtering, and control, if not outright invention of practices intended to create the desired image of the people's artistic genius.

44. Cornel West, "A Matter of Life and Death," *October* 61 (1992): 20–23.

45. Michael Herzfeld, *The Social Production of Indifference: Exploring the Symbolic Roots of Western Bureaucracy* (Oxford: Berg, 1992). We could also apply the Goffmanian terms of "front" and "back" in describing national identities (Erving Goffman, *The Presentation of Self in Everyday Life* [Penguin, Harmondsworth and New York, 1982]).

46. "Previously identity forming was based on family and work, now it is based on consumption" (Dunn, 1998: 64).

47. Where identity could be seen as "a reservoir of civilization deficiencies" (Alexander Kiossev, *Catalogues of the Absent*, in *The Bulgarian Canon? The Crisis of Literary Heritage* [Sofia: A. Panov, 1998], 12).

48. In postmodern society, "difference sells" (Douglas Kellner, *Media Culture: Cultural Studies, Identity and Politics between Modern and Postmodern* [London: Routledge, 1995]). Cf. also Arjun Apadurai, *Modernity at Large. Cultural Dimensions of Globalization* (Minneapolis: University of Minnesota Press, 1996).

III

Sexuality, Trauma, and Myth

10

Queer Serbs

Branka Arsić

On June 30, 2001, the first gay parade in the history of Belgrade took place. Unexpectedly, however, the participants of the parade were met with violence, attacked by their fellow citizens who happened to be on the streets and for whom a gay parade disgraced the "Serbian nation." The police were called to protect them but beat them instead, injuring a large number. This essay is dedicated to all those participants of that parade who were victims of police violence and that of their fellow citizens.

Specters in the Small Town

In his study of the "spirit" of the small town, *Filozofija Palanke,*[1] Radomir Konstantinović has determined the fundamental "feeling" of the parochial mind as the feeling of being "excluded from the world": we (me) are here where everything is *in order*; the chaos of the world, the chaos of the Other is on the other side of the mountain, there where we are not. This feeling (self-exclusion from the world of the other conceived of as exclusion by the other, and followed by mourning over this exclusion) is the effect of a complicated structure of interpolations and extrapolations as well as of the degeneration of interpellation into what we will call "psychotic interpellation." Let us proceed step by step.

To say that the mind of the province, the parochial mind, is overwhelmed by the feeling of its exclusion from the world is to refer to the labor of exclusion and inclusion of the other (or the world) from the world, and to the constitution and identification of the world. Simply: the parochial mind is rooted in a doubling and not in the multiplication of the world. On the one hand, the world is where we are, *there is no other world*, and we are therefore the people of the world (the parochial mind can be recognized by its insistence on its not being parochial, on its "worldliness," by its constant self-legitimation). If our world is the whole world then this world has to be closed (this is precisely the logic of the absolute and the parochial mind is a totalizing mentality: its demand is the demand for the "ideally closed"[2]). On the other hand, precisely because it identifies its world as the whole world or as the only possible world, this mind reads its gesture of self-closure and exclusion of the other as opening its world to the other: for if there is no other world outside of this world then our world has to be an absolutely open world. The parochial mind, therefore, delusionally recognizes the closedness of its world as an openness toward the other which, however, does not exist either because it does not live in that world or because it can live in that world only by accepting it unconditionally as its own world (thus becoming one of us, or one of ours, the one who is the same, easily readable and recognizable). The "openness" of the parochial mind, therefore, relies on the *totalization of its closedness,* on the *globalization of the local* (in the Serbian version this attitude is expressed in the sentence Serbs commonly use to address foreigners. Addressing them in Serbian they say: "Speak Serbian so that the whole world can understand you" ["*Govori srpski tako da te ceo svet razume*"]).

Needless to say, this totalization or absolutization has the structure of everything that is (that wants to be) absolute: like everything absolute this absolute is not whole; on the contrary, it is based on a "hole." The blind spot of this "total" parochial mind is precisely the other, the world outside its world, outside "us," the world that does not exist but that curiously enough constantly returns as a "non-existent" world, as the absent world; the world of others, as the world of difference, visits our world time and again, and visits it as an absence, as a non-visitor, as a sight that will remain blind to us, that will not see us or see through us for we are the impenetrable wall of sameness, safe within the identity of our little town or of our big state, in any case the identity of our race (two more favorite Serbian sayings: "only harmony among Serbs can save Serbs," and "united we stand.") "United we stand" means: by our very bodies, by our very lives (for the individual does not exist here, she is miraculously transformed into "we," and the death of the individual does not count, or it counts only insofar as it provides the resurrection of the "we") we build the wall that will save us, that will separate us, but separate us from whom? Precisely from that non-existent world that threatens us in its non-existence: the world of others is present as the spectral world, *difference is an apparition,* others are ghosts of otherness and therefore the constant threat, the *eternal trauma.* For if they are specters they are as a death that remains eternally alive. The unhappiness of the "ideally closed" parochial mind lies in its inability to rid itself of others.

The spectralization of the other is both the effect and cause of self-spectralization. To the extent that (spectral) difference belongs to the other, time, as the work of difference, also belongs to the other. Time is spectral; an eternally apparitional difference haunts the eternity of our identity excluded from time, excluded from history: "history belongs to the other;"[3] (one should notice the paradox of this self-enclosed mind: whereas the other is spectral because it is the work of history, the work of time or the work of difference, this mind itself is spectral because it is outside of time, in an eternal eternity). Therefore, we live in eternity, in the infantilism of our immortality, in the unchangeability of our identity, our system of values, our way of life, a way of life that we never change, which means that we never live. Every change is a little death and that is why for the parochial mind there is no change: there is no death. Death as individual death is always insubstantial for it cannot disturb the life of our identity and what is more, it can only reaffirm it (it can be a fine occasion for the collective mind to mourn over itself: s/he is dead therefore we are endangered which only means that we are still "we," that we are still "together"; this is the source of "our" collective enjoyment in individual death). To put it differently: for this mind the experience of death occurs only as experience of the possible death of its "community" (of the endangerment of the nation or race), and it reads it as the death of the world as such, as the twilight of the world (one should keep in mind that according to Lacan the expectation of the "twilight of the world," the idea that if something were to happen to us the world would not be the same, that it would be the end of the world, is a fundamental feature of psychosis). And because there is no other world outside our own the endangerment of our world threatens the world as such (in the Serbian version this was formulated in the following paranoid way: we are surrounded by the spectral spaces of Islam, it haunts us in all possible ways, it is the hidden intruder upon our identity. We are therefore invited to defend the world from Muslim fundamentalism. If we do not succeed in this it will be the end, the absolute disaster of the world. Such was the attitude invoked to justify crimes against Muslims).

Psychotic Interpellation

The spirit or mentality determined here as the spirit of provincialism is, therefore, the spirit imbedded in the collective and in race (even when it is "liberally" open it is open only because it is "closed" and exclusive, or only because it is open exclusively for the totalization of its own world). But if this mind is the outcome of self-spectralization and the spectralization of the other, if it exists in a world without a world, how then does it constitute itself in its identity? What presupposes this question is, of course, the Hegelian insight that the other is the condition of possibility of identity, that the "I" can recognize itself only if it is recognized by the other whom it "previously" recognized in its otherness. Or, to use a different vocabulary to which we will often refer in the analysis that follows: the "I" can exist in its subjectivity only if it is interpellated, only if the Other calls it, names it, subjects it, and thus constitutes it. According to Althusser's presupposition one has to know that s/he is interpellated and subjected, s/he has to be able to appropriate reflexively her own subjectedness insofar as it is precisely the knowledge by which she mediates her situation that constitutes her as a subject. The "formula" of Althusserian interpellation therefore says: you have to know that you are subjected, you have to appropriate and live your subjectedness in order to constitute yourself as subject (of power). Your freedom, as the freedom of the subject of power is the effect of your subjection. The best example of this freedom produced by complete subjection is the way in which we learn and appropriate language. We say that one is a "native speaker" not because there are "natural" and "artificial" languages but because we are able to speak a language by following all its rules and laws *without thinking about them at all*, feeling free within them; in other words, when we are completely imbued with the law of a language, completely constituted by it, or completely subjugated by it, we stop thinking about it because we ourselves are that very law. The force of law is then our very nature—that is why we are native speakers. On the other hand, a foreign language remains foreign precisely to the extent that we are not able to appropriate all its laws, because we continue to think about them: we do not feel free because we are not completely subjected, because we still resist the law.

The same Althusserian logic of interpellation should be valid for the process of production of identity of a nation or race. The Hegelian philosophy of war was precisely a function of that insight: the identity of the nation is constituted only through a traumatic intervention of the Other so that exposure to the possibility of being subjected to the other, the fight for life and death, the exposure of the nation to the experience of its death, the collectivity of the experience that faces the nation with the agony of its "disappearance," is what actually constitutes its identity. The Hegelian philosophy of war is, therefore, a predictable outcome of the narrative of master and slave. However, the contemporary technology of war escapes the master-slave logic insofar as today it is possible to wage a war in which one side remains always already immortal, and is not exposed to the possibility of its own death. This dramatically changes the structure of the Hegelian, but also of the

Althusserian argument and calls for a reformulation of the strategy of interpellation and therefore of the strategy of constituting an identity. (In other words, it demands a reformulation of the very concept of the political insofar as the latter presupposed the concept of sovereignty, self-appropriation through procedures of interpellation, procedures that have to be reflexive if subjection is to function as the condition of subjectivation.)

If the Althusserian conception of interpellation can be reformulated then this reformulation will be brought to bear precisely on the instance of self-reflexive appropriation of one's situation. In other words it becomes necessary to raise the question: is an interpellation without self-reflexive appropriation possible, is it possible for interpellation to take place without the subject's knowledge of it? Judith Butler clarifies:

Consider the situation in which one is named without knowing that one is named, which is, after all, the condition of all of us at the beginning. . . . The name constitutes one socially, but one's social constitution takes place without one's knowing. . . . One need not know about or register a way of being constituted for that constitution to work in an efficacious way. For the measure of that constitution is not to be found in a reflexive appropriation of that constitution, but, rather, in a chain of signification that exceeds the circuit of self-knowledge. The time of discourse is not the time of the subject.[4]

Simply put, interpellation can function successfully, the subject can be subjectivized through his subjection to subjectivation, to the intervention of the Other, without his knowing that he has been caught in the loop of interpellation: interpellation functions even if nobody turns to answer the call of the policeman or of God. For interpellation to be effective the self-reflexive appropriation of its procedure is not necessary; the only necessary condition is the infinite, impersonal functioning of the Other.

Our question (how the mind enclosed within itself constitutes its identity) could therefore be formulated in the following way: what happens with interpellation, with the whole circulation of subjection-subjectivation when the Other is absent? If the mind sunken into the agony of race is the mind that always already presupposes the exclusion of the Other, if the Other cannot constitute it because it is outside of my "already constituted" world, how then can this world of "ideal closedness" constitute and identify itself? How is interpellation possible at all if the mind of the ideally closed race (or nation) steps out of the time of the other? This is to say: if we follow Judith Butler and allow that interpellation is possible without the subject's knowledge of it, and if we accept the fact that the time of discourse is not the time of the subject, what then happens with interpellation when the subject steps out of the time of discourse, when the discrepancy between time of discourse and time of the subject disappears so that all time becomes the time of the subject (the time of eternity)? Following Lacan from the seminar on psychoses, we will determine this interpellation as *psychotic interpellation*. Within the structure of this interpellation the circulation of subjection-subjectivation is an effect of the exclusion of the Other: "the cycle contains an exclusion of the big Other. The circuit closes on the two small others. . . ."[5] Instead of the big Other there emerges a little other (produced by the subject itself) who addresses the subject not from reality but from the real that the subject experiences as exteriority: the voice of the interpellating Other that subjectivized the subject and that is produced by the subject itself is the voice that, as far as the subject is concerned, arrives "from without."

What is of utmost importance here is precisely to understand that the subject does not know that the other who interpellates it is, actually, the little other produced by the subject itself. This structure of interpellation, therefore, inverts the logic of that described by Butler: here the subject knows that it is interpellated but does not know that it interpellates itself ("she does not know that she is saying this, but she says it nevertheless," says Lacan); in other words, it does not know that the big Other is absent and that it itself now functions as the big Other: "the Other being truly excluded, what concerns the subject is actually said by the little other, by shadows of others. . . ."[6] The subject spectralizes itself (as well as others) and becomes its own apparitional other (its own shadow), thus subjecting itself to itself, recognizing itself by itself. A simple example of this type of interpellation is the voice one can hear in the New York cab: "Welcome to New York, the capital of the world." This voice of the big Other that establishes a city as capital of the world is actually the voice of the little other insofar as it comes from the interiority of the city itself, from its "belly," and can be heard only there; the voice that comes from interiority is the voice that is heard as if coming from "without."

Of course, the fact that the symptoms of this interpellation can be detected everywhere only affirms Lacan's thesis that remarkably enough we always participate in a psychotic interpellation and that we always understand it well: "Naturally, I understand—which proves that we all have a little something in common with delusionals."[7] This structure of interpellation taken to its extreme is precisely the structure that establishes the "nature" of the mind caught in the "agony" of race (or nation) and wrapped up in its world as the only possible world, outside of which there is no other world. The process of self-recognition here unfolds within a closed world, within its delusional order as in a situation in which the little other (addressed directly) is produced as big Other (as the whole symbolic field constituting and affirming the identity of the whole nation): the hundreds of thousands of people gathered to give support to their leader Slobodan Milošević are there not in order to hear their leader, not in order to send a political message to the others, but simply in order to close the circle of a delusional order, to give support to themselves for the war/s, to recognize themselves. For their leader does not speak, they are the ones who speak or, more precisely, it is they who passionately cry out one single sentence: "Slobodan, we love you," after which the other answers: "I love you, too," thus closing this self-establishing circle, or, to put it differently, thus establishing self-constitution within the order of a "paranoid delusion." All individual "I"s or egos are here annihilated, they have sunk into the collective alter ego, become the amorphous "totality" of the shadows of the others that ask another little other to give it an answer—I love you too. As is the case with all psychotic delusions, "the *ego* speaks through the intermediary of the *alter ego*,"[8] through the intermediary of the collectivity or the national "spirit." In this case, everything happens as if the nation (which, according to Freud, could be a "part" of the ego ideal) had "swallowed" the ego, as if the ego had fallen into the ideal and now existed in such an "ideal" way, as a shadow. And the message that returns to all those gathered there affirms (and thus "seals") the self-constitution of the collectivity of the race in its ideal closedness; for whoever receives this message, "I love you too" means: I am affirmed and I am loved only as We, therefore, *I am We*, the only "I" that is possible for me is the I of the We, I exist only through my nation (or race) and as that nation.

The Marital Life of the Philosopher and the Nation as Family

To say that the "I" exists only as We is to say that I exist only by the way of non-existence: the particularity of my desires is negated along with the particularity of my body. The negated individual body has been resurrected within the spectral *national spirit* (which is the spirit that "lives on" live bodies: the individual deaths of all those killed in war are experienced as the prolongation of the life of that very spirit), within a closed set of shadows, within a body without body that lives its apparitional life as "pure" life, as dead life that ensures the fantasmatic identity of the race (or nation). "We" therefore lives only in the sameness of its delirious identity, in a life without change (however, since life without change is impossible this life has to be conceived of only as an idea about life, a fantasy or the shadow of life). The idea of the ideally closed life finds its embodiment in the celebration of life as routine, of life as "pure habit." Life as routine is a styled life, life with clear "boundaries," life as repetition; it is the life that dreams about its predictability. That is why it is (or wants to be) pure life. "Between purity and routine there exists a powerful causality that sometimes takes the form of their identity, so that one should talk about routine only as of pure routine and about purity as routine purity."[9] The life of routine celebrates habit as a preservation of "what has been," as the life that is no longer alive and that, precisely thanks to its death, is pure. This life is rooted in the family insofar as the family provides the subjugation of individuals to collective norms and ideals and reshapes their individual life into the life of the community (no solitary or isolated life is pure).

In the nineteenth-century dictionary of Serbian language written by Vuk Stefanović Karadžić, which Radomir Konstantinović calls the "Serbian Discourse on Method," one can read the following under the entry "Ćiril Philosopher:" "Serbs narrate that on the day of Ćiril birds look for a mate to build a nest and to lay eggs. Whoever does not find a mate hangs himself."[10] On the one hand, there are birds, the "collectivity" named by the name of the species, whose family life is the life of the reproduction of the species (building the nest, laying eggs). On the other hand, the only bird here named by the proper name (Ćiril), the only bird that does not bear the mark of the species is the bird of thought and of philosophy. Such a bird does not build the nest and does not dedicate his/her life to the reproduction of the species; his/her sexual life is not "promised" to the prolongation of the life of the species and therefore has to be understood as "perverted." Such a bird does not find a spouse and does not obey the norms and laws of the community: it is a solitary bird that does not affirm the life of the community. It does not, therefore, belong to the community, or, to put it differently, anybody who thinks and whose sexual life is "perverted" (whose sexuality is not purely reproductive) is excluded from the life of the community and sentenced to death by that community (one should note that Karadžić says that that is what "Serbs narrate;" the narrator of this little narrative is therefore the spectral narrator, the "national spirit" itself).

The spirit of the race is essentially anti-philosophical and its anti-philosophical attitude is the outcome of its unmistaken presumption that the one who thinks never identifies himself with the "national spirit." For this "collective mind" the philosopher (insofar as she thinks) is also the one who, by refusing the collective identity, refuses the pure marital "bond" as the bond of the pure. This is precisely to say that for this "collective" mind marital "love" is only a manifestation of service to the race and nation, only an aspect of love for the race, love for the race being the fundamental experience of love. And, by the same token, any other kind of love, any love between an I and a You (whatever their gender might be) that does not obey the demand of the collective subverts its life; that is why it is expelled from the collective spectral life and sentenced to death: "The philosopher is always a Ćiril philosopher, thinking without race . . . a danger for the tribe, which is going to sentence him to death. There is life only within the race that objectivizes . . . for the race everything outside it is non-life, death itself, the synonym for foreignness and strangeness."[11]

If the philosopher is the figure of thinking without race then the homosexual is the figure of the body without a race. For the spectral "national spirit" the paradigmatic figure of the strange (or foreign) body becomes a homosexual body conceived here as a body that insists on the particularity of its desire, on the life of its life that does not want to die and fade into the apparitional spirit. Let us consider here the way in which the president of the "Movement for the Fatherland—Dignity," Nebojša Krstić, reacted to the gay parade that took place in Belgrade in June 2001, stating that such parades are nothing other than the mocking of morality, mocking of the *family, of the spiritual and national identity* of the Serbian people who have already suffered a great deal. "Just force," he demands, "must be used to resolutely strike at all the local damned homosexuals. . . . They should all be punished mercilessly and justly sentenced to death or life imprisonment if we wish the Serbian nation to survive."[12] Needless to say, this is a crystal clear example of the psychotic interpellation: I think only what Serbian people think; I am communicating the message I have received from the big Other, who in this case is only my fantasy (the fantasmatic shadow of others); I am relating therefore the message I have received from the "real," from my own delirious world in which I do not exist as I, in which I exist only as the spectral collectivity that speaks through me and says: the family exists only as the existence of national identity which is spiritual; the family exists as negation of the body, as pure spirit which is the spirit of the race: identity is always and only the identity of the bodiless spirit of the race. (One should notice here a curious contradiction, namely, that this bodiless and asexual spirit is gendered as heterosexual; should we conclude from this that it is precisely heterosexuality which forecloses sexuality insofar as heterosexuality is what here provides the pure life of the body and therefore the way out of sexuality? The reasoning of this mind would therefore be understood as follows: we are excluding homosexuality because we are excluding sexuality as such; sexuality is possible only as homosexuality; by insisting on so-called heterosexuality we are actually insisting on the pure, bodiless life of the spirit).

In order to try to discover what this President of the Movement for the Fatherland (the president who presides over his father) is talking about and to whom he is talking we should be reminded of Lacan's psychotic patient and her delirious butcher:

She confided to me that one day, as she was leaving her home, she had a run-in in the hallway with an ill-mannered sort of chap, which came as no surprise to her, since this shameful married man was the steady lover of one of her neighbors. . . . On passing her . . . he had said a dirty word to her, a dirty word that she was disinclined to repeat to me because, as she put it, it devalued her. Nevertheless . . . after five minutes of chat we were on good terms with one another and on that subject she confessed to me with a conceding laugh that she was not completely innocent in this matter for she herself had said something in passing. This something, which she confessed to me . . . was this—*I've just been to the butcher's*. . . . I said—*I've just been to the butcher's*, and then she blurts it out to us, what did *he* say? He said—*Sow!* . . . What does she say? She says—*I've just been to the butcher's*. Now, who has just been to the butcher's? A quartered pig. She does not know that she is saying this, but she says it nevertheless. That other to whom she is speaking, she says to him about herself—*I, the sow, have just been to the butcher's*.[13]

Now, if our answer to the President of the Movement for the Fatherland were to be as follows: "We understand that when you are addressing us you are trying to send us a message about your sexuality that haunts you," we would be wrong. For such an answer would only mean that we were returning his message in the inverted form or else that he was within the logic of "true speech," that his speech "commited us" as Lacan would say and thus made the Other speak. The whole trick of his speech is, however, "hidden" precisely in the "fact" that he does not address us at all. He is the president of a movement, of a motion, or of a life that lives for its father; he is the very life of his father who, therefore, is not dead; he is talking to his father, this shadow of the other is what is addressed here. And this father lives on his "son's" body, the son gives life to his father, he becomes the lover of his father who gives birth to his father and thus becomes the father of his father who is all the time his brother insofar as both of them "reach" their spectral life through the "spectral" womb of their mother, the Land. This delirious spirit of the "spiritual race" is therefore the spirit whose father is always alive, whose father is the father that cannot die. The father before the instance of the "taboo" therefore, the father who supports the fantasmatic loop of sexual intercourse between brothers. "Brothers" means here precisely brothers, not "brotherhood." For brotherhood is based on homosocial bonds that are possible only if they are mediated by women or others (strangers and foreigners), whereas the "dream" of a brother that dreams of the possibility of sexual intercourse with a brother excludes not only women but also everyone else who does not have the same father. (That is why for such a brother who communicates with his father the *figure* of the homosexual is so disturbing: the homosexual would be the one who proved the possibility of the life of the individual body in spite of the death of the father).

Woman Buried Alive

The Serbian myth about the foundation of the city (which should be the foundation of the nation and race) presupposes that the nation can be constituted only after it has been constituted. This myth, in short, and according to the version given in the poem "Building of the City on the Bojana River," narrates a tale of three noblemen brothers who are building the city (which also means the wall, the border). Race, kinship, and kingdom already exist (one of the brothers is the king) which means that the city, supposed to constitute the "kingdom" is constituted on the foundation of what it has to constitute, as if kingdom and race existed in non-existence (kingdom without kingdom, race without race). However, the building of the city somehow always fails: everything that the brothers build during the day gets ruined during the night. The building of the city disturbs a fairy who will, at some point, address one of the brothers (the king) to tell him that she will allow the existence of the city only if one of their wives is sacrificed: only if they build one of their wives into the walls of the city. According to the predictable logic of the myth, the wife of the youngest brother will be built into the foundations of the city, the prettiest and the smartest one, in a word, the woman. The myth vividly describes how this woman slowly disappears into the walls, how the parts of her body slowly become invisible while she is begging for her life, until, in the end, her voice gets silenced within the walls. One could, of course, say that this myth is like any other myth of foundation insofar as it relates the constitution of the race through the exclusion of the stranger or woman. The race is rooted in the exclusion of the woman's gaze and voice (in the exclusion of the gaze and voice of the other): the wall of the city is thus a veil that covers her eyes and blocks her voice; voiceless, gazeless, she will be forever alive in the crypt of the city, in the city as crypt.

However, this strategy of foundation and exclusion has its particularities. For this exclusion is not a "primordial" exclusion that would take place within the imaginary space of a myth that "precedes" the symbolic and constitutes it (in that sense this is not a myth). In other words, this exclusion is not similar to the one described in Plato's *Timaeus*: the feminine here is not conceived of as *chora*, it is not a nurse-receptacle who "freezes the feminine as that which is necessary for the reproduction of the human, but which itself is not human and which is in no way to be construed as the formative principle of the human form that is, as it were, produced through it."[14] The feminine is not formlessness as the potency of forms, it is not outside of the distinction between form and matter; on the contrary, it is already caught in the distribution of forms, formed as a woman, launched in a symbolic network that assigns to it symbolic tasks and functions. The paradox of this situation is that a phantasm is to be transformed into the symbolic through the exclusion of the already existing symbolic field; the already existing order (family, kinship, kingdom, race, nation) is sacrificed in the sacrifice of the woman (who is also wife, mother, sister, or queen). The "new symbolic field" is therefore built on the grave of the "symbolic," insofar as the whole city is the crypt of the buried female body, of a buried kingdom and race. This myth is therefore the myth of the foundation of another type of "race," not only the race that would be the effect of homosocial bonds (that always presupposes difference, the other), but the psychotically "pure" race of brothers who are literally brothers, who are building the city as the city of eternal life that would make it possible for the race to exist eternally as a pure race, as the race that never changes (and such a race is always founded on the "same" blood of brothers; wherever there is the dream of the purity of the race there is also blood). The symbolic field established in this way is therefore the imaginary based on the "funeral" of the symbolic (for to build a woman into the city walls does not mean to get rid of the body or of nature, but to get rid of the established symbolic ties); as the effect of this "funeral," the new city, the city of men in which the power of production and forming will belong also exclusively to men (for the city is built by three hundred male workers) should emerge. In this sense, the negation of the symbolic and the establishing of new symbolic relations (for example, the establishing of a kinship in which the kin would be exclusively men, for the woman is buried after she gives birth to her children, so that the new city is the city of sons, brothers, fathers; the establishing of exclusively male families in which woman would not function even as a "mediator" that transferred the name by being named) functions as the negation by which the imaginary tries to establish itself as the symbolic. What does that mean?

Here we should be reminded of the Lacanian distinction among different ways in which symbolic, imaginary, and real are represented: "the symbolic, represented by the signifier, the imaginary, represented by meaning, and the real, which is discourse that has actually taken place in a *diachronic* dimension."[15] That the imaginary is represented by meaning means that it is structured according to the desire of the particular, individual ego, that it is always a "personal little meaning" that only becomes the "whole reality" thanks to the existence of the symbolic that introduces "difference" between desires and the possibility of the "inter-subjective" exchange of desires, which means the possibility of the subjection of a desire to the desire of the Other: "There's no doubt that meaning is by nature imaginary. Meaning is, like

the imaginary, always in the end evanescent, for it is tightly bound to what interests you, that is, to that in which you are ensnared. You would know that hunger
and love are the same thing, you would be like any animal, truly motivated. But
owing to the existence of the signifier your personal little meaning—which is also
absolutely heart-breakingly generic, human all too human—leads you much
further."[16] But, what happens when the imaginary within itself produces the big
Other as the signifier whose demands it now follows? In that case, the imaginary
absolutizes its own "little meaning," constitutes a diachronic discourse, falls into
the real that becomes the whole reality, a discourse outside of time (without the big
Other), in an eternity of time as eternal reality that should provide the eternal realization (satisfaction) of the personal little meaning or of that "in which you are
ensnared," of the desire in which you are captured. In other words, the real becomes
the whole reality—the psychotic procedure for establishing reality. This procedure
is at stake in the Serbian myth of the construction of the nation-city as a city of
men.

For the sacrifice of the woman is here the effect of the big Other, but a big Other
who is already the shadow of the big Other, its specter visible and hearable only
within the imaginary of one of the brothers. The sacrifice of the woman is not
ordered by God or by a universal law but by a fairy with whom only one of the
brothers can communicate. This fairy is not, therefore, the specter visible to many
(like Hamlet's ghost, which is why the order that Hamlet receives is the order of
the big Other) but is the shadow of the shadow that emerges within a delirious
world. And this woman-fairy says to the king that he will be allowed to build the
city only if he first satisfies her, her desire, only if he gives her his own wife. The
fairy is a woman who wants a woman. To put it simply, the fairy that addresses
the king is a lesbian fairy looking for a woman. What is more, she is the lesbian-
signifier (that functions as the big Other) who has the power to disturb the established symbolic field of heterosexual and homosocial bonds, who has the power to
subvert family and kingdom. She functions as the signifier that causes the "twilight
of the existing world" and the imposition of the reality of her own demand. In a
word, the fairy functions as the lesbian phallus: "the lesbian phallus may be said to
intervene as an unexpected consequence of the Lacanian scheme, an apparently contradictory signifier which, through a critical mimesis, calls into question the ostensibly originating and controlling power of the Lacanian phallus, indeed, its
installation as the privileged signifier of the symbolic order."[17] In the case we are
analyzing the lesbian phallus demands the murder of the mother-wife (here, therefore, oedipalization presupposes the murder of the mother, and not the murder of

the father, so that the "oedipalized" son can be the perfect daughter-woman to his father).

However, if this lesbian phallus is here only the shadow of the big Other produced within an imaginary that wants to satisfy its own desire (the desire for male homosexual eroticism), then its function is to enable the prohibition on homosexuality imposed by the symbolic law itself to be overcome. For what is the outcome of this installation of the lesbian phallus that demands that the woman be murdered? The outcome of this situation is that not only is the guilt caused by homosexual desire (insofar as that desire is prohibited by the law) overcome, but also the guilt caused by murder: the lesbian phallus is here the law that demands a murder so that murder becomes a lawful act which only proves the thesis that "what operates under the sign of the symbolic may be nothing other than precisely that set of imaginary effects which have become naturalized and reified as the law of signification."[18] Insofar as this murder is ordered from the place of the (imaginary) law, the men who kill the woman (woman is here the figure of any type of strangeness and otherness) can "lawfully" sink into the "oceanic feeling" that allows any murder and allows them to be guilt-free.

That is the logic of these mythical brothers. It reads as follows: even if we wanted to we would never be able to rid ourselves of our wives in such a way, we would have to follow and respect another symbolic law, but that is now happily subverted by the order that orders the murder, thus making of it an ethical gesture. On the other hand, if the prohibition established by the symbolic order prohibits homosexuality then this prohibition is now also happily overcome: "Prohibitions, which include the prohibition on homosexuality, work through the pain of guilt. Freud offers this link at the end of his essay when he accounts for the genesis of conscience, and its self-policing possibilities, as the introjection of the homosexual cathexis. In other words, the ego-ideal which governs what Freud calls the ego's 'self-respect' requires the prohibition on homosexuality. This prohibition against homosexuality is homosexual desire turned back upon itself."[19] Taking into account every word of this elaboration of the prohibition on homosexuality, the strategy adopted by brothers who want to establish the city of man as the city of race and nation would now read as follows: since their homosexuality is demanded they, the brothers, the men, are destined to homosexuality, which means that they have to suffer it against their will and desire, that they have to follow the new rules of the new symbolic order. And by responding to the demand of the big Other who is here the Lesbian, they are still (according to this fantasmatic loop) heterosexual insofar as they are the perfect men of a female Other, insofar as they respond to her demand, which sentences them to homosexuality. And what is more, if the ego-ideal requires the prohibition on homosexuality then thanks to the twist enabled by the installing of the lesbian phallus, homosexuality is here what affirms the ego-ideal: we are not homosexuals, we only have to act as homosexuals, it is demanded of us, therefore, we can preserve the ego-ideal which governs the ego's "self-respect." (Only now does it become clear why this new kingdom has to be established only after the kingdom and the state has been established or why it has to be established only after the establishing of the social bonds that imposed the prohibition on homosexuality). What is gained by this imaginary detour is precisely the freeing of homosexual desire that now obeys the law that orders that very desire. In other words, homosexual desire can now be fulfilled by following the law that forbids heterosexual desire.

Another important consequence of this "ploy" should be noticed here, namely that this fantasy does not fantasize only about murdering the woman nor about the absolute absence of the stranger (only brothers will remain among us), but also about the exclusion of the lesbian. This lesbian phallus, which is here as it were a "subgod," has the paradoxical nature of the evil demon (who insists on killing) and the honest goddess; for the fairy will keep her word: after she gets what she wants, and she wants the woman's body, she will withdraw, she will leave the brothers alone in their city. Very simply: this myth fantasizes about the arrival of the absolute separation of the sexes after the "twilight of the world;" the sexes will be separated in such a way that they will never again meet; in our city there is no place for women, for the stranger, for foreigners, but also, no place for the female homosexuality.

Let us be clear here: so far we have been analyzing the *repressed* content of the founding myth (is there any other?). To explain why this content is repressed would mean undertaking a complicated analysis of the way in which the repression of homosexual eroticism functions; it would mean analyzing the "transformation" of homosexual desire into the feeling of guilt, etc. It would require an explanation of the complicated mechanism according to which "this prohibition against homosexuality *is* homosexual desire turned back upon itself."[20] But that is not the aim of this analysis. We wish rather to elaborate the way in which the repressed content of this myth is exploited to mobilize nationalism and how nationalism manifests itself as a male homosocial bond that reacts in a panic against homosexual desire. In this respect another aspect of the myth we were analyzing could be of some help, the one that plays a decisive role in the constitution of national consciousness as consciousness of the body of the "national land." This refers to a simple logic of exclusion: namely the fact that there is no such thing as an absolute exclusion insofar as what is excluded is always included in what has excluded it precisely as what is excluded.

What is excluded comes back, time and again, to haunt the field from which it is excluded and this coming back has at least a twofold function; on the one hand, it is the uncanny presence of an absence, but, on the other hand, precisely by being the uncanny specter of the gesture of exclusion it incites the desire for repetition of that same gesture: since what is excluded is never "totally" excluded, the gesture of its exclusion has to be repeated again and again. The return of the specter thus enables the repetition of exclusion. For example, the woman built into the city becomes, as it were, the naturally artificial foundation of the artificial building (of the city, race, nation, border, and so on). But to build the woman into the city walls does not mean to get rid of her. For, her body will go through a miraculous process of "transubstantiation," her body will become the body of the city or of the territory; the dead woman lives as the very body of the bodiless nation and the so-called "national spirit" is nothing other than the life of a dead woman. To defend the "national" territory would therefore mean to defend The Woman. For the mind sunken into nationalism the only woman is the nation and the "national territory" (which explains the sentences dear to the nationalist: I am married to my country, I live for my country, my country is my highest duty, and so on). Nationalism would therefore presuppose (among other things) the investment in the territory of the heterosexual cathexis, in such a way that this heterosexual investment enables and produces the homosexual male race. In other words the logic of this circle reads as follows: we exclude the other so that homosocial bonds can be transformed into the life of the "pure" race that lives on itself and within itself (within its male body-mind) but since what was excluded returns, it by the same token mobilizes that body-mind of the pure race, reestablishes it, and provokes the repetition of the gesture of exclusion.

The Dead Female Lover

It is therefore not an accident that Serbian late romanticism renewed this myth of foundation in its own effort to signify the twentieth century as the century without women, as the century that will finally mark the entrance into the eternal life of the male race. The motif of the dead female lover is certainly the canonical motif of romanticism (taken from Edgar Allan Poe and Charles Baudelaire). On the other hand, in Serbian late romanticism this motif has been rearticulated by means of a renunciation of the body itself, the life of the body, which is to say life as such; it represents as a mournful celebration of eternally living death. The dead woman's body therefore opens up the possibility of the self-spectralization of the body, of the killing of the body that led to the re-establishment of the bodiless national spirit in the dawn of the First World War. Serbian romantic poet, Sima Pandurović, offers these lines:

That distant gaze, the pale cloud on the forehead of our ladies
Hides a secret:
A mute non acceptance, a ruined desire,
A passion that was alive but is no more.

It seems that we,
The tired children of this century,
Are no longer interested in the other, beautiful sex,
That we cannot be seduced by the hope and chastity of future seasons.[21]

One should notice here how the ambivalence between the two stanzas produces a strange circulation of performatives and constatives: a performative that announces and promises mourning over the lost woman (life, passion, love, etc.) with all reproaches that usually accompany mourning (for she is the one who is dead, that is why I cannot obtain my enjoyment and attain my desire, that is why I have to give up my heterosexuality), is interrupted by a constative (We, the tired children of this century, are no longer interested in the other, beautiful sex) that introduces a different performative, one that is not the effect of the spectral presence of the pale woman, not the effect of her death. As if the diagnosis of tiredness now referred to the absence of interest in "the other sex," as if this absence of interest were not the effect of ruined female desire: we are no longer interested in the "other, beautiful sex" but because we are tired of that interest, not because the woman is "dead."

This tiredness, this ruination of desire, which is at first articulated as the ruination of heterosexual desire (and we could say as the announcement of an interest in the "same" sex) ends in the ruination of desire as such, in the spectralization of desire (as a renunciation of hope in the future, a renunciation of life). But what happens to the desire renounced by the national romanticism that tirelessly celebrates the "national spirit"? If to give up desire means only to displace it then we could ask: where did this desire of national romanticism go, where did it find its shelter? And how is it possible that the "tired children of this century" still have the strength to celebrate the race and to fight for it? Could it be that this desire (that gave up the body and therefore life) found its "home" in the bodiless "national spirit"? This is precisely what another Serbian romanticist and warrior, Dr. Petrović, confirms.

This man who was a delighted romanticist (and even wrote a long, boring verse tragedy about Serbian "evil" destiny, Serbian suffering, etc.) had fought in several wars until in the First World War his leg was amputated in the German military camp. There, in that camp, he passed through a painful process of self-analysis whose main object was precisely his nationalism; the notes about this process of self-inspection are preserved in the journal he kept in German under the title *Beilage zur Nirwana*, in which he reveals the truth of his nationalism and patriotism as the truth of his desire: "Thus limping on my crutches I often find myself in the situation of falling down in order not to crush an ant; but I am capable of shooting the whole squad of enemy soldiers without any feeling of guilt; the desire for crime, the one I cannot comprehend, produced in my soul the mask of patriotism."[22] This crime committed in the name of patriotism (which patriotism never "interprets" as a crime, "the crime . . . I cannot comprehend"), this crime conceived of as the defense of the nation from the "evil" other is the effect of the displacement of desire, or more precisely of the decoding and re-coding of desire: desire that is forced to give itself up, desire that is forced to renounce life returns in the form of a desire for death: "Death is felt rising from within and desire itself becomes the death instinct, latency, but it also passes over into these flows that carry the seeds of a new life."[23]

This new life is the life that Gilles Deleuze and Felix Guattari, following Wilhelm Reich, call the "life of traditional bonds" or the "life of the archaic" in which desire that renounced its own interest invests itself in the non-life or spectral life, thus spectralizing itself, thus making of life an apparitional life; "traditional bonds" or the life of death, the life of the archaic can take the form of folkloric life or a form "capable of nourishing a modern fascism as of freeing a revolutionary charge" or the form of "regionalism or nationalism." In all those cases, however, it is a question of the desire that renounces its interests but finds its means of remaining in life through a detour that affirms death or that affirms spectral life: "desire can never be deceived. Interests can be deceived, unrecognized, or betrayed, but not desire. Whence Reich's cry: no, the masses were not deceived, they desired fascism, and that is what has to be explained."[24]

The Blind City

One of the paths that could lead to an explanation of the complicated mechanism of this detour resides in the relationship between the process of subjectivation and its representation within the symbolic field, or more precisely its representation within the imaginary that propels subjectivation within the symbolic field. In other words, is it accidental that the process of subjectivation is connected to the building of the "new city"; is it accidental that by mirroring the process of subjectivation of the subject the "new imaginary city" at the same time mirrors repressed desire, precisely the desire whose repression had constituted the subject in the first place? Let us go back for a moment to the first example we were analyzing, to the example of the "myth of foundation." In that case we were faced with a kind of a "revised" subjectivation: an already subjectivized nation (or race) subjectivizes itself anew, this time, however, making visible what was invisible and vice versa, making invisible what was visible or visibly represented in the first effort of subjectivation: woman was transformed into the invisible foundation of the city that was never visible for those within the city for they could not see the very place they occupied; and what was not visible "before" the city, the male homosexual desire that was concealed by homosocial bonding, that is to say, by bonding that required women, now became visible. That again means that according to the way in which this imaginary imagines the city, the city dwellers are men (woman is not a city dweller and what is more she is not a citizen, she does not belong to us, and to our race). How are we, therefore, to understand the relationship between the subjectivation of the subject and the building of the imaginary city? Does this imaginary city take something over from the logic of the city and if so, what?

Hubert Damisch refers to the change that Jacques Callot introduced in the way the city was represented to the gaze (its own gaze). He, no doubt, still used Brunelleschi's perspective (what is more, one could say that "all views of the city current in our own time are tributaries, in one way or another, of the perspective configuration—perspective being essentially constructive, if not urban"[25]). However, he changed the position of Brunelleschi's spectator:

> Jacques Callot engraved the same sites exploited by the Florentine architect in his experiments . . . but introduced into the corner of his compositions, in the position of the observer, a figure on an artificial hill taking in the spectacle of the city offered by his elevated perch. However crude in iconographic terms, this procedure nonetheless evidences a concern to obtain . . . *a more comprehensive vision of the city*. . . . The observer is no longer immediately implicated in the spectacle, being positioned at eye-level and at a reasonable proximity, as with Brunelleschi. Rather, he is moved simultaneously backward and upward.[26]

In other words, he invented a spot "in motion" that was outside of the city even though it was a "part" of it; he invented an internal exteriority as the necessary condition for viewing the city in its wholeness (thus announcing the arrival of the panoramic view).

What, in this invention, is of utmost importance for our analysis is the fact that it mimes or mirrors the position and strategy of the modern subject, able to be the subject only insofar as it is able to distance itself from itself in order to apprehend or to see itself, to see through itself; or to put it differently, able to be the subject, able to subjectivize itself only if it subjects itself to its own gaze. According to

Damisch, nineteenth-century architecture will apply this invention to the "internal" architectural organization of the city thus making the city visible to itself: "But only in the nineteenth century did architects multiply panoramic prospects by erecting all manner of belvederes and terraces, bridges, viaducts, elevated trains."[27] And even though the panoramic view is always a view seen from a point of view, even though every totality is only an aspect of totality, that does not change the fact that structurally, the modern city is visible to itself, that it mirrors itself (Damisch calls it "the narcissistic city"), that it wants to see itself seeing. (The same goes for the subject: the fact that it always fails to apprehend itself does not negate the insight that the subject is always the very effect of its effort to apprehend itself.)

According to the hypothesis we are advancing here, the imaginary mythical city would be the inversion of the narcissistic city and its logic of self-mirroring. It would be based on the idea of its total non-transparency, the result of dreaming the possibility of escaping subjectivation, the dream of the city as a cave or uterus, in any case of the city that would be uncannily canny, the city of pure oblivion and absolute blindness that forecloses any possibility of self-mirroring. By saying this we are not referring to Freud's example from *Civilization and its Discontents* where he tried to compare the archeological layers of Rome to the logic of the unconscious; for the main aim of Freud's example was to point to the simultaneous existence of different pasts within the same present of the unconscious (in the same way in which the ruins of the city exist beneath its "present foundation"). According to David Wills' interpretation of the Freudian comparison between the archeological layers of Rome and the layers of the unconscious, Freud's theory "asks us to defy . . . the space-time coordinates of an architectural and archaeological chronology in favor of the impossibility of a historical simultaneity. It is the same idea that was imagined by means of the magic writing-pad, the idea of successive imprints upon the unconscious 'surface' that *do not obscure each other but remain accessible and legible.*"[28]

In contrast to Freud we are trying to refer to the possibility of dreaming about a city (or about subjectivation) that would be fundamentally inaccessible to itself, fundamentally blind to itself; such a city would not be unconscious of its own unconscious or of its own past, on the contrary it would be without any split within its own present, it would be without any external point or site from which it could be visible to itself. Such a city, therefore, could not be narcissistic insofar as narcissism presupposes precisely the split of Narcissus, the split of the self-image that in vain tries to form one with itself. The paradox of Narcissus is that Narcissus is possible only as effect of the other, only as effect of fundamental loss or a fundamental split.

"The blind city," on the contrary, would be the effect of the psychotic dream of the invention of the artificial (built or produced) uterus; it would be based on the psychotic paradox of the prosthetic uterus, that is to say it would be a psychotic world in which the symbolic falls into the real thus producing not the "past in ruins" (which is what Freud referred to) but the future in ruins: "If one is capable of envisaging a reconstruction of Roman architectural history one is equally capable of projecting an architectural future, one that, like the past, will above all be strewn with ruins, with buildings and bodies in all sorts of dysfunctional stress and indeed just plain dead."[29] Following Wills we will say that the "blind city" or prosthetic uterus is precisely the psychotic detour taken by desire in order to project life as the life of "plain dead" bodies, as the spectral life of death. The prosthetic uterus therefore, is neither simply the natural cave of the unconscious nor the world of the symbolic that splits the subject and brings about the labor of self-appropriation: it is the world in which there are gaps and splits but only happy ones, only ones that can be overcome in death or in "eternal" life. Or, differently, it is a world where the signifier is substituted for by personal meaning and where the Other is substituted for by the shadows of others. Or, again, it is a metonymic world in which the partial object substitutes for totality and where non-vision substitutes for the panoramic view.

We will explain the logic of the functioning of the blind city by referring to the recent example from Serbian history. In 1999, for more than seventy days Belgrade (and also other Serbian cities) was turned into a blind city by NATO bombing. And turned into the blind city quite literally: it was bombed with graffiti bombs that left the city without electric power for days (literally in darkness). The tower on the outskirts of the city (that had a twofold role: being at the same time the place from which a panoramic view of the city was possible and of a TV transmitter that enabled national TV to function and therefore enabled information to be transmitted) was bombed. Bridges were inaccessible; the national TV station was bombed: in a word the city was "freed" from any possibility of seeing itself, it became inaccessible to itself. This, however, was not all. For this bombing also caused a radical destabilization of the symbolic field: the headquarters of the police and army were destroyed so that it was almost impossible to see a policeman on the street, important information if one takes into account that in Althusser it is precisely the voice of a policeman that functions as the privileged example of interpellation and therefore of subjectivation. Now, what interests me is the way in which desire was released in this blind city and how this emergence of desire on the surface of the city transformed "true speech" into delusional speech.

I am referring to the fact that the reactions of the inhabitants of the city were mostly expressed through graffiti written on the facades of Belgrade buildings. Those graffiti had two main features: their subject was always the first person plural (we) and their content was always the threat of homosexual intercourse or sodomy. After the night when Belgrade was for the first time bombed into total darkness by the special bombs, many of the facades in the center of the city emerged in the light of the day covered by graffiti that expressed the same desire: "Sidjite dole, guze će da bole!" (Come down, your asses will hurt!) Now, one can say that this is quite predictable, the helpless reaction of a threat expressed by somebody who feels threatened, frightened, or endangered. But things are not that simple for at least two reasons: first, because of the "position" of the one to whom this message is addressed; second, because of the nature of the extreme punishment of the other (of the enemy) that is in question here. One should notice that the reaction to the situation of existential crisis in which one's bare life is endangered is not a symmetrical threat, a threat that would say: "I'll hit your planes," "I'll track you down," which is to say any kind of threat that threatens the life of the other but instead a threat that promises a "punishment" worse than death. According to this thinking the only thing that is worse than a bullet in the head is a dick in the ass. The strategy of this punishment therefore reads as follows: I will leave you in a life that is not worth living, I will punish you with a life that is more horrible than any imaginable death.[30]

If we presume that for the sender of this message punishment by sexual intercourse is the worst possible punishment, or the threat of the worst possible injury, then we could also say that the speech that pronounces it (and promises it) is an example of hate speech. Now, what does hate speech do? It "constitutes the subject in a subordinate position." And even though the subordinated subject, the one who is addressed by hate speech, does not have to be aware that he/she is addressed by it in order for that speech to be effective (as we already noted by referring to Judith Butler's analysis of such speech). The subject still has to be part of the same social field or network. The fact that "one need not know about or register a way of being constituted for that constitution to work in an efficacious way."[31] says at the same time that one can be constituted by it (even without knowing it), which is possible only if one is caught within the same social field as the one who speaks the hate speech. In that sense, hate speech still has the structure of what Lacan calls "true speech" insofar as true speech "founds the position of the two subjects." To put it differently, true speech "makes the other speak as such."[32] However, in the case we are analyzing this condition is not fulfilled. The Other whom this speech addresses is simply absent (no NATO soldier ever entered the streets of Belgrade). It is not that the other is unaware of the hate speech addressed to him/her, but that the other is not addressed by it at all, since in no way can he/she be affected or constituted by it and, what is more, the one who speaks it knows that the object of his/her speech can in no way be affected by it. What remains of the whole complicated structure of hate speech is only one delusional moment of it: "the one who speaks hate speech is imagined to wield sovereign power, to do what he or she says when it is said,"[33] the one who speaks it delusionally imagines her/himself doing what his speech is speaking about, one imagines or one sees oneself doing the "injurious" act and takes enjoyment from it.

This detour through the absent Other is necessary precisely because it is not a question here of any "simple" unconscious desire but of (psychotically) closed reality (what we call the "blind city"). According to Lacan, "in psychosis . . . reality itself initially contains a hole that the world of fantasy will subsequently fill." But this "point of rupture" will be filled by a detour, that is to say by the logic of projection according to which what is projected returns from the outside: "It is incorrect to say that the internally suppressed sensation . . . is once again projected outwards. . . . But instead we must say that what is rejected returns from without."[34] It is important to notice that this without is a "without" constituted by the "shadow of the other," by the very absence of the Other. In the "blind city" the message, of the "text" we are analyzing, writes the repressed desire addressed to the Other who will never see it (who will never get it); it is, therefore, a message addressed to the gaze of its sender that will project itself in the place of the gaze of the Other and through this absent gaze will return the message to itself from "without," thus announcing to the sender the final enjoyment of his repressed desire ("final" insofar as enjoyment is always foreclosed, insofar as the subject does not have access to her/his enjoyment, or insofar as the subject can "appropriate" her/his enjoyment only at the price of not being the subject anymore). In other words, the one who sends the message is the one who will receive his/her own message; he/she, therefore, does not only put her/himself in the position of the one who promises punishment but also in the position of the one who is punished by her/his own punishment; thus punishing her/himself he takes her/his enjoyment for her/himself and vanishes as the subject. The dream of absolute sovereignty thus ends up in the reality of absolute desubjectivation.

Acknowledgments

I am grateful to the following people for their help with the preparation of this essay: Dušan Bjelić, who kindly put at my disposal the results of Lucinda Cole's and his own research on Serbian sexuality; David Wills, who not only corrected my English but found himself subjected to more Serbian nationalist polemic than he deserved, thus helping me to define the limits of my own tolerance for and argumentation against such rhetoric; Roger Conover, thanks to whose suggestions I further elaborated some of the examples referred to.

Notes

1. Radomir Konstantinović's book *Filozofija Palanke* (*Philosophy of Provincialism*) was first published in Belgrade in 1969. In it the philosopher elaborates the "philosophy" of race, the way the "spirit" of race thinks and is connected to the "philosophy" (in the sense of mentality) of the small town, or the "philosophy" of provincialism. The literal translation of the title of the book would be "The Philosophy of the Province" in the sense of provincialism. One thing should be emphasized: Provincialism (or parochialism) functions in Konstantinović's analysis as a technical term, as a concept that is not specifically related to "small (Serbian) towns," but to provincialism as such. However, in the second part of his book Konstantinović applies his analysis to Serbian provincialism in particular (mostly through analysis of Serbian poetry). His analysis of Serbian nationalism was undertaken some twenty years before that nationalism assumed its most violent form (1989–2000). Konstantinović's volume was a "cult" book for generations of Belgrade theorists in their attempt to think against mainstream (nationalistic) "theory"; in short, in their attempt to think.

2. Konstantinović, *Filozofija*, 8.

3. Ibid., 7.

4. Judith Butler, *Excitable Speech. A Politics of the Performative*, (New York: Routledge, 1993), 30, 31.

5. Jacques Lacan, *The Psychoses 1955–1956*, ed. J. A. Miller, trans. Russell Grigg (New York: Norton, 1997), 52.

6. Ibid, 53.

7. Ibid, 48.

8. Ibid, 42.

9. Konstantinović, *Filozofija*, 13.

10. Quoted in Konstantinović, *Filozofija*, 204.

11. Konstantinović, *Filozofija*, 206.

12. http://www.b92.net/specijal/gay-parada/tema_dana.phtml (Serbian); http://www.yumediacenter.com/english/as/2001/7/a030701e.asp (English)

13. Lacan, *The Psychoses*, 48, 49, 52.

14. Butler, *Bodies That Matter: On the Discursive Limits of "Sex"* (New York: Routledge, 1993), 42.

15. Lacan, *The Psychoses*, 63.

16. Ibid, 54.

17. Butler, *Bodies*, 73.

18. Ibid, 79.

19. Ibid, 65.

20. Ibid.

21. "Mrtva Draga" ("A Dead Darling"), quoted in Konstantinović, *Filozofija*, 321.

22. Konstantinović, *Filozofija*, 216.

23. Gilles Deleuze and Felix Guattari, *Anti-Oedipus. Capitalism and Schizophrenia*, trans. R. Hurley, M. Seem and H. R. Lane (Minneapolis: University of Minnesota Press, 1993), 223.

24. Ibid., 257.

25. Hubert Damisch, *Skyline: The Narcissistic City*, trans. John Goodman. (Stanford: Stanford University Press, 2001), 11.

26. Ibid., 11, 12.

27. Ibid., 12.

28. David Wills, *Prosthesis*. (Stanford: Stanford University Press, 1995), 100.

29. Ibid.

30. These graffiti (unfortunately my efforts to provide a photo failed) were written mostly on the facades of the buildings of the pedestrian zone of the city (Knez Mihajlova Street), and as I remember, were greeted with satisfaction by the majority of pedestrians. The curious thing was that even those who "supported" the NATO bombing, thinking that Milosević's nationalism could be defeated only by force, had recourse to a similar "discursive" strategy, supporting the bombing but in an inverted form, placing themselves in what they imagined the "feminine" position to be. Thus a male acquaintance of mine told me: "If they introduce ground troops I'll gladly give a blow job to the first black G. I." This is, however, a double self-victimization insofar as he is congratulating himself not only for his willingness to renounce his masculinity and to give someone a blow job, but even for going so far as to renounce his racial "preferences." Simply, his "anti-nationalistic" stance is actually racist and homophobic. It therefore doubles and mirrors the ideology of those it is directed against.

31. Butler, *Excitable*, 31.

32. Lacan, *The Psychoses*, 37.

33. Butler, *Excitable*, 16.

34. Lacan, *The Psychoses*, 46.

11

Sexualizing the Serb

Dušan I. Bjelić and Lucinda Cole

Testicles are a national symbol, a trademark of the race; other peoples have luck, tradition, erudition, history, reason (but balls belong to us alone).
Danilo Kiš[1]

The above quotation, however ironic, foreshadows recent attempts on the part of critics and scholars to "explain" the Serb, usually in order to account for widespread rape during the break-up of Yugoslavia. Notable sociologists, anthropologists, women's studies scholars, political theorists, and psychoanalytic critics have contributed to this discussion in ways that sometimes support and sometimes reject essentialist descriptions of Serbian identity.[2] What has emerged is what Michel Foucault would identify as a *discourse*, a system of more or less organized statements whereby Serbs, and especially Serbian men, become marked as "objects of knowledge."[3] Some of this work emanates from Yugoslav-successor countries, some from England and the United States. In both cases, for obvious and understandable reasons, such scholarship has been dominated by attention to questions of gender—the real and imaginary power of men over women. We do not wish to deny this power, or that it has been exercised in often brutal ways over the past ten years. But if Foucault's work has taught us anything, it is that the paths of both sexuality and power are far less predictable than our discipline-bound paradigms might allow them to appear.

This article begins, then, by "de-sexualizing" the Serb. If "balls" have indeed become for some Serbs a "trademark of the race," what were the discursive conditions, what was the sexual *dispositif*,[4] that made this identity possible? Since any association between sex and national identity is the product of a series of discursive maneuvers, ours is partly an historical question requiring a return to the early modern period. Beginning in the nineteenth century, as one Foucaultian scholar has argued, the deployment of sexuality "was generalized to an unprecedented degree, and it became more explicit than ever in dominant European systems of representation—particularly in the context of constructing difference."[5] Such differences were produced largely through anthropological studies of sexual practices with such titles as *Strange Sexual Practices in All Races of the World* (1933) or *The Scented Garden: Anthropology of the Sex Life in the Levant* (1934), in which the Serbs and other comparatively "primitive" people were sexualized, usually in contradictory ways. Together, these books worked not only to solder a link between desire and nation but to do so in ways legitimated by "science." Thus Havelock Ellis proclaimed close to a century ago: "The question of sex—with the racial questions that rest on it—stands before the coming generations as the chief problem for solution."[6]

In contrast to Ellis and others who seek to "know" the sexual proclivity of a nation, we examine how the Serbian nation defined itself with the help of a largely Occidental[7] *scientia sexualis*. We argue that the striving for "Greater Serbia" was partially dependent upon a massive deployment of sexuality often mischaracterized as either "barbaric" or "fascist."[8] Unlike either French or German models of sovereignty, Serbian nationalism is founded neither on the promotion of a universal citizenry nor on the creation of an organic unity, but on a modern principle of governmentality, in the Foucaultian sense, wherein "sex" functions as a new form of explicitly political knowledge. From this perspective, if "testicles" have indeed become a kind of "national symbol" in the eyes of Serbs and the world, prior to such a relatively stable signification is a common and markedly "modern" understanding of how, in the global theater of power, "sex" works.

I.   Early Sexologists and the South Slav Syndrome

It is by now a truism of postcolonial analysis that, for the West, the "East" or the "Orient" is associated with sensuality, sexuality, and the feminine. The Balkans are with difficulty assimilated to the Orientalist paradigm just described, in part because representations of the Balkans seem to lack what Maria Todorova calls "the overtly sexual overtones of Orientalism."[9] As she elaborates, men rather than women are usually the focus of literature on the Balkans, and the "standard Balkan male," unlike his exotic and usually feminized Eastern counterpart, most often appears as "uncivilized, primitive, crude, cruel, and, without exception, disheveled."[10] Todorova's generalization may be complicated, however, when we turn away from literature and poetry in favor of travel writing and sexual anthropology, where the "standard Balkan male" is not only sexed but sexed in particular ways, as in the familiar example of Rebecca West. In *Black Lamb and Grey Falcon*, West describes three men on Korčula, an island in Croatia, looking at a boat. "It is strange," she writes, "it is heartrending, to stray into a world where men are still men and women still women": "These were men. They could beget children on women, they could shape certain kinds of materials for their purposes that made them masters of their worlds."[11] Representing Slav men as almost archetypally heterosexual, she describes them only in terms of procreative impulses. Yet this "real masculinity" turns out to be pressed into the service of reform at home. As others have noted, the passage taken as a whole exhibits what one writer calls "benevolent racialism," whereby West locates in Balkan men "the opposite of everything she dislikes about England"—specifically, an advanced market economy and the effete kind of men it presumably engenders.[12] Thus she continues:

I thought of two kinds of men that the West produces: the cityish kind who wears spectacles without shame, as if they were the sign of quality and not a defect, who is overweight and puffy, who can drive a car but who knows no other mastery over material, who presses buttons and turns switches without contemplating the result, who makes money when the market goes goes up and loses it when the market goes down; the high-nosed young man, who is somebody's secretary or is in the Foreign Office, who has a peevishly amusing voice and is very delicate, who knows a great deal but far from all there is to be known about French pictures. I understand why we cannot build, why we cannot govern, why we bear ourselves without pride in our international relations. It is not that all Englishmen are like that, but that too many of them are like that in our most favoured classes.[13]

"Slav virility" therefore turns out to be predicated mostly on a series of absences: the absence of industry, technology, government, even French paintings. Such byproducts of industry, West opines, have undermined "in certain classes" the stability of gender difference and even the hegemony of heterosexual desire.[14] She interprets these lacks in a positive way, but the same characterization, as we shall see later, is easily collapsed into a discourse of the noble savage.

The point to be emphasized here is that West's text posits an English crisis in masculinity and helps give it shape by projecting a premodern and therefore "natural" heterosexuality onto the men from Korčula. Orientalist or not, then, this passage exhibits the twofold nature typical of the process of "othering" described most precisely by Irvin Schick, author of *The Erotic Margin: Sexuality and Spaciality in Alterist Discourse*. During the modern period, he writes, travel writing and related disciplines such as anthropology were not "merely the intellectual arm of imperialism" but also played "a central role in the process of self-definition" for Western European nations.[15] In other words, they were both externally and internally directed. Although he does not treat the Balkans, Schick traces the process of "sexualization" by following a modified Foucaultian paradigm easily transferred to other geo-ethnic contexts.

Briefly, one recalls, Foucault claimed that since the eighteenth century, sex increasingly served as a means to power, or, more precisely, as a means by which power began to operate in an entirely new way. Contrary to the Freudian "repression hypothesis" and its representation of power as a law, taboo, or means of repression, power for Foucault begins to organize itself through sexual pleasure; "it delineates, employs, proliferates, and arouses pleasure—not merely for the sake of pleasure, of course, but ultimately as a means of establishing control over life and death."[16] From Foucault's perspective, we—Eastern and Western Europeans, Danilo Kiš and Rebecca West—exist in a society of "sex," or rather, in a society "with a sexuality."[17] One of the "discursivities" through which sexuality was deployed was psychology. Another, as Schick points out, was sexual anthropology and its first cousin, xenological pornography or "ethnopornography," meaning collections and explicitly erotic novels (such as *The Lustful Turk*) set in exotic locales. While Rebecca West's description of men in Korčula is decidedly less titillating than, say, *A Private Anthropological Cabinet of 500 Authentic Racial-Esoteric Photographs and Illustrations* (1934), which features the naked breasts of women from all over the world, as part of a self-reflexive regime of sexual discursivities, it could have served more or less the same functions.

Within the context of sexual anthropology, works specifically pertaining to Serbs or South Slavs (as distinct from Turks and "Orientals") include *The Sexual History of the World War*, published in 1941, the same year as *Black Lamb and Grey Falcon*. Written by Dr. Magnus Hirschfeld, "Founder and Director of the Institute for Sexual Science, In Collaboration with World-Famous Physicians, Scientists, and Historians," the book belongs to a series, *Encyclopedia Sexualis*, dedicated to Hirschfeld but also to Dr. Iwan Bloch. Bloch's many accomplishments included a biography of the Marquis de Sade. In general, *The Sexual History of the World War* is indebted to the Freudian repressive hypothesis: War is an extension of the "erotic process" whereby suppressed eros produces "destructive sadistic powers"[18] during wartime. As Hirschfeld puts it, "The sexual misery of peacetime, the hypocritical morality of the ruling classes, perverts the natural impulses and finally bursts out in aberrant reactions."[19] A catalogue of wartime perversities—"Intended for circulation among Mature Educated Persons Only," the book includes chapters on prostitution, venereal diseases, "war eunuchs," "amatory adventures of female spies," "eroticism behind military drill," "the bestialization of man," "sadism, rape, and other atrocities"—in short, like de Sade's texts, *The Sexual History* provides a "catalogue of perversities," textually constructed pleasures suitable, presumably, only to those "mature" and "educated" enough to regulate pleasure in accordance with "normal" definitions of sexuality.

Hirschfeld casts aberrant sexual practices within an explicit theory of development, nowhere more so than in his discussion of "atrocities," in which he lumps Serbian crimes together with those of other South Slavs. Although "in general" atrocities "receded" during the First World War, Hirschfeld claims that rapes and "individual acts of cruelty, often with a definite erotic cast" were perpetrated "principally by the more primitive groups, such as Russians, South Slavs, Turks, Kurds, as well as the colonial contingents."[20] While the "Turkos" or "Black French warriors" most often practiced bodily mutilation,[21] "among the Southern Slavs, sadistic murders, castrations, and rapes were very frequent."[22] Hirschfeld's explanations for such atrocities are uncannily familiar to those who have followed reports of recent Balkan conflicts. They include a history of war in the Balkans ("one long and breathless fight for existence"[23]); an educational system that promotes "Guslar songs," or ballads of knighthood featuring scenes of torture[24]; and, significantly, a general gullibility to war propaganda, whereby fictions of the enemy's cruelty provoke retaliatory violence.[25] He bases these conclusions largely upon the writing of Professor Freidrich Krauss, who was stationed in Vienna during the Balkan Wars. As the latter writes: "While Balkan Slavs, no less than the Slavs of the north and the west are kindly and peaceful in their peasant and middle-class groups" their "minds are more easily poisoned."[26] Krauss's experience reinforces Hirschfeld's larger empirical premise that "these peoples have remained behind the rest of Europe in civilization and have retained their primitive traditions."[27] In other words, for both men, descriptions of Balkan "atrocities" fulfilled a certain function in the process of the "advanced" European's self-definition.

One can see most clearly how this identity formation works in Hirschfeld's discussion of rape. Hirschfeld begins by admitting that rape is "a sexual crime, always connected with war."[28] Reasons for wartime rape include alcohol, "protracted sexual abstinence," and the status of war as a "sexual stimulant," although he assumes that the ready availability of prostitutes probably cut down on the number of rapes committed in the First World War. "The field- and halting station brothels, no matter how disgusting, diminished the number of cases of rape during the war."[29] There follows a strikingly disturbing argument, at least to twenty-first century ears, about how the relative absence of rape among "advanced" Europeans was "a disappointment to many"—especially to women—since "public opinion was set on having a vast increase of this crime in the war areas."[30] He elaborates:

The erotic fantasy of the time wallowed in deeds of violence in the sexual realm which were attributed to the enemy, particularly to the Germans in Belgium. The soldiers of every land went to war with the conscious or unconscious resolve of indulging upon the field of honor in the pleasures of love and, whenever necessary, forcibly seizing them. "Women and cities must surrender." While the Germans were represented as embodying all vice and crime, Italian fliers on the Southwest front dropped down, among the Austrian soldiers, leaflets informing them that, while they were fighting against Italy, the Russians would make a triumphant entry into Hungary, occupy their houses and violate their wives. A French poem of that time began with the words: "Germans, we shall possess your daughters."[31]

So far, Hirschfeld has established that while all men are *potential* rapists, those of the advanced civilizations mostly fantasized about rape or threatened their enemies with rape by Russians—and this, in a decidedly literary manner, through songs, leaflets, and poems. Now he goes on to imply that any *actual* sexual contact between Western European soldiers and women of occupied lands should not be read in terms of rape, but as a kind of mutual seduction partially facilitated by the women themselves:

For the women, the brutality and aggressiveness of the man is, to a certain degree, accompanied by pleasure. The reasons for this are obvious. The conquest of woman and the act of copulation, presupposes, on the men's part, a definite joy in attacking. The woman who, in the act of love, is the one that gives herself, reacts to this with passion. The normal woman desires to be conquered by the man, to be forced; and only one step separates her from the female masochist who wishes, not only to be overwhelmed, but also to be raped and brutalized. Though the science of sex psychology is young, this point is ancient, for as far back as two thousand years ago, the great teacher of love, Ovid mentioned this matter to his disciples.[32]

His conclusion, then, is while men of Northern and Central Europe fantasized about rape, and even threatened rape, and while women of the occupied lands wanted to be raped, such desires were not for the most part realized—except, of course, in the case of the South Slavs and a few other "members of the more primitive groups."

Driving the above passage is an Occidentalism only slightly less apparent than its sexism. Clearly sexuality is being instrumentalized for the purpose of drawing boundaries between self and other. This "other," however, is not marked by absolute difference, but embodies what Todorova has argued about the Balkans as a whole: The Balkan suffers (or enjoys) an ambivalent status within the Western European imagination, represented less as absolute "other" than as "incomplete self."[33] Now, within Hirschfeld's Freudian paradigm, an "incomplete" self is an unrepressed self— in other words, a self dominated by unregulated libidinal impulses. Looking back on the above passages, then, we can see how the psychoanalytic and ethnocentric discourses reinforce one another. The Slav appears to exercise "natural" violent impulses, which "civilized" soldiers resist, sublimate, or displace, instead writing about rape or acting it out with prostitutes. In either case, the South Slav performs the Northern European's desire for sexual violence, manifests his pleasure, and in so doing, marks himself as part of an inferior race. As Hirschfeld wrote earlier: "War is that type of enterprise in which atavistic criminals, psychopaths unhindered by cultural repressions, and all sorts of primitives, are much better suited than civilized human beings who first have to go through the process of regression."[34] To restate this Freudian argument in Foucaultian terms: through Hirschfeld's text, the South Slav is *sexualized* in ways that legitimize and reinforce the writer's *scientia sexualis* and the cultural imperialism to which it is tethered. The Slav "makes real" what, according to the Freudian repressive hypothesis, would otherwise remain a part of the silent unconscious, that is, men's desire to rape and the "average" woman's desire to be ravished. In this sense, the Southern Slav's perversion brings into visibility "normal" sexual behavior simultaneous with a notion of ethnic difference.

Hirschfeld's discussion of inter-ethnic conflict may be relevant to the overdetermined nature of some recent scholarship as well. When he tries to articulate differences among Balkan peoples, Hirschfeld relies heavily upon the report of Professor Krauss, excerpting sections pertaining to mutual accusations between the Bulgarians and Serbs, each of whom charged the other with homosexual rape and castration. One Serb of "the academic class," Krauss claims, described the actions of Serbs in Macedonia.[35] They cut off the heads of men, consorted with their wives and daughters, established flesh markets, raped captured boys and men, and perhaps castrated the enemy. Krauss's ethnographic report interests us for two related reasons. First, as we have seen, he has already suggested that such reports are fueled by self-perpetuating "war propoganda" whereby "minds"—and especially Balkan minds—are "easily poisoned," which raises the thorny issue of verifiability. Second, as an ethnographer, he is nevertheless compelled to comment upon the "truth" of such claims, which usually amounts to marking one of two competing accounts as legitimate. In this case he takes the side of the Serbs against a Serb, offering as evidence a ballad in his collection wherein, upon invading Bulgaria, Serbs, rather than raping, "simply put every living thing to the sword."[36]

This example illustrates the familiar tendency to respond to reports of war atrocities by essentializing ethnic identity—who castrates, who buggers, who mutilates—and by countering one narrative with another. Whether or not this predicament is "postmodern," as some recent writers have suggested, it certainly created and continues to create a kind of epistemological vertigo, both nightmare and goldmine for the sexual anthropologist whose professional identity is dependent upon his willingness to make and support a judgment. To make matters worse, the very material that founds judgment and provokes moral outrage is also the stuff of pornography; a fine line, in other words, divides anthropology from ethnopornography, science from the erotic.[37] Thus, in supporting his own position, Krauss turns to a Belgrade newspaper article written during the Balkan Wars: The article accuses the victorious Bulgarians "of killing mothers and leaving the infants at their breasts until the poor things also died; of cutting off the sexual parts of male children and beating women on the naked abdomen."[38] Demonstrating full awareness of these troubled boundaries, Krauss reasserts his purely professional interest. He claims he has not the stomach to describe "the manner in which the sadistic conquerors took delight in the sufferings of the helpless entrusted to their keeping," but continues to describe them anyway, only because he is "constrained . . . as an ethnologist and investigator of primitive human impulses" to continue this "worthwhile project."[39]

We shall return to the problem of truth, desire, and *scientia sexualis* later in this essay. At this point, it should be clear that by the end of the First World War Balkan men were associated with a brutal sexuality, whereas Northern Europeans, while symptomizing predictable desires in the face of war, were represented as being capable of more complex psychological and erotic responses. (Indeed, Freud himself is reported to have said that Balkan people are incapable of repression and therefore of undergoing analysis.[40]) A last example of this phenomenon should suffice, this one drawn from popular culture. The 1942 film *Cat People* features a Serbian woman who tries but fails to enter into "civilized" sexual relations. Haunted by fears that sexual desire will transform her into a raging, mutilating panther, the inheritance of the Serbian village she tried to escape, Irene remains abstinent and eventually tries to kill the female friend her once-patient American husband now wants to marry. Irene is an almost exact rendering of Hirschfeld's Balkan, marked by a sexuality that is both dangerous and generative of endless interpretation. The sympathetic husband, for example, initially dismisses her stories as "superstition"; the girlfriend perceives them as a sign of emotional disturbance; the psychiatrist reinterprets them as repressed desire. The South Slav syndrome, now firmly attached to a Serb, compels her to become a screen for the sexual fantasies of the people around her. That the psychiatrist is eventually mutilated at her hands—or paws—paradoxically "makes real" her otherness, marked by the savagery and cruelty she both embodies and represents, against which the "normal" heterosexual desires of the husband and his new girlfriend are cast in clear relief.

That one of the first extended and mainstream Western depictions of a "Serbian" sexuality appears in female form should not be surprising; the "feminine" has often functioned to mark sexuality. That the sexually troubled Irene seems, at first glance, to be diametrically opposed both to the "freedom loving" or "brave warrior" Serb of novels and Western travel accounts is perhaps less predictable. Within the context of sexual anthropology, however, the "South Slav" had before the World Wars often been "feminized" or assimilated to an "Eastern" sensibility. As Dr. K. H. Ulrich had written about Slavic homosexuality earlier in the century: "That idea which scintillates in the golden goblet of the *Symposium* you will find alive today only in the Orient and among the South Slavic races, to a degree for which there is no comparison in the cool German nature"; South Slavs even surpass the Greeks in "depth of passion."[41] Moreover, within ethnographic writing, sexual cruelty, primitivism, the feminine, and reckless courage are often explicitly linked. At least according to Hirschfeld, with whose work *Cat People* was contemporary, sexual cruelty is a feminine trait most often found in "primitive groups" which, as we have seen, includes the Serbs. As he writes of castration: "In previous wars and especially revolutionary struggles this practice was not infrequently perpetrated by women," which is to suggest that Balkan men are in some ways more psychologically akin to women than to civilized men.[42] According to this Orientalist chain of logic, then, soon to be altered by the rise of Communism, the first Serb man was not a "man" at all but, by virtue of his unregulated libido, a dangerous and unreadable creature, half-woman, half-beast, and therefore an object both of fascination and fear.[43]

II. *Scientia Sexualis* **Among the Serbs**

Such is the pre-history—or part of it, anyway—of *scientia sexualis* and the Balkans. To understand the relationship between this discourse and present conflicts first requires acknowledging that while materially governments in the Balkans have risen and fallen, while economic regimes and ideologies have come and gone, what remains relatively stable is the discourse of sexuality within which such ideological changes are operationalized. Second World War military policies on sexual behavior, party policy surrounding birth control, debates surrounding the status of women, the absence of debates surrounding the presence of gays—all these factors and more contributed to nationalist and anti-nationalist struggles in ways that scholars, both feminist and otherwise, have begun to explore within the Yugoslav successor states, usually in overtly instrumentalist attempts to alter public policy. Working both within and against such material, we want to focus in this section on the relationship between nationalism and *scientia sexualis* in the former Yugoslavia with the goal of beginning to describe the social rhetoric of Serbian nationalism, and the role sexuality plays within it.

At some point during the 1990s, Freudianism, Jungianism, and other "sexual sciences" became less the province of an intellectual elite and more part of a national campaign to define and regulate "normal" sexuality. A host of sexologists or sexual "experts" emerged whose works are characterized by a radical self-consciousness about how Serbs have been represented by the global community. Obviously, these books are at least partially reactive. They attempt to construct a narrative of self capable of combatting, on the one hand, the "primitivizing" assumptions of traditional Western European sexology (Serbs are incapable of repressing natural impulses) and, on the other, a host of new characterizations following the Bosnian war, wherein Serb sexuality, somewhat paradoxically, now appears as "postmodern" in its sheer self-consciousness. For example, Catherine MacKinnon writes in "Turning Rape into Pornography: Postmodern Genocide": "the world has never seen sex used this consciously, this cynically, this elaborately, this openly, this systematically, with this degree of technological and psychological sophistication, as a means of destroying a whole people."[44] Self-essentializing works such as *What Kind of People Are We Serbs?: Contribution to the Characterology of the Serbs* cannot be read apart from this context.

Consciously or unconsciously, most sexperts appeal to what is perceived as a Western sexual standard. Professor Jovan Marić, author of the above text, provides chapters on such topics as "Relation to the Leader: Serb Oedipal/Anal Structures" and "The Serb Mental Quartet: Sorrow, Endurance, Masochism, and Stubborness." In "Serb Spirituality: Jokes and Serb Sexuality," he reassures his readers of their "normalcy" in relation to the rest of Europe by proudly reporting that when it comes to sexual performance, Serbs "are in a good standing."[45] He continues: "In our view, Serbs are efficient, that is very successful, in sexual activity and this is a rare domain in which, I am quite sure, we can equally compete with the rest of the Europe."[46] (Marić employs an interesting logic: Because there are so few sex therapists in Serbia, there must be few clients in need.) Isidora Bjelica, the political artist, publicist, and founder of the organization "Only Women Can Save the Serbs," seems to concur. In her book, *Self-Portrait With Men*, Bjelica offers a gallery of powerful Serb males, sexual profiles of men she has known or can imagine, usually described in relation to non-Serbian men. The sex appeal of Radovan Bigović, a well-known young Orthodox priest, is in his "urban image," she writes; he is a "Hollywood star from a David Lynch movie."[47] Even when the Serbs in question are gay or bisexual, as in the case of a writer Miodrag Bulatović, their sex appeal is based on which Westerners they had sex with: "He simultaneously fucked Gala and Dali."[48] Regardless of their ideological or sexual orientation, then, Serbs are, in Bjelica's analysis, "sexy" and "unique" partly by virtue of their proximity to Western masculinity. Naturally, Slobodan Milošević most closely approximates this sexual ideal. Bjelica argues that his sex appeal is tethered both to his "good clothes" and his authority, which for her creates feelings of security and excitation simultanously. Bjelica compares the "Butcher of Belgrade" to Mick Jagger, but the former is judged to be superior by virtue of his monogamy: "Although a peer of Mick Jagger," she writes, Milošević "built his image on quite different values by being faithful to a single woman."[49]

At issue here is a process of strategic self-stereotyping, born simultaneously of defensiveness in the face of Western representations and the desire to display what Michael Herzfeld refers to as "collective confidence," "alleged national traits" that "offer citizens a sense of defiant pride in the face of a more formal or official morality and, sometimes, of official disapproval, too."[50] Far from being directed toward the West, these are modes of "cultural intimacy," self-stereotypes "that insiders express ostensibly at their own collective expense."[51] In this case, in fact, the immediate trigger is not the United States, but Slovenia. As Bjelica continues in her description of Milošević:

Slovenes, who don't like him anyway, claim that his last name should be read as an anagram. The secret is in his predecessor. The pioneering, soft core French magazine *Louis* published Broz's caricature, editing his face against the contours of Mickey Mouse. The caption read, "Tito is the only one who showed Stalin." Milošević also showed the world! This is what Clinton and Albright could not forgive him.[52]

Without having seen the cartoon in question, we assume that it pictured Tito exposing his penis in a show of defiance, his Mickey Mouse head a reference to pro-American sentiment that would be anathema to Stalin. The wordplay can be explained as follows: in Serbian, "Milo" means "dear" and "šević" means "fucking." Slovenes used this word play as a put down, but Bjelica appropriates the Slovene joke, revaluing it: "Dear-fucker," or "known to be good in bed," is for her the essence of Serbian power and a means by which Serbs assert their national "balls." In keeping with his last name, "Dear-fucker," Milošević has "shown his dick" to the world (*inat*),[53] and this is what "Clinton and Albright could not forgive him."

The above example suggests that while "balls" are featured prominently in nationalist discourse and figure as an emblem of masculine power, the apparent obsession with balls among both men and women is really a reification of a more complicated sexual and cultural formation. This formation even contradicts other nation-making strategies, such as the appeal to "tradition" insofar as sexual discourse is deeply indebted to a modern conception of power. Power in the modern era, as Foucault has insisted, works through the codification of pleasure. In this new form of "governmentality," he writes, "the mechanisms of power are addressed to the body, to life, to what causes it to proliferate, to what reinforces the species, its stamina, its ability to dominate, or its capacity for being used."[54] This insight strikes us as crucial to understanding nationalism in general, and Serbian nationalism in particular. Both turn upon an "analytics of sexuality" manifest, for example, in the ability of the government to secure conformity through pleasure, rather than torture. (Thus pornography first appeared on Yugoslav television during the Bosnian War; similarly, during the October 2000 election demonstration, Mirjana Marković's television station *Politika* ran a pirated copy of *The Matrix*, not yet released in theaters, in order to keep Serbian youth at home.) What Foucault calls "biopower" replaced an earlier "symbolics of blood," in which "power spoke *through* blood," he writes, and where "blood was a reality with a symbolic function."[55] In the new context, by contrast, "power spoke *of* sexuality and *to* sexuality; the latter was not a mark or a symbol, it was an object and a target."[56] In casting their men as good lovers, then, the Serb sexologists both assert a "collective confidence" and model their nation on modern democracies, assimilating themselves to modern themes, including but not limited to "health, progeny, race, the future of the species, the vitality of the social body."[57]

One corollary of this argument is that analyses emphasizing "ethnic purity" as the basis of nation-building in Serbia are radically partial, at best. Foucault argues that while these two forms of power—a "symbolics of blood" and an "analytics of sexuality"—were initially grounded in two very "distinct regimes of power," they are now not easily separated. Racism "in its modern, 'biologizing,' statist form" clearly involves both; Nazism, he claims, was the "most cunning and the most naïve . . . combination of the fantasies of blood and the paroxysms of a disciplinary society," although the role of sexuality has been less thoroughly explored.[58] In contemporary Serbia, the emphasis is perhaps inverted. Despite the occasional rhetoric of war propaganda, "pure blood" is decidedly less important to the current moment than is the more generalized idea of "Slav virility."[59] Thus, ethnogenetic narratives of self often incorporate, rather than exclude, the blood of the Turk. Marić, for example, claims that Serbs inherited their sexual prowess from Turks: "If we take into account that our ancestors inherited something positive from the Turks," he writes, "then their relationship toward women could be included in a genetic inheritance, in those collective Jungian archetypes (and some recent studies point out that genetic predispositions are decisive when it comes to the quality and quantity of some sexual potentials and functioning)."[60] Here, the "sexual unconscious" egregiously trespasses Samuel P. Huntington's "fault lines" of civilization.[61] Ethnic difference, correspondingly, is reconsidered through a sexual analytics, as in the case of Nada Todorova, a Serb academic who employs a deeply psychoanalytic logic in the following characterization of Muslim sexuality. Since *The Tales of the Arabian Nights* are "full of eroticism," she claims,

it is certain that they (the Muslims) read them carefully during puberty; their effect on the personality of the latter is clearly evident. In committing atrocities (rapes) in Bosnia-Herzegovina, (their) conscious, sub-conscious, and unconscious levels or personality have been at work.[62]

In both of the above cases, *scientia sexualis* helps ground a newly racialized account of sexuality, or a newly sexualized account of ethnicity, through which Muslims are simultaneously represented as the genetic source of Serbian virility and as the perpetrators of mass rape.

III. The Case of MacKinnon

Such ethnosexual discourse is not confined to late twentieth-century Yugoslavia. The most obvious and controversial example in the United States is Catherine MacKinnon's *Ms. Magazine* piece, mentioned above. Published in 1993, "Turning Rape Into Pornography: Postmodern Genocide" introduced a mainstream American audience to the Serb rape in Bosnia. Briefly, MacKinnon's article claims a) that before the war, Yugoslavia's pornography market "was the freest in the world," which meant that b) pornography was heavily consumed by Serbs who c) during the war constructed rape camps in which d) pornography was found. MacKinnon, like the sexologists, essentializes the Serb in ways that legitimize her theory. Her long-standing argument that pornography leads directly to violence against women had, of course, already been attacked by equally prominent North American feminists, including Eve Sedgwick and Judith Butler. Butler had accused MacKinnon of "representational realism,"[63] or treating signs of sexual fantasies as referents, and Sedgwick had accused her of reducing all aspects of sexuality to the single category of gender.[64] In her *Ms.* article MacKinnon does both, as in the following pronouncement: "Serbian aggression against non-Serbs is as incontestable as male aggression is against women in everyday life."[65] Here MacKinnon equates masculinity with aggression and Serbs with masculinity, by analogy defining an entire ethnic group in terms of a particular sexuality. (All women appear as real or potential victims.) Such essentializing doubtless would not go unremarked were the subject, say, African American or Jewish, but in this case, at least to many readers, the link between ethnicity and sexuality appeared as natural—or as "incontestable"—as gender difference itself. In other words, because MacKinnon located "proof" of her theory in an "other" located "elsewhere"—and because no one wanted to appear to be supportive of wartime rape—American feminists remained markedly silent.

Scholars of Eastern Europe, however, criticized this piece on political, theoretical, and empirical grounds. Vesna Kesić, to offer but one example, questions MacKinnon's characterization of the former Yugoslavia as saturated with pornography, and we would like to amplify that point.[66] Although a history of Yugoslav pornography lies beyond the scope of this paper, it is fair to say that the Yugoslav market follows—indeed, is deeply indebted to—the pornography market in the United States. Nude photographs of women reflected a more general "liberated" attitude toward sexuality initiated by *Playboy Magazine* in 1969; Yugosavia's nude beaches, a subject of fascination for Americans, were artistically rendered by Leroy Neiman in the July/August issue of that year. *Start* magazine, published in Croatia, distributed throughout Yugoslavia, and attacked by MacKinnon, capitalized on that trend, representing itself as part of a larger liberatory phenomenon. As Kesić argues, *Start* was "very Western-oriented and mostly-anti Communist," and the appearance of Playboy-type centerfolds in the 1980s corresponded "with the trend toward social liberalization and the decline of the socialist regime."[67] Local girls were included slowly and very cautiously at the end of the 1980s, she reports, a claim reinforced by the history of porn films in the region.[68] Indeed, visiting Vojvodina last year, we noted that Serbian late-night pornography is rarely in Serbian; instead the actors speak German, French, or even English. Pictures of bare-breasted women in the daily papers are often old reprints of non-Yugoslav actresses and models from German, Italian, and American newspapers. Videos, modeled on those of MTV, feature Yugoslav women singing, for example, a Shania Twayne song, dressing like Shania Twayne, and even imitating her body movements. One could, of course, explain such borrowings as an effect of "globalization," but our point is more specific: Whether we like it or not, pornography is an effect of modern forms of governmentality, not its barbaric other.

Modern, not post-modern—this point strikes us as crucial, and it can be illustrated through the following account from *Time* magazine in February 1993, at the peak of mass rapes:

White Eagles have made rape a gesture of group solidarity. A man who refuses to join the others in rape is regarded as a traitor to the unit, and to his Serbian blood. Sometimes, that impulse to bond with the male group becomes a kind of perverse inflaming energy inciting to rape. Lust is only a subsidiary drive. And sometimes, young men in war may commit rape in order to please their elders, their officers, and win a sort of father-to-son approval. The rape is proof of commitment to the unit's fierceness. A young man willing to do hideous things has subordinated his individual conscience in order to fuse with the uncompromising purposes of the group. A man seals his allegiance in atrocity.[69]

While the American writer uses the language of psychoanalysis in his report—"lust is only a subsidiary drive"—his description is easily assimilated to Foucault's discursive model. Here, the individual is subject to a "total institution" whose purpose is to break down the structures of "naturalized" sexual behaviors and to produce or reinforce an institutional, or national, identity. This process involves a modern element of power which Foucault identifies, paradoxically, with both Immanuel Kant and the Marquis de Sade. As Andrew Cutrofello explains modern power, in Kant's "moral geometry" the European Enlightenment found a weapon with which to resist nature and to assert the freedom of subjectivity.[70] Kant's philosophy, in other words, was both a symptom and an effect of a new social discipline, now reified and cast in ontological terms. So, however, is Sade's *apathy*, with its cold detachment from sensory life.[71] Thus Kantian morality (*ascesticism*) and Sadean debaucheries (*apathy*) are not really diametrically opposed, in that both represent pleasure in the power of self-assertion—the power of subjective freedom—against any external determination, including sexual mores. Rape both requires and reinforces *apathy*, so *apathy* functions as a *technique* of power. The military, or at least the specific paramilitary group, de-naturalizes the sexual desire of a single soldier—subordinates "individual conscience," as the reporter would have it—creating a subjectivity congruent with the interests of the new nation and its military authorities. Rape in this analysis has nothing to do with postmodernism but shares the logic of the disciplinary state. Already fully established as a modern principle of power, sadism and its techniques may, in the case of the Serbian nation and others, carry "it to the point," to return to Foucault, "where it is no longer anything but a unique and naked sovereignty: an unlimited right of all-powerful monstrosity."[72]

Whether we like it or not, then, wartime rape and other deployments of sexuality—anti-abortion legislation, population control, the maschismo promoted and practiced by politicians—in fact connect countries of the former Yugoslavia to Western industrialized nations, rather than marking them as "pre-" or "postmodern" societies. In order to test this thesis, one need only examine so-called war pornography in the United States. These extensive and graphic representations of the conflicts in the Balkan states are designed for the entertainment—sometimes the erotic entertainment—of U.S. citizens. And especially since the election of George W. Bush and his appointment of John Ashcroft as attorney general, the media has been inundated with "pro-life" commercials disturbingly analogous to the population-control arguments or any Serbian Orthodox priest.[73]

That sexuality in Balkan countries is now (or was recently) *more explicitly and even more hysterically* attached to national power—to the question of state—is understandable. In other industrialized countries, and particularly in the United States, sexuality has all through this century served as what Althusser would call an "ideological state apparatus." But perhaps the Yugoslav-successor countries, partly due to Communism, are not yet fully adept at this game. Power, we should recall, works most effectively when it masks itself, and rape is a markedly direct deployment of power, as are the populist literatures of the Serbian sexologists, with their embarrassingly obvious insistence on "sexual normalcy." That both deviation and defense are part of the same *sexual dispotif* should alert us, however, to the double-edged nature of a piece such as MacKinnon's. MacKinnon seems to recognize, as we do, that empirically tracing "mass rape" to a handful of politicians is impossible. Rape is an individual crime. Her solution (in this article at least) is a sensationalistic act of ethnopornography in which a country (Serbia) appears as a metonym for the universal rapist, a man who, inflamed by pornography, acts out his (presumably natural?) aggression in heterosexual rape. Whether or not one supports the explicit feminist *goals* of MacKinnon's article, it is important to recognize its implicit discursive function. While helping to create the conditions for The Hague's recent convictions of three Serbian men for "crimes against humanity," it simultaneously worked to sexualize Serbs *as a group* even while in the United States, according to the National Victims Center, 1.3 adult women are raped every minute. By virtue of MacKinnon's tremendously popular piece, Hirschfeld's arguments about South Slavic "sexual cruelty" and even "primitives" as a group are now more tightly linked to the Serbs as a people. Under these circumstances, it is easy to see why, when the U.S. soldier Frank Ronghi sodomized and murdered an eleven-year-old ethnic Albanian, his plan was "to blame the Serbs."[74]

V.   The Defense of Dragojević

"Serbs as a people" includes Yugoslav film director Srdjan Dragojević, whose depiction of masculinities in *Pretty Village, Pretty Flame* can be usefully, if briefly, compared to MacKinnon's account. The film as a whole in no way apologizes for Serbian behavior, but it attempts to evoke, as Oliver Stone's *Platoon* does for the U.S. experience in Vietnam, empathy for the Serb "experience" of the Bosnian war. In so doing, the film indirectly raises the issue of rape.

The story unfolds through a series of flashbacks from the perspective of Milan, a wounded Serb soldier, whose childhood best friend in eastern Bosnia was a

Muslim, Halil. With the arrival of war, the two found themselves fighting without enthusiasm for different sides. Eventually Milan and six members of his platoon become trapped in a tunnel, along with the American journalist Lisa Kinel, who had been searching for a story about the Serbian rape of Muslim women. Her video camera records much of what happens in the tunnel, including the strange suicide of Velja, arguably the most "misogynist" member of the Serbian platoon. In this scene, he brings a gun to his head, unlocks the trigger, and Lisa Kinel looks at him inquisitively. Velja catches her eye, smiles, and asks: "One kiss for a dead man?" After a long silence, Lisa Kinel smiles at him and hands the camcorder to another character, Speedy. In a recorded image, viewers see Lisa kissing Velja tenderly. Overwhelmed by feelings, Velja drops the gun from his head, giving her a passionate embrace. He declares to the camcorder: "This is real Hollywood slobbering!" While Lisa sobs on his shoulder, he continues, "This is worth living for, guys. . . . At least a while longer!" Then, "I was just kidding. So long." He puts the barrel into his mouth and through the camcorder we see him pull the trigger.

The threat of rape magically turns to romance. One has the sense that Velja's suicide ought to "redeem" Serbs in the eyes of those so fascinated by their sexuality, or at least to redefine Serbian sexuality so as to contest Western media representations (outside the film, those of Beverly Allen and MacKinnon; inside the film, the story-in-progress by Lisa Kinel). It temporarily displaces the image of the Serb rapist by evoking a more traditional character, that of the fearless and romantic warrior; much like Prince Lazar in the Battle of Kosovo, Velja exchanges life for death, chooses heaven rather than earth, and the female of an alien people facilitates this transition. Simultaneously, his kiss with Lisa is pointedly described as "*Hollywood* slobbering," where Hollywood functions as the new principle of transcendence, perhaps the most important source of gender stereotypes for the Serb soldiers and the American reporter alike. Velja sacrifices himself, in other words, at the hyperreal altar of heterosexual romance, exchanging life for the singular pleasure of an American romantic moment. ("This is worth living for, guys!") The performance as a whole, Velja's willingness to die with some "Hollywood slobbering," re-sexualizes the male Serb in ways that might be soothing to a Serbian audience and palatable to a Western one.

Dragojević was, of course, aware of the difficulties of being marked as Serb. When asked by a reporter from *Vreme* whether people in the United States can truly understand the work of a Serbian filmmaker, Dragojevic joked that most Americans care less about one's origin than about one's ability to generate profit. Significantly, however, he immediately turns to the issue of sexual identity:

As far as the "Serbian question" is concerned, I was told by old-timers that, in spite of the propaganda offensive against the Serbs, between 1991 and 1994, men emphasized with pride their Serbian ethnic identity, which assured them the reputation of a "macho" or "true" man (both categories in deficit over here). But after Krajina, Bosnia, and in particular, the "unresolved results" in Kosovo, it was better to tell a girl that you were a Slovene, even, rather than a Serb.[75]

Dragojević's "defense" of Serbs does little to dismantle the idea that sexuality can be inferred from ethnicity. Serbs, he seems to be saying, are "real men," while the Americans and, to a lesser extent, the Slovenes, are not. In retrospect, we can see how Velja enacts this essential ethnic masculinity. The kiss constitutes a kind of Faustian pact in which Velja becomes a man fastened (albeit temporarily) to what Foucault calls the "charm of sex"—seductive, horny, and deeply heterosexual. Dragojević's Serbs, similarly, are highly performative: Sometimes Serbs in America, he reports, assume the role with pride, sometimes they pretend to be Slovenes ("I was just kidding, folks"), depending upon how the Real Man Serb is presently valued, and upon whether or not that image is useful in getting a girl in bed. Admittedly, one recognizes Dragojević's statements as indirect discourse, whereby the director offers the perspective of "old timers" while distancing himself, however slightly, from this attitude. One might even argue that he acknowledges "ethnic sexuality" as a discursive rather than natural phenomenon—as a mere matter of reputation, or a kind of cliché. In both readings, however, the issue of masculinity is profoundly overdetermined by what is only alluded to, wartime rape, which he dismisses as a "propaganda offensive" against the Serbs. Both in this interview and in the film, then, Drogojević gestures toward and then occludes the Serb rapist by offering an alternative model of male Serb sexuality that replicates the logic of the Serbian sexologists. As in the *scientia sexualis* literature, the self-promoting Real Man Serb was intended to serve as a partial corrective to rapidly consolidating and essentializing views. It does so, but only by hauling in the apparatus of heterosexual romance with its corresponding myth of the testicular male. From this perspective, Dragojević's "defense" of Serb sexuality ultimately shares the same problem as MacKinnon's attack: namely, both focus relentlessly on "man" and "woman" and, in so doing, both reinforce the apparatus of gender difference.

VI.   A Politics of Perversion

Because mainstream sociological analysis often conflates "sex" with "gender" and "sexuality" with "heterosexuality," object-choice often becomes invisible or irrelevant in discussions of national and global identity. Even a brief look at local politics in contemporary Serbia reveals the crippling partiality of that position. Revising this section for publication, we read in a Belgrade newspaper that a group of masked skinheads with bats and beer bottles demolished the office of the Social Democratic Union, a party led by Serbia's Deputy Prime Minister Žarko Korać. Several activists were sent to the emergency room with injuries. In 1997 this same skinhead group had attacked the Social Democratic Union for opposing the bombing of Sarajevo; this time the party seems to have been targeted for supporting the legalization of homosexual marriage. Right-wing groups are able to link such apparently disparate phenomena as the bombing of Sarajevo and the question of homosexuality by virtue of a logic not immediately apparent to those on the outside, because it turns on the fact that Yugoslav psychiatry treats homosexuality as a disease;[76] periodically, moreover, homosexuality is also portrayed as a peculiarly "Western" disease. According to Dušan Maljković, deputy executive director of the Campaign Against Homophobia, homophobia has now "taken a radical twist, and is finding a place in Serbian geo-political thinking."[77] What follows is an attempt to explore the logic of nationalist heterosexuality as that plays out in Serbia's homophobic *scientia sexualis*.

The most graphic example of homophobia pressed into the service of national identity formation is a book by Ratibor-Rajko Djurdjević titled *The Faggot Brigade*, a copy of which we found in an Eastern Orthodox bookstore. (It is one of Djurdjević's sixteen works published by the Christian Orthodox Press.) Born in Serbia, Djurdjević left for the United States when the Communists rose to power in Yugoslavia. He graduated with a degree in clinical psychology from the University of Colorado, studied with Victor Frank in Vienna, and joined the board of the American Psychological Association (APA) until it reversed its view on homosexuality (the APA now treats homosexuality as a lifestyle rather than as a pathological behavior). Djurdjević returned to Yugoslavia in protest, having written a letter to Max Zigel, president of the American Society of Psychology, in which he blamed Marx, Freud, and Skinner for the decay of the professional science of psychology, and for the legitimation of homosexuality, which he regarded as a direct attack on the Christan foundations of the human soul. Sounding like the poor cousin of right-wing Christian fundamentalists in the United States, Djurdjević begins *The Faggot Brigade* from the assumption that the United States, the center of world power, is the principle conspirator against the integrity of Serbian national culture. In his account, Talmudic Jews (as distinct from Mosean Jews) took over American society, shaping its version of Judeo-Christian culture, which has now begun to infect the Serbs. "The tragedy of the people of the second Yugoslavia," he writes, "is a consequence of the Judaic plans to establish a New World Order, and to make the Serb godless is proof that the secular epidemic has been spreading among the progeny of Holy Sava."[78] Pornography, AIDS, drugs, globalization, Marxist-liberalism, secularism, anti-Semitism, and abortion all stand as symptoms of this takeover. American Jews share their power with homosexuals, so the purpose of this book is to disprove Freud's claim that homosexual tendencies are universal. Djurdjević historicizes homosexuality, claiming that pre-civilized societies, including those of Vikings, Native Americans, and Mongols, all prosecuted homosexuality, which must mean that Freud was proselytizing lies.

While it is easy to dismiss Djurdjević's *oeuvre* as an extended paranoid fantasy, what made it possible was an historically heteronormative discourse on sexuality traceable to the early modern period. His text, then, is symptomatic in much more than a personal sense. Foucault, one recalls, argued that in the nineteenth century, the persecution of "the peripheral sexualities entailed an *incorporation of perversions* and a new *specification of individuals*."[79] By virtue of this process, the "homosexual became a personage, a past, a case history, and a childhood, in addition to being a type of life, a life form, and a morphology, with an indiscreet anatomy and possibly a mysterious physiology."[80] While Djurdević is anti-Freudian, he is not anti-psychoanalytic, and he capitalizes on the tendency of Yugoslavian psychiatry to treat homosexuality as a disease, assimilating this pathology to global political discourse. Thus in addition to being endowed with a personal psychology whose effects may be treated, Djurdjević's homosexual is also endowed with a national heritage; he (and homosexuals are usually *he* in Serbia, lesbianism being much less visible) can trace his origins to the United States. Now homosexuals are *both* diseased and "enemies of Serbia." As Maljković puts it: "Where the threat [of homosexuality] used to be the lack of children, now it's perceived as not only 'non-productive, but a life-destroying force,' directly related to the visible centers of globalizing power such as the U.S. or NATO."[81]

Even among those less directly invested in a nationalist agenda, one often sees the desire to treat homosexuality as a Western phenomenon. In the *Vreme* interview excepted above, a reporter asked Srdjan Dragojević to reflect upon and compare American and Serb sexuality. Assuming a somewhat constructivist position, Dragojević explains the prevalent phenomenon of American homosexuality, which is sometimes "puzzling" for a Serb audience, as a product of the logic of capital. It is a fact, he claims, that a member of the homosexual community (male or female, regardless) earns more than a heterosexual does. Because they can afford better cars and more expensive houses, homosexuals are far better consumers than heterosexuals; consequently, "homosexual culture" has been established and protected at the highest level.[82] In Dragojević's elaborate sociological fantasy, gayness turns out to be another symptom of a decadent capitalist West. It does not dawn on him that the liberalization of homosexuality in the United States may have less to do with the calculus of capital than with the painful but persistent struggle of a gay community against heterosexual hegemony. In any case, his desire to locate a "cause" for same-sex desire while attributing heterosexuality to "nature" aligns him with the right-wing Djurdević, however much their attitudes toward a Greater Serbia differ.

The "homosexual" constituted by both discourses is, in the words of David Halperin, "an impossibly contradictory creature, not a natural reality but a fantasmatic projection, an incoherent construction that functions to stabilize and to consolidate the cultural meaning of heterosexuality by encapsulating everything that is 'other' than or 'different' from it."[83] Simply the negation of a particular sexual/ political formation, whether conservative or progressive, homosexuality is simultaneously understood and politicized in ways that have partially determined the responses of the gay community, some of whose efforts, not surprisingly, are directed toward re-education. One of the goals of Arcadia, for example, a Serbian gay rights organization, is to introduce sexual education in schools, "based on the latest scientific knowledge."[84] Same-sex relationships, writes one spokesperson, "would be treated as one of the normal forms of expressing human sexuality."[85] In this ambition, one witnesses the appropriation of *scientia sexualis* as part of what Foucault calls a "reverse discourse." Having been pathologized, he writes, "homosexuality began to speak in its own behalf, to demand that its legitimacy or 'naturality' be acknowledged, often in the same vocabulary, using the same categories by which it was medically disqualified."[86]

This reverse discourse is the backbone of *Serbian Diaries*, one of the few gay literary productions to emerge from the Yugoslav-successor states. It is presumably the "memoirs" of Boris L. Davidovich, who, when asked whether having sex with a man is "unnatural," replies: "It's as natural as having sex with a woman." He then justifies this claim on scientific and historical grounds:

The most famous sexologists and scientists, such as Hirschfeld, Weininger, Freud, Marcuse, Kinsey and others, think that humans are essentially bisexual. That means that there's a potential in each of us to be both heterosexual and homosexual. Judeo-Christian morality is to be blamed for the fact that homosexuality has been "pushed out" from human nature and put under a ban."[87]

Later, Davidovich writes about his childhood friend, Vlada, who eventually gets married: "In Freudian terms he had left the so-called homosexual stage of development behind him, while I stayed in it for my whole life."[88] In this ontogenetic account, borrowed from Freud, Davidovich endows himself with a pathology. In other words, his text actively *produces* sexuality in ways reminiscent of gay-liberation politics in the United States.

This point might be emphasized. For Foucault, sexuality operates according to a strategic model through discourses, "tactical elements or blocks operating in the field of force relations."[89] The discourses of "bio-power" carved out "normal" sexual relations, but in so doing, they simultaneously create "abnormalities," including "the perverse adult." Foucault's insistence on perceiving sexualities in terms of positive power relations (what reciprocal effects of power and knowledge particular discourses ensure) offers a clear alternative to models of power based on the law, wherein power is conceived in a very narrow way: in terms of the dominant and dominated, the powerful and the powerless. Identity, from this perspective, including sexual identity, is never completely stable, but neither is power. As Foucault puts it, "there is not, on the one side, a discourse of power, and opposite it, another discourse that runs counter to it."[90] In practice, this means that a specific discourse—say, Freudian or Lacanian psychology—may be appropriated for both progressive and conservative ends, and sometimes simultaneously. Having said that, it is also true that, for Foucault, to reverse a discourse does not mean merely to provide a mirror image of it, or to replicate it. "On the contrary," writes Halperin: To "recapitulate in an affirmative vein, as the nineteenth-century homosexual emancipationist did, the oppressive, medicalizing discourse to which they were subjected, while strategically reversing the object- and subject-positions assigned by it to themselves and to the medical authorities, respectively, is, in Foucault's eyes, to perform a significant act of political resistance."[91] This appropriation helped to create a space whereby gay identity could manifest itself as a creative project. It carved out a subject position from which gays could begin to speak about themselves.

Within the Yugoslav context, *Serbian Diaries* is therefore a significant book. Presumably the journal of a gay Belgrade professor (though constructed in a much more formal arrangement than its pretense to be a diary would suggest), it covers the pre-war years 1986–1989 ("Freedom From Communism"), then picks up again in 1991, ending in 1993 ("War and Disaster"). Three major themes unify the memoir. The first pertains to the sexual adventures of the aging professor, his pleasures and pains, as he attempts to seduce men in Belgrade. This explicitly sexual (MacKinnon might say "pornographic") narrative is interwoven with a theoretical one, wherein the narrator comments on how sexologists and psychologists have represented homosexuality, both in the past and in the present. Within this context, he discusses, among other people Isidora Bjelica and Ratibor-Rajko Djurić. The third theme concerns nationalism and war. Although these three registers may be isolated for the purpose of analysis, in fact they are tightly interwoven, as in the following comment: "If it wasn't for sex" he writes,

which was the main reason why I met individuals of all races and nations, I probably wouldn't have such strong anti-nationalist and cosmopolitan feelings. Don Juan cannot be a nationalist because he likes all the women in the world. I am not a nationalist because I like all the young and beautiful men of the world. The sources of my cosmopolitanism and my love of all men are not to be found in my mind or in my heart, but in my cock and my arse, that is in my sex drive; it was later that my reason accepted this impulsive tendency, gave it a rational form and created an anti-nationalist attitude."[92]

In this passage, one witnesses a political and sexual alternative to the heterosexist *scientia sexualis* of Davidovich's nationalist contemporaries. Davidovich's discourse of bodies and pleasures disrupts a nationalist narrative inextricably tethered to a reproductive sexuality. As a radical reappropriation of Freud, it also reinforces the flexible nature of *scientia sexualis*. Although Radovan Karadžić and his mentor, Jovan Rašković, are both psychiatrists, they neither invented nor completely control the discourse they so effectively employ.[93]

Indeed, despite its constant appeals to Freud, *Serbian Diaries* can be read as a very Foucauldian text. Foucault always insisted that homosexuality did not name an already existing structure of desire, but that the task of the homosexual was "to *become* homosexual, not to persist in acknowledging that we *are*."[94] This comment and others like it have been explained as part of Foucault's "queer" sensibility, where "queer," in the words of Halperin, involves an identity without essence; it "demarcates not a positivity but a positionality vis-à-vis the normative."[95] Rather than "designate a class of already objectified pathologies or perversions . . . it describes a horizon of possibility whose precise extent and heterogeneous scope cannot in principle be delimited in advance."[96] By virtue of his off-center subject position, Davidovich resists some aspects of heteronormativity, both in positive and negative ways. In the midst of Communist-inspired injunctions against homosexuality, for example, which also portrayed same-sex desire as a "product of the Imperialist West," he reports on sexual adventures with a Serb, three Bosnians, two Macedonians, a Slovene, and a Herzegovinian, culminating with a member of a non-aligned nation and, finally, a traveler from the former Soviet Union. Throughout the book he mounts a critique of what he calls "the patriarchy," which he acts out in sexual ways. In a chapter titled "A Good Husband and Father" he writes: "So, I felt like I humiliated the man, a husband and a father, by letting him suck my cock and even gulp down my sperm. I know I am ridiculous with my ideas of the revenge I get on straight men, the establishment and the wider society. I sometimes wonder to what extent my sexual excitement results from some other non-sexual motivation."[97] Although his are not always happy unions—at several points Davidovich is beaten by his object of desire, and the journals indicate a Baudelarian *ennui*—together they demonstrate the kind of "ethical self-fashioning" that, according to Foucault, regards the self as a strategic possibility, not as something that can be known in advance.

One shouldn't push that interpretation too far, however. Like most of the texts we have already seen, *Serbian Diaries* upholds a rigid and essentialist understanding of masculinity, perhaps a by-product of the Freudian paradigm. One example of this, we hope, will suffice. The narrator attends a conference on the position of gay people in society and, enraged at an "effeminate" speaker from Bosnia whose "looks, gestures, way of speaking and what he said, were just suited to confirm the worst prejudices of the heterosexual public" writes a letter condemning the spokesperson.[98] "I estimate," he writes, "that ninety percent of all gays look normal," and to have such a "disgraceful effeminate" spokesperson was counterproductive.[99] This "heterosexual public," we assume, includes rabid homophobes such as Djurdjević, but also more mainstream psychologists such as Jovo Toševski, who writes in his *Hidden Sexuality* (1993) that "the normal man must hate homosexuals, otherwise his manliness is questioned."[100] Clearly, the term "normal" in both cases is interchangeable with "heterosexual." Davidovich later takes himself to task for this public letter of condemnation—"with that I proved I was no better or more tolerant than the wider society"—but he "cannot get rid of [his] dislike for effeminate homosexuals."[101] He complains, "I do not regard effeminate gays as 'true and normal' homosexuals, and I often feel the need to challenge their right to represent us gay men."[102] Even though the desire to construct a "manly homosexual"— a heterosexual-like homosexual—may be understandable where heterosexual masculinity is a privileged identity (and where anyone suspected of being gay might be beaten), this strategic positioning of the "true homosexual" has to be seen as part of the *dispotif* outlined above. Davidovich seeks an essential identity, and *to the extent that he is regarded as representative*, Serbian gay men have balls, too.

VII. Conclusions

In a 1983 book called *Sexual Practices: The Story of Human Sexuality*, Edgar Gregersen provides a series of maps charting sexual behavior in the world. While

Northern Europe is characterized by sadomasochism (severe), fetishism, homophilia (not necessarily tolerated), and, of course, the missionary position, the Balkans are marked only once, and this as a region that practices circumcision. In a chapter titled "Europe and European Outposts," we learn, among other things, that married Serbs have sex infrequently, though "sex hospitality" was probably widespread in the former Yugoslavia.[103] There is evidence to suggest that while wives are expected to be faithful, "the brother of a woman's husband may take some sort of sexual liberties with her."[104] In the rural Balkans, we are told, "sex with a wife," a "sacred object," is not regarded as "fun," a situation sharply distinguished from sex with "gypsies, singing girls from cafes, widows who have become prostitutes, foreigners—and particularly Scandinavian tourists."[105] One could go on, but the point should be clear: in the absence of anything but the most formulaic and "primitivizing" evidence about the Balkans and sexuality, the region easily serves as a screen for all kinds of fantasmatic projections from the West which, in turn, become part of the fodder for Serbian identity formation. Indeed, it is probably not at this point possible to speak of a Serb sexuality, if one can ever speak of a "Serb sexuality," formed apart from a history of science, novels, ethnography, film, and even feminist writing produced largely by and for Westerners. Knowledge-production and sexual identity being inextricably linked, Serbs themselves, nationalist and antinationalist, gay and straight, have adopted these representations, including a Western *scientia sexualis*, making what Michael Herzfeld calls "strategic adjustments to the demands of the historical moment."[106] If Danilo Kiš is correct in his assumption that Serbs have become a nation of balls, obviously this identity did not emerge *sui generis*: "Sex" has a history in the former Yugoslavia, one deeply imbricated with modernity, intimately related to the history of Western sexuality, tightly allied with heterosexual pleasure, and, we would insist, impossible to infer from the ballad tradition.

This history, as we have attempted to demonstrate, is not entirely stable, but increasingly evidences strategic, self-sterotyping, and shifting forms of othering typical of the modern democratic state. Recently, some two years after President Bill Clinton and two months after Senator Gary Condit, Serbia experienced its first political sex scandal. Vuk Obradović, a member of Zoran Djindjić's new Serbian Cabinet and chair of a powerful committee investigating political and economic corruption, was accused of sexual harassment. Two days after Milošević's extradition to The Hague, soccer fans attacked gay activists at what is being billed as Serbia's first gay-rights parade. Both events attest to the tightening of links between sexuality and state power endemic to the modern disciplinary regime.

Under these volatile circumstances, where people put their bodies on the line for sexual rights and freedoms, it is not clear what role postmodernism could or should play. Particularly in sociological scholarship on the Balkans, at issue have been two different models of "the subject": one based on the juridical model and connected to matters of law, the other strategic and connected to a more diffuse model of power. This article, obviously, relies on the latter. While one cannot use Foucault to prosecute a criminal case, there may nevertheless be value in a Foucaultian approach, in part because by foregrounding significant relationships between knowledge and power, it allows us to see not only the contours of present-day nationalisms, but their constitutive materials, including the otherwise invisible discourses of sexuality on which collective identity is built. It forces us to acknowledge that there is no easy escape from this discourse, no alternative to the tyranny of sex. However, to the extent that *scientia sexualis* reinforces, rather than dismantles, stable ethnic and sexual identities, we follow Foucault in suggesting that it may be time to break away from the "agency of sex," a strategy that would also apply to identity politics (what he calls "counterattacks on the deployment of sexuality"). In other words, it may be time to *depsychologize* sexuality, to treat it, in Halperin's words, as a "device whose operation can be analyzed rather than as a thing whose nature can be known."[107] Otherwise, as we have seen, old sexual identities are easily reinscribed in ethnically essentializing ways. While our historical deconstruction and focus on "bodies and pleasures" run the risk of being dismissed as war propaganda or a postmodern flight from the "real," through such tactics the tyranny of sex, the terror of heterosexuality, and the hegemony of sexual desire will perhaps come into clearer view.

Notes

1. Danilokiš, *Čas Anatomije* (Sarajevo: Svetlost, 1990), 68.

2. Recent scholarship in sociology includes, for example, Keith Doubt, *Sociology After Bosnia and Kosovo: Recovering Justice* (New York: Rowman & Littlefield, 2000); in anthropology, Robert M. Hayden, "Rape and Rape Avoidance in Ethno-National Conflicts: Sexual Violence in Liminized States," *American Anthropologist* 102, no. 1 (March 2000): 27–41; in psychology, Branka Arsić (ed.), *Žene, Slike, Izmišljaji* (Beograd: Centar za Ženske Studije, 2000); and in political theory, Anna M. Agathangelou, "Nationalist Narratives and (Dis)Appearing Women: State Sanctioned Sexual Violence," *Canadian Women's Studies/Les Cahiers de la femme* 19, no. 4 (2000): 12–21. Most of the work, however, including some previously mentioned, is both interdisciplinary and feminist in methodology. See, for example, Wendy Bracewell, "Rape in Kosovo: Sex, Gender and Serbian Nationalism," *Nations and Nationalism* 6, no. 4: 563–590; Maja Korać, "Ethnic Conflict, Rape, and Feminism: The Case of Yugoslavia," *Research on Russian and Eastern Europe*, no. 2 (1996): 247–266; Lepa Mladjenović, "Where Do I Come From?" *Index on Censorship* 24, no. 4 (1995): 72–74; Julie

films in Serbia, largely due to the rising costs of film production in Hungary: "It is very logical," says Stanković, "every significant capitalist, including those from the porn industry, looks for the most optimal environment for investment. It is generally thought that our environment would be a perfect investment. Therefore, the big porn producers contemplate penetrating our market." (http://www.glas-javnosti.co.yu/danas/srpski/R00102001.shtm, 10/20/2000)

69. Lance Morrow, "Unspeakable," *Time* (February 22, 1993), 50.

70. Andrew Cutrofello, *Discipline and Critique: Kant, Poststructuralism, and the Problem of Resistance* (Albany, New York: State University of New York, 1994), 39–41. Immanuel Kant discusses the problem of social discipline in *Critique of Pure Reason*, translated from German to English by Norman Kemp Smith (New York: St. Martin's Press, 1965), A711/B739, A713/B741.

71. Cutrofello, *Discipline and Critique*, 44. On Sade and modernity, see also Gilles Deleuze, *Masochism* (New York: Zone Book, 1991), 81–90; Jacques Lacan, "Kant with Sade," translated from French to English by James B. Swenson, Jr., *October* 51 (Winter 1989); Marcel Henaff, *Sade: The Invention of the Libertine Body*, translated from French to English by Xavier Callahan (Minneapolis: University of Minnesota Press, 1999), 230.

72. Foucault, *The History of Sexuality*, 149.

73. The most obvious example of the latter phenomenon is the population policy constructed and employed by Slovenia, Croatia, Serbia, and most of the other former Yugoslav states. The Serbian Orthodox Patriarch Pavle, for example, as Julie Mostov reports, broadcast a Christmas message in 1995 warning that the low birthrate among Serbs was a "plague" visited on the nation, and admonishing mothers who had lost their only children to the war that they had no right to complain. He added that if the birth rate did not increase significantly in ten years, Serbs would be a national minority in their own country and would have nothing to say about their own fate, 518–519.

74. Roger Cohen, "US soldier jailed for killing girl," (http://www.theage.com.au/news/20000803/A45851-2000Aug2.html)

75. *Vreme* 469 (2000): 34.

76. Under the Penal Code of June 30, 1959, which categorized it as "indecent acts against nature," sex between men was made illegal in the former Yugoslavia. During the 1970s, when power devolved to the eight states and republics, Serbia and Kosovo retained the ban. (In Vojvodina, sex between men was decriminalized with a discriminatory age of consent of eighteen.) Male homosexuality was described as "unnatural debauchery," subject to a penalty of up to one year imprisonment. Homosexuality in Serbia was decriminalized in 1994, even while, significantly, the homophobic rhetoric and persecution of homosexuals escalated. On this issue, see Bracewell, "Rape in Kosovo." In Croatia, see Tatjana Pavlović, "Women in Croatia: Feminists, Nationalists, and Homosexuals" in Ramet, *Gender Politics*, 1999). For broad reporting, see *Campaign Against Homophobia: A Semi-Annual Report*, No. 1- January–June 1998 (http://www.ilga.org./information/europe) which includes reports on the media in Serbia.

77. "Sheltering from the Hard Rain," *Gay Times*, July 1999 (http://www.ilga.org/information/europe/sheltering_from_the_hard_rain_.htm)

78. Dr. Ratibor Djurdjević (Pederska Brigada: Perverznjaci Mrze Hrista (Bedgrad: HTUS, 1997), 11.

79. Foucault, *The History of Sexuality*, 42–43.

80. Ibid., 43.

81. "Sheltering from the Hard Rain."

82. *Vreme* 469 (2000), 34.

83. David M. Halperin, *Saint Foucault: Toward A Gay Hagiography* (New York and London: Oxford University Press, 1995), 61.

84. Campaign Against Homophobia: A Semi-Annual Report.

85. Ibid.

86. Foucault, *The History of Sexuality*, 101.

87. Boris Davidovich, *Serbian Diaries*, translated from Serbo-Croat by Dragan Vujanić (London: The Gay Men's Press, 1996), 17.

88. Davidovich, *Serbian Diaries*, 37.

89. Foucault, *The History of Sexuality*, 101–102.

90. Ibid., 101.

91. Halperin, *Saint Foucault*, 59.

92. Davidovich, *Serbian Diaries*, 91–92.

93. On the role of psychiatry in ethnic cleansing see Steven M. Weine, *When History is a Nightmare: Lives and Memories of Ethnic Cleansing in Bosnia-Herzegovina* (New Brunswick, New Jersey: Rutgers University Press, 1999), 87–146.

94. In Halperin, *Saint Foucault*, 79.

95. Ibid., 62.

96. Ibid.

97. Davidovich, *Serbian Diaries*, 52.

98. Ibid., 10–11.

99. Ibid., 11.

100. Reported in *Campaign Against Homophobia*.

101. Davidovich, *Serbian Diaries*, 12.

102. Ibid., 12.

103. Edgar Gregerson, *Sexual Practices: The Story of Human Sexuality* (New York: Franklin Watts, 1983), 276.

104. Ibid.

105. Ibid., 275.

106. Herzfeld, *Cultural Intimacy*, 5.

107. Halperin, *Saint-Foucault*, 121.

12

Muslim Women, Croatian Women, Serbian Women, Albanian Women . . .

Vesna Kesić

Two images have been haunting me since the wars began in the former Yugoslavia in 1991. The first one is of men's heads (or upper bodies) at round tables, leaning over maps. That image first appeared in the local and international press in 1990 and 1991, during the now almost forgotten series of meetings of the six newly elected presidents of Yugoslav republics who were unsuccessfully trying to find a political solution for the country's political crisis. (The media called them "the traveling circus.") Men's heads also came together at the "secret" meetings between presidents Franjo Tudjman and Slobodan Milošević, during the wars in Croatia (1991–1992) and in Bosnia (1992–1995), and at the meetings held in Washington in 1994 and in Dayton in 1995. During the war in Kosova, Serbian and KLA leaders did not meet officially, though there was that strange episode of Ibrahim Rugova's "visit" to Belgrade. But one can just as easily imagine Serbian and Albanian political leaders and war commanders bending over maps and making decisions about borders. International leaders or NATO commanders discussing war affairs can easily be imagined in this pose. Men decided on national boundaries, on territorial borders; they shape the past and future of nations, and they make decisions that affect human lives.

The second image is of women: women refugees carrying the remnants of their belongings in plastic bags; women dragging frightened and exhausted children; weeping women, angry women, women impregnated by rape, traumatized women. Whatever happens, women are depicted as bodies. The few women in combat units, or even one participating at the decision making level, make no difference. Amid all the vicious circles of violence in these wars, this remains constant: Women are bodies in pain, regardless of which ethnic group is at some point recognized as aggressor and which as victim. Croatian women, Bosnian women, Muslim women, Serbian women, Albanian women . . . and this is not only in the wars of the former Yugoslavia.

Wars are gendered activities, right from the beginning. Jacklyn Cock states that war both "uses and maintains the ideological construction of gender in the definitions of 'masculinity' and 'femininity.'"[1] Men, she stresses, go to war to protect and defend national values, territories, and borders, and to protect and defend "their" women and children. Women are cast in the role of "the protected" and "the defended," or, in the words of another woman from another part of the world, the German filmmaker Helke Sander, women are "the liberated" and men are "the liberators."[2] Liberators themselves, like the Allied soldiers in Germany in 1945, often abuse women.[3]

At the beginning of the wars in the former Yugoslavia, Croatian feminists who assisted displaced and refugee women from Bosnia, Herzegovina, and Croatia, regardless of their ethnicity or nationality, wrote: "Women did not participate in making (irresponsible) political or military decisions, and yet war and its misery more and more acquire women's and children's faces."[4] We were positioning the sexual violence of war within the larger matrix of patriarchal power relations and patriarchal violence against women. Women's groups in Belgrade and Zagreb noticed that domestic violence increased during the war and acquired new forms. Disillusioned men and frustrated soldiers attacked or threatened their partners with guns, rifles, bombs, or military knives. Feminists pointed out the congruity between ethnic chauvinism and sexism: In both, differences are exaggerated, "Others" are perceived stereotypically, as of minor human value and as a threat to the nation and masculinity; domination and hierarchy are perceived as natural and worth the infliction of cruelty and violence.

For taking this position, some feminists and women's groups were immediately denounced as "traitors of the nation," they were met with rage, exposed to defamation, even accused of betraying women. Rape as a weapon of war was entirely positioned within the category of ethnicity as a part of "genocidal" strategy, and women were turned into metaphors: "A raped Croat or Bosniak woman stands for a raped Croatia or Bosnia." At the same time, the rapists' existence as "men" and military figures was obliterated by their ethnicity. Serbs (Croats, Muslims) rape, not Serbian (Croatian, Muslim) militaries and paramilitaries. On one hand, to be a woman in a war zone meant one stood a good chance of being raped. On the other, to be a feminist within the nation provoked political, and sometimes even bodily, threat. I must admit that I was surprised and frightened by such responses, not so much for my life (everybody was in danger), but because I had not expected such heated animosity would be aroused by the feminist attempt to analytically disentangle gender from ethnicity.

In the early 1990s, political contention and division emerged among different Croatian and Bosnian women's groups over the explanation of the mass rapes in Bosnia. Should we emphasize the "gender" or the "ethnic" dimension of this compound violence against women? The debate took place within a political context of induced nationalism and ethnic hatred. International feminist groups and scholars soon picked up the dispute. As Robert M. Hayden recently remarked: "Within the former Yugoslavia, long-established feminists tended to maintain gender as central to their analyses, seeing rape as a common weapon of war, directed mainly against women."[5] Hayden, though, simplifies when he categorizes the gender approach of local feminists as a "global feminist view." This understanding probably results from the fact that the texts and statements of local feminists were rarely translated or considered in their original forms. In the majority of cases, these texts entered Western scholarly discussion through second hand or partial references.[6] In my opinion, local feminist analyses of Yugoslavia's collapse and its wars of succession were rather complex and well conceptualized. But Hayden is right when he states that the "gender approach" was contrasted with a "genocidal rape" approach that saw the rapes of Muslim women in Bosnia as a unique historical phenomenon, "a rape warfare" conducted by Serbs against Muslim and Croatian women in which rape was a unique form not only of war, but of genocide. That view was first developed and used by local groups, as Hayden rightly points out by quoting Dubravka Žarkov, in accordance with the nationalist governments and the controlled media in which reports of sexual violence, whether true or not, became common propaganda.[7] That view was appropriated and followed by some, but far from all, Western feminist scholars.[8]

The U.S. law professor Catherine MacKinnon became particularly embroiled in the political debates among locals, taking the actively nationalist side.[9] The locally prevailing "genocidal" concept, whose theory and politics MacKinnon supported internationally, still resonates in local discussions. There is an ongoing debate over the "real character" of mass rapes in Bosnia, in which a Croatian journalist, informed by MacKinnon's main local partners in Croatia, upholds the concept of "genocide by procreation" as the only acceptable understanding of these "unique crimes."[10] According to this interpretation, Serbs raped with the intention of impregnating Bosnian and Croatian women and forcing them to give birth to "little chetniks."[11] Ultimately, their intention was to destroy the Muslim and Croatian ethnic groups in Bosnia. My response to this notion was that the concept of "genocide by procreation" appropriates and reinforces racist ideology, because it accepts that the nation or ethnic group can be destroyed by procreation, that is, by its enlargement through the dilution of "ethnic blood."

During the NATO bombing of Yugoslavia and the exodus of Kosovo Albanians to neighboring countries, similar messages started to reach the world: Serbs rape "to destroy the spirit of the brave soldiers of the Kosova Liberation Army."[12] Women's bodies, individually tortured and in pain, are transformed into national symbols and presented as symbolic battlefields that embody national values.

Feminist discourse contests the fusing of gender and ethnicity, which, in nationalist rhetoric, works as a homogenizing and hegemonic practice. To Judith Butler's insight that sex is always already gendered,[13] I want to add that when women become victims in nationalist wars, gender becomes ethnicized, or subordinated to ethnicity, even before it appears as an "autonomous" discourse. Feminist discourse on gender deconstructs the simple divisions of "aggressors and victims," "our rights" and "their wrongs," the differences constructed as insurmountable, and all the other reductions needed for waging wars. My hypothesis is that militarized patriarchy and ethnic nationalism intersected and became enmeshed at the roots of the violence in these wars. This mix of ethnic and gender representations, symbols, and images has generated extremely violent practices, particularly in terms of the sexualization of war violence. Men of all ethnicities, when turned into soldiers and trained in patriarchal institutions to "build" or "defend" the nation, are prone to rape.[14] The question to answer is: How does sexual desire get invested into constructions of ethnicity and nationalism? How does it become "collectivized" and transformed into war violence?

The Indian anthropologist Veena Das, who has studied violence connected to communal riots between ethnic and religious groups since the Partition of India, claims that the imagining of nationalist projects already includes the appropriation of women's bodies as objects "on which the desire for nationalism could be brutally inscribed and a memory for the future made."[15] The magnification of the image of the nation through icons, rhetoric, and mythology draws its energy from the image of a magnified, patriarchally constructed, masculine sexuality. When the distinction between "magnified images" of the nation and of women dissolve, and "the nation becomes a magnified image of the beloved worshipped in the abstract, it becomes possible to inflict all kinds of violence on all those who resist this or who create counter images, equally enlarged."[16] In brief, the desire for nationalism easily can be metamorphosed into sexual violence, women's bodies objectified and abstracted, and their pain and suffering disavowed. To conclude with Das's possibly exaggerated but still meaningful insight into the narratives that recall both Indian and Pakistani violence against women during the Partition of India: "if men emerged from colonial subjugation as autonomous citizens of an independent nation, then they emerged simultaneously as monsters."[17]

At this point it might be useful to recall the history of the former Yugoslavia and the events that demonstrate the gendered dimension in the intensification of ethnic conflict and the incitement to violence. Among all the "beginnings" or "triggers" said to have touched off the wars that have now lasted for a decade, one has become obscured with time. Sometime during the years 1986 and 1987, at a time when relations between "Serbia proper" and Kosova (then still a Yugoslav province with political autonomy within Serbia) were already disturbed but not yet violent, a moral panic took hold in Belgrade about "widespread" Albanian rapes of Serbian women, including Orthodox nuns. The alleged rapes were explained as an attempt by Albanians to terrorize the Serbs and drive them out of Kosova. The emphasis was immediately placed on the ethnic dimension of these rapes; facts were neglected and numbers exaggerated. Although it was rather soon proved that Kosova police had registered only one rape of a Serb woman by an Albanian man, and subsequent research showed that rapes in Kosova basically did not cross ethnic lines, the allegations of inter-ethnic rape generated fear and helped form the basis of the future culture of terror. To make matters worse, two Albanian leaders from the "old communist guard" stated publicly that it was only natural that young Albanians obtain some pleasure from Serbian women. These things happen, the leaders claimed, because of the well-known chastity of Albanian women and the fact that Albanian culture forbids sex outside of marriage. Feminists from Slovenia, Croatia, and Serbia already at that point demanded that the crime of rape, as the gravest violence against women, be kept separate from ethnic quarrels. But, of course, nobody listened.

When nationalist politicians came to power throughout Yugoslavia in the 1990 elections, women's bodies became everybody's business. They were the objects of demands, projections, and restrictions. After the elections, women almost disappeared from national parliaments, where before they had made up between 16 and 30 percent of deputies; many women's rights, including the right to legal and safe abortion, were threatened. With the onset of war, women were used in nationalist propaganda. Eventually, all of the warring factions committed rapes and other kinds of sexual violence—although not all at the same rate, which certainly makes a difference, politically and legally. Women were tortured and abused in many different ways in war zones: They were systematically raped, gang raped, held as slaves, bodily searched by male militias at check points, exploited by prostitution, or forced into prostitution because it was the only way to survive. Even United Nations soldiers in Bosnia visited the war brothels. The Bosnian Islamic Community pronounced raped women "shehids," or holy warriors. The Serbian Orthodox and Croatian Catholic churches appealed to women to give birth to more nationals. Indeed, the churches treated women as demographic reservists. Both Orthodox and

*the religious aspect to this –
women were held up as symbols.*

Catholic churches issued dramatic warnings that the national birth rates of their respective nations were among the lowest in the world, and that they faced the threat of becoming "minorities in their own countries." The states strongly supported this stance.

In the patriarchal construction of gender, women's primary role is the biological reproduction of family and nation. In its ideological definition of femininity, a woman's chastity, her and her family's honor, are the highest "values." And her chastity becomes everybody's business—the defenders' and the aggressors'. It is only seemingly a paradox that exactly those values—culture, tradition, honor, female chastity—that nationalist warriors defend against "modernity's nihilism and globalization" are the values that they readily attack and destroy when they belong to others, be they of different gender or ethnicity.

The tragic consequences for women in such militarized, patriarchal cultures extend beyond the battlefield. During the war in Kosova, an article in *The New York Times*[18] reported Kosova women's shame, their fear of rejection and expulsion should their experience of rape become known. The meaning of patriarchal masculinity and family honor was articulated in one Albanian man's statement that he would divorce his young wife even if they had twenty children. Some women reported that they would rather die than be raped.[19] Although nothing as bad as the "honor killings"[20] of the Middle East was reported from Bosnia or Kosova, articles like this one painted a traditional picture of an "Oriental" society, where family's and men's honor is the only force that moves events. The reporter may have had the best intentions to protect the women, but the real political background and the power relations at work are lost in such representations, which depict events that are not necessarily widespread and not always true.

While working with Bosnian refugees in Zagreb, we have witnessed cases where women needed a long time to come out with "what else" happened to them during the war, because the trauma of rape is usually very deep and the surroundings are often perceived as unsupportive and threatening. But I also know of cases where women talked self-confidently, where their husbands and children knew what had happened, showed their deepest sorrow and compassion, and did everything to help the women overcome the consequences of their experiences.

In any case, almost everybody rightly concludes that victims of sexual war violence suffer twice—first, the torture of rape, and second, the attitudes of a patriarchal community. I claim that there is also a third dimension that has to do with how these rapes are represented and recognized. In the former Yugoslavia (and probably elsewhere), as soon as the rapes were reported, contestations about their character, circumstances, and numbers began. At the beginning, the state, or some political group representing the state, characterized rapes as "genocidal" and exaggerated the numbers.[21] For example: In 1992, the Croatian side claimed ten thousand rape victims in Croatia. The Bosnia and Herzegovina State Commission for collecting data on war crimes released the number of fifty to sixty thousand victims by the end of 1992; but some "patriotic" women's groups set the number at 120,000 raped women in Bosnia and Croatia. All of those "facts" were met with eagerness "to help" and sometimes even further exaggeration from the different actors abroad. Catherine MacKinnon herself helped disseminate these exaggerated figures and ethnically informed explanations.[22]

There is a popular saying that the news from the Balkans has to be checked not twice, but three times. The notion of stereotyped "cultural difference" has been created and sealed through this seemingly reasonable appeal for objectivity and reliability. But how is it that so many intellectuals from the West, trained in the tradition and spirit of "objectivity" and "reasonability," have fed into this "Balkan irrationality"?

The next phase in gendering the war propaganda was the "counterattack" from the side that was allegedly wrongly accused, which was in this case the Serbs. When the first "realistic" data started to appear, Serbian nationalists and their international supporters started to defend a "Serb cause." Pointing at the exaggerated numbers, they protested that nothing "really serious" had happened. Only "a couple thousand" women were raped. "The international plot against Serbia" was to be blamed for everything. Often during this third use of "women's bodies as battlefields," as Susan Brownmiller would put it, I was glad that the women refugees would be the last to learn about these "wars of interpretation," which produced yet another dimension of humiliation for the women—from exaggeration to denial.[23]

What is here contested, dispensed with, and instrumentalized for nationalistic, political, military, or other, sometimes "merely professional" (journalistic), purposes are women's bodies in pain. Because war rapes and other forms of violence against women were so tightly enmeshed within the categories of nation and ethnicity, they could be recognized as a war strategy, subjected to indictments as war crimes, and juridically sanctioned—in short, taken seriously—only if they occurred in large numbers (whatever "large" means), if they were "systematic" and "followed a pattern," and if they supported the claim of genocide or ethnic cleansing. Even then, if perpetrators were brought to court, it was left to women to prove, argue, and corroborate their crimes.

The media is an important purveyor of representations of war crimes against women. It has been stressed many times that due to the growing number of women reporters and to the women's human rights movement, the media has played a crucial role in assuring that war rapes in the former Yugoslavia and Rwanda were the first in history not to pass unnoticed or get pushed under the carpet. Nonetheless, it should not be forgotten that the media has its own rationale. Whether journalists are motivated by commercial interests, by the desire to break a good story, or by empathy and a concern for justice can be debated.[24] Regardless, Western media reflect (or create) a particular perception of these "distant events" that happen in the non-West (even if it is a part of Europe that is recognized as both "near," and thus like "us," and "far," and thus not like "us.") Both of the *New York Times* articles mentioned earlier—on the doom of women in the Arab world, and on raped Kosova women—present the situation of women in these parts of the world as so exceptional, so different, so exotic that nothing like it can be imagined in the West. "Exceptionalizing" is a way of creating cultural differences, which we still don't know how to approach; whether to respect and nourish them, because they represent diversity, or to contest and confront them, because they may violate universal human rights.

Sometimes I wonder—without attempting to minimize the harshness of some women's situations, or to deny that sometimes social, legal, and cultural differences can threaten life—what the so-called West is so shocked about. Is the situation for women in Kosova or Bosnia really so different from the one in the United States or in Western Europe? For how many years has a raped woman been able easily to step into a U.S. or Western European court and testify that she was raped without feeling threatened or ashamed? Without fearing that she will be asked how short her skirt was, or why she was out on the streets so late? And without fear that her husband, boyfriend, even family will reject her, especially if her background is not a middle-class white one, but, let's say, a Puerto Rican one. It is commonly understood among feminists that Susan's Brownmiller's *Against Our Will* and a strong feminist movement articulated around women's human rights have made the difference in the perception of rape, its social characterization, and the legal procedures available to combat it.[25] But this means that the changes were achieved in a period of a mere twenty years or less, and the question still remains: How many women have benefited from them?

We have barely begun to uncover the deep origins of male violence against women in the home, on the streets, in offices, in the media, and especially in wartime. Feminist theory has certainly contributed to understanding these origins and to the search for ways to confront them. German historian Mechtild Rumpf argues that the state monopoly on violence, as defined by Weber and other classical theorists of the state, was a myth all along, insofar as it pertains to family and gender relations.[26] Through patriarchal marriage and family structures—which have been regarded as civilizing since the Enlightenment—violence remains structurally anchored in society. "In (state) monopolized violence, the everyday violence of patriarchy went on," states Rumpf. Similarly, Carole Pateman argues that the sexual contract between men and women, which she believes precedes the patriarchal contract envisioned by Hobbs, Lock, and Rousseau, gives to the "fraternity" of men rights to enjoy equal sexual access to women and sex.[27] Thus, not all violence comes from the state. Neither, however, does it all come from culture. The violence inflicted by state actors—or by those whose political project is to "imagine" the state or the nation—combined with social-patriarchal violence, should be held responsible for the gender-specific forms of war violence, even in the "Wild Balkans."

Women still have a long way to go to achieve full citizenship and equality. In the case of the former Yugoslavia, I can entirely embrace Jacklyn Cock's suggestion from South Africa: Changing gender relations is one of the prerequisites for reducing the risk of war in the future.[28] But "gender relations" are not a simple derivation from "cultural specificities." They are the fundamental power relation in most existing and historical societies, and this relation is tightly connected to and intertwined with all other power and social relations, including political and economic ones. A "Western approach," be it by "helpful sisters" or the "well-meaning" media, is not helpful if it fails to address the issue with the same political and theoretical seriousness with which violence against women was discussed in the West itself—nor if it keeps on emphasizing "cultural differences."

Notes

1. Jacklyn Cock, *Colonels and Cadres: War & Gender in South Africa* (Cape Town: Oxford University Press, 1991), x.

2. Helke Sander, Barbara Johr, eds. *Befreir und Befreite: Krieg, Vergewaltigung, Kinder*, (Munich: Verlag Antje Kunstman, 1992).

3. The authors documented that within a month of the Allies entering Berlin, 70 percent of German women were raped. The majority of perpetrators were from the ranks of the Red Army, but the U.S., French, and British soldiers raped as well.

4. Rada Borić, ed. *Centar za žene zrtve rata: Zbornik* (Zagreb: CZZR, Ženska Infoteka, 1994), 43.

5. M. Robert Hayden, "Rape and Rape Avoidance in Ethno-national Conflicts: Sexual Violence in Liminalized States," *American Anthropologist* 102, no. 1 (2000): 27–41.

6. Several reprinted documents in *Zbornik* (see supra note 4) underline that our primary request was that the data on abused women not be interpreted, and thereby opened to nationalist misuse, before "everything ends" and the full picture of what was happening on all sides made available. We stressed the need to pursue research on the concrete circumstances of these events.

7. Hayden, "Rape and Rape Avoidance in Ethno-national Conflicts," 29.

8. See Beverly Allen, *Rape Warfare: The Hidden Genocide in Bosnia-Herzegovina and Croatia* (Minneapolis: University of Minnesota Press, 1996); Catherine MacKinnon, "Turning Rape into Pornography: Postmodern Genocide," *Ms.*, July–August 1993, 24–30; C. MacKinnon, "Rape, Genocide, and Women's Human Rights," *Harvard Women's Law Journal* 17 (spring 1994): 5–16.

9. Vesna Kesić, "A Response to Catharine MacKinnon's Article, 'Turning Rape into Pornography: Postmodern Genocide'" *Hastings Women's Law Journal* 5, no. 2 (summer 1994): 267–280.

10. Mirko Petrić, "O povijesnom revizionizmu Vesne Kesić," *Zarez, dvotjednik za kulturna i društvena zbivanja* 2, nos. 45–46 (2000): 52; M. Petrić, "O feminizmu i nacionalizmu," *Zarez* 3, no. 49 (2001): 44, 45; V. Kesić, "Ideologizacija tudje patnje," *Zarez, dvotjednik za kulturna i društvena zbivanja* 3, no. 47 (2001): 52; V. Kesić, "Od Vještica iz Rija do povijesnih revizionistica," *Zarez* 3, no. 49 (2001): 44, 45.

11. Chetnik is a historic term for Serbian paramilitaries, dating from the time of the Ottomans, and used for the official units of Draža Mihajlović during the Second World War.

12. Elisabeth Bumiller, "Deny Rape or Be Hated: Kosovo Victim's Choice," *New York Times*, June 22, 1999, A1.

13. Judith Butler, *Gender Trouble: Feminism and the Subversion of Identity* (London: Routledge, 1990), 6, 7; 109–111.

14. This does not, of course, mean that all soldiers rape. Sexual abuses are predominantly inflicted on ethnically or religiously different others. But they also occur in civil wars among members of the same ethnicity, and they are performed by freedom fighters or fundamentalists of all kinds (for example, in Algeria), and within gender-mixed military units (cases of rape among U.S. troops during the Gulf War).

15. Veena Das, "Language and Body: Transactions in the Construction of Pain," in *Social Suffering*, ed. A. Kleineman, V. Das, and M. Lock (Berkeley: University of California Press, 1997), 67–91.

16. Ibid., 74.

17. Ibid., 86.

18. Ibid., supra note 12.

19. This is not a common finding in "civilian" rape cases. Women usually express joy that they survived, no matter how grave the physical and psychological consequences might be, and even if their lives remain miserable for a long time.

20. Douglas Jehl, "Arab Honor's Price: A Woman's Blood," *New York Times*, June 20, 1999: section 1, 1.

21. Some of these numbers were released as official; some were released by officials in unofficial circumstances, for example, at meetings or to the media; some were from unofficial

sources, like women's or other groups actually working closely with the governments, or guided by patriotic or nationalistic motives. However, the confusion over numbers was huge. The Center for Women War Victims, a feminist group in Zagreb that declared its independence and non-nationalistic politics, stated in its founding act, "The Letter of Intentions," in November 1992:

Data on raped women should be centralized and adequately processed only when "all that" [meaning the wars] is over and it must be done under the supervision of international experts. Until then, every unchecked use of numbers and data we shall consider as manipulation hurting the women. (*Zbornik*, 1994, 121)

22. Kesić, "A Response to Catherine MacKinnon's Article 'Turning Rape into Pornography: Postmodern Genocide,'" 276, 277.

23. The European Community's Investigative Mission, established in 1992, reported in February 1993 an approximation of twenty thousand raped women. The United Nations Commission of Experts collected over 4,500 reports of rape and sexual assault, not all of them equally documented. It rendered an approximation—achieved by extrapolation—of well over twelve thousand victims of rape and sexual assault. M. Cherif Bassiouni, former chairman of the commission, states that the commission's findings "lend credibility of the estimate of twenty thousand cases of rape and sexual violence" that was released by the European Community in 1993. The UN Commission also estimated that "the large majority of reported victims were Bosnian Muslims. The second largest group is unidentified as to ethnic background. The third group is Bosnian Serbs, followed by Croats. (M. Cherif, M. Bassiouni, and Marcia McCormick, "Sexual Violence: An Invisible Weapon of War in the Former Yugoslavia," *Occasional Papers no. 1* (International Human Rights Law Institute, De Paul University College of Law, 1996), 44, 10, 11.

24. Not to mention already notorious, but not unrealistic journalist's request: "Anybody here been raped and speaks English?"

25. Susan Brownmiller, *Against Our Will: Men, Women, and Rape* (New York: Simon & Schuster, 1975).

26. Mechtild Rumpf, "Staatliche Gewaltmonopol, nationale Souveraenitaet und Krieg: Einige Aspekte des 'maenlichen Zivilisationsprozesses,'" *L'Homme, Zeitschrift fuer Feministische Geschichtswissenschaft*, "Krieg," 3, no. 1 (Vienna: Boehlau Verlag, 1992), 8–10.

27. Carole Pateman, *The Sexual Contract* (Stanford, Calif.: Stanford University Press, 1988, chapter 1).

28. Ibid., supra note 1, x.

13

Hypnosis and Critique: Film Music for the Balkans

Stathis Gourgouris

The exigency of thinking about the Balkans today directs us beyond the radical immediacy of events.[1] I say this against my "better judgment" because, even in those uncommon instances of rapid understanding of the magnitude of events, something always feels elusive, uncanny, uncircumscribable. Perhaps because deep meditation cannot, in the end, withstand the barrage of continuous immediacy—or to put it otherwise, because thought about history-in-depth cannot withstand the barrage of history-in-the-making—the apparent failure to conceptualize the Balkans beyond their elemental historical, cultural, and political boundaries has become increasingly acute. It seems that the more pressured we feel to account for rapidly unfolding events, the greater difficulty we encounter in making sense of them beyond a simple accounting.

Now, I hardly mean to diminish those serious attempts to chronicle the labyrinthine trajectory of events in the Balkans during the last decade, often and rather wisely composed in mind of the complex and multivalent history of the region. Such chronicles certainly entail in-depth meditation on the complex determinations of the events in question. But even in such cases, something intangible eludes one's grasp and becomes maddening precisely because in its elusiveness, it registers history's unboundable mark. This sense of concrete intangibility, which I take to be necessary to the challenge of making sense of history, becomes even more urgent when contemplating the Balkans.

Investigating the objective parameters of this claim is beyond the scope of this essay. Yet, I would still risk the speculation that the complex of forces in the Balkans—both social-historical and psycho-symbolic—is such that no event eschews its instantaneous metaphorization, its centrifugal translation into an ever-increasing inventory of images that subsequently become the abyssal source of the event's concrete interpretation.[2] The metaphorization of "things Balkan" seems endemic to any attempt to make historical sense of the enormous dispersal of social-historical forces in the region during the last decade.

The instantaneous metaphorization of events demands that we confront history as a representational flux which remains actually uninterruptible, even though each attempt at self-reflection in its midst registers, from the standpoint of reflection, a tentative (and surely limited) interruption. This paradoxical perception should not confound us. While submitting ourselves as historical subjects to the uninterruptible flux of history, we can still remain attuned to those moments of interruption for which our corporeal existence is often the conduit. The elucidation of such moments becomes imperative if one is committed to making tangible the means by which historical events are liquified in their metaphorization, entering the symbolic realm as moments of self-reflection or self-interrogation.

While recognizing the undeconstructible presence of the real in history, I am drawn more toward the metaphorized restaging than the pure event. I have a hunch that the inherent performativity of the real in history is best conceptualized in such reflexive and interrogative restagings, perhaps because the performative condition of all historical events becomes discernible in their secondary elaboration, in the "event" of their metaphorized existence. This existence may find various forms within the range of aesthetic or socio-political ritual: from festive commemorations in public to the most private reimaginings in art, from gestures of overt political efficacy to gestures of obscure symbolic reorientation. Precisely because the immediacy of the event cannot be outmaneuvered, no matter what the philosophical armory, and yet also because no socially effective event escapes its instantaneous metaphorization and subsequent ritualization, its reality is double and is thus confirmed, like the dream-work it involves, in the instance of its secondary elaboration, or in strict Freudian terms, secondary revision.

In *Dream Nation*, I argued that secondary revision is a crucial component in society's negotiation with its imaginary significations, as it provides the connecting threads between a society's dream-work and its real effects, thus making history real in the same gesture that makes reality historical.[3] Extending this argument (conducted specifically in regard to the genre of national history and its task as secondary revision immanent to the nation's dream-work in the nineteenth century), I would say that nowadays, in a more incidental or less determinate fashion, film carries out an analogous dream-task, even if often against the grain of forged identities. Even the most traditional formalist history of film in the twentieth century cannot evade the way in which film partakes of the national inventory of images and phantasms, whether it stages them in the most epic collectivist or most private individualist manner. But unlike national history, which is a genre whose peculiar performativity is still folded into the compulsion to narrate, film exceeds strict narrative boundaries and works instead through a *synesthetic* entwinement of iconic, sonic, and textual *images* to which narration, even in the most "realist" cases, remains necessarily incidental. The secondary elaboration of national fantasy in film—whose aim, consistent with that of national history, is the achievement of fantasy's reality effect—occurs in the formal juxtaposition of images drawn from the inventory of the national imaginary, and yet, at their very instance of perform-ance, drawn back into the ceaseless process of society's imaginary (re)institution. Such instances of "reabsorption" entail either confirmation or interrogation of the identitary terms that hold the social phantasm together; there is simply no neutral (re)circulation of imaginary significations, insofar as no performative instance can be reduced to mere repetition, even at the extremes of social conformism. In every case, an explicit translation (*metaphora*) takes place, even if the recipient of the staged phantasms is also the source.[4]

What I mean to examine here is the operative mode of such retrieval and reab-sorption of the social imaginary, and I will do so by focusing on two directors whose methods of filmic metaphorization of "Balkan" phantasms are unique and much discussed. Even at that, I will not directly address the iconic or even textual aspects of filmic vision, but rather a more neglected and arguably less tangible aspect: film music. So, in invoking the well-known directors Theo Angelopoulos and Emir Kusturica, I will in fact address the much lesser known (in the West) composers whose music has shadowed these directors' efforts for most of their careers: Eleni Karaindrou and Goran Bregović. I should say right off that the relative obscurity of these composers is thoroughly undeserved; they have forged a film-musical idiom as unique and groundbreaking as those of Nino Rota, Ennio Morricone, Bernard Herrmann, or Carl Stallings. Perhaps their marginal status (by film industry stan-dards) is symptomatic of their insistence on composing music for films that remain outside the Hollywood market; the notoriety accorded to their film-makers is grounded precisely in their defiant distance from the industry. But both composers also approach film music as full-fledged musical practice, which places them at even further distance, since it subverts the standard reception of film music as a "para-genre" that merits no proper theorization. In addition, both composers are exceed-ingly aware of film music's intrinsic performativity, which becomes explicit in that their music is *internal* to the film's narrative structure, but most important, in that their musical idiom itself provides an exemplary occasion to explore the process of "instantaneous metaphorization" that concerns me here. The *co-incidence* of all these elements reverses one's sense of "partial" focus in having decided to concentrate on film music instead of film.[5] Film music provides a unique opportunity to contemplate the workings of social imaginary signification precisely because of its ambiguous status as a genre, which is compounded by its contingent relation to a primarily visual genre that is itself peculiarly situated within the traditional grammar of narrative modes. In this respect, "film music for the Balkans" emerges as a bona fide historical figure. It carries the metaphorical instance of a specific social-historical domain into the terrain of self-interrogation, at the same time that, as a category, it is blatantly constructed. Ultimately, the impetus in this essay is to traverse the "category" of film music, and in doing so to grasp the terms of such self-interrogation in the interplay between society's mythic performativity and its sublimation, as they can be traced in the two *synesthetic* experiences I examine below.[6]

I.   The Framework of Film Music as a Genre

Film music's condition of inaudibility, shared by musicologist and spectator alike, is built into its very history and may have much to do with the perception of film music as "parasitical" genre. The fact that radical theories in film studies in recent years are exclusively scopic in conception and vocabulary is telling enough, as are the countless film industry statistics demonstrating that audiences remain in large part oblivious to the presence of music in films.[7]

Film music has had a relatively short life in the course of music history, springing forth essentially without tradition. Far from following the lines of contemporaneous music development, film music consisted from the outset of a collage of different musical domains, histories, and soundscapes. Film music reinvokes long-gone musical traditions in the same instance as contemporary ones (or even in the same instance as it invents new sound categories), seemingly free of the burden that weighs on serious artistic conceptions: namely, the self-imposed demand to account for history's distinct mark on artistic composition. This constitutive historical hybridity affects the overall development of film music to such an extent that we cannot review its history (brief as it is) in the same terms in which we view the concurrent history of music at large.

The origins of film music more or less coincide with the history of film-making itself—at least, in its earliest industrial phase. Film music was an essential part of the silent movie, although its traces from this era remain a phantom; evidence of its existence is confined to the occasional review in early twentieth century local newspapers.[7] The silence of early motion-pictures made music necessary, and it may not be far-fetched to suggest that music would not be an element of motion-pictures today were it not an integral part—a formal phantom presence—of movie heritage from the silent era. Let us keep in mind that in the later industrialized silent era, the errant pianist or lone nickelodeon accompanying the image was often replaced by an enormous orchestra (luxuriously endowed, especially in urban centers with large movie theaters), which accompanied the mute image on the screen with loud and bombastic sound structures, conducted by well-placed maestros in search of quick and generous remuneration. It is this particular model of sound accompaniment, in its full material base, that gets transferred into the new motion pictures as the silent movie era folds into oblivion.[8]

But the historical specificity marking the origins of film music dates it unambiguously as a modern musical genre, concurrent with the impact of various experimentalisms in classical music and the early popularization of jazz forms. As such, film music emerges away from classical music territory, strictly speaking, and closer to the ethos of popular music, with which eventually it comes to share production values and techniques as it becomes a full-fledged industry in itself. From this point of view, the frequent presence of classical music phrasings or quotations within the hybrid form of film music (particularly true in the early days of Hollywood, but still present today in various cliché forms) should not be seen merely as nostalgic invocation of serious music (or beautiful music), but rather as its freehand industrialization.

To recognize the origins of film music as modern is to date it within the period when the classical music ethos declines as an integral expression of bourgeois art. The decline in opera attendance was the most succinct sociological expression of a shift toward what Theodor Adorno famously described in the 1930s as "the fetish character of music and the regression of listening." At that point, orchestral music and the various theatrical forms it supported deteriorated either to mere repetition and restaging of compositions belonging to the previous two centuries (i.e., it became *classical*) or to ostentatiously melodic compositions tantamount to what today, in another music-industrial context, is categorized as "easy-listening" (Richard Strauss is the exemplar here). On the other hand, even as mass audiences withdraw from orchestral music, the so-called new music ethos at the time, whose most influential purveyors would have to be Schoenberg, Stravinsky, and Bartok, established itself. Against this backdrop, film music appeared to be the most deviant sort of "modern" music, first, because it was by definition implicated in a commercial enterprise (the budding motion picture industry)—which is to say that it automatically reached large audiences—and second, because, although modern in origin, it is retro in practice, favoring either direct quotations of nineteenth century music or standard tonal-chromatic emulations. Either way, film music seems to have been disjointed from the context of its inception at the very moment of its inception. Herein may lie the refiguration of its peculiarity as a form into its subservience as a genre.

In addition, there is an insurmountable elementary problem: Film music depends, by definition, on the nature of another art form. As its very name suggests, film music (or, more tellingly, soundtrack music) has been conceived, since the beginning, as subservient to another mode of artistic production and, given the historical particulars, subjected to a distinct mode of *industrialized* production. Indeed, the industrial development of popular music as we know it, from swing to rock n' roll and beyond, owes a great deal to the unique production values and techniques that film music developed during Hollywood's glory years. The matter was sealed after Hollywood's financial restructuring, following the 1948 Paramount decree and the acquisition of recording companies by major film studios in order to centralize the marketing of both film and music. It is one of the banal realities of Los Angeles life, traceable in the most quotidian aspects of everyday existence, that the movie industry and the music industry are one and the same corporate complex and preside over the imaginary horizon of the city not unlike the automobile industry did in Detroit during the Fordist era.

This intrinsic formal and historical peculiarity of film music demands its own terms of historical and formal analysis, which is why, although it is part of the overall domain of music history, film music has been largely excluded from musicological discussion. It should come as no surprise that even in the field of film studies, film music is hardly considered an autonomous area of study, and it is rarely a topic of scholarly discussion or publication.[9] This makes the pioneering collaboration of Theodor Adorno and Hanns Eisler in *Composing for the Films* (first published in English in 1947) more crucial and indispensable today than in its own time.[10] The project's history exemplifies the forceful idiosyncrasy of both authors. Although both were schooled in Schonbergian aesthetics (Eisler was the master's star pupil at one time, and Adorno studied with Alban Berg before he abandoned music composition for philosophy), and although both were active members of the German Marxist intelligentsia in American exile during the war, they were quite distinct in personality and in ideological conviction regarding the relation between cultural politics and everyday life. Yet, beyond their shared fate in exile and mutual respect for each other's musical acuity, what bound them together was precisely their individual hard-headedness, the singular rigor with which they devoted themselves to thought as political practice and to music as social resistance.

Composing for the Films draws heavily on Adorno's groundbreaking formalist and sociological critiques of industrialized culture and on Eisler's acute observation of the conditions for film-music composition in Hollywood at that time.[11] The book delivers a devastating condemnation of the entire institution of composing music for films. But it also furnishes the first mindful history of the genre, as well as a glimpse into the radical artistic possibilities for film music as a form. The critique points to several factors that made film music composition in the high days of Hollywood mere hack work, but all of them eventually come down to one point: Films are super-sophisticated (and super-profitable) commodities serving essentially as large scale advertising venues for the supreme commodity, which is the proliferating image of Hollywood itself, and of its star-studded lifestyle. This fetishistic objective was translated into harnessed conditions of production: The orchestras were always composed of a set number and a set sort of instruments (due to union rules), and the producers held all the rights to the use and composition of film music. This harnessed structure was in turn translated into highly standardized sound structures: the leitmotif or *ostinato*; the melodic cliché (which literally represented in sound what was projected as image); the soundtrack which strove towards self-erasure (for it had to remain unobtrusive at all costs); the pyrotechnic orchestration that simulated the image in galloping action (in contemporary industry terms, "mickey-mousing"); the often racist folk melody cliché; the predictable quotation of a classical phrase; and the ridiculous security of stock phrasings at predictable junctures. Adorno and Eisler could not foresee the overturning of this regime and the real development of the genre of film music, which naturally coincided with the development of independent avant-garde film in Europe during the 1960s. Adorno, primarily under the influence of the young Alexander Kluge, did have a chance to greet this new turn in film with some insightful comments, but he never addressed the issue of music in a similar vein.[12]

Eisler and Adorno's observations sprang from the classic-industrial Hollywood films, but the lucrative film-music hack work they scrutinized continues to have its day in Hollywood soundstages. It is part of the historical nature of Eisler and Adoron's vanguard vision that these two believers in the viability of new musical forms emerging through film—they thought that Schonberg's music was the most appropriate for *King Kong* because it matched the supernatural terror of the image[13]—would not have a chance to witness the rise of the serious film music composer.

As modern music developed into increasingly dissonant structures, culminating in free jazz and psychedelic rock improvisation by the late 1960s, as well as more abstract structures with the advent of electronic music and *musique concrete*, film-making also opened up to what I would call a modern musical conceptualization (almost entirely outside of Hollywood). And so film music was liberated from the exigencies of industrial commodification. The signature of Nino Rota, for example, without whom, I dare say, Fellini's films would not be Fellini's films, opens the genre of film music composition into a *bona fide* musical form. Despite possible charges against an "auteurist" bias, something analogous (though for some nearly blasphemous) could be said about Bernard Herrmann and his scorings of certain Hitchcock films. Yet, beyond even Rota or Herrmann, the presence of Ennio Morricone in the last forty-some years of film composition history is exemplary of the sort of autonomous musical innovation I am suggesting. Morricone's versatility of sound is simply astounding. This is the only way to express how the pioneering sonic atmosphere of Sergio Leone's spaghetti westerns, or the twisted horror soundtracks written for Dario Argento's precise vision, could adapt themselves to major Hollywood productions such as *The Mission* or *The Untouchables* without compromising the music's autonomous and tangible trace. No doubt, Sergio Leone's decision to film *Once upon a Time in the West* (1968) starting from an already written musical score elevates this film to a visual oratorio of the strangest and most extraordinary nature—and the hardest evidence that film music need not be subordinated to the image.

II.   Film Music for the Balkans

The two cases I examine below belong to this kind of experimental tradition and would not have been possible had not the conditions of film-music composition during the 1960s altered the original Hollywood bind. Eleni Karaindrou has emerged as Theodoros Angelopoulos's musical voice in a way that parallels Rota's relation to Fellini. Goran Bregović became for a time such a voice for the famous Yugoslav film-maker Emir Kusturica, enriching with his frenetic sound both *Time of the Gypsies* (1990) and *Underground* (1995), as well as his one venture into Hollywood, *Arizona Dream* (1993). On the face of it, the two composers are rather dissimilar in musical orientation and in approach to sound itself. Yet they share a notion of music's autonomy within a perfectly integrated cinema. This dialectic permeates both composers' forms, so that despite the differences among the cinematic experiences, the film-music experiences are alike. This likeness encompasses both terrains of interrogation that concern me here: on the one hand, the "instantaneous metaphorization" of events and, on the other, film music as a mode of "hypnosis and critique" that makes this metaphorization possible.

Critique from the Standpoint of Suspension

Eleni Karaindrou is unprecedented in Greek film history. An easy way to explain this is by saying that Angelopoulos is unprecedented in Greek film history. A more difficult, but more appropriate, way would be to analyze the role of music in Greek film through the decades, which is decidedly beyond the scope of this essay. A brief sketch, as background for our purposes, would point to the use of popular song in the classic popular films of the late 1950s and 1960s, which served both as entertainment and as moral instruction (by either melodrama or slapstick satire, both performed with outrageous extravagance). These films tended to use songs as breaks in the dramatic or comedic action, like miniature music videos made with "Stone Age" technology and occasionally performed by the protagonists (which meant they had to show a tolerable talent for singing), or else by actual popular singers of the day, who otherwise had no role in the action and no narrative presence in the film. The crowning figure of this genre is the eminent composer Manos Hatzidakis, whose songs from that era nurtured an entire generation in a particular musical aesthetic that, in many ways, has yet to be surpassed.

An essential note on Hatzidakis and these songs: It is difficult to imagine producing a serious study of their significance not merely to Greek music (or Greek film music), but to the contemporary Greek imaginary as a whole. Even a book would not cover the task, for one would need to put some heavy listening time into an enormous *oeuvre* in order to comprehend the ingenious conceptualization and execution of this music, given the musical and cultural material available from this period. Hatzidakis became distinguished internationally as a film-music composer (after his Academy Award for *Never on Sunday*), but little attention has been paid to his thoroughly radical approach to the orchestration and arrangement of these light-headed and singable tunes. The songs became enormously popular and influential in Greece, and were sung by large numbers of urban dwellers, who remained unconscious, however, of the vanguard musical sensibility. In these early versions of what later became trademark songs and were reproduced in many variations, one discerns the curious balance of basically jazz background atmospheric rhythms (without playing jazz signatures) with heavy treble electric bass sounds and vibraphones covering all corners of the compositional frame, laid underneath an array of oboes and trumpets and thin two-dimensional string arrangements (whose sonic breadth, nonetheless, puts Phil Spector to shame)—all this as groundwork for the legendary melodies that incorporate traditional *rebetiko* references into essentially classical arrangements with stunning ease. The result is simply unique and unreproducible.

Like any serious Greek composer, Karaindrou is well versed in Hatzidakis. This is particularly evident in her sense of spacing. Moreover, her ability to produce traditional popular songs of the highest order demonstrates her deep knowledge of the form. But her own style is unique in the Greek soundscape. It has been amply noted that Karaindrou's sound is not Greek as such, but rather meta-Greek—an ambiguous term that tries to account for the synthesis of a post-classical, Europeanized musical attitude with traces of Balkan harmonies.[14] Karaindrou made her mark as film composer with her characteristically suspended orchestral structures: elongated chordal passages over which a solo instrument (often an oboe or, in later years, the brazen tenor saxophone of Jan Garbarek) repeats a haunting melody, whose line is simple but whose texture elicits a rich range of associations.

Karaindrou's soundscapes are uniquely appropriate to the cinematic vision of Theodoros Angelopoulos, although she has written music for other film-makers in much the same style. Angelopoulos's films produce an unusual cinematic idiom to which there is no appropriate European equivalent (except perhaps some of Bergman's long shots in his early black and whites, but Angelopoulos treats the shot with an unnervingly ineffable eye as compared to Bergman's explosively repressed anxiety). Angelopoulos draws his visual energy from painting, with elongated frames that create a sense of suspension, not unlike those of Sergio Leone (though the referential frame is obviously different).[15] The shots are so long that the audience finds itself trapped in impressionistic contemplation, a mode of thought that utilizes the language of dreams. His films forbid close-ups or any other sort of personalization of the action. Rather, they develop with sweeping pan shots and various distancing techniques that refine the Brechtian *Verfremdungseffekt* into something so subtle that it becomes insidious. In his groundbreaking film *The Traveling Players* (1975)—which became in many non-European countries emblematic of the kind of film-making that was dubbed "Third Cinema" (along with Tomas Guitierrez Alea's seminal *Memories of Underdevelopment*)—Angelopoulos pioneered his famous 360-degree pan, in which the characters depicted in the beginning of the shot would be seen in the same spot some ten years later at the end of the shot, as the camera comes around full circle. This technique succeeded in showing the dual aspect of historical movement: namely, the fact that historical time occurs simultaneously both as circularity and as a series of leaps and ruptures. In fact, Angelopoulos' cinema succeeds in depicting historical time in a way that was previously the sole property of modernist fiction.

In this respect, Angelopoulos's time is monumental and Karaindrou's music renders it in palpable terms. What occurs in her music is a simultaneously visual and aural landscape that hypnotizes the spectator, who expects to exercise his or her mastery over the historical narrative but fails. Of course, I am speaking of Greek audiences, and particularly of Greek leftists, who would be Angelopoulos's addressees—precisely the ones most in need of induced suspension of historical givens. I am not sure what effect this music would have on audiences unfamiliar with the minutiae of the specific social-historical experience. I suspect the effect would tend toward a more exclusively aesthetic one. The "hypnotic" sound is nonetheless recognized as such within its proper context; this may account for Karaindrou's contract for release of her music with Manfred Eicher, the producer of the recognized German label ECM, which has recorded a number of encounters between top European jazz musicians and American artists who favor the inter-section of jazz arrangements with so-called atmospheric or ambient sound.[16] Karaindrou's sound is literally imagistic and even sublime—it is too huge to be understood analytically. The refusal to embrace history according to one's ideolog-ical expectations is precisely what opens history wide within oneself; this is Angelopoulos's greatest filmic achievement, and Karaindrou's musical expression provides an additional sensory dimension.

Yet, Karaindrou's success with Angelopoulos goes beyond the elongated chordal structures that accompany the films' slow, wide-angle shots. She also manages to tame traditional Greek elements and incorporate them into a culturally mys-terious musical language. In film music she wrote before her collaboration with Angelopoulos, Karaindrou already demonstrated a range of such transformative abilities. In her main motif for Christophoros Christophis's first film *Wandering* (1979), one observes an uncanny interweaving of folk elements (particularly in the choice of instrumentation) and an Eisler-like style of composition and arrangement. Karaindrou's elegiac theme for Christophis's subsequent film *Rosa* (1982) and her classic "Rosa's Aria"—written for mezzo-soprano and orchestra and originally sung by the composer herself with stunning bareness—show her profound understand-ing of the German *lieder* tradition, particularly according to Eisler and Brecht's groundbreaking meditation on the song as a political-theatrical form.[17]

But Karaindrou is equally at ease incorporating straight Greek folk elements. Written for mezzo-soprano and acoustic guitar, her song "The Price of Love"— from the classic film of the same title by Tonia Marketaki (1983)—shows Karain-drou's capacity to extend the vocabulary of the song form to a strange intersection between a Brechtian understanding of the *lied* form and a Greek new-wave sound (a simple, stripped-down, ballad form that characterizes urban political youth culture of the mid-1960s). In the context of the film, this contemporary song form produces a subtle disruption.[18] In a different and perhaps bolder gesture, the song written for her first collaboration with Angelopoulos (*Voyage to Kythera*, 1984) is a masterful composition in a bonafide *xasapiko* song form: a superb piece that captures the entire history of the genre, a history of displacement and refugee life (*rebetiko*). The evocative lyrics, written by the composer herself, capture the disruptive nostalgia of the film: An old political prisoner returns from decades of exile to his native island to face the enormous changes that have shaped society during his absence. But Karaindrou dares something further with this traditional theme: She reworks it into a jazz quartet (alto sax-piano-bass-drums) that gingerly picks through the variations in such *style* as to shatter any ethnocentric investment in the otherwise stunning folk melody. The mastery of classical and jazz idioms here is uncanny—perfect for the context of a film about cultural dissolution and betrayal, interminable displacement and undomesticated difference.

Karaindrou's music for *Ulysses' Gaze* (1995), Angelopoulos's overt meditation on the Balkans, is even more minimalist and hypnotic than her previous works. Perhaps closer to a classical idiom, with occasional subtle and muted strains of waltz, but hardly folkish and certainly hardly Balkan,[19] the music permeates the film, ethereal yet palpable, like mist. In this respect, it evokes one of Angelopoulos's dearest atmospheric settings—all the more significant here, considering that mist is the sole full-screen image for a three-minute span, while the film's culminating violence takes place off-screen. Indeed, more than in any other film, Karaindrou's music is foregrounded in this one as a muted drama unfolds beyond the bounds of the screen. This arrangement is shattered only once: when, emerging from the screen's mist, the anonymous film-maker (played by Harvey Keitel) faces the bodies of his murdered friends and breaks into a long, piercing wail, before the music re-emerges and gradually permeates the landscape again like water breaking on the shore. This culminating scene is one of Angelopoulos's and Karaindrou's most masterful moments, in a film that comes closer than all its predecessors to the magnificence of *The Traveling Players*.

Ulysses' Gaze was Angelopoulos's most rigorous meditation in some years. He decided to film on location throughout the Balkans (his first ever shooting outside of Greece) in a genuine attempt to render historical reality in a cinematic idiom. This is hardly to say that he opts for a documentary vision. On the contrary, his cinematic evocation of historical reality is so rigorous precisely because the stark realism of the film is mythographic at its core. Paradoxically, the mythical element does not register through the explicit use of the Odyssean journey (which is after all the central allegory of most of Angelopoulos' films), but through the continuous superimposition of various historical temporalities, all channeled through the body of the anonymous protagonist in his encounter with the Balkan terrain. In this sense, the film engages with the *mythistorical* core of the Balkans in its various geographical, political, and cultural transformations over the course of the twentieth century. The object of the protagonist's quest is the first film ever shot in the Balkans, at the beginning of this turbulent century, which had remained undeveloped and thus lost as a witness to history. Hence, the impetus of this film is to seek the point of historical emergence, to search for the original metaphorical instance. Yet the quest is not merely archaeological. The point is not to unearth a lost relic; it is, as the protagonist says at one point, to unlock a lost gaze. In other words, the trajectory is reversed: One does not seek to bring the past up to date in order to peer into the past; rather, one seeks to discover the past intact within the present, in order to enable the past to fill the present with its gaze. This is the profound truth behind the obsession with creating a mysterious chemical solution that will revive a lost filmic gaze—both vanished traces of the past—in the midst of a vanishing present, namely, war-torn Sarajevo.

Ulysses' Gaze is boldly constructed so as to foreclose any opportunity for nostalgia, even while its vision is predicated on the obsession with making history anew in the midst of a dying historical present. There is something harsh here, even while one is treated to a sumptuous cinematic vision, a sublime and deeply humane depiction of a ravaged historical landscape. This "harshness" is likely due to Angelopoulos's own ineffable gaze that generally characterizes his cinematic mythography, echoed here specifically by the protagonist's professed inability to love his loved ones beyond his obsession. Karaindrou's music, here more than in any other Angelopoulos film, provides the soul of this beautifully restrained, sublime cinematic coldness. A deeply sensuous and thoughtful music, unafraid of sentimentality but free from any nostalgia, the score to *Ulysses' Gaze* actually provides the subtle critical mindfulness (*psyche*) that Angelopoulos's universe demands but never directly shows.

Critique from the Standpoint of Excess

Goran Bregović's path into film music is substantially different from Karaindrou's. While Karaindrou's musical initiation owes much to her formal education (in classical orchestration and ethnomusicology in Paris, to which we must add her formative exposure to the Parisian jazz scene of the late 1960s and early 1970s), Bregović burst onto the musical scene around that time as a rock guitarist. His subsequent impact on Yugoslav culture (ranging from the strictly musical to the wider political and aesthetic realm) was simply enormous. As a founder (in 1973) and main song-writer for the Sarajevo group Bijelo Dugme, Bregović has linked the range of his musical invention with an entire generation of Yugoslav youth, perhaps the last gen-eration to develop its imagination simultaneously against both the homogenizing aesthetics of the state and the nationalist exclusivity that brought about Yugoslav society's demise.

Bijelo Dugme was dubbed by music critics at the time "the Beatles of Yugoslavia," and its stature and enormous popularity among Eastern European youth certainly justifies the extravagance of the term. Musically, Bijelo Dugme epitomized the rich and diverse rock scene in Yugoslavia (which had been, along with Czechoslovakia, at the forefront of musical innovation and political gravity in Eastern European countries since the late 1960s).[20] Bijelo Dugme's sound ranges from its earliest hard glam rock (including the transgendering images characteristic of the glam move-ment in England during the early 1970s) to straight rhythm-and-blues signatures, heavy rock ballads (in the style of "heavy-metal" ballads of the 1980s), occasional excursions into "progressive rock" territory, new-wavish upbeat signatures (some-times with brass backing, bordering on funk), or often times uncategorizable, exper-imental tunes, arranged for acoustic instruments. The recognizable influences thus range from classic, even mainstream, rock elements flowing from the West at the time (unlike the Czech scene, which was formed under the musical influences of Frank Zappa and the Velvet Underground—hardly a mainstream sound) to more regional elements, as "secondary revisions" of already assimilated rock patterns (for example, certain of Bijelo Dugme's ballads sound very much like the Italian rock remoldings of Lucio Dalla). Yet, most important, Bregović made a point from the outset of incorporating local (Bosnian) folk elements into the material, often inter-twining them with straight rock rhythms and instrumentation—as, for example, in the resolutely "Balkan"-sounding choral passage overlaid on the heavy R&B rhythm of the classic "Ako možes, zaboravi" (1983), which features some stunning blues guitar lines by Bregović himself.

This latter aspect of Bijelo Dugme would become the formal bridge to Bregovic's later film music work. By the late 1980s, as Yugoslavia began to enter its irreversible death-dive, Bijelo Dugme's repertoire became decidedly anti-nationalist via a sub-versive invocation of folk elements, while Bregović declared it necessary to dismantle the straight rock sound in favor of the collage of elements that characterizes con-temporary "ethnic music."[21] At this juncture, Bijelo Dugme's long term position at the forefront of a subversive anti-Statist politics entered its last phase, with the des-perate warning against "the stupid war" (Bregović's words) about to be waged. Not

The whole occasion of "Ya Ya" is wonderfully complicated. Kusturica shrewdly chooses to stage this scene in the early 1960s, before in fact Yugoslav rock culture became a fully fledged genre of resistance. The fact that this genre, as *secondary revision*, stages its own presence (and claims its own present tense) through its deconstructive action as film music, thus produces a deliberate temporal disjuncture. But Kusturica's staging also foregrounds the antagonistically ironic image of American music as the secret fetish of "hip" Party functionaries, those beneficiaries of the system who surely knew nothing about rock culture but nonetheless flattered themselves as exclusive agents of modernization. The view is thoroughly refracting. Bregović boldly *Balkanizes* the form, creating a moment when the "indigenous" culture renders the "invading" culture in its own idiom. The sampled Lee Dorsey refrain is made to echo the "indigenous" translation-metaphorization (the nursery rhyme "Ringe Ringe Raja" as sarcastic R&B), while the hybrid arrangement (tubas doubling the electric bass parts, the contrapuntal quasi-folk melody inserted between the refrains) lends a centrifugal dimension to an otherwise thoroughly imitated form. In a strange way, the appropriate subversive response to cultural imperialism is precisely this centrifugal gesture: externalizing yourself within your own culture. This is a dialectical gesture. To one extent, it is itself the outcome of imperialized existence. Edward Said insists that, in the last instance, imperialism is always about identity, and it is precisely in the signifying terrain of identity where the experience of externalization belongs. To another extent, however, it is a resistant gesture in the most basic sense: a derailment or a defraying of the very language of imperialist culture. To construct and sustain an "external" standpoint from within is indeed to act against acculturation to the global idiom. This is how "ethnic music" can still be renewed: by being performed against the grain, relieved from the quicksand of nostalgic fetish.

Yet, following the same logic of the charges against Kusturica, Bregović himself has been accused of fetishizing the "indigenous," Bosnian or gypsy music. No doubt, his genius is one of absorption and appropriation. He does it in a great variety of forms, not only the traditional, but also the "classical" and the "modern," the tango and the techno. In a way, the overall musical landscape of *Underground* may be seen as an autonomous document of the musical trajectory of Yugoslavia in the second half of the twentieth century. The connecting thread—the thread of secondary revision—is precisely the cannibalization of one's refracted, indigenous musical forms. Bregović is explicitly drawn to variation, recirculation, rearrangement, repetition, continuous self-quotation, continuous blurring of the "original" instance and the instance of its reproduction—indeed in the vein of the classic Brazilian *cannibalismo*.

Outside the terrain of Bijelo Dugme and their overtly blues voicings, Bregović has consistently sought to refract his self-quotation through the vocal expression of expertly selected world singers. Thus, Bijelo Dugme's brilliant "Ako možes, zaboravi" recurs ten years later in the music for *Arizona Dream* as "TV Screen," with English lyrics and vocals by Iggy Pop (as part of a set of songs performed by Iggy Pop in quasi-recitation mode, somewhere between Lou Reed and the Residents); Bijelo Dugme's ballad "Ružica si bila" is rewritten as "Greek ethnic" and sung by Alkestis Protopsalti (1991) or as "Polish ethnic" and sung by Kayah (1999), or yet again, as choral piece in the film score to *Queen Margot* (1994); similarly, a heavy "choral" electric guitar riff from Bijelo Dugme's heavy-metal ballad "Ne gledaj me tako i ne ljubi me više" is recast in sumptuous funereal pomp (with sheets of low background horns) for the Protopsalti recording, yet also reappears famously in *Queen Margot* as the chant "Elo Hi" performed by Ofra Haza; the instrumental tango from the film music to *Kuduz* (1989) is rewritten for the sensuous voice of Cesaria Evora in *Underground*; and, of course, the legendary *Ederlezi*, from the score to *Time of the Gypsies*, has seen the most extensive variation, repetition, refraction, cannibalization.

In a sense, the recirculation and restaging of motifs that has become Bregović's trademark since Bijelo Dugme is itself a method of composing film music. Bregović, meanwhile, ever one to go against his own grain, has recently announced his unwillingness to compose more film music: "Film is an hysterical environment that does not suit my way of life."[28] His new endeavor is to manage a fifty-piece orchestra that stages multimedia events practically continuously around the globe. The only available recording from this phase is the performance presented on the occasion of Thessaloniki being declared Cultural Capital of Europe in 1997 and released with the suggestive title *Silence of the Balkans* (1998). Bregović's turn to large, live, multimedia performances is certainly consistent with his self-conscious openness to performativity and theatricality ever since Bijelo Dugme's glam days. Yet this particular work, which incorporates many aspects of his film-music repertoire, but also may be said to recast the film-music experience as theatrical performance away from the permanent inscription on celluloid, reveals a possible turn toward sparseness and silence as main organizational and compositional principles, a turn away from Bregovićs previous desire for an "aesthetics of noise."

The *co-incidence* of this turn with the collapse of Sarajevo's multiethnic and multicultural world cannot go unnoticed. Bregović is forced by the circumstances of deathly silence to loosen his referential frame, to adopt a hybrid, "globalized" idiom—for lack of a more accurate term. Instrumentally, the music sounds more

"Western," less for its turn to string orchestration and more for adopting the overall hybrid aesthetics of "world music." Bregović's choice to interweave softer string-orchestral structures with more prominent techno-rhythmic structures, while allowing the familiar brass gypsy rhythms to recede to the background, becomes his own contemporary evidence of dispersal in the region's long history of cultural crossings and experimentation. His homage to Thessaloniki, the most ancient city of the Balkans—which is to say also, the most ancient site of dispersal—is at once appropriate and ironic in a variety of ways. The occasion is the celebration of Thessaloniki, not as a Balkan site, but as Europe's Cultural Capital; the language of the songs performed is English, while the work speaks of the silence of the Balkans; the Balkans no longer speak but through the translation of silence. It is not surprising that the work closes with a wordless (but not voiceless) piece, whose snappy, hypnotic, "Balkan-reggae" beat (with tubas, again, playing the off-time bass line)—somewhat reminiscent of the ironic Iggy Pop funk piece "Get the Money" from *Arizona Dream*—is much too happy to be true: It is titled "Mocking Song."

III.   The Psychic Framework of Hypnosis and Critique

From a certain standpoint that I don't discuss here directly, one might say that, in both Karaindrou and Bregović, the primary conceptualization of film music is ritualistic. Constructed less on the methodological basis of the film frame, and not quite as commentary on the content of the images (at least in any evident sense), these two different musical idioms coincide as liturgical practices. Their rhythms are virtuosic and rigorous, yet improvisational, if necessary; their melodies are distinctive and autonomous; their atmospheres, corporeal. The easy pronouncement would be to call Karaindrou "Western" and Bregović "Eastern." But, besides the fact that it would essentially ignore most of the music written for *Arizona Dream* or *Queen Margot* (both indeed closer to *Silence of the Balkans*), this folklorization of Bregović would be as problematic as the notion of "Balkanization" is to describe the allegedly inherent tendency of the Balkan peoples to disintegrate into ever more trivial structures. Bregović relies on folk elements but what he does with that tradition breaks it apart. The crucial question is how each composer builds a specific context for critical meditation. In Karaindrou's suspended soundscapes, a hypnotic atmosphere stretches time, much like Angelopoulos' shots, so that history does not vanish in a flash—so that in slow, hypnotic motion, history becomes more accessible to critique. Yet even in Bregović's most frenetic time signatures, the same sort of suspended meditation is achieved through *ekstasis*: The experience of history is a centrifugal whirlwind, absorbing us but never letting us rest on solid ground. In this respect, hypnosis and critique are not meant as antagonistic terms. Nor do they denote opposing poles occupied by each composer in singular plenitude. They pertain to both Karaindrou and Bregović, each notion making the other possible as primary methodological forces in both projects.

Conceiving the matter in this way requires that we counter the widespread prejudice against hypnosis and its connotations of trickery or stupefaction, external manipulation by magic, or internal collapse of one's ability to discern and judge—in other words, to use one's *krisis*. Since Freud's expulsion of hypnosis (including his own contribution to it as a therapeutic practice) from psychoanalysis, the signification of hypnosis receded further into the murky terrain of the magical and the mystical. Freud was explicit in his claim that psychoanalysis proper (*eigentliche*) begins where hypnosis ends, because he sought to shield transference, the keystone of psychoanalytic practice, from being tainted with the charge of suggestion. This was, in many ways, Freud's rupturing gesture against the epistemology and methodology from which psychoanalysis fashioned itself as an autonomous discipline. Yet, even though Freud's descendants (including Lacan) held to and even refined the taboo against hypnosis, further distancing psychoanalysis from its "prehistory," no rupture is wholly clean. As Mikkel Borch-Jacobsen shows in a series of subtle and incisive readings, Freud's repudiation of hypnosis actually involved a great deal of equivocation and retrogression.[29] In ruminations, second thoughts, and remarks, Freud repeatedly ends up (re)affirming the richness of hypnosis as the paradigmatic signification of one's deep relation with the other, as the unchartable and enigmatic terrain of what he terms *Gefuhlsbindung*—"the emotional tie" that, as Borch-Jacobsen is quick to show, is none other than the social bind itself, the space in which the profound relation to the other becomes tangible as the actual foundation of society.

Obviously, there are greater implications to this than mere revision of the history of psychoanalysis. Borch-Jacobsen's groundbreaking contribution is to recognize that in his official purging of hypnosis from the theory of transference, Freud also occluded the performative dimensions of the analytic encounter, thus burdening transference (and the whole therapeutic method) with a requisite narrative task. The denial of the performative nature of transference is implicated directly in the consistent emphasis throughout the psychoanalytic tradition on the power of language. The "talking cure" is taken all too literally as the essence of the analytic encounter, whereby the transference experience consists of the analysand's self-abandonment to his or her inner psychic narrative conducted nonetheless through the "mirroring" silence of the analyst. As such, the whole epistemological universe of *Vorstellung*, the fact that the human psyche *socializes itself* within and by means of the interminable flux of affective representations (of self and otherness, of the here and the elsewhere), in plain words, the work of the imagination itself, is sidelined in favor of privileging an order of language, a symbolic structure, and most important, a narrative conceptualization of the phantasmatic universe itself.[30]

In the process, the theatrical element of analysis is lost; the psyche's *Phantasiebildung* is dedramatized and its unfolding in the therapeutic process is, as Borch-Jacobsen claims, "demimetized." What enables one to think of the dismantling of mimetic conditions is the wager that the analytic encounter hinges on the possibility of automanifestation before the void of the analyst's silent mirror, to refer (somewhat freely) to Lacan's famous schema. As such, an "interminable" flow of language is to replace the interminable flow of phantasmatic presentation; or, to put it otherwise, the free association of images by which the psyche recognizes and alters itself is replaced by the spoken representation of those images, whereby verbal free association assumes inherent symbolic value and, via the analyst's interpretive authority (which the analysand ultimately is to appropriate, embody, and produce on his own), achieves a (wishfully) coherent narrative of the unconscious self. This is how image is translated into word and, if I may, *Phantasiebildung* into the psyche's own *Bildunsgroman*.

Yet, Freud's meticulous attention (throughout *The Interpretation of Dreams*) to the way in which dream-work is iconographic at its core—in dreams, even language is bound up in image—testifies to the ultimate trickery required in order to re-fashion dreams into a therapeutic narrative. Taken strictly, it is tantamount to a conjurer's gesture. In the temporal frame of the unconscious, words are iconic, and for precisely this reason, the conscious translation of images to words, posited as an act of practical disenchantment, is actually an enchantment in reverse: an act of making an object vanish in order to replace it with itself dressed in different clothes. Apart from the fact of its self-occultation, which psychoanalytic theory has traditionally evaded, I find this magical act hardly problematic. On the contrary, it serves to remind us that the "talking cure" is hardly mere verbal externalization (and, ideally, transcendence) of one's unconscious activities, but is undeconstructibly performative: therapeutic delirium is not unlike a staged performance in which one speaks as an other, a kind of self-hypnosis that enables radical self-interrogation and entails, in the last instance, self-alteration, the revolutionary gesture *par excellence*.

It is certainly not accidental that, in this brief foray into the internal antagonisms of psychoanalytic history regarding hypnosis, we have returned to the terms posited at the outset regarding the "instantaneous metaphorization" of events in the Balkans as key to reading history's interminable flux of social imaginary representations— society's fantasies about itself and its other(s). As in *Dream Nation*, my concern here has been to explore society's own conditions for placing its *Phantasiebildung* under performative interrogation. Societies create their own mythography (whether or not they admit it or even know it) and, of course, they are constantly sublimating their innermost fantasies, for good or ill. In both of these *co-incidental* practices, a performative reality is always at the forefront, regardless of whether it is acknowledged as such. This performative reality incorporates the radical singularity of all historical events which, at the very instance of coming into existence as events—at the very instance they emerge into history and make history—vanish into their insurmountable metaphorization, which feeds society's process of mythography and sublimation.

The instances of film music I have examined here, precisely because they exemplify the hybrid, *synesthetic*, excessive capacity of the genre, elucidate this process in a unique way. Indeed, through their music, Karaindrou and Bregović make the unconscious ground of their societies' imaginaries *sensible*: tangible as well as comprehensible, perhaps against the grain of logical analysis but certainly not outside the range of self-reflection that the film experience provokes. This is not the sort of film music that works as emotional manipulation behind the scenes, as it were. Its staging is hardly veiled. On the contrary, its excessive hypnotic effect alerts one further to the performative nature of the history the film engages, as the spectator and listener is drawn into the theatrical whirlwind of the visual and aural ritual. Precisely at the most heightened moment of suspense or excess, the spectator is driven furthest out onto the stage of his or her own investment in the very social imaginary the film interrogates. Such a position no doubt provokes a critical moment, and a moment of crisis.

Notes

1. This essay would not have been realized without the generosity of Dušan Djordjević Mileusnić.

2. My thinking here is grounded on the foundational signification of the notions of metaphor (in Greek, *metaphora*) and translation (in Latin, *translatio*), which inhere in the representation of transposition, the gesture of moving from one domain to another. In this transposition, a transformation of space and object cannot be avoided; meaning demands the full range of creative/destructive *poiesis*. Moreover, given a crucial association incidental to the English language, the notion of *translation* of funereal relics should resound in full force.

3. See *Dream Nation: Enlightenment, Colonization, and the Institution of Modern Greece* (Stanford University Press, 1996), 261–266.

4. Beyond rethinking here certain arguments from *Dream Nation* that pertain to the workings of the national fantasy, I have also incorporated a great deal, particularly in regard to the conceptualization of Yugoslavia's national fantasy, from Renata Salecl's exceptional book *The Spoils of Freedom: Psychoanalysis and Feminism After the Fall of Socialism* (New York: Routledge, 1994).

5. In this essay, I use the term *co-incidence*, much like I use it in *Dream Nation*, to refer to the impossibility of the singular emergence of any event or act in history, the impossibility of any event or act to occupy an exclusive space without being leaned on by (and leaning on in turn) an other. Needless to say, the logic of co-incidence presupposes a non-identitarian logic of time.

6. In this sense, this essay occupies the crossroads of two projects I am currently working on: one, on society's mythographic capacity; the other, on the politics of sublimation. See indicatively *Literature as Theory (for an Antimythical Era)*, forthcoming with Stanford University Press and "Philosophy and Sublimation" in *Thesis Eleven* 49 (May 1997): 31–44.

7. The consummate works on this subject are Rick Altman's "The Silence of the Silents" *Musical Quarterly* 80:4 (1997): 648–718 and Martin Marks's *Music and the Silent Film: Case Studies 1895–1924* (New York: Oxford University Press, 1997).

8. Incidentally, the recent turn in new music circles to score original compositions for classic silent films, frame by frame, is a retro fashion that elaborates on this foundational significance of music to the art of film-making. It makes sense that the favorite objects of such retroactive contemporary scoring are classic German expressionist films (*Metropolis*, *The Cabinet of Dr. Caligari, Nosferatu*), which are submitted with equal ease either to elaborate orchestrations (as, for example, by the San Francisco based experimental group The Clubfoot Orchestra) or to the stripped-down industrial-noise aesthetic of the legendary German group Faust—in both cases, though on rare occasions, performed live from the cinema's orchestra pit. Another notable effort along these lines would be the scoring of several Buster Keaton films by the experimental guitarist Bill Frisell.

9. For a concise overview of the relevant history, methodology, and bibliography see Claudia Gorbman, "Film Music," in *The Oxford Guide to Film Studies*, ed. John Hill and Pamela Church Gibson (Oxford: Oxford University Press, 1998), 43–50.

10. See Theodor Adorno and Hanns Eisler, *Composing for the Films* (London: The Athlone Press, 1994).

11. It is noteworthy, however, that the book was published under Eisler's name only, as Adorno, in an exemplary gesture of Brechtian cunning (rather ironic, considering their contentious relation), withdrew his authorial signature so as not to be implicated in the mounting investigation against Hanns Eisler by the House Committee on Un-American Activities. Adorno restored his signature in the German translation and publication of the treatise shortly before his death in 1969. An excellent discussion of the background and various permutations of this collaboration is found in Albrecht Katz, *Hanns Eisler: Political Musician* (Cambridge: Cambridge University Press, 1982), 169–194.

12. See Theodor Adorno's 1966 essay "Transparencies in Film" (Thomas Levin, trans.) in *New German Critique* 24–25 (fall/winter 1981–82): 199–205.

13. *Composing for the Films*, 36.

14. This is how Karaindrou's sound is described by Andrew Horton in his book *The Films of Theo Angelopoulos: A Cinema of Contemplation* (Princeton: Princeton University Press, 1997), 51. Horton's book, the first full study of Angelopoulos, is no doubt valuable, and his understanding of the basic terms of Angelopoulos's cinema is accurately and meticulously depicted. However, one cannot help but be struck by the curtailed horizon of critical contemplation, particularly since, by the author's own admission, this is what Angelopoulos's cinema uniquely produces. The evident unwillingness to consider, beyond scant and shallow references, the significance of Karaindrou's music (which is, to my mind, indispensable to the unique "Angelopoulos-effect") is just one of the many puzzling shortcomings of this study.

15. Horton elaborates on various influences and affinities along these lines, including notably Robert Bresson, Miklos Jancso, and Kenji Mizoguchi. See *The Films of Theo Angelopoulos*, 73–88.

16. Eleni Karaindrou's most accessible discography is represented by her ECM recordings: the compilation *Music for Films* (1991), as well as the complete soundtrack recordings for Angelopoulos's films *The Suspended Step of the Stork* (1992) and *Ulysses' Gaze* (1995) that features the viola playing of Kim Kashkashian. But the extraordinary Greek recording of her extant music from theatrical performances, titled *Anekdotes Echographeseis* [Unpublished Recordings], released in 1991, demonstrates best her resilience and comfort with a wide-ranging musical idiom.

17. The complete soundtracks of both of Christophis' films have been re-released in a sumptuous CD edition by the Greek label Lyra as Eleni Karaindrou, *Rosa/Periplanes* (1997).

18. The profoundly radical significance of this song—as well as of the film itself—is based on the sundering ambiguity of the Greek title *Atimetes agapes*. The word *time*, consistent with its ancient signification, means simultaneously both honor and price. This becomes trenchant insofar as the film shows, in dramatically horrendous sequences, that honor both comes at a price and cannot possibly have a price. This untenable situation for the woman protagonist in the film is borne out brilliantly by the dialectic of the word on which her world hinges—Karaindrou's barest song arrangement and haunting melody captures it perfectly. The song reaches its dialectical culmination in the last verse "honor has no price" which simultaneously signifies the reverse: "price has no honor." One cannot imagine a more Brechtian verse.

19. I am at a loss as to where Andrew Horton sees "a feisty folk tune at the core" of this "decidedly more 'Balkan' than Greek" music. (See *The Films of Theo Angelopoulos*, 185.)

20. The two most informative texts in English on the history of rock in Yugoslavia are Sabrina Petra Ramet's "Shake, Rattle, and Self-Management: Making the Scene in Yugoslavia," in *Rocking the State: Rock Music and Politics in Eastern Europe and Russia*, ed. Sabrina Petra Ramet (Boulder: Westview Press, 1994), 103–131; and the chapter on "Rock Music" from her book *Balkan Babel: Politics, Culture and Religion in Yugoslavia* (Boulder: Westview Press, 1992), 81–104. For a more contemporary, detailed account of the demise of rock's subversive mode and the complicity of popular music with nationalist regimes, see Eric D. Gordy's "The Destruction of Musical Alternatives," in his recent book *The Culture of Power in Serbia: Nationalism and the Destruction of Alternatives* (Pennsylvania State University Press, 1999), 103–162.

21. See Goran Bregović's revealing 1989 interview with Sabrina Petra Ramet: "Whoever Doesn't Listen to This Song Will Hear the Storm" in *Rocking the State*, 133–139.

22. See Bregović's interview with Ramet, 139.

23. The group's notorious mastermind, Dr. Nele Karaljić, a legendary rock personality of its own, wrote some of the music for Kusturica's most recent film *Black Cat, White Cat* (1998).

24. The various permutations of youth culture in the making of post-Second World War Yugoslavia have been expertly discussed by Renata Salecl—most important, the various contradictory significations of youth culture according to the social-historical instance and the state's demands for "normalization." We must not forget, as Salecl warns us, that "no such thing as youth exists in itself: youth by 'nature' is always mediated by the symbolic network, by the ideology that defines it" (*The Spoils of Freedom*, 44). In this respect, even the real danger that youth culture poses to social authority (totalitarian or otherwise) is itself mediated by the social imaginary that authorizes it—which is hardly to dismiss the reality of its danger, but it is to relativize the professed ontology of this danger.

25. Such is Dina Iordanova's position in her review, "Conceptualizing the Balkans in Film," *Slavic Review* 55, no. 4 (winter 1996): 882–890. She sees *Underground* as a "film about robust survivalism" and "the personal politics of parasitism," marked by a "Byzantine mentality and opportunism." In other words, she sees it as resolutely *Balkan*. I say this in light of her claim that Angelopoulos is "the only one daring enough to assert that universal problems lurk within the peculiar Balkan universe." There is some sort of reverse "Balkanism" at work when the notorious narcissistic investment of a Bernard Henri-Levy (in his documentary *Bosna!*) is taken as history's truth, while Kusturica is practically rendered a Serbian state propagandist. No doubt, the Western film establishment exoticizes Kusturica's vision. But to measure matters using this Western fetish as a (negative) standard is indeed to subscribe to a Western semantics of what is Balkan—and indeed that the Balkan *is* an element untouched by the force of metaphor—precisely the sort of thing Iordanova rightly wishes to undo.

26. Salecl, *The Spoils of Freedom*, 58–73, 99–111.

27. This characteristic Bogart-Bacall reference is quoted by John Wrathall in his review "Gypsy Time," *Sight and Sound* 7, no. 12 (December 1997): 11–13.

28. Quoted in the Greek newspaper *Eleutherotypia*, May 31, 2000.

29. See Mikkel Borch-Jacobsen, *The Emotional Tie: Psychoanalysis, Mimesis, and Affect* (Stanford: Stanford University Press, 1992).

30. It is to Borch-Jacobsen's credit that he traces precisely how this gesture is conducted by Lacan, in a brilliant rethinking of the residual Levi-Straussian structuralism in Lacan's understanding of language.

14

Simonides on the Balkans

Petar Ramadanović

According to a legend told by Cicero and Quintilian, Simonides of Ceos, the famous Greek poet, invented the art of memory.[1] A wealthy man, Scopas of Thessaly, commissioned Simonides to compose a paean celebrating a boxing champion. The poet devoted half of the ode to Castor and Pollux, the mythical prototypes of boxers. So Scopas decided to pay Simonides only half of the promised sum. The other half, Scopas said, should be paid by the Dioscuri. And the gods did indeed repay Simonides—by inviting him to come out of the house in which the boxing victory was being celebrated just before it collapsed. "In the interval of his absence," Cicero writes in book two of *De Oratore*,

the roof of the hall where Scopas was giving the banquet fell in, crushing Scopas himself and his relations underneath the ruins and killing them; and when their friends wanted to bury them but were altogether unable to know them apart as they had been completely crushed, the story goes that Simonides was enabled by his recollection of the place in which each of them had been reclining at table to identify [the bodies] for separate interment.[2]

Cicero concludes that Simonides invented a new method for remembering when he succeeded in identifying the corpses of the feasters. Simonides was able to do this because he recreated the order in which the guests were sitting before the house collapsed. In this way, it was discovered that order aids memory.

Almost two thousand years after Cicero, Dubravka Ugrešić, a writer from the former Yugoslavia, tells again the legend of Simonides's invention of the art of memory. In an essay titled "The Confiscation of Memory," she writes:

Simonides, asked by the relatives to identify the victims, does not manage to do his mnemotechnical job, because suddenly the remaining walls collapse, killing him and the relatives who had come to bury their dead. The new witnesses of the scene, struck by this double misfortune, are, admittedly, in a position to identify the victims, but only those they remember from the places where they happened to be when the remaining walls collapsed. And so each one remembers and mourns his own. The other victims—not to mention the original ones—do not exist.[3]

This time around, Simonides is himself caught in the collapse of the house. And while, upon his death, others assume his role, they are able to reconstruct only partially the past that has disappeared. Which is to say that if Ugrešić repeats history, she also marks a change in her repetition. Namely, there is a multiplication of misfortune and a particularization or isolation of experience as each new witness "remembers and mourns his own." There are thus Serbs, Croats, and Muslims instead of Yugoslavians.

The legend that revealed to the Romans that order illuminates memory is in the Balkans today a legend about the impossibility of witnessing catastrophe. What was for the Romans a story about the origin of a method of reconstructing the past in its totality is for Ugrešić a story of repeated collapse and the loss of any vantage point from which the past, the dead, can be known. In the Balkans, Ugrešić says, the "story slips away in the opposite direction and instead of being about *remembering* it becomes a story about *forgetting*."[4]

The remaining walls of the house collapse and we may imagine that they do so continually, over and over again as if history in the Balkans were nothing but this collapsing, a caving in of being, witnessing, and memory onto themselves. What has happened to the illuminating powers of order? Why can't the contemporary Balkan poet tell what is under the rubble and restore the dead for proper burial? Why can't she redeem the loss? Why has Simonides's mnemotechnical job become a historically impossible task? Why has the history of remembering become a history of forgetting? Why can't we identify and reappropriate the dead and continue our lives?

We might presume that there was a specific moment when a drastic shift occurred in history. Before certain material changes—before, for example, the advent of the modern subject, the formation of nation-states, or the capitalist mode of production—people were able to witness fully their catastrophes, to know their pasts, to bury and mourn their dead properly. No such moment is, however, in evidence in Ugrešić's retelling of the legend. Instead, when Ugrešić attempts to identify the initial victims, to do what we could call the work of history proper, her project ends up under the rubble. It cannot be overemphasized that Ugrešić begins to tell the Roman legend in the way it was told by Cicero, but that in the process something goes awry and the remaining walls collapse. It is as if the original legend, the story of the invention of the art of memory, had suddenly revealed its nether side: that it was all along a story of forgetting.

When the walls collapse, so does the very foundation of any mnemotechnical job, including story-telling. The Yugoslavian version of the legend thus addresses the

who speaks in Danner's articles: a contemporary Simonides who pretends to know what he sees, and who pretends to be able to use power (of order, for example) without himself being affected by it.

IV

For Ugrešić, whose story relies on assumptions and demands quite different than Danner's, even a two-thousand-year-old legend is caught up in contemporary events. The wall that falls on Simonides in her rendition of the Balkan wars is a technological device of the same order as Simonides's invention of mnemotechnology. It delimits the familiar inside from the threatening outside, nature from culture, the dead from the living, past from present. So when the first catastrophe (the collapse of the roof) is repeated in the second catastrophe (the collapse of the remaining walls), there is nothing to prevent the past, chaos, ghosts, from rushing in. There is nothing to maintain the repression or postpone the return of the repressed.

Now, those who have survived the catastrophe can replace this wall with another figurative or actual wall and create a space of provisional peace. In my opinion, Danner's articles and, more importantly, the Dayton peace agreement with which the war in Bosnia ended, form such a new wall built in place of the collapsed one. Bosnia now has the option of fortifying the wall so that it can withstand the pressure of the past. At the same time, after Dayton, it is also possible for Bosnia, as well as for the international community, to look for other ways to deal with the disaster besides bringing Bosnia to order—ways other than those dictated by the logic of national interests, moral outrage, guilt, and even by the notion of human rights that is shaped by such interests, attitudes, or feelings. For the walls will (it seems inevitable) not only reinforce the logic of the fortification of identity along ethnic lines, but also become a source of permanent threat, a petrified memory that is threatening precisely because Bosnia would have forgotten its forgetting, would have forgotten what has been walled away in Dayton.

V

If the history of the Balkans teaches us something, it is that walls are murderous even if they do not kill. There is something in the structure of peace in the Balkans that is warlike, and that a generation or two later, leads to a breakdown of the force of stabilization and hence to another collapse. In saying this, I am not arguing that another structure could replace the wall. I certainly do not want to suggest resuscitating the hybrid identity politics symbolized by the bridge connecting the multiethnic Bosnia of the past and celebrated by the official Yugoslavian ideology during communism. No new edifice, metaphorical or otherwise, can set things right, for in this war we have seen that everything ever built in Bosnia—especially bridges, walls, and sacred structures—can come tumbling down. Furthermore, as another Balkan legend has it, a building requires a sacrifice if it is to stand. It is this sacrifice, this foundational violence, that Bosnia has not been able to survive. The future of Bosnia, the future of the former Yugoslavia whose ghost looms large over the Balkans, cannot be supported by a sacrifice. Bosnia cannot be built up against the force that came rushing in—against, that is, the past that went unrecognized by the very history of remembering, whose violent logic Ugrešić's story discloses.

Along similar lines, one could argue that there is a need to change established styles of writing on wars, genocides, and other disasters, be it history or reportage, literature or cinema. A change would require of writers like Danner more introspection, humility, and sensitivity. Not least, it would demand that they be aware of the processes involved in creating their own identities, including, for example, projection, and the fascination with death and destruction.

VI

When the remaining walls of Scopas's house fall down, there is a compulsion to continue Simonides's job, and those whom Ugrešić calls "new witnesses" are "struck by ... [a] double misfortune." At the same time, after the wall collapses on Simonides, we can witness a certain truth about history that was not previously available in quite the same way. We return now to Cicero's *De Oratore* to see more closely what the mnemotechnical device invented by Simonides is, for in it lies the real difference between Ugrešić's story and its Roman version, and the reason why we need to find a different strategy for building and witnessing.

I continue to read Cicero's work from the place I left off at the beginning of my essay. After he makes the claim that Simonides identified the crushed bodies by his recollection of the order in which Scopas's guests were sitting around the table, Cicero concludes, "*hac tum re admonitus invenisse fertur ordinem esse maxime qui memoriae lumen afferret.*"[13] The key word of the sentence is "*ordo*"—line, row, series, order, regularity, arrangement. But what "*ordo*" denotes for Cicero is not at all self-evident. For example, there is no guarantee that the order Simonides discovers is the arrangement in which the feasters who died were sitting before the catastrophe, and not instead the order, perhaps even a certain law of memory, imposed in the very process of remembering. Also, it is not evident that there is a continuity—an order—between the events before, during, and after the collapse of the house. Is it then order that illuminates memory, or is it memory that illuminates the functions of order? Is this the order of things, a sequence of events, or the order of time? Is it first the order of things, the order of time, or the order of memory?

But let us start with a simpler question: How are we to translate Cicero's *"hac tum re admonitus invenisse fertur ordinem esse maxime qui memoriae lumen afferret"*? One possible way is: "admonished by this, he is said to have discovered that it is order, most of all, that brings light to memory." The dative, *"memoriae,"* says that light is brought *to* memory. And because *"lumen afferret"* translates into the English verb "to illuminate," it is order that illuminates memory. The "most of all" or "especially" (*maxime*), means here "more than any other thing." In other words, humans have not yet invented something that would illuminate memory more than this thing called "order."

About illumination Cicero will say that it "cannot be used to draw out the memory if no memory has been given to us by nature, *but it can undoubtedly summon it to come forth if it is in hiding.*"[14] Bearing this in mind, Cicero's sentence does not say that Simonides's discovery of *"ars memoriae"* defines the moment when memory is invented but the moment when order and memory are related. In fact, Cicero uses the verb *"protollo"*[15] for Simonides's "invention" of the art of memory. *Protollo* can be translated as "to invent," but it also means, because of its stem *tollo*, "to put forth, stretch forward" and "to raise, lift up, elevate." Simonides's invention is, hence, a putting forth, a raising or lifting up of the art of memory. We can then conclude that the light of order, and order by way of light, is brought to memory, which has been given to human beings by nature. Order draws memory out from hiding. And this is the way in which memories of the past are discovered and recalled.

But whether discovery, recall, illumination, and elevation are synonymous or complementary processes, that which order cannot apprehend remains in the dark and out of human reach. Memory is hence that which is *brought to light*, and remembering is a process of illumination of dark sites. Moreover, memory is a thoughtful, skillful, and artificial extension of order against the unknown. If this is so, with the art of memory we remember only that part of the past that can be ordered. While memory illuminates certain elements of the past, it—the luminosity itself, the shining itself—further obscures that which remains in the dark.

Order is, hence, constituted as a substitute for what Cicero assumes to be the chaotic, dead state in which things were when the roof collapsed. As it lifts the darkness, order takes the place of whatever was there prior to it and clears up the confusion of body parts, preparing them for proper interment. In a sort of double gesture, then, Cicero places order (and the invention of the art) at the beginning and considers order to be the beginning before there is nothing. If, then, Simonides's account of the disaster is a representation of the event, this is because it is a convincing, reasonable reconstruction of the event and not because it is a testimony to what happened.

In analyzing the art of memory in this way I am not dismissing the usefulness and power of order and reason. Quite the contrary. The purpose of my readings of both Cicero and Danner is to point to a few places in their texts—both of which reconstruct the past—where order and reason turn into their opposites and, in effect, obscure that which we want and need to know. In Cicero, this happens when order (the art of memory, the history) is regarded as capable of fully defining and representing the state of affairs under the collapsed roof.[16] The ordering of the events does not reveal or transform or redeem the chaos of the catastrophe. It only helps us to translate the events into terms that seem less threatening and hence easier to understand and remember.

As far as reason is concerned, it is reasonable first, to doubt Simonides's finding—not his reassembling of the dead bodies but certainly the tropes (order and memory, for example) that Cicero uses. Second, it is not at all reasonable to believe that the disturbance we feel when we face a catastrophe has to do with the dead rather than with the living (and their fascination and over-identification with the dead). Third, perhaps most important, it is not reasonable to think that the rationalization of catastrophic events, the interment of the corpses, can take the place of mourning the disaster. Reason might be the effect of trauma, a capacity we have developed to cope with what is incomprehensible. But even so, reason cannot—does not—do away with the event itself.

The art of memory fixes the dead (the memories) in an orderly manner, according to the terms of living order. With the proper identification and burial of the bodies, the elements of memory that are unrecoverable and un-orderable are pushed into oblivion and pacified.[17] What we are left with as the result of this process of reconstructive recollection is not the meaning of the past or the past event, but the meaning of the order which has become the substitute for the past, and which is known under the name of history. Cicero, in other words, does not witness the collapse of the roof but the birth of an art of memory that conforms to the political order of the Roman empire. The corpses of the dead feasters are walled away, not to be seen.

In Ugrešić's story, on the other hand, the act of remembering inaugurated by Simonides is interrupted and Simonides the poet disappears in the catastrophe he was supposed to decipher. He falls prey to his fantasy of omnipotence, to the very power of telling apart order from disorder, peace from chaos, light from dark, memory from forgetting, body part from body part. He falls prey to the very history his discovery has inaugurated in the Roman version. Registering Simonides's death, Ugrešić also stages the advent of a different subjectivity precisely when she exposes repetition and fragmentation as the rules of history in the Balkans. The new witness is in a position not only to witness a historic catastrophe, Simonides's death, but also the catastrophe of its (the subject's) own becoming. The witness is witnessing the advent of history just as the subject is being created. And this is a lasting process, not an act—a process that leads, ultimately, to an awareness of what self-assertion (for example, national independence) entails.

If in witnessing the catastrophe we try to confront the fantasy fundamental to identity creation, Bosnia may be able to start over for the first time. To be sure, nothing can be promised to the war-ravaged Balkans. We can, however, pay heed to the potential squandered in the late 1980s, when ethnicity became the primary aspect of identity, and self-determination, ethnic particularization, and the nation-state became historical tasks superseding all other rights, interests, and needs. Any agreement after the Dayton accords would hence entail an appointment with an unknown past. And this is the appointment Bosnia—and the Balkans in general—cannot miss, for Bosnia itself is nothing but this date with a history that is not Bosnia's own.

For Europe (as its Hamlet-like hesitation to act amply demonstrates), Bosnia is the fold from which history comes, the place where history is created. And not only the history of the twentieth century—the "unimaginable" that happens again as "ethnic cleansing," the First World War that started in Sarajevo—but also the cultural prehistory of Europe, since Bosnia is the site where its East and West, its Greek and Roman roots intersect. If Bosnia, which bears the scars of European religious, historical, and political divisions, and reminds Europe of its deepest wounds, does not show up for this date with history, the next war will force it to do so.

If this sounds too abstract, let me add that a new agreement after Dayton would entail, among other things, an assumption of responsibility for what was done when what is now the past was the shared present. That past is repeating itself in Kosovo as I write this (in the summer of 1998), between the Albanian demand for a separate state and the Serbian repression of Albanian identity.

VII

Balkan history does not need a cure. Rather, we—both former Yugoslavians, as well as Europeans, and perhaps others—need the courage to face the repetition of history, the courage to encounter the dead and our own mortality without turning those who have died into the property of the living. In other words, we need to learn not how to reassemble the dead or bury them properly, but how to survive (that is, outlive) our identification with them. What is needed is not a new *pax Romana*, but the realization that every repetition of history is also a moment when we can start over, a moment of opening toward a plurality of possibilities, rather than simply or necessarily an opportunity for another slaughter. At any rate, regardless of which exact route this working through of historical trauma takes, it will have to involve overcoming the fantasy that was fundamental for identity creation in the Balkans. For only a people that has overcome the fantasy of its annihilation or extinction can co-exist with another people. Only the poet who has traversed the fantasy of her death, the poet who has, in other words, recognized herself in Simonides under the rubble and has survived that identification, can in some way address the future in and after a disaster.

This fantasy of collective annihilation is, of course, also a fantasy of our humanity and about that which makes us human.

In this essay I dealt with two different attitudes toward the past: One, Cicero's and Danner's, is an attempt to reconstruct the past; the other, Ugrešić's, is an attempt to witness the past at the moment of its becoming (emergence, eruption) in the present. The first one leads to a forgetting of the past precisely when the author believes that he has discovered what happened. The second offers an insight into the very process of history-making. The first one is the story of a bystander who observes an event from a safe distance. The second one speaks as if the survivor of a disaster always stands amid the ruins, her life permanently threatened by an event which, in our rational judgment, we believe to have happened some time ago.

We should now recognize that the two versions of the Simonides legend complement each other. Taken together, they reveal the two sides of the exigency of catastrophe: on the one hand, the necessity to commemorate the dead, and, on the other, the rupture, the break, the oblivion, whose remembering is beyond the powers of both poets and scholars, and, indeed, beyond tragedy.

We, Ugrešić and I, and others who left Yugoslavia unable to take sides, can neither remember nor forget Yugoslavia—the former Yugoslavia, a former "we." Of course, the roof and the walls of Scopas's Balkan house do not cease collapsing. We continue to be caught inside—inside the forgetting, inside the confusion of this disaster without a key. But we also continue to turn away.

Notes

1. Simonides is the author of some of the most famous Greek epitaphs. He is also known for demanding high fees for his services. Among the verses attributed to him is, as Bernard Knox writes, "the most famous two-line epitaph in all history":

Traveler, take this word to the men of Lakadaímon:
We who lie buried here did what they told us to do. (247)

Simonides also wrote the epitaph "for the Spartan prophet who foresaw his death at Thermopylae but refused to withdraw":

This is the grave of that Megístas, whom once
the Persians and Medes killed when they
crossed Spercheíos River; a seer who saw
clearly the spirit of death advancing upon him,
yet could not bring himself to desert the
Spartan kings. (251)

Bernard Knox, ed., *Classical Literature* (New York: Norton, 1993).

2. Cicero, *De Oratore,* trans. E. W. Sutton (Cambridge, Mass.: Harvard University Press, 1948), 467.

3. Dubravka Ugrešić, "The Confiscation of Memory," trans. Celia Hawkesworth, *New Left Review* 218 (1996): 39. Ugrešić, one of the most acclaimed writers in the former Yugoslavia, left her native Croatia at the beginning of the war.

4. Ibid., 39.

5. Katherine Kearns, *Psychoanalysis, Historiography, and Feminist Theory: The Search for Critical Method* (Cambridge: Cambridge University Press, 1997), 1.

6. Mark Danner, "Bosnia: The Turning Point," *New York Review of Books* 45, no. 2 (1998): 35.

7. Ibid., 35.

8. Mark Danner, "The US and the Yugoslav Catastrophe," *New York Review of Books* 44, no. 18 (1997): 64.

9. Danner, "Bosnia," 41.

10. Ibid., 41.

11. Ibid., 41.

12. Ibid., 35.

13. Cicero, *De oratore*, 466.

14. Ibid., 473 (emphasis added).

15. Ibid., 464.

16. The art of memory is also the gift humans receive after the catastrophe. It is an outcome of the sacrificial exchange, a skill humans gain as a reimbursement for death and suffering.

17. The Latin word "pax" (peace) is etymologicaly related to "pango" which means "to fasten, to fix" as Heidegger explains in *Parmenides*. See Martin Heidegger, *Parmenides*, trans. A. Scjuwer and R. Rojcewicz (Bloomington: Indiana University Press, 1992), 41.

Contributors

Grigoris Ananiadis teaches political philosophy and social theory at the University of the Aegean (Lesbos) and is a member of the editorial board of the political and cultural journal *Synchrona Themata*. His most recent publication in English is "Carl Schmitt and Max Adler: The Irreconcilability of Politics and Democracy" in C. Mouffe, ed., *The Challenge of Carl Schmitt*, 1999. He is currently doing research on Hans Kelsen's contribution to political and social theory.

Branka Arsić is assistant professor of history of modern philosophy at SUNY Albany. Her publications include books: *Dictionary* (coauthor with Mrdjan Bajic), 1995; *Reason and Madness: Some Aspects of Descartes Meditations on First Philosophy*, 1997; *View and Subjectivity: Some Problems of Berkeley's Theory of Vision*, 2000; *Women, Images, Imaginings* (ed.), 1999. Her articles were also published in various journals and magazines: *Women's Studies, Belgrade Circle Journal, Philosophical Yearbook, Theoria, Viewpoints*, and in a few collections.

Milica Bakic-Hayden is adjunct professor in the religious studies department, University of Pittsburgh. Her published articles include "Orientalist Variations on the Theme 'Balkans': Symbolic Geography in Recent Yugoslav Cultural Politics," *Slavic Review* (spring 1992); "Nesting Orientalisms: The Case of Former Yugoslavia," *Slavic Review* (winter 1995).

Dušan I. Bjelić is associate professor of criminology at the University of Southern Maine. His areas of research and publication are ethnomethodology/science, and media and culture. His book *Galileo's Pendulum: Science, Sexuality and the Body-Instrument Link,* is forthcoming from SUNY Press.

Adrian Cioroianu is a candidate for a doctorate at Laval University. He is the author of history textbooks and studies on the history of mentalities, history of Romanian communism, political discourse, and propaganda in communist regimes, and the cult of communist leaders' personalities. He is an editorial board member of the magazines *Dilema* and *Sfera Politicii* and a member of the board of directors of the "Institute for Political and Economic Research," Bucharest.

Lucinda Cole teaches literary theory and women's studies at the University of Southern Maine. She is the author of several articles on the cultural construction of masculinities; she has most recently completed a coedited book, *Homegrown Terrorism: "America" and Political Violence in the 90s.*

Ivaylo Ditchev is associate professor of cultural anthropology at Sofia University. He is the director of the Center for Social and Political Anthropology. His research work includes Balkan communism (Bulgaria, Albania, and Macedonia), gift ethics and modernity, European integration, and the transformation of political cultures. Recent books: *Albania-Utopia: Behind Closed Doors of the Balkans*, 1996 (editor, coauthor); *To Give without Losing: Exchange in the Imaginary of Modernity*, 1997; *Gift in the Age of its Technical Reproductability*, 1999.

Vesna Goldsworthy teaches modern English literature and drama at the University of London and St. Lawrence University, New York. She is the author of *Inventing Ruritania: The Imperialism of the Imagination*, 1998, and has contributed to a number of articles and books including, most recently, *The Cambridge Guide to Women's Writing in English*, 1999; *Representing Lives: Women and Autobiography*, 1999; *Routledge International Encyclopaedia of Women's Studies*, 2000.

Stathis Gourgouris is assistant professor of comparative literature at Princeton University and the author of *Dream Nation: Enlightenment, Colonization, and the Institution of Modern Greece*, 1996, and *Literature as Theory (for an Antimythical Era)*, forthcoming. He has also written essays on psychoanalysis, legal theory, political theory, music, and the theater. He is a translator of Greek poetry into English (most recently Yiannis Patilis's *Camel of Darkness*, 1997) and the author of four volumes of poetry in Greek (his most recent being *Introduction to Physics*, 2000).

Vesna Kesić is a prominent Croatian feminist and an antiwar activist. She has published many articles and has participated in many public debates in and outside of Croatia, on issues of women and war. Her essay "A Response to Catharine MacKinnon's article 'Turning Rape into Pornography: Postmodern Genocide,' " published in *Hastings Women's Law Journal*, has received worldwide attention.

Alexander Kiossev teaches cultural history of modernity at the University of Sofia. He was a lecturer in Bulgarian language and literature at the University of Gottingen, Germany. Since 1989 he has been a member of the research group Periphery investigating the Western images of the Eastern changes. In the period between 1995 and 1999 he was the leader of the group project Creation and Destruction of Symbolic World of Communism. From 1987 to 1989 he was leader of the group Synthesis, an interdisciplinary and opposition group of young artists, writers, academics, and students. His publications include a book on the history of Bulgarian poetry and many theoretical essays. He was the editor of the book *Post-Theory, Games, and Discursive Resistance: The Bulgarian Case*, 1995.

Tomislav Z. Longinović is a professor of Slavic and Comparative Literature at the University of Wisconsin-Madison and a novelist who writes both in Serbian and English. His publications include a comparative study of the Slavic novel *Borderline Culture*, 1993; and novels *Moment of Silence*, 1990 and *Lonely America*, 1994.

Rastko Močnik teaches theory of discourse and epistemology of the humanities at the University of Ljubljana. His recent publications include: *Altercations*: Essays on Totalitarianism, the Alternative, Nationalism, 1998; *How Much Fascism?: Essays on Post-communist Politics,* 1998; *Theory for Our Times. Levi-Strauss, Mauss, Durkheim*, 1999; *Three Theories: Ideology, Nation, Institution*, 1999. His articles include: "After the Fall," 1999; "Der 18.

Brumaire des oestlichen Fruehlings," 1992; "Das 'Subjekt, dem unterstellt wird zu glauben' und die Nation als eine Null-Institution," 1994; "Auf dem Weg zur Kulturellen Hegemonie?," 1994.

Petar Ramadanović is an assistant professor in the English department at the University of New Hampshire.

Ugo Vlaisavljević is professor of the history of contemporary ontology and epistemology at the University of Sarajevo. He has written *Ontology and Its Legacy* (1995) and *The Phenomenological Constitution of the European Community. A Re-Reading of the Vienna Lecture* (1996). He is also author of numerous articles on the philosophy of language and coeditor of the journal *Dialogue*.

Obrad Savić teaches history of social theory and philosophy at the University of Belgrade. He has been the editor of many theoretical journals: *Theoria, Philosophical Studies, Text,* and *Belgrade Circle Journal*. He published and edited several books and collections of articles: *Philosophical Reading of Freud*, 1988; *Musil and Philosophy*, 1990; *European Discourse of War*, 1995; *Politics of Human Rights*, 1999. He was one of the founders and acting president of the Belgrade Circle NGO. During the period of communism (1975–1985) he was an active member of the Belgrade Dissident Group. His recent publications include *Forgetting Futures: On Memory, Trauma, and Identity* (2001) and *Topologies of Trauma (Contemporary Theory)*, edited with Linda Belau (2002).

Index